ACCA

PAPER P7

ADVANCED AUDIT AND
ASSURANCE
(INTERNATIONAL)

PRACTICE & REVISION KIT

In this June 2007 new edition

- We discuss the **best strategies** for revising and taking your ACCA exams

- We show you how to be well prepared for the **December 2007 exam**

- We give you **lots of great guidance** on tackling questions

- We include **genuine student answers** with BPP commentary

- We show you how you can **build your own exams**

- We provide you with **three** mock exams including the **Pilot paper**

- We provide the **ACCA examiner's answers** as well as our own to key exam questions and the Pilot Paper as an additional revision aid

Our **i-Pass** product also supports this paper.

FOR EXAMS IN DECEMBER 2007

First edition June 2007

ISBN 9780 7517 3376 1

British Library Cataloguing-in-Publication Data
A catalogue record for this book
is available from the British Library

Published by

BPP Learning Media Ltd
BPP House, Aldine Place
London W12 8AA

www.bpp.com/learningmedia

Printed in Great Britain by
WM PRINT

We are grateful to the Association of Chartered
Certified Accountants for permission to reproduce past
examination questions. The answers to past
examination questions have been prepared by BPP
Learning Media Ltd.

Contents

Review form & free prize draw

Question index

The headings in this checklist/index indicate the main topics of questions, but questions often cover several different topics.

Questions set under the old syllabus *Audit and Assurance Services* (AAS) paper are included because their style and content are similar to those which appear in the P7 exam. The questions have been amended to reflect the current exam format.

BPP LEARNING MEDIA

Part E: Reporting

Mock exam 1

Mock exam 2

Mock exam 3 (Pilot paper)

Planning your question practice

Our guidance from page 29 shows you how to organise your question practice, either by attempting questions from each syllabus area or **by building your own exams** – tackling questions as a series of practice exams.

Topic index

Listed below are the key Paper P7 syllabus topics and the numbers of the questions in this Kit covering those topics.

If you need to concentrate your practice and revision on certain topics or if you want to attempt all available questions that refer to a particular subject, you will find this index useful.

Syllabus topic	Question numbers
Advertising, publicity and obtaining professional work	8
Analytical procedures	18, 21, 39, ME1 Q1, ME2 Q1
Assurance services	47, ME2 Q6
Audit evidence	25 – 35, 39, ME1 Q3, ME 2 Q3
Audit planning	10, 15, 16, 36
Audit reports	48 – 58, ME1 Q4, ME2 Q4, ME3 Q4
Audit strategy	23
Brands	19, 27
Confidentiality	1, 3, ME2 Q5
Construction contracts	16, 41
Deferred taxation	26
Discontinued operations	27, 39
Due diligence	41, 42
Ethics	2 – 13, 46, ME1 Q5, ME2 Q5, ME3 Q5
Forensic audits	ME3 Q2
Fraud and error	11, 12, 36
Going concern	50
Government grants and assistance	28, 31
Group audits	36, 40, 57, ME1 Q1, ME3 Q1
Intangible assets	31, 34, 39
Internal audit	38, ME1 Q2
Internal financial control effectiveness	23, 36, ME2 Q1
Inventory	19, 35, 37, ME3 Q2
Investments	28
Laws and regulations	58
Leases	21, ME2 Q3
Management representations	21, ME1 Q4
Materiality	18, 56
Money laundering	ME3 Q5
Non-current assets	18, 20, 26, 29, 32, 34, ME1 Q3
Opening balances and comparatives	48, 54
Other information	55
Outsourcing	38, ME1 Q2
Prospective financial information	ME2 Q2
Provisions and contingencies	25, 28, 29, 32, 33, 34, 37, 41
Quality control	13, ME3 Q3
Risk assessments	14 – 21, 23, 37, 43, 44, 45, 46, ME1 Q1, ME2 Q1, ME3 Q1
Segmental information	15, 33
Subsequent events	51
Using the work of others	16, 35, ME2 Q3

Using your BPP Practice and Revision Kit

Tackling revision and the exam

You can significantly improve your chances of passing by tackling revision and the exam in the right ways. Our advice is based on recent feedback from ACCA examiners.

- We look at the dos and don'ts of revising for, and taking, ACCA exams
- We focus on Paper P7; we discuss revising the syllabus, what to do (and what not to do) in the exam, how to approach different types of question and ways of obtaining easy marks

Selecting questions

We provide signposts to help you plan your revision.

- A full **question index**
- A **topic index** listing all the questions that cover key topics, so that you can locate the questions that provide practice on these topics, and see the different ways in which they might be examined
- **BPP's question plan** highlighting the most important questions and explaining why you should attempt them
- **Build your own exams**, showing how you can practise questions in a series of exams

Making the most of question practice

At BPP we realise that you need more than just questions and model answers to get the most from your question practice.

- Our **Top tips** provide essential advice on tackling questions, presenting answers and the key points that answers need to include
- We show you how you can pick up **Easy marks** on questions, as we know that picking up all readily available marks often can make the difference between passing and failing
- We summarise **Examiner's comments**
- We include **marking guides** to show you what the examiner rewards
- We refer to the **BPP 2007 Study Text** for detailed coverage of the topics covered in each question
- A number of questions include **Analysis** and **Helping hands** attached to show you how to approach them if you are struggling
- We include **annotated student answers** to some questions to highlight how these questions can be tackled and ways answers can be improved.
- In a bank at the end of this Kit we include the **examiner's answers** to the Pilot paper and other questions. Used in conjunction with our answers they provide an indication of all possible points that could be made, issues that could be covered and approaches to adopt.

Attempting mock exams

There are three mock exams that provide practice at coping with the pressures of the exam day. We strongly recommend that you attempt them under exam conditions. **Mock exams 1 and 2** reflect the question styles and syllabus coverage of the exam; **Mock exam 3** is the Pilot paper. To help you get the most out of doing these exams, we not only provide help with each answer, but also guidance on how you should have approached the whole exam.

BPP)))
LEARNING MEDIA

Passing ACCA exams

Revising and taking ACCA exams

To maximise your chances of passing your ACCA exams, you must make best use of your time, both before the exam during your revision, and when you are actually doing the exam.

- Making the most of your revision time can make a big, big difference to how well-prepared you are for the exam

- Time management is a core skill in the exam hall; all the work you've done can be wasted if you don't make the most of the three hours you have to attempt the exam

In this section we simply show you what to do and what not to do during your revision, and how to increase and decrease your prospects of passing your exams when you take them. Our advice is grounded in feedback we've had from ACCA examiners. You may be surprised to know that much examiner advice is the same whatever the exam, and the reasons why many students fail don't vary much between subjects and exam levels. So if you follow the advice we give you over the next few pages, you will **significantly** enhance your chances of passing **all** your ACCA exams.

How to revise

☑ Plan your revision

At the start of your revision period, you should draw up a **timetable** to plan how long you will spend on each subject and how you will revise each area. You need to consider the total time you have available and also the time that will be required to revise for other exams you're taking.

☑ Practise Practise Practise

The **more exam-standard questions** you do, the **more likely you are to pass** the exam. Practising full questions will mean that you'll get used to the time pressure of the exam. When the time is up, you should note where you've got to and then try to complete the question, giving yourself practice at everything the question tests.

☑ Revise enough

Make sure that your revision covers the breadth of the syllabus, as in most papers most topics could be examined in a compulsory question. However it is true that some topics are **key** – they are likely to appear often or are a particular interest of the examiner – and you need to spend sufficient time revising these. Make sure you also know the **basics** – the fundamental calculations, proformas and report layouts.

☑ Deal with your difficulties

Difficult areas are topics you find dull and pointless, or subjects that you found problematic when you were studying them. You mustn't become negative about these topics; instead you should build up your knowledge by reading the **Passcards** and using the **Quick quiz** questions in the Study Text to test yourself. When practising questions in the Kit, go back to the Text if you're struggling.

☑ Learn from your mistakes

Having completed a question you must try to look at your answer critically. Always read the **Top tips guidance** in the answers; it's there to help you. Look at **Easy marks** to see how you could have quickly gained credit on the questions that you've done. As you go through the Kit, it's worth noting any traps you've fallen into, and key points in the **Top tips** or **Examiner's comments** sections, and referring to these notes in the days before the exam. Aim to learn at least one new point from each question you attempt, a technical point perhaps or a point on style or approach.

☑ Read the examiners' guidance

We refer throughout this Kit to **Examiner's comments**. As well as highlighting weaknesses, Examiners' comments often provide clues to future questions, as many examiners will test areas that are likely to cause students problems. ACCA's website also contains articles by examiners which you **must** read, as they may form the basis of questions on any paper after they've been published.

Read through the examiner's answers to key exam questions and the Pilot paper included at the back of the Kit. In general these are far longer and more comprehensive than any answer you could hope to produce in the exam, but used in conjunction with our more realistic solutions, they provide a useful revision tool, covering all possible points and approaches.

☑ Complete all three mock exams

You should attempt the **Mock exams** at the end of the Kit under **strict exam conditions**, to gain experience of selecting questions, managing your time and producing answers.

How NOT to revise

☒ Revise selectively

Examiners are well aware that some students try to forecast the contents of exams, and only revise those areas that they think will be examined. Examiners try to prevent this by doing the unexpected, for example setting the same topic in successive sittings or setting topics in compulsory questions that have previously only been examined in optional questions.

☒ Spend all the revision period reading

You cannot pass the exam just by learning the contents of Passcards, Course Notes or Study Texts. You have to develop your **application skills** by practising questions.

☒ Audit the answers

This means reading the answers and guidance without having attempted the questions. Auditing the answers gives you **false reassurance** that you would have tackled the questions in the best way and made the points that our answers do. The feedback we give in our answers will mean more to you if you've attempted the questions and thought through the issues.

☒ Practise some types of question, but not others

Although you may find certain topics challenging, you shouldn't just practise those questions. Make sure you attempt questions covering the whole of the syllabus.

☒ Get bogged down

Don't spend a lot of time worrying about all the minute detail of certain topic areas, and leave yourself insufficient time to cover the rest of the syllabus. Remember that a key skill in the exam is the ability to **concentrate on what's important** and this applies to your revision as well.

☒ Overdo studying

Studying for too long without interruption will mean your studying becomes less effective. A five minute break each hour will help. You should also make sure that you are leading a **healthy lifestyle** (proper meals, good sleep and some times when you're not studying).

How to PASS your exams

☑ Prepare for the day

Make sure you set at least one alarm (or get an alarm call), and allow plenty of time to get to the exam hall. You should have your route planned in advance and should listen on the radio for potential travel problems. You should check the night before to see that you have pens, pencils, erasers, watch, calculator with spare batteries, also exam documentation and evidence of identity.

☑ Select the right questions

You should select the optional questions you feel you can answer **best**, basing your selection on the topics covered, the requirements of the question, how easy it will be to apply the requirements and the availability of easy marks.

☑ Plan your three hours

You need to make sure that you will be answering the correct number of questions, and that you spend the right length of time on each question – this will be determined by the number of marks available. Each mark carries with it a **time allocation** of **1.8 minutes**. A 25 mark question therefore should be selected, completed and checked in 45 minutes. With some papers, it's better to do certain types of question first or last.

☑ Read the questions carefully

To score well, you must follow the requirements of the question, understanding what aspects of the subject area are being covered, and the tasks you will have to carry out. The requirements will also determine what information and examples you should provide. Reading the question scenarios carefully will help you decide what **issues** to discuss, **techniques** to use, **information** and **examples** to include and how to **organise** your answer.

☑ Plan your answers

Five minutes of planning plus twenty-five minutes of writing is certain to earn you more marks than thirty minutes of writing. Consider when you're planning how your answer should be **structured,** **w**hat the **format** should be and **how long** each part should take.

Confirm before you start writing that your plan makes **sense,** covers **all relevant points** and does not include **irrelevant material.**

☑ Show evidence of judgement

Remember that examiners aren't just looking for a display of knowledge; they want to see how well you can **apply** the knowledge you have. Evidence of application and judgement will include writing answers that only contain **relevant** material, using the material in scenarios to **support** what you say, **criticising** the **limitations** and **assumptions** of the techniques you use and making **reasonable recommendations** that follow from your discussion.

☑ Stay until the end of the exam

Use any spare time to **check and recheck** your script. This includes checking you have filled out the candidate details correctly, you have labelled question parts and workings clearly, you have used headers and underlining effectively and spelling, grammar and arithmetic are correct.

How to FAIL your exams

☒ Don't do enough questions

If you don't attempt sufficient questions on the paper, you are making it harder for yourself to pass the questions that you do attempt. If for example you don't do a 20 mark question, then you will have to score 50 marks out of 80 marks on the rest of the paper, and therefore have to obtain 63% of the marks on the questions you do attempt. Failing to attempt all of the paper is symptomatic of poor time management or poor question selection.

☒ Include irrelevant material

Markers are given detailed mark guides and will not give credit for irrelevant content. Therefore you should **NOT** braindump all you know about a broad subject area; the markers will only give credit for what is **relevant**, and you will also be showing that you lack the ability to **judge what's important.** Similarly forcing irrelevant theory into every answer won't gain you marks, nor will providing uncalled for features such as situation analyses, executive summaries and background information.

☒ Fail to use the details in the scenario

General answers or reproductions of old answers that don't refer to what is in the scenario in **this** question won't score enough marks to pass.

☒ Copy out the scenario details

Examiners see **selective** use of the right information as a key skill. If you copy out chunks of the scenario which aren't relevant to the question, or don't use the information to support your own judgements, you won't achieve good marks.

☒ Don't do what the question asks

Failing to provide all the examiner asks for will limit the marks you score. You will also decrease your chances by not providing an answer with enough **depth** – producing a single line bullet point list when the examiner asks for a discussion.

☒ Present your work poorly

Markers will only be able to give you credit if they can read your writing. There are also plenty of other things that will make it more difficult for markers to reward you. Examples include:

- Not using black or blue ink
- Not showing clearly which question you're attempting
- Scattering question parts from the same question throughout your answer booklet
- Not showing clearly workings or the results of your calculations

Paragraphs that are too long or which lack headers also won't help markers and hence won't help you.

Using your BPP products

This Kit gives you the question practice and guidance you need in the exam. Our other products can also help you pass:

- **Learning to Learn Accountancy** gives further valuable advice on revision

- **Passcards** provide you with clear topic summaries and exam tips

- **Success CDs** help you revise on the move

- **i-Pass CDs** offer tests of knowledge against the clock

- **Learn Online** is an e-learning resource delivered via the Internet, offering comprehensive tutor support and featuring areas such as study, practice, email service, revision and useful resources

You can purchase these products by visiting www.bpp.com/mybpp.

Visit our website www.bpp.com/acca/learnonline to sample aspects of Learn Online free of charge. Learn Online is hosted by BPP Professional Education.

BPP
LEARNING MEDIA

Passing P7

Revising P7

Topics to revise

Paper P7 is a challenging higher level paper consisting of two compulsory case-study style questions in Section A (worth a total of 50-70 marks) and two out of three short scenario questions in Section B.

In her examiner's approach to this paper, Lisa Weaver, the P7 examiner, has stated that planning and risk assessment are key areas which are likely to form part of a compulsory question. Evidence is also likely to feature in Section A. Reporting could come up in either a compulsory or optional question, similarly ethical and professional issues. Current issues could come up anywhere on the paper so it is important that students do not ignore this area and make sure they keep up to date by reading *student accountant* and reviewing the accountancy and financial press.

One of the general features of Professional level papers is the availability of professional marks. These will generally be awarded in Section A and comprise four to six marks. They will be awarded for the degree of professionalism with which answers are presented. For example, if you are asked to set out your answer as a letter or a report, marks will be awarded for presentation. Other professional marks could be awarded for the form of your answer such as the structure or logical flow of arguments. You should assume that if a question asks for a certain format, that there will be some professional marks available.

To summarise, although this paper contains an optional element, we **strongly advise** that you do not selectively revise certain topics – any topic from the syllabus could be examined anywhere on the paper. Selective revision will limit the number of questions you can answer and hence reduce your chances of passing.

Question practice

Question practice under timed conditions is essential, so that you can get used to the pressures of answering exam questions in **limited time** and practise not only the key techniques but allocating your time between different requirements in each question. Our list of recommended questions includes 25-30 mark Section A and 15-20 mark Section B questions. The key to success in this paper is question practice. It is essential that you attempt as many questions as you can in full. Having completed a question you must try to look at your answer critically. Try to learn at least one new point from each one you attempt – a technical point or a point on style or approach. This will help your answers to improve over time.

Passing the P7 exam

Displaying the right qualities and avoiding weaknesses

(a)   Reading time

You have 15 minutes of reading time – make sure you use it wisely. Given that Section A will consist of two compulsory questions, worth 50-70 marks in total, you could spend the time analysing and planning these questions and doing them first, and then choose and tackle the optional questions from Section B.

(b)   The following are examples of things to avoid – and note our comments about action to take in each case.

Failure to complete the paper	This problem can be avoided by ensuring that you have a very disciplined exam technique and that you set times in which to answer questions and, when that time is over, you move on to the next question. Lots of practice at answering questions in timed conditions will help you to discipline yourself in this way. Remember, it is easier to get marks at the outset of answering a question (when all the marks are still available) than to get the last few remaining marks for a question (when you have made all the easy points and are struggling with the most difficult aspects of the question).
Not reading the question	We recommend that you read each question more than once. Try to force yourself to read slowly as well. Although the exam is time-limited, reading the question properly is a good investment.
Lack of comprehension and analytical skills	These are higher level skills which you have to learn at this level and the best way to enhance them is to practise as many questions as you can. In addition, once you have completed your own answer, you should always work through the suggested answer referring back to the question so that you can see the links that have been made.
Lack of lower level assumed knowledge	You should endeavour not to commence your P7 studies until you have completed your F8/2.6 studies. It is not possible to pass P7 unless you have a very firm understanding of basic auditing theory.
Lack of awareness of current issues	You should ensure that you keep up to date with current issues in the auditing and business world, by reading examiner articles as a minimum, but preferably by keeping an eye on the accountancy press throughout your studies.
Failure to respond in a practical/commercial way	The answer to this problem is to practice lots of questions, read other people's answers to questions in this Kit and on the ACCA website and to try and think about how you would respond in practice if it were one of your clients.
Lack of relevant practical experience	You may not be able to do anything about this if your are not employed in a relevant field. However, if you can, do. For example, if you can discuss with your managers the necessity of getting relevant experience and they are able to meet that need, try and obtain as much relevant experience as you can. If not, the best you can do is follow the advice for the previous point, which should stand you in good stead.
Inability to reach a conclusion/make a decision	You must get into the habit of drawing conclusions where the requirement is to do so. Again, practise questions where this is required, and, when reading questions note whether you are required to draw a conclusion or make a decision.
Poor exam technique/time allocation	This point links to the first point made above. There is a great deal of guidance concerning exam technique in this kit. Read it and put it into practice.

Tackling questions

You'll improve your chances by following a step-by-step approach along the following lines.

Step 1 **Read the requirement**

Identify the knowledge areas being tested and see precisely what the examiner wants you to do. This will help you focus on what's important in the scenario.

Step 2 **Check the mark allocation**

This shows the depth of answer anticipated and helps you allocate time.

Step 3 **Read the scenario/preamble**

Identify which information is relevant to which part. There are lots of clues in scenario-based questions so make sure you identify those which you should use in your answer.

Step 4 **Plan your answer**

Consider the formats you'll use and discussion points you'll make.

Step 5 **Write your answer**

Stick carefully to the time allocation for each question, and for each part of each question.

Exam information

Format of the paper

		Number of marks
Section A:	2 compulsory questions	50-70
Section B:	Choice of 2 from 3 questions	30-50
		100

Time allowed: 3 hours

Section A of the P7 paper will comprise two compulsory 'case study' type questions, worth in total 50 to 70 marks. These questions will include detailed information, such as extracts from financial statements and audit working papers. The questions themselves will include a range of requirements, covering material from across the syllabus.

Section B of the paper will consist of three questions, from which two should be attempted. These questions will include short scenarios as the basis for the question requirements.

Additional information

Candidates need to be aware that questions involving knowledge of new examinable regulations will not be set until at least six months after the last day of the month in which the regulation was issued.

The Study Guide provides more detailed guidance on the syllabus. Examinable documents are listed in the 'Exam Notes' section of ACCA's *student accountant*.

Pilot paper

Section A

1   Business risks for a group, support letter, horizontal group audits
2   Forensic auditing, tests on inventory

Section B

3   Quality control policies and procedures
4   Audit reports
5   Money laundering guidance, ethical and professional issues

The Pilot paper is Mock exam 3 in this Kit.

Examinable documents

Knowledge of new examinable regulations will not be assessed until at least six calendar months after the last day of the month in which the document was issued, or the legislation passed. The relevant last day for issue for the June examinations is 30 November of the previous year, and for the December examinations, it is 31 May of the same year.

The study guide offers more detailed guidance on the depth and level at which the examinable documents should be examined. The study guide should therefore be read in conjunction with the examinable documents list.

The accounting knowledge that is assumed for Paper P7 is the same as that examined in Paper P2. Therefore, candidates studying for Paper P7 should refer to the Accounting Standards listed under Paper P2.

Title
International Standards on Auditing (ISAs)
Glossary of Terms
International Framework for Assurance Assignments
Preface to International Standards on Quality Control, Auditing, Assurance and Related Services

ISA 200	Objective and General Principles Governing an Audit of Financial Statements
ISA 210	Terms of Audit Engagements
ISA 220	Quality Control for Audits of Historical Financial Information
ISA 230	Audit Documentation
ISA 240	The Auditor's Responsibility to Consider Fraud in an Audit of Financial Statements
ISA 250	Consideration of Laws and Regulations in an Audit of Financial Statements
ISA 260	Communications of Audit Matters with Those Charged with Governance
ISA 300	Planning an Audit of Financial Statements
ISA 315	Understanding the Entity and its Environment and Assessing the Risks of Material Misstatement
ISA 320	Audit Materiality
ISA 330	The Auditor's Procedures in Response to Assessed Risks
ISA 402	Audit Considerations Relating to Entities Using Service Organisations
ISA 500	Audit Evidence
ISA 501	Audit Evidence – Additional Considerations for Specific Items
ISA 505	External Communications
ISA 510	Initial Engagements – Opening Balances
ISA 520	Analytical Procedures
ISA 530	Audit Sampling and Other Means of Testing
ISA 540	Audit of Accounting Estimates
ISA 545	Auditing Fair Value Measurements and Disclosures
ISA 550	Related Parties
ISA 560	Subsequent Events
ISA 570	Going Concern
ISA 580	Management Representations
ISA 600	Using the Work of Another Auditor
ISA 610	Considering the Work of Internal Auditing
ISA 620	Using the Work of an Expert
ISA 700	The Independent Auditor's Report on a Complete Set of General Purpose Financial Statements
ISA 701	Modifications to the Independent Auditor's Report
ISA 710	Comparatives

Title

ISA 720	Other Information in Documents Containing Audited Financial Statements
ISA 800	The Auditor's Report on Special Purpose Audit Engagements

International Auditing Practice Statements (IAPSs)

IAPS 1000	Inter-bank Confirmation Procedures
IAPS 1010	The Consideration of Environmental Matters in the Audit of Financial Statements
IAPS 1013	Electronic Commerce: Effect on the Audit of Financial Statements
IAPS 1014	Reporting by Auditors on Compliance with International Financial Reporting Standards

International Standards on Assurance Engagements (ISAEs)

ISAE 3000	Assurance Engagements other than Audits or Reviews of Historical Financial Information
ISAE 3400	The Examination of Prospective Financial Information

International Standards on Quality Control (ISQCs)

ISQC 1	Quality Control for Firms that Perform Audits and Reviews of Historical Financial Information and Other Assurance and Related Services and Engagements

International Standards on Related Services (ISRs)

ISR 4400	Engagements to Perform Agreed-Upon Procedures Regarding Financial Information
ISR 4410	Engagements to Compile Financial Information

International Standards on Review Engagements (ISREs)

ISRE 2400	Engagements to Review Financial Statements
ISRE 2410	Review of Interim Financial Information Performed by the Independent Auditor of the Entity

Exposure Drafts (EDs)

ISA 240	(Redrafted) The Auditor's Responsibility to Consider Fraud in an Audit of Financial Statements
ISA 260	(Revised) The Auditor's Communication with Those Charged with Governance
ISA 300	(Redrafted) Planning an Audit of Financial Statements
ISA 315	(Redrafted) Understanding the Entity and its Environment and Assessing the Risks of Material Misstatement
ISA 320	(Revised) Materiality in the Identification And Evaluation of Misstatements
ISA 330	(Redrafted) The Auditor's Procedures in Response to Assessed Risks □□ ISA 540 (Revised) Auditing Accounting Estimates And Related Disclosures (Other than Those Involving Fair Value Measurements and Disclosures)
ISA 600	(Revised) The Audit of Group Financial Statements
ISA 701	The Independent Auditor's Report on Other Historical Financial Information
ISA 705	Modifications to the Opinion in the Independent Auditor's Report
ISA 706	Emphasis of Matter Paragraphs and Other Matters Paragraphs in the Independent Auditor's Report
ISA 800	The Independent Auditor's Report on Summary Audited Financial Statements
	Proposed Amendments to the Preface to the International Standards On Quality Control, Auditing, Assurance and Related Services

Title

Other Documents

ACCA's 'Code of Ethics and Conduct'

IFAC's 'Code of Ethics for Professional Accountants'

ACCA's Technical Factsheet 94 – Anti Money-Laundering (Proceeds of Crime and Terrorism)

The Combined Code (of the Committee on Corporate Governance) as an example of a code of best practice

IAASB Paper 'Financial Reporting on the Internet: Responsibilities of Directors and Management'

IAASB Paper 'First Time Adoption of International Financial Reporting Standards – Guidance for Auditors on Reporting Issues'

Useful websites

The websites below provide additional sources of information of relevance to your studies for *Audit and Assurance Services.*

- www.ft.com

    This website provides information about current international business. You can search for information and articles on specific industry groups as well as individual companies.

- www.bpp.com

    Our website provides information about BPP products and services, with a link to the ACCA website.

- www.accaglobal.com

    ACCA's website. Includes student section.

- www.ifac.org

    This site has links to the International Auditing and Assurance Standards Board for up-to-date information on auditing issues.

Planning your question practice

Planning your question practice

We have already stressed that question practice should be right at the centre of your revision. Whilst you will spend some time looking at your notes and Paper P7 Passcards, you should spend the majority of your revision time practising questions.

We recommend two ways in which you can practise questions.

- Use **BPP's question plan** to work systematically through the syllabus and attempt key and other questions on a section-by-section basis

- **Build your own exams** – attempt questions as a series of practice exams

These ways are suggestions and simply following them is no guarantee of success. You or your college may prefer an alternative but equally valid approach.

BPP's question plan

The BPP plan below requires you to devote a **minimum of 40 hours** to revision of Paper P7. Any time you can spend over and above this should only increase your chances of success.

Step 1   **Review your notes** and the chapter summaries in the Paper P7 **Passcards** for each section of the syllabus.

Step 2   **Answer the key questions** for that section. These questions have boxes round the question number in the table below and you should answer them in full. Even if you are short of time you must attempt these questions if you want to pass the exam. You should complete your answers without referring to our solutions.

Step 3   **Attempt the other questions** in that section. For some questions we have suggested that you prepare **answer plans or do the calculations** rather than full solutions. Planning an answer means that you should spend about 40% of the time allowance for the questions brainstorming the question and drawing up a list of points to be included in the answer.

Step 4   Attempt **Mock exams 1, 2 and 3** under strict exam conditions.

Syllabus section	2007 Passcards chapters	Questions in this Kit	Comments	Done ☑
Revision period 1				
Professional and ethical considerations				
Confidentiality	2	1	Answer in full. This is a good question that tests your knowledge of ethical guidance and then applies it in a scenario context.	☐
Objectivity	2	2	Answer in full. This question appears to be set in a complex scenario so is a good one to do to test your ability to think logically and sensibly.	☐
Ethical and professional issues	3	3	Answer in full. This question based on a scenario is important to attempt because you need to be able to identify the ethical and professional issues raised.	☐
		4	Answer in full. This question is set with three mini scenarios and could be similar to one you could expect in the real exam. Take each in turn and consider it separately and logically.	☐
		7, 8	Plan an answer to these questions.	☐
Revision period 2				
Practice management				
Professional and practical issues	4, 5	9	Answer in full. This question set in the context of three mini scenarios, considers professional and practical matters, as well as ethical considerations regarding independence.	☐
Tendering	5	10	Answer in full. This is an excellent case study style question on the issue of tendering. You need to be able to critically appraise the information in the scenario to produce a relevant, well-thought out answer.	☐
Fraud and irregularity	3	12	Answer in full. This question looks at irregularities occurring in a small company, providing detailed information you need to appraise. Therefore this is a good question to get practice of Section A type questions.	☐
	6	11	Plan an answer to this question.	☐
Revision period 3				
Audit planning and risk assessment				
Audit risks and acquisition	6, 12	14	Answer in full. This past exam-standard question will be useful to you in practising both identifying and explaining audit risks and thinking through group issues relating to an acquisition.	☐
Business risks, acquisitions and analytical procedures	6, 7, 10	21	Answer in full. This could be a typical Section A question on risk, together with audit work to perform on specific areas. You are also asked to discuss the reliance you could place on analytical procedures and management representations.	☐

Syllabus section	2007 Passcards chapters	Questions in this Kit	Comments	Done ☑
Business risks, audit strategy, tendering and controls	6, 7	24	Answer in full. This question provides more good exam practice as it indicates the type of question the examiner could ask in this area. It is also a wide-ranging question, as you can expect a case study question at this level to be.	☐
Business and audit risks, audit strategy	6, 7	17	Answer in full. This question provides more practice of identifying audit and business risks.	☐
Audit risks and audit work	6, 9	22	Answer in full. This is an excellent recent old syllabus exam question where you have to identify the audit risks from the scenario in part (a) and then set out the audit work you would perform on specific areas in part (b).	☐
Planning materiality, audit risks and audit work	6, 9	18	Answer in full. This is a 30 mark exam-standard question. It's a good one to practise as it's scenario-based and very time-pressured.	☐
		20	Plan an answer to this question.	☐
Revision period 4 *Audit evidence, evaluation and review*				
	8, 9, 10	27	Answer in full. This question is a good one to practise as it looks at audit evidence in the context of three issues.	☐
		34	Plan an answer to this question.	☐
		26	Answer in full. Remember that 'matters' include issues such as risk, materiality, accounting treatments (including disclosure). For part (b) make sure that you answer in terms of the evidence you would expect to find and *NOT* the procedures you would perform.	☐
		25	Plan an answer to this question.	☐
		30	Answer in full. This question covers some tricky areas, particularly the area of revenue, so it is a good one to make sure that you run through completely, if you have time.	☐
		33	Plan an answer to this question.	☐
Revision period 5 *Group audits*				
Group audit and audit of stock	8, 11	35	Answer in full. You must be comfortable with a question set in a group context. A question on groups was set in the Pilot paper.	☐
Revision period 6 *Audit-related services and assurance services*				

Syllabus section	2007 Passcards chapters	Questions in this Kit	Comments	Done ☑
Due diligence exercise, group audit planning issues	12	40	Answer in full. This past pilot paper question is both exam style and standard and is therefore good practice for your exam. Working through part (a) of this question (set in a due diligence context) is very useful practice for your exam.	☐
		41	Answer in full. This question on due diligence is a very good question for you to practise.	☐
		42	Answer in full. This is another good question where you should be able to score well in part (a) on defining due diligence. In part (b) you have to use the scenario to identify matters to consider.	☐
Business risk assessment/ management Performance measures	15	45	Answer in full. Work through this recent exam question to ensure you can identify and explain business risks. Part (c) is a useful small part on performance measures too – make sure you try it.	☐
Revision period 7 *Internal audit, prospective financial information and social and environmental audits*				
Outsourcing	16	46	Answer in full. This is a good question on outsourcing in a scenario situation.	☐
Prospective financial information	14	47	Answer in full. If you have time, you should also work through this question, on PFI and comparing audit engagements with other types of assurance engagements.	☐
Revision period 8 *Reports*				
Going concern and audit reports	17	50	Answer in full. Audit reports are a key topic and likely to feature somewhere in the paper. This past exam question is good practice and includes a real student answer.	☐
Subsequent events and audit reports	17	51	Answer in full. This is a recent exam question on audit reports, including a short part on subsequent events.	☐
Other information	17	55	Answer in full. This question looks at other information in documents containing financial statements and the possible impact on the audit report.	☐
Opening balances and audit reports	17	54	Answer in full. This question considers opening balances and auditors' responsibilities. It also considers the implication of two specific matters on the audit reports of the individual company and the group	☐
Comparatives and audit reports	17	48	Answer in full. This question looks at comparatives and then asks you to critique an extract from an audit report.	☐

BPP
LEARNING MEDIA

Build your own exams

Having revised your notes and the BPP Passcards, you can attempt the questions in the Kit as a series of practice exams. You can organise the questions in the following way:

	Practice exams		
	1	2	3
Section A			
1	17	18	21
2	35	36	37
Section B			
3	1	5	25
4	26	27	28
5	29	30	31

Whichever practice exams you use, you must attempt **Mock exams 1, 2 and 3** at the end of your revision.

Questions

REGULATORY ENVIRONMENT AND PROFESSIONAL AND ETHICAL CONSIDERATIONS

Questions 1 to 12 cover Regulatory environment and Professional and ethical considerations, the subjects of Parts A and B of the BPP Study Text for Paper P7.

---

1 Confidentiality (AAS Pilot paper) (amended)   36 mins

(a) Explain the importance of the role of confidentiality to the auditor-client relationship and discuss current guidance in this area.   **(8 marks)**

(b) Your firm acts as auditor and adviser to Blake Seven, a private limited company, and to its four directors. The company is owned 50% by Brad Capella, 25% by his wife Minerva and 10% by Janus Trebbiano. Brad is the chief executive and Janus the finance director. Janus's sister, Rosella Trebbiano, has recently resigned from the executive board, following a disagreement with the Capellas. Rosella has now formed her own company, Blakes Heaven, in competition with Blake Seven.

Rosella is currently negotiating with her former co-executives the profit-related remuneration due to her and the sale of her 15% holding of shares in Blake Seven to one or all of them.

Rosella has contacted you to find out Brad's current remuneration package since he refuses to disclose this to her. She has also requested that your firm should continue to act as her personal adviser and become auditor and adviser to Blakes Heaven.

Required

Comment on the matters that you should consider in deciding whether or not your audit firm can comply with Rosella's requests.   **(12 marks)**

                (Total = 20 marks)

2 Aventura International (AAS 12/01)   27 mins

Aventura International, a listed company, manufactures and wholesales a wide variety of products including fashion clothes and audio-video equipment. The company is audited by Voest, a firm of Chartered Certified Accountants, and the audit manager is Darius Harken. The following matters have arisen during the audit of the group's financial statements for the year to 30 June 2007 which is nearing completion:

(1) During the annual physical count of fashion clothes at the company's principal warehouse, the audit staff attending the count were invited to purchase any items of clothing or equipment at 30% of their recommended retail prices.

(2) The chief executive of Aventura International, Armando Thyolo, owns a private jet. Armando invoices the company, on a monthly basis, for that proportion of the operating costs which reflects business use. One of these invoices shows that Darius Harken was flown to Florida in September 2006 and flown back two weeks later. Neither Aventura nor Voest have any offices or associates in Florida.

(3) Last week Armando announced his engagement to be married to his personal assistant, Kirsten Fennimore. Before joining Aventura in March 2007, Kirsten had been Voest's accountant in charge of the audit of Aventura.

Required

Discuss the ethical issues raised and the actions which might be taken by the auditor in relation to these matters.

Note. Assume it is 11 December 2007.   **(15 marks)**

3 Corundum (AAS 6/02)   27 mins

The audit of the financial statements of Corundum, a limited liability company, for the year ended 30 June 2007 is nearing completion and the company's annual general meeting is to be held next week.

The current audit firm, Skarn, has not sought to be reappointed as it is Corundum's policy to change auditors periodically. Nuee Ardente, a firm of Chartered Certified Accountants, has accepted nomination as auditor for the year ending 30 June 2008.

It has just come to light that a provision which should have been made in the financial statements for the year ended 30 June 2007 has been omitted in error. This is of such significance that the financial statements which are soon to be issued cannot be considered to be reliable. However, the financial statements have been approved through the company's internal processes and the directors do not propose to amend them at this late stage but will not agree to a modified auditors' report. Skarn has discussed the matter with Nuee and obtained verbal assurances that if Skarn were to sign an unmodified report, the comparative information in the financial statements for the year ending 30 June 2008 would not be restated.

The company outsourced all legal and company secretarial work to Adam Flysch, a qualified legal practitioner, who worked from home using his own computer. Adam died suddenly. Corundum does not routinely keep copies of minutes and legal documentation.

Required

Identify and discuss the ethical and other professional issues relating to the above matters.

Note. Assume it is 11 December 2007.   **(15 marks)**

4 Isthmus (AAS 12/02)   27 mins

You are an audit manager of Kloser, a firm of Chartered Certified Accountants. You are assigning staff to the final audit of Isthmus, a company listed on the stock exchange, for the year to 31 December 2007. You are aware of the following matters:

(1)   Isthmus has recently issued a profits warning. The company has announced that the significant synergies expected from the acquisition of Vanaka, a former competitor company, have not materialised. Moreover, it has emerged that certain of Vanaka's assets are significantly impaired. Your firm's corporate finance department, assisted by two audit trainees, carried out due diligence work on behalf of Isthmus before the purchase of Vanaka was completed in December 2006.

(2)   Mercedes, the assistant manager assigned to the interim audit of Isthmus, has since inherited 5,000 $1 shares in Isthmus. Mercedes has told you that she has no intention of selling the shares until the share price recovers from the fall to $1.95 which followed the profit warning.

(3)   Anthony, an audit senior, has been assigned to the audits of Isthmus since joining the firm nearly three years ago. He has confided to you that his father owned 1,001 shares in Isthmus but sold them only days before the profits warning at a share price of $7.95. You are assured that Anthony did not previously know that his father had the shares.

Required

Comment on the ethical and other professional issues raised by the above matters and their implications, if any, for staffing the final audit of Isthmus for the year to 31 December 2007.

Note. Assume it is 11 December 2007.   **(15 marks)**

5 Question with analysis: Depeche (AAS 6/03) (amended)

36 mins

You are a manager in Depeche, a firm of Chartered Certified Accountants. You have specific responsibility for undertaking annual reviews of existing clients and advising whether an engagement can be properly continued. The following matters arose in connection with the audit of Duran, a company listed on a Stock Exchange, for the year to 30 June 2006.

(1)   The audit team included a manager, two supervisors, two qualified seniors and six trainees. The final audit, which lasted approximately five weeks, was very time-pressured and the team worked late into the night towards the end of the audit. Duran's staff were very supportive throughout and paid for evening meals that were brought in so that the audit team could work with minimum disruption.

(2)   Duran's chief finance officer, Frankie Sharkey, was so impressed with the commitment of the audit staff that he asked that Depeche pay them all a bonus through an increase in the audit fee. In October 2007, Depeche paid all the members of the team below manager status a bonus amounting to a week's salary. The bonus was processed through Depeche's payroll, in the same way as overtime payments, and recharged to Duran as part of audit expenses.

(3)   One of the points initially drafted for possible inclusion in the report to the company's audit committee concerned the illegal dumping of drums, containing used machine oil, on nearby wasteland. Notes of discussions between the audit manager and Frankie show that it is the company's unwritten policy to disregard the local environmental regulations and risk incurring the fines, which are only small, as it would be costly to use the nearest licensed disposal unit. The matter is not referred to in the final report.

Required

(a)   Comment on the ethical and other professional issues raised by each of the above matters.

(12 marks)

(b)   Discus the appropriateness of available safeguards and advise with reasons whether or not Depeche should continue as the auditor to Duran. **(8 marks)**

Note. Assume it is 11 December 2007. **(Total = 20 marks)**

5 Question with analysis: Depeche (AAS 6/03) (amended)

36 mins

You are a manager in Depeche, a firm of Chartered Certified Accountants. You have specific responsibility for undertaking annual reviews of existing clients and advising whether an engagement can be properly continued. The following matters arose in connection with the audit of Duran, a company listed on a Stock Exchange, for the year to 30 June 2006.

| Hospitality … judgement impaired? | (1)   The audit team included a manager, two supervisors, two qualified seniors and six trainees. The final audit, which lasted approximately five weeks, was very time-pressured and the team worked late into the night towards the end of the audit. Duran's staff were very supportive throughout and **paid for evening meals** that were brought in so that the audit team could work with minimum disruption. |

| Threat to independence | (2)   Duran's chief finance officer, Frankie Sharkey, was so impressed with the commitment of the audit staff that he asked that Depeche pay them all **a bonus through an increase in the audit fee**. In |
| Why restricted to juniors? | October 2007, Depeche paid all the members of the team **below manager status** a bonus amounting to a week's salary. The bonus was processed through Depeche's payroll, in the same way as overtime payments, and recharged to Duran as part of **audit expenses**. — Audit fee |

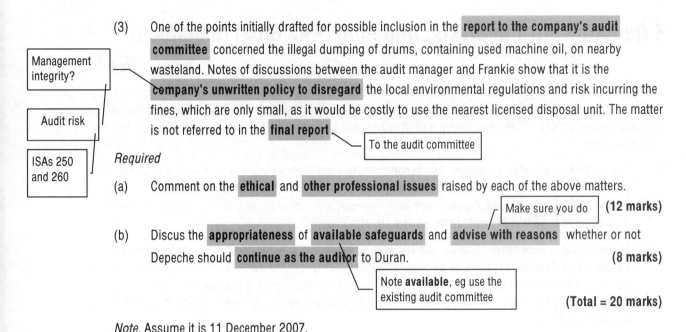

(3)   One of the points initially drafted for possible inclusion in the **report to the company's audit committee** concerned the illegal dumping of drums, containing used machine oil, on nearby wasteland. Notes of discussions between the audit manager and Frankie show that it is the **company's unwritten policy to disregard** the local environmental regulations and risk incurring the fines, which are only small, as it would be costly to use the nearest licensed disposal unit. The matter is not referred to in the **final report**.

Management integrity?

Audit risk

ISAs 250 and 260

To the audit committee

Required

(a)   Comment on the **ethical** and **other professional issues** raised by each of the above matters.

Make sure you do   **(12 marks)**

(b)   Discus the **appropriateness** of **available safeguards** and **advise with reasons** whether or not Depeche should **continue as the auditor** to Duran.   **(8 marks)**

Note **available**, eg use the existing audit committee

(Total = 20 marks)

Note. Assume it is 11 December 2007.

6 Bartolome (AAS 6/05)   27 mins

You are an audit manager in Bartolome, a firm of Chartered Certified Accountants. You have specific responsibility for undertaking annual reviews of existing clients and advising whether an engagement can be properly continued. The following matters have arisen in connection with recent assignments:

(a)   Leon Dormido is the senior in charge of the audit of the financial statements of Moreno, a limited liability company, for the year ending 31 December 2007. Moreno's Chief Executive Officer, James Bay, has just sent you an e-mail to advise you that Leon has been short-listed for the position of Finance Director. You were not previously aware that Leon had applied for the position.   **(5 marks)**

(b)   Chatam, a limited liability company, is a long-standing client. One of its subsidiaries, Ayora, has made losses for several years. At your firm's request, Chatam's management has made a written representation that goodwill arising on the acquisition of Ayora is not impaired. Your firm's auditors' report on the consolidated financial statements of Chatam for the year ended 30 September 2007 is unqualified. Your firm's auditors' report on the financial statements of Ayora is similarly unqualified. Chatam's Chief Executive, Charles Barrington, is due to retire in 2008 when his share options mature.   **(6 marks)**

(c)   Pinzon, a limited liability company and audit client, is threatening to sue your firm in respect of audit fees charged for the year ended 30 June 2007. Pinzon is alleging that Bartolome billed the full rate on air fares for audit staff when substantial discounts had been obtained by Bartolome.   **(4 marks)**

Required

Comment on the ethical and other professional issues raised by each of the above matters and their implications, if any, for the continuation of each assignment.

Note. The mark allocation is shown against each of the three issues.   **(Total = 15 marks)**

7 Boleyn (AAS 12/06)   27 mins

(a)   IFAC's 'Code of Ethics for Professional Accountants' is divided into three parts:

Part A – Applicable to All Professional Accountants
Part B – Applicable to Professional Accountants in Public Practice
Part C – Applicable to Employed Professional Accountants

Required

Distinguish between 'Professional Accountants', 'Professional Accountants in Public Practice' and
'Employed Professional Accountants'.   **(3 marks)**

(b)   As a newly-qualified Chartered Certified Accountant in Boleyn & Co, you have been assigned to assist the
ethics partner in developing ethical guidance for the firm. In particular, you have been asked to draft
guidance on the following frequently asked questions ('FAQs') that will be circulated to all staff through
Boleyn & Co's intranet:

(i)   What Information Technology services can we offer to audit clients?   **(5 marks)**
(ii)   Can we entertain our clients as a gesture of goodwill or is corporate hospitality ruled out? **(3 marks)**
(iii) Can audit teams cross sell services to their clients?   **(4 marks)**

Required

For EACH of the three FAQs, explain the threats to objectivity that may arise and the safeguards that should
be available to manage them to an acceptable level.

Note. The mark allocation is shown against each of the three questions.

(Total = 15 marks)

PRACTICE MANAGEMENT

Questions 8 to 13 cover Practice management, the subject of Part C of the BPP Study Text for Paper P7.

8 Hawk Associates (AAS 6/04)   27 mins

You are a training manager in Hawk Associates, a firm of Chartered Certified Accountants. The firm has suffered a reduction in fee income due to increasing restrictions on the provision of non-audit services to audit clients. The following proposals for obtaining professional work are to be discussed at a forthcoming in-house seminar:

(a)   'Cold calling' (ie approaching directly to seek new business) the chief executive officers of local businesses and offering them free second opinions.   **(5 marks)**

(b)   Placing an advertisement in a national accountancy magazine that includes the following:

'If you have an asset on which a large chargeable gain is expected to arise when you dispose of it, you should be interested in the best tax planning advice. However your gains might arise, there are techniques you can apply. Hawk Associates can ensure that you consider all the alternative fact presentations so that you minimise the amount of tax you might have to pay. No tax saving – no fee!'   **(6 marks)**

(c)   Displaying business cards alongside those of local tradesman and service providers in supermarkets and libraries. The cards would read:

'Hawk ACCA Associates
For PROFESSIONAL Accountancy, Audit,
Business Consultancy and Taxation Services
Competitive rates. Money back guarantees'

(4 marks)

Required

Comment on the suitability of each of the above proposals in terms of the ethical and other professional issues that they raise.

Note. The mark allocation is shown against each of the three issues.   **(Total = 15 marks)**

9 Fox & Steeple (AAS 6/06)   27 mins

You are an audit manager in Fox & Steeple, a firm of Chartered Certified Accountants, responsible for allocating staff to the following three audits of financial statements for the year ending 30 June 2008:

(a)   Blythe Co is a new audit client. This private company is a local manufacturer and distributor of sportswear. The company's finance director, Peter, sees little value in the audit and put it out to tender last year as a cost-cutting exercise. In accordance with the requirements of the invitation to tender your firm indicated that there would not be an interim audit.

(b)   Huggins Co, a long-standing client, operates a national supermarket chain. Your firm provided Huggins Co with corporate financial advice on obtaining a listing on a recognised stock exchange in 2006. Senior management expects a thorough examination of the company's computerised systems, and are also seeking assurance that the annual report will not attract adverse criticism.

(c)   Gray Co has been an audit client since 2001 after your firm advised management on a successful buyout. Gray provides communication services and software solutions. Your firm provides Gray with technical advice on financial reporting and tax services. Most recently you have been asked to conduct due diligence reviews on potential acquisitions.

Required

For these assignments, compare and contrast:

(i)   The threats to independence
(ii)   The other professional and practical matters that arise
(iii)   The implications for allocating staff   **(15 marks)**

10 Azure (AAS 6/02)   45 mins

Azure sells inclusive tours (ie international flights, hotel accommodation and meals) to two million customers. All hotels are independently owned and operated. The company employs 5,000 people and uses 11 leased aircraft. Azure has a representative office at each of 13 holiday locations. Your firm has been invited to tender for the audit of Azure for the year ending 30 June 2008. As the prospective audit engagement manager, you have been asked to identify the principal audit risks and other planning issues, including audit strategy, to be presented as part of your firm's written submission. The invitation to tender indicates that written submissions will be used as a means of shortlisting for the presentation stage.

You have obtained the following information from Azure's Annual Report 2006.

(i)   Holidays are sold through Azure's retail travel agency, IsoTours, which has 29 outlets (2005: 31). Direct sales through call centres is the fastest growing distribution method and Internet bookings are now offered.

(ii)   The internal financial control system includes:

     –   Divisional planning and budgeting systems and regular Board reviews of actual results compared to budget and prior year comparatives;

     –   An internal audit function and a review of internal audit reports by the Audit Committee.

(iii)   Financial extracts ($m):

	2006	2005
Revenue (Note i)	942.8	763.7
Operating profit before tax	27.3	25.7
Tangible non-current assets	109.1	80.3
Trade receivables	29.7	18.2
Cash and cash equivalents	138.6	91.0
Current liabilities (Note ii)	(237.2)	(200.5)
5% Convertible debt due 2010 (Note iii)	(73.0)	-

Notes

(i)   Revenue represents gross revenue receivable from inclusive tours and travel agency commissions. Revenues and expenses relating to inclusive tours are taken to the income statement on holiday departure.

(ii)   Revenue received in advance included in current liabilities amounts to $69.9 million (2005: $61.4 million)

(iii)   Debt will be redeemed at its principal amount on 7 January 2010 unless it is converted at the option of the debt holder any time before 31 December 2009.

(iv)   Annual commitments under non-cancellable operating leases are as follows ($m):

	2006	2005
Less than one year	4.3	2.5
Between one and five years	16.7	17.9
Five years or more	17.4	12.7
	38.4	33.1

Required

(a) Explain the audit planning issues which should be included in the written submission as requested by Azure.

(15 marks)

(b) Suggest and comment on appropriate selection criteria which should be used by Azure in its evaluation of submissions received. **(10 marks)**

Note. Assume it is 11 December 2007. **(Total = 25 marks)**

11 Turnals

45 mins

Turnals, a private limited company, is a manufacturing company with 120 employees, a projected revenue of $12 million, and estimated profit before tax of $1.5 million. During the current year the directors' attention had been brought to a recently discovered fraud perpetrated by Mr Jones, the purchasing manager. He had set up a fictitious business that had invoiced Turnals for goods that had never been supplied. The fraud had been going on for two years. Mr Jones was immediately suspended from all duties and the police informed.

Mr Jones had responsibility for obtaining competitive quotes, checking and initially approving new suppliers. Final approval was authorised by the managing director but in practice this was a formality. Mr Jones also raised most of the purchase requisitions based on information supplied by the storekeeper and approved any requisitions made by other members of staff.

The storekeeper's responsibility was to match each delivery note to a copy of the purchase requisition before the goods were taken into inventory. The two documents were then sent to Mr Jones who matched them with the purchase invoice before passing the invoice to the purchase ledger cashier for payment. When the storekeeper was on holiday the system of internal control specified that a deputy should perform the delivery note matching procedure. In practice this had always been done by Mr Jones.

The fraud took place during the storekeeper's holidays. It was discovered when the cashier had to query one of the fraudulent invoices with the storekeeper because Mr Jones was absent on company business.

Subsequent investigation revealed that approximately $50,000 had been misappropriated by Mr Jones.

Garner and Company are the auditors of Turnals. They are a firm with 12 partners and 60 audit staff. During the interim audit of Turnals last year they recorded and tested the internal control of the purchase system. They made no comments to management.

Garner and Company had acted as management and systems design consultants during the implementation of Turnals's purchase system. As a result the directors believe that Garner and Company should be liable for the losses suffered by Turnals as they employed the audit firm in a dual capacity.

Required

(a) Describe the regulations and other audit practices that are designed to avoid conflicts of interest in the provision of non-audit services to an audit client. **(8 marks)**

(b) Compare and contrast the auditor's responsibility for the detection and reporting of fraud and error. Your answer should distinguish fraud from error. **(5 marks)**

(c) Discuss why the following audit procedures may have failed to detect the above fraud:

  (i) Evaluation of the prescribed system of controls
  (ii) Tests of control on the authorisation of new suppliers
  (iii) Analytical review procedures **(7 marks)**

(d) Discuss the basis on which Turnals believe they have a claim against their auditors and the likelihood of its success. **(5 marks)**

(Total = 25 marks)

12 TS Circuits

45 mins

You are the audit manager in charge of the audit of TS Circuits, a small private company specialising in the manufacture of printed circuit boards. The company was formed four years ago by Trevor Steven Conroy, the managing director, who owns 90% of the shares with the remaining 10% being owned by his wife.

During the interim audit, the audit manager uncovered some irregularities. As part of a trade receivables' circularisation the audit team had sent out a copy of the last month's sales ledger statement to selected customers for confirmation, rather than the normal procedure of requiring confirmation of just the outstanding balance. Past experience had shown that this practice often made it easier for customers to confirm their outstanding balance. One customer, Gilling Electrical, replied to confirm the outstanding balance, but disagreed with its composition. They claimed that an amount shown as being settled by credit note had actually been settled by a cheque payment. On investigation by the audit manager a copy of the credit note was traced. It showed that the credit note had been issued as a credit against the original invoice for a circuit board that had failed due to a design fault. As a precaution the audit manager checked all other credit notes issued and it was discovered that approximately $50,000 of credit notes had been issued to customers in respect of design faults on circuit boards.

The managing director was interviewed about the above irregularities. When presented with the reply letter from Gilling Electrical, the managing director explained that some customers (on his instructions) had made out cheques to TSC. He had then added 'onroy' after the TSC so that he could bank them in his personal bank account in the name of T S Conroy. The audit manager then confirmed with Mr Conroy that this practice has extended to all of the credit notes issued in relation to 'design faults'. Mr Conroy was informed that the matter would be discussed with the engagement partner.

At the meeting with the engagement partner, Mr Conroy said that he did not see any real problem with this practice. He made the point that the company was 100% owned by himself and his wife; it was therefore his money. Also his loan account to the company was over $50,000, so he owned more than the amount of the cheques he had personally banked.

The draft financial statements (without correction of the irregularities above) show that the company's profitability has declined in the current year to about break-even point, and the summarised draft balance sheet is as follows.

	$'000	$'000
Non-current assets		
Plant and equipment		200
Current assets		
Inventory	64	
Receivables and prepayments	36	
		100
Total assets		300
Equity		
Ordinary shares $1 each		20
Retained earnings		2
Current liabilities		
Bank overdraft	45	
Sales tax	22	
Income tax	63	
Payables	70	
Corporation tax	14	
		214
Loan account		64
		300

The bank overdraft is secured against the company's plant and equipment and supported by a personal guarantee from Mr Conroy.

Required

(a)   Discuss the arguments in favour of, and those against, small companies being subject to an annual audit.

(10 marks)

(b)   Describe the financial effect that the irregularities will have on the (uncorrected) financial statements; and identify the users to whom the auditor may be potentially liable if they are not corrected.   **(8 marks)**

Note. You are NOT required to recalculate the financial statements.

(c)   Advise the engagement partner on the further actions he should take in relation to the irregularities.

(7 marks)

(Total = 25 marks)

13 Benson   45 mins

Benson Co is a medium sized listed entity, managed by its owners who bought it out from a large listed company six years ago. The share capital is owned by four directors. One of the original directors, Alistair Fisher, has recently passed away and his shares and his place on the board have been taken up by his son, John Fisher.

A large loan from the bank which helped to finance the management buy-out was paid off in the previous period. This year, the directors have negotiated another loan from the bank to help finance an expansion into Europe.

You work for a firm of chartered certified accountants called Andrews, Baker and Co (ABC). ABC became involved with Benson at the time of the buy-out when it provided advice to two of the (current) directors. The firm has been involved with the business ever since, acting in the capacity of tax advisers, management consultants, and personal tax advisers for all the directors. It has also been involved in some special projects for Benson, taking part in an investigation due to a suspected fraud two years after the buy-out, and putting together projections and budgets for the potential expansion into Europe.

ABC was invited to tender initially for the audit, but its tender had the highest fee, and Mr Fisher senior, who was the managing director at the time, strongly believed that an audit was a statutory necessity which the company should obtain as cheaply as possible. The audit was given to a smaller firm of auditors, XYZ, but ABC was engaged to provide what Mr Fisher always termed, 'the useful stuff – worth paying for'.

The fee income from Benson has been considerable over the years. Two years ago, when the work was done on the expansion, it represented 20% of the income of the firm for that year.

The increase in size of the business since the expansion has led to the current auditors, XYZ, resigning. Rather than going through another tender, the directors have decided to offer the audit to their business advisers, ABC, as they believe that it provides synergy to combine the two roles, and that synergy may result in a lower overall cost to the company of accountancy and related services.

ABC has accepted the audit work. The first audit is due to start in three weeks time. At a recent board meeting, attended by the partner who has been in charge of the work provided by Benson, and his colleague, who has been appointed as the audit engagement partner, the directors discussed plans to float the company on a stock exchange in the foreseeable future.

Required

(a)   Explain the current ethical and legal considerations in connection with accepting appointment as an auditor.

(7 marks)

(b)   Discuss whether the conduct of ABC has been ethical in its dealings with Benson during the course of their relationship, and how Benson's prospective listing might change the ethical situation.

(10 marks)

(c)   ABC has appointed an audit engagement partner who has not previously been involved with the client to the audit of Benson. What other quality control procedures and policies should ABC have in place in relation to the audit of Benson to safeguard audit quality?   **(8 marks)**

(Total = 25 marks)

14 Alakazam (AAS 12/01)   45 mins

Your audit client, Alakazam, sells and distributes telecommunications equipment and accessories to retail outlets. The company has expanded rapidly since the appointment of a new chief executive, Leon Izzardo, in September 2006.

In October 2006, the company purchased exclusive national distribution rights to an imported WAP phone for a two-year period. During 2006 and 2007, the company has doubled its customer base and is close to achieving national coverage with its distribution network. Employee numbers have increased rapidly from 36 to 103. Head office administrators, including accounts staff, have risen from 10 to 25.

In October 2007, the central distribution and servicing department was moved away from the head office into larger premises. This was necessary to handle not only the increased inventory levels and pre-delivery checks necessary, but also the rising level of after sales warranty work caused by manufacturing defects in the WAP phones.

Sales of the WAP phone, which now account for 80% of Alakazam's revenue, have recently started to fall.

You have been assigned the task of planning the audit of the financial statements of Alakazam for the year ended 31 March 2008.

Required

(a)   Describe the principal audit risks arising and how the audit strategy will be directed to take account of them in the overall audit plan.   **(14 marks)**

(b)   Mr Izzardo has now targeted Neodex, a private limited company, for acquisition by Alakazam in 2008. Your firm has just completed a review of Neodex's published financial statements for the year to 31 December 2006 and held brief discussions with its two directors. The main findings were as follows:

   (1)   Shares in Neodex are owned equally by the technical director, Stefan Koyla, and marketing director, Georgio Neratu, who set up the company three years after graduating from university.

   (2)   Neodex has successfully developed a small range of specialised data interface network servers (DINS) which significantly reduce the costs of communication systems. Each unit sells for $3,500 - $5,000. Monthly sales are increasing slowly but steadily since Georgio presented the products at an IT exhibition earlier this year.

   (3)   Between them, Stefan and Georgio assemble and package DINS in a small rented office. The manufacture and assembly of the principal component (a circuit board) is outsourced. Stefan would like to recruit an assistant so that he has time to prototype his new design for the Virtual Private Network (VPN) market.

   (4)   Neodex has only one employee who acts as telephonist, receptionist, secretary and bookkeeper.

   Required

   (i)   Outline the principal matters to be considered by Alakazam in deciding whether or not to acquire Neodex.   **(5 marks)**

   (ii)   Explain the implications of the acquisition for the conduct of your audit of Alakazam for the year to 31 March 2008.   **(6 marks)**

   Note. Assume it is 11 December 2007.

                                                                        (Total = 25 marks)

15 Meadow (AAS 12/02)

45 mins

You are an audit manager in Robert Bracco, a firm of Chartered Certified Accountants. One of your audit clients, Meadow, is a company listed on a stock exchange with a 30 September accounting year-end. The principal activity of Meadow is retailing under the Vazandt brand name. The retail industry has recently suffered from a reduction in consumer spending.

Meadow has two operating divisions: Domestic and International. Each retail division is sub-divided into four business units: Ladieswear, Menswear, Home Furnishings and Foods. The International retail business consists of three broad geographic areas: Africa, South America and the Far East. Robert Bracco is represented by affiliated offices in all relevant countries.

You have obtained the following information from Meadow's draft financial statements:

(1) Financial extracts

	For the year ended 30 September	
	2007	2006
Income statement	$m	$m
Revenue	2,585.0	2,638.8
Total operating profit	129.1	120.0
Provision for loss on operations to be discontinued (Note i)	(83.8)	-
Finance cost (net)	(4.7)	(4.8)
Profit before tax	40.6	115.2

	As at 30 September	
	2007	2006
Balance sheet	$m	$m
Tangible non-current assets		
Land and buildings	950.5	964.0
Store fit-out, fixtures and equipment	448.9	481.8
Inventory (Note ii)	164.2	165.9
Trade and other receivables	22.5	36.9
Cash and cash equivalents	53.7	104.6

Notes

(i)   The company has announced its intention to close loss-making businesses in Africa, subject to the full consultation that the Board recognises will need to take place. The decision to close would be taken only after consultation with employee representative bodies and if no other solution is found during the consultation. Net closure costs of $83.8m have been provided, covered future trading losses, losses on disposal of assets and redundancy costs.

(ii) Inventory is valued at the lower of cost and net realisable value. Cost is ascertained using the retail method (ie current selling price less normal gross profit margin).

(2) Segmental information

	Revenue		Operating profit	
	2007	2006	2007	2006
	$m	$m	$m	$m
International				
Africa	99.0	96.7	(11.8)	(9.0)
South America	264.0	250.5	11.1	5.3
Far East	38.3	38.9	2.8	(1.2)
Total International	401.3	386.1	2.1	(4.9)
Domestic	2,183.7	2,252.7	127.0	124.9
Total operating activities	2,585.0	2,638.8	129.1	120.0

	Number of stores	
	2007	*2006*
International		
Africa	14	13
South America	86	87
Far East	4	4
Total International	104	104
Domestic	107	106
Total	211	210

(3) International restructure

On 29 September 2007, the company announced the intention to:

– close all African operations (representing 14 stores); and
– sell the South American businesses

Required

(a) Using the information provided, identify and explain the principal audit risks and other matters to be considered when planning the approach to the final audit of Meadow for the year ended 30 September 2007.

(17 marks)

(b) Describe the audit work that you would undertake to determine whether the accounting treatment and disclosure for the:

(i) Segmental information
(ii) International restructuring

are appropriate.

(8 marks)

Note. Assume it is 11 December 2007.

(Total = 25 marks)

16 ABC (AAS 6/03)

45 mins

ABC, a limited liability company, undertakes construction contracts, which include offices, factories, warehouses, schools and bridges. ABC's customers include businesses and local government departments. Recent cut-backs in local government expenditure have resulted in fewer contracts being started this year than budgeted.

The statement of accounting policy for construction contracts in ABC's financial statements is as follows:

'Revenue is recognised using the percentage of completion method, calculated on the basis of costs incurred as a percentage of expected total costs.

'Anticipated losses are provided for in full as soon as the possibility of loss is forecast.'

Direct costs attributed to specific contracts include:

(1) Architects' design costs, legal fees and engineering assistance
(2) Materials issued to the site
(3) Site supervision (apportioned foremen's salaries)
(4) Site labour costs (allocated from the payroll and subcontractors' invoices)
(5) Costs of hiring portable buildings and leasing plant and equipment
(6) Depreciation of plant, equipment and vehicles
(7) Transportation costs of resources (e.g. materials and plant) between sites
(8) Insurance and telephone

Indirect expenses incurred by ABC's head office which relate to construction activities are attributed to projects at 70% of direct costs.

You are the auditor of ABC. Last year your firm qualified the auditors' report due to a lack of evidence to support the client's schedules of estimated costs to completion. During the year, a quantity surveyor joined the client's management team to:

(1)   Supervise monthly physical counts at the major construction sites;

(2)   Monitor costs to date against monthly rolling budgets; and

(3)   Prepare year-end schedules, by contract, of total costs to completion (i.e. direct costs incurred to the balance sheet date, attributable overheads and estimated costs to completion).

You are satisfied that the quantity surveyor is appropriately qualified and experienced.

Required

(a)   Identify and explain the principal audit risks to be considered when planning the approach to the final audit of ABC for the year ending 31 March 2008.   **(12 marks)**

(b)   Explain the nature and extent of the reliance which you should seek to place on the work of the quantity surveyor.   **(5 marks)**

(c)   Describe the audit work to be performed in respect of total costs to completion.   **(8 marks)**

Note. Assume it is 11 December 2007.   **(Total = 25 marks)**

17 Question with analysis: Hydrasports (AAS 12/03)   54 mins

Hydrasports, a limited liability company and national leisure group, has sixteen centres around the country and a head office. Facilities at each centre are of a standard design which incorporates a heated swimming pool, sauna, air-conditioned gym and fitness studio with supervised childcare. Each centre is managed on a day-to-day basis, by a centre manager, in accordance with company policies. The centre manager is also responsible for preparing and submitting monthly accounting returns to head office.

Each centre is required to have a licence from the local authority to operate. Licences are granted for periods between two and five years and are renewable subject to satisfactory reports from local authority inspectors. The average annual cost of a licence is $900.

Members pay a $100 joining fee, plus either $50 per month for 'peak' membership or $30 per month for 'off-peak', payable quarterly in advance. All fees are stated to be non-refundable.

The centre at Verne was closed from July to September 2007 after a chemical spill in the sauna caused a serious accident. Although the centre was re-opened, Hydrasports has recommended to all centre managers that sauna facilities be suspended until further notice.

In response to complaints to the local authorities about its childcare facilities, Hydrasports has issued centre managers with revised guidelines for minimum levels of supervision. Centre managers are finding it difficult to meet the new guidelines and have suggested that childcare facilities should be withdrawn.

Staff lateness is a recurring problem and a major cause of 'early bird' customer dissatisfaction with sessions which are scheduled to start at 07:00. New employees are generally attracted to the industry in the short-term for its non-cash benefits, including free use of the facilities – but leave when they require increased financial rewards. Training staff to be qualified life-guards is costly and time-consuming and retention rates are poor. Turnover of centre managers is also high, due to the constraints imposed on them by company policy.

Three of the centres are expected to have run at a loss for the year to 31 December 2007 due to falling membership. Hydrasports has invested heavily in a hydrotherapy pool at one of these centres, with the aim of attracting retired members with more leisure time. The building contractor has already billed twice as much and taken three times as long as budgeted for the work. The pool is now expected to open in February 2008.

Cash flow difficulties in the current year have put back the planned replacement of gym equipment for most of the centres.

Insurance premiums for liability to employees and the public have increased by nearly 45%. Hydrasports has met the additional expense by reducing its insurance cover on its plant and equipment from a replacement cost basis to a net realisable value basis.

Required

(a) (i) Identify and explain the business risks which should be assessed by the management of Hydrasports.

(8 marks)

(ii) Explain how each of the business risks identified in (i) may be linked to financial statement risk.

(8 marks)

(b) Describe the principal audit work to be performed in respect of the carrying amount of the following items in the balance sheet of Hydrasports as at 31 December 2007:

(i) Deferred income   **(3 marks)**
(ii) Hydrotherapy pool   **(3 marks)**

(c) Suggest performance indicators that could be set to increase the centre managers' awareness of Hydrasports' social and environmental responsibilities and the evidence which should be available to provide assurance on their accuracy.

(8 marks)

Note. Assume it is 11 December 2007.   **(Total = 30 marks)**

17 Question with analysis: Hydrasports (AAS 12/03)   54 mins

Hydrasports, a limited liability company and national leisure group, has sixteen centres around the country and a head office. Facilities at each centre are of a standard design which incorporates a heated swimming pool, sauna, air-conditioned gym and fitness studio with supervised childcare.

> Local managers restricted

> Control risk

Each centre is managed on a day-to-day basis, by a centre manager, **in accordance with company policies**. The centre manager is also responsible for preparing and submitting monthly accounting returns to head office.

> Asset?

Each centre is required to have a **licence** from the local authority to operate. Licences are granted for periods between two and five years and are **renewable** subject to satisfactory reports from local authority inspectors. The average annual cost of a licence is $900.

> Cannot operate if not renewed

> Can company provide services already paid for?

Members pay a $100 joining fee, plus either $50 per month for 'peak' membership or $30 per month for 'off-peak', payable quarterly **in advance**. All fees are stated to be **non-refundable**.

> Accounting issues

> Is this legally true in practice?

> Provisions

The centre at Verne was closed from July to September 2007 after a chemical spill in the sauna caused a serious accident. Although the centre was re-opened, Hydrasports has recommended to all centre managers that sauna facilities be suspended until further notice.

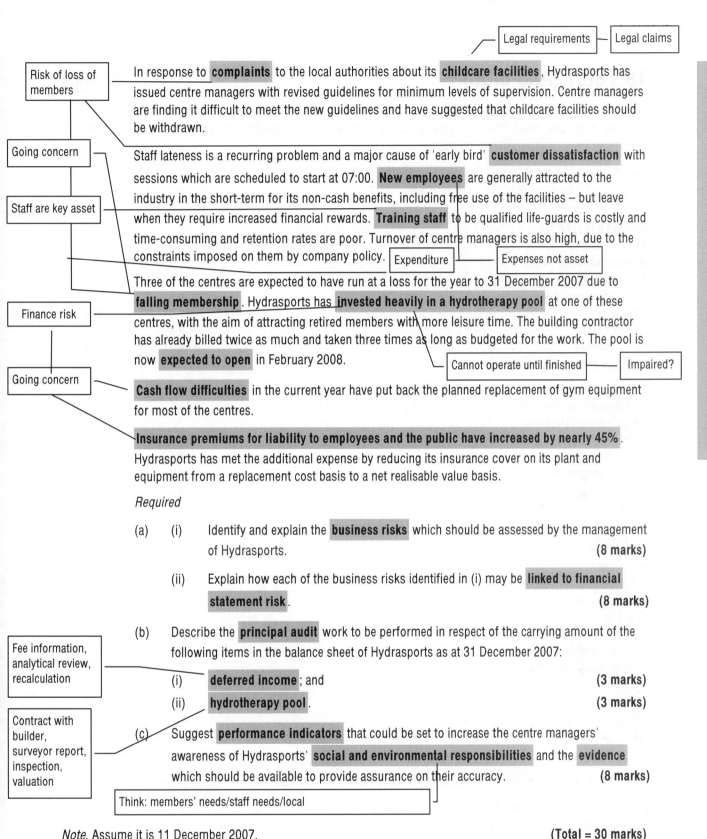

Legal requirements — Legal claims

Risk of loss of members

In response to **complaints** to the local authorities about its **childcare facilities**, Hydrasports has issued centre managers with revised guidelines for minimum levels of supervision. Centre managers are finding it difficult to meet the new guidelines and have suggested that childcare facilities should be withdrawn.

Going concern

Staff are key asset

Staff lateness is a recurring problem and a major cause of 'early bird' **customer dissatisfaction** with sessions which are scheduled to start at 07:00. **New employees** are generally attracted to the industry in the short-term for its non-cash benefits, including free use of the facilities – but leave when they require increased financial rewards. **Training staff** to be qualified life-guards is costly and time-consuming and retention rates are poor. Turnover of centre managers is also high, due to the constraints imposed on them by company policy.

Expenditure — Expenses not asset

Finance risk

Three of the centres are expected to have run at a loss for the year to 31 December 2007 due to **falling membership**. Hydrasports has **invested heavily in a hydrotherapy pool** at one of these centres, with the aim of attracting retired members with more leisure time. The building contractor has already billed twice as much and taken three times as long as budgeted for the work. The pool is now **expected to open** in February 2008.

Cannot operate until finished — Impaired?

Going concern

Cash flow difficulties in the current year have put back the planned replacement of gym equipment for most of the centres.

Insurance premiums for liability to employees and the public have increased by nearly 45%. Hydrasports has met the additional expense by reducing its insurance cover on its plant and equipment from a replacement cost basis to a net realisable value basis.

Required

(a) (i) Identify and explain the **business risks** which should be assessed by the management of Hydrasports. **(8 marks)**

(ii) Explain how each of the business risks identified in (i) may be **linked to financial statement risk**. **(8 marks)**

(b) Describe the **principal audit** work to be performed in respect of the carrying amount of the following items in the balance sheet of Hydrasports as at 31 December 2007:

Fee information, analytical review, recalculation

(i) **deferred income**; and **(3 marks)**
(ii) **hydrotherapy pool**. **(3 marks)**

Contract with builder, surveyor report, inspection, valuation

(c) Suggest **performance indicators** that could be set to increase the centre managers' awareness of Hydrasports' **social and environmental responsibilities** and the **evidence** which should be available to provide assurance on their accuracy. **(8 marks)**

Think: members' needs/staff needs/local

Note. Assume it is 11 December 2007. **(Total = 30 marks)**

18 Yates (AAS 6/06)

54 mins

Your firm has successfully tendered for the audit of Yates Co, a private national haulage and distribution company with over 2,000 employees. This long-established company provides refrigerated, bulk and heavy haulage transport services to time-sensitive delivery schedules.

You have obtained the following financial information from Yates:

For the year to 31 December	2007 Draft $m	2006 Actual $m
INCOME STATEMENT		
Revenue (Note 1)	161.5	144.4
Materials expense (Note 2)	88.0	74.7
Staff costs	40.6	35.6
Depreciation and amortisation	8.5	9.5
Other expenses	19.6	23.2
Finance costs	2.9	2.2
Total expenses	159.6	145.2
Profit/(loss) before taxation	1.9	(0.8)
BALANCE SHEET		
Intangible assets (Note 3)	7.2	6.2
Tangible assets (Note 4)		
Property	55.1	57.8
Vehicles and transport equipment	16.4	16.0
Other equipment	7.4	9.3
Inventories	0.6	0.5
Trade receivables (Note 5)	13.7	13.4
Cash and cash equivalents	3.4	2.8
Total assets	103.8	106.0
Provisions		
Restructuring (Note 6)	9.7	10.8
Tax provision	3.0	3.3
Liabilities		
Finance lease liabilities (Note 7)	5.4	4.4
Trade payables	13.8	13.1
Other liabilities (Note 8)	8.5	7.9
Total liabilities	40.4	39.5

Notes

(1) Revenue is net of rebates to major customers that increase with the volume of consignments transported. Rebates are calculated on cumulative sales for the financial year and awarded quarterly in arrears.

(2) Materials expense includes fuel, repair materials, transportation and vehicle maintenance costs.

(3) Purchased intangible assets, including software and industrial licences, are accounted for using the cost model. Internally generated intangible assets, mainly software developed for customers to generate consignment documents, are initially recognised at cost if the asset recognition criteria are satisfied.

(4)   Movements on tangible non-current assets have been drafted as follows:

	Property $m	Vehicles and transport equipment $m	Other equipment $m	Total $m
Historical cost				
Opening balance at 1 January 2007	75.7	25.6	17.8	119.1
Additions	1.4	2.7	1.1	5.2
Disposals	(2.5)	(2.6)	(1.4)	(6.5)
Closing balance at 1 December 2007	74.6	25.7	17.5	117.8
Depreciation and impairment losses				
Opening balance at 1 January 2007	17.9	9.6	8.5	36.0
Depreciation and impairment loss	2.4	1.9	2.5	6.8
Disposals	(0.8)	(2.2)	(0.9)	(3.9)
Closing balance at 31 December 2007	19.5	9.3	10.1	38.9
Carrying amount at 31 December 2007	55.1	16.4	7.4	78.9
Carrying amount at 31 December 2006	57.8	16.0	9.3	83.1

Depreciation is charged using the straight-line method assuming the following useful lives:

	Years
Property	6 to 60
Vehicles and transport equipment	3 to 8
Other equipment	3 to 15

(5)   Trade receivables are carried at their principal amount, less allowances for impairment.

(6)   The restructuring provision relates to employee termination and other obligations arising on the closure and relocation of distribution depots in June 2006.

(7)   Finance leases are capitalised at the date of inception of the lease at fair value or the present value of the minimum lease payments, if less.

(8)   Other liabilities include amounts due to employees for accrued wages and salaries, overtime, sick leave, maternity pay and bonuses.

Required

In respect of the financial statements audit of Yates Co for the year ending 31 December 2007:

(a)   Calculate preliminary materiality and justify the suitability of your assessment.   **(6 marks)**

(b)   Identify and explain the financial statement risks to be taken into account in planning the final audit.

(12 marks)

(c)   Explain the extent to which you should plan to place reliance on analytical procedures as audit evidence.

(6 marks)

(d)   Briefly describe the principal audit work to be performed in respect of the carrying amount of the following items in the balance sheet:

(i)   trade receivables; and   **(3 marks)**
(ii)   vehicles.   **(3 marks)**

Note. Assume it is 11 December 2007.   **(Total = 30 marks)**

19 Harrier Motors (AAS 6/04)

45 mins

Harrier Motors deals in motor vehicles, sells spare parts, provides after-sales servicing and undertakes car body repairs. During the financial year to 31 December 2007, the company expanded its operations from five to eight sites. Each site has a car showroom, service workshop and parts storage.

In November 2007, management appointed an experienced chartered certified accountant to set up an internal audit department.

New cars are imported, on consignment, every three months from one supplier. Harrier pays the purchase price of the cars, plus 3%, three months after taking delivery. Harrier does not return unsold cars, although it has a legal right to do so.

Harrier offers 'trade-ins' (ie part-exchange) on all sales of new and used cars. New car sales carry a three year manufacturer's warranty and used cars carry a six-month guarantee. Many used cards are sold for cash.

An extensive range of spare parts is held for which perpetual inventory records are kept. Storekeepers carry out continuous checking.

Mr Joop, the sales director, selects a car from each consignment to use for all his business and personal travelling until the next consignment is received. Such cars are sold at a discount as ex-demonstration models.

Car servicing and body repairs are carried out in workshops by employed and sub-contracted service engineers. Most jobs are started and finished in a day and are invoiced immediately on completion.

In November 2006, Harrier purchased a brand name, 'Uni-fit', which is now applied to the parts which it supplies. Management has not amortised this intangible asset as it believes its useful life to be indefinite.

Required

(a) Using the information provided, identify and explain the audit risks to be addressed when planning the final audit of Harrier Motors for the year ending 31 December 2007. **(12 marks)**

(b) Identify and briefly explain the principal matters to be addressed in Harrier Motors' instructions for the conduct of its physical inventory count as at 31 December 2007. **(6 marks)**

(c) Describe the audit work to be carried out in respect of the useful life of the 'Uni-fit' brand name as at 31 December 2007. **(7 marks)**

Note. Assume it is 11 December 2007. **(Total = 25 marks)**

20 Shire (AAS 12/05)

43 mins

Shire Oil Co ('Shire'), a listed company, is primarily an oil producer with interests in the North Sea, West Africa and South Asia. Shire's latest interim report shows:

	30 June 2007 Unaudited $'000	30 June 2006 Unaudited $'000	31 December 2006 Audited $'000
Revenue	22,000	18,300	37,500
Profit before tax	5,500	4,200	7,500
Total assets	95,900	92,300	88,400
Earnings per share (basic)	$1.82	$2.07	$3.53

In April 2007, the company was awarded a new five-year licence, by the central government, to explore for oil in a remote region. The licence was granted at no cost to Shire. However, Shire's management has decided to recognize the licence at an estimated fair value of $3 million.

The most significant of Shire's tangible non-current assets are its 17 oil rigs (2006 – 15). Each rig is composed of numerous items including a platform, buildings thereon and drilling equipment. The useful life of each platform is assessed annually on factors such as weather conditions and the period over which it is estimated that oil will be extracted. Platforms are depreciated on a straight line basis over 15 to 40 years.

A provision for the present value of the expected cost of decommissioning an oil rig is recognised in full at the commencement of oil production. One of the rigs in South Asia sustained severe cyclone damage in October 2007. Shire's management believes the rig is beyond economic recovery and that there will be no alternative but to abandon it where it is. This suggestion has brought angry protests from conservationists.

In July 2007, Shire entered into an agreement to share in the future economic benefits of an extensive oil pipeline.

You are the manager responsible for the audit of Shire. Last year your firm modified its auditor's report due to a lack of evidence to support management's schedule of proven and probable oil reserves to be recoverable from known reserves.

Required

(a)   Using the information provided, identify and explain the audit risks to be addressed when planning the final audit of Shire Oil Co for the year ending 31 December 2007.   **(12 marks)**

(b)   Describe the principal audit work to be performed in respect of the useful lives of Shire Oil Co's rig platforms.   **(6 marks)**

(c)   You have just been advised of management's intention to publish its yearly marketing report in the annual report that will contain the financial statements for the year ending 31 December 2007. Extracts from the marketing report include the following:

'Shire Oil Co sponsors national school sports championships and the 'Shire Ward' at the national teaching hospital. The company's vision is to continue its investment in health and safety and the environment.

'Our health and safety, security and environmental policies are of the highest standard in the energy sector. We aim to operate under principles of no-harm to people and the environment.

'Shire Oil Co's main contribution to sustainable development comes from providing extra energy in a cleaner and more socially responsible way. This means improving the environmental and social performance of our operations. Regrettably, five employees lost their lives at work during the year.'

Required

Suggest performance indicators that could reflect the extent to which Shire Oil Co's social and environmental responsibilities are being met, and the evidence that should be available to provide assurance on their accuracy.

(6 marks)

Note. Assume it is 11 December 2007.   **(Total = 24 marks)**

21 Cerise (12/04) (amended)   54 mins

Cerise, a limited liability company, manufactures computer-controlled machinery for production-line industries such as cars, washing machines, cookers, etc. On 1 September 2007, the shareholder-managers decided, unanimously, to accept a lucrative offer from a multi-national corporation to buy the company's patented technology and manufacturing equipment.

By 10 September 2007 management had notified all the employees, suppliers and customers that Cerise would cease all manufacturing activities on 31 October 2007. The 200-strong factory workforce and the majority of the accounts department and support staff were made redundant with effect from that date, when the sale was duly completed.

The marketing, human resources and production managers will cease to be employed by the company at 31 December 2007. However, the chief executive, sales manager, finance manager, accountant and a small number of accounting and other support staff expect to be employed until the company is wound down completely.

Cerise's operations extend to fourteen premises, nine of which were put on the market on 1 November 2007. Cerise accounts for all tangible non-current assets under the cost model (ie at depreciated cost). Four premises are held on leases that expire in the next two to seven years and cannot be sold or sub-let under the lease terms. The small head office premises will continue to be occupied until the lease expires in 2010. No new lease agreements were entered into during 2007.

All Cerise's computer-controlled products carry a one-year warranty. Extended warranties of three and five years, previously available at the time of purchase, have not been offered on sales of remaining inventory from 1 November onwards.

Cerise has three-year agreements with its national and international distributors for the sale of equipment. It also has annual contracts with its major suppliers for the purchase of components. So far, none of these parties have lodged any legal claim against Cerise. However, the distributors are withholding payment of their account balances pending settlement of the significant penalties which are now due to them.

Required

You are required to answer the following in the context of the final audit of the financial statements of Cerise for the year ending 31 December 2007:

(a)   Using the information provided, identify and explain the financial statement risks to be taken into account in planning the audit.   **(12 marks)**

(b)   Explain how the extent of the reliance to be placed on:

(i)   Analytical procedures; and   **(5 marks)**
(ii)   Management representations,   **(5 marks)**

should compare with that for the prior year audit.

(c)   Describe the principal audit work to be performed in respect of the carrying amount of the following items in the balance sheet:

(i)   Amounts due from distributors; and   **(4 marks)**
(ii)   Lease liabilities.   **(4 marks)**

Note. Assume it is 11 December 2007.   **(Total = 30 marks)**

22 Geno Vesa Farm (AAS 6/05)   47 mins

Geno Vesa Farm (GVF), a limited liability company, is a cheese manufacturer. Its principal activity is the production of a traditional 'Farmhouse' cheese that is retailed around the world to exclusive shops, through mail order and web sales. Other activities include the sale of locally produced foods through a farm shop and cheese-making demonstrations and tours.

The farm's herd of 700 goats is used primarily for the production of milk. Kids (ie goat offspring), which are a secondary product, are selected for herd replacement or otherwise sold. Animals held for sale are not usually retained beyond the time they reach optimal size or weight because their value usually does not increase thereafter.

There are two main variations of the traditional farmhouse cheese; 'Rabida Red' and 'Bachas Blue'. The red cheese is coloured using Innittu, which is extracted from berries found only in South American rain forests. The cost of Innittu has risen sharply over the last year as the collection of berries by local village workers has come under the scrutiny of an international action group. The group is lobbying the South American government to ban the export of Innittu, claiming that the workers are being exploited and that sustaining the forest is seriously under threat.

BPP
LEARNING MEDIA

Demand for Bachas Blue, which is made from unpasteurised milk, fell considerably in 2006 following the publication of a research report that suggested a link between unpasteurised milk products and a skin disorder. The financial statements for the year ended 31 March 2007 recognised a material impairment loss attributable to the equipment used exclusively for the manufacture of Bachas Blue. However, as the adverse publicity is gradually being forgotten, sales of Bachas Blue are now showing a steady increase and are currently expected to return to their former level by the end of March 2008.

Cheese is matured to three strengths – mild, medium and strong – depending on the period of time it is left to ripen which is six, 12 and 18 months respectively. When produced the cheese is sold to a financial institution, Abingdon Bank, at cost. Under the terms of sale, GVF has the option to buy the cheese on its maturity at cost plus 7% for every six months which has elapsed.

All cheese is stored to maturity on wooden boards in GVF's cool and airy sheds. However, recently enacted health and safety legislation requires that the wooden boards be replaced with stainless steel shelves with effect from 1 January 2008. The management of GVF has petitioned the government health department that to comply with the legislation would interfere with the maturing process and the production of medium and strong cheeses would have to cease.

In 2006, GVF applied for and received a substantial regional development grant for the promotion of tourism in the area. GVF's management has deferred its plan to convert a disused barn into holiday accommodation from 2007 until at least 2009.

Required

(a) Identify and explain the principal audit risks to be considered when planning the final audit of GVF for the year ending 31 March 2008. **(14 marks)**

(b) Describe the audit work to be performed in respect of the carrying amount of the following items in the balance sheet of GVF as at 31 March 2008:

    (i)   Goat herd **(4 marks)**
    (ii)   Equipment used in the manufacture of Bachas Blue **(4 marks)**
    (iii) Cheese **(4 marks)**

(Total = 26 marks)

Note. You are not required to apply the principles of IAS 41 *Agriculture* in answering this question. Assume it is 11 December 2007.

23 Taurus Traders (AAS Pilot paper)   45 mins

As manager responsible for prospective new clients you have visited Taurus Traders, a limited liability company, which supplies a range of specialist materials to the building industry. The chief executive and majority shareholder, Mr Aquila, has asked your firm to make a proposal for the company's audit and provision of financial advice.

During your initial meeting you have ascertained the following:

Turnover has grown from $4 million to $7 million in the last two years and the company is profitable. Further growth is anticipated as Mr Aquila has plans:

(1) To increase the company's customer base by making certain materials available to the public through builders merchants, and

(2) To expand the product base by setting up an overseas operation to manufacture silicon carbide components.

Mr Aquila negotiates prices directly with both suppliers and customers. A part-qualified accountant was recruited earlier this year to help with credit control and to set up more formal accounting systems and procedures. A desk-top computer provides basic sales, receivables, inventory and payroll information. The software was written to Mr Aquila's requirements by his wife's brother. Most purchases require foreign currency translation and are recorded manually. Each month-end there are varying, small and unreconciled differences on the receivables and payables ledger control accounts.

The annual budget significantly understates actual revenue and expenses because of higher than expected growth. Management accounts are produced infrequently on an ad hoc basis.

For management accounting purposes, cost of sales is calculated as a percentage of sales value of different product categories. Historically, this method has proved reasonably reliable when compared to the year-end valuation of the annual physical inventory count. However, margins on product lines have recently become much more varied.

Taurus is currently experiencing a high level of returns of faulty materials. These are returned to inventory if they cannot be sold at a discount for cash.

Mr Aquila is negotiating a bank loan to finance the cost of planned new premises. Contracts with the builders have been signed and building work has commenced. The bank is waiting for a profit forecast before giving final approval to a $2 million loan.

Taurus Traders has increasingly tended to exceed its agreed overdraft facility. Mr Aquila has indicated that a large receipt from a major customer, expected at the end of next month, is to be used to clear tax payment arrears and repay his loan of $52,000.

Mr Aquila is recently married and has purchased a luxury apartment and a new car. He is dissatisfied with the firm of accountants which currently prepares and audits the annual financial statements. He attributes this to the firm's failure to reconcile the ledgers. He also claims that the firm has been unable to suggest how his remuneration package can be increased to meet his personal needs.

Required

(a)   Identify and describe the principal business risks relating to Taurus Traders.   **(11 marks)**

(b)   Identify and comment on the factors that should influence the partner in deciding whether or not the firm should make a proposal for this engagement.   **(5 marks)**

(c)   Justify an appropriate audit strategy for the first audit of Taurus Traders.   **(6 marks)**

(d)   Suggest two procedures that Taurus Traders could implement immediately to improve its accounting procedures and financial controls.   **(3 marks)**

(Total = 25 marks)

24 Indigo (AAS 12/05)   47 mins

Your firm was appointed as auditor to Indigo Co, an iron and steel corporation, in September 2007. You are the manager in charge of the audit of the financial statements of Indigo, for the year ending 31 December 2007.

Indigo owns office buildings, a workshop and a substantial stockyard on land that was leased in 1995 for 25 years. Day-to-day operations are managed by the chief accountant, purchasing manager and workshop supervisor who report to the managing director.

All iron, steel and other metals are purchased for cash at 'scrap' prices determined by the purchasing manager. Scrap metal is mostly high volume. A weighbridge at the entrance to the stockyard weighs trucks and vans before and after the scrap metals that they carry are unloaded into the stockyard.

Two furnaces in the workshop melt down the salvageable scrap metal into blocks the size of small bricks that are then stored in the workshop. These are sold on both credit and cash terms. The furnaces are now 10 years old and have an estimated useful life of a further 15 years. However, the furnace linings are replaced every four years. An annual provision is made for 25% of the estimated cost of the next relining. A by-product of the operation of the furnaces is the production of 'clinker'. Most of this is sold, for cash, for road surfacing but some is illegally dumped.

Indigo's operations are subsidised by the local authority as their existence encourages recycling and means that there is less dumping of metal items. Indigo receives a subsidy calculated at 15% of the market value of metals purchased, as declared in a quarterly return. The return for the quarter to 31 December 2007 is due to be submitted on 21 January 2008.

Indigo maintains manual inventory records by metal and estimated quality. Indigo counted inventory at 30 November 2007 with the intention of 'rolling-forward' the purchasing manager's valuation as at that date to the year-end quantities per the manual records. However, you were not aware of this until you visited Indigo yesterday to plan your year-end procedures.

During yesterday's tour of Indigo's premises you saw that:

(i)   sheets of aluminum were strewn across fields adjacent to the stockyard after a storm blew them away;
(ii)   much of the vast quantity of iron piled up in the stockyard is rusty;
(iii)   piles of copper and brass, that can be distinguished with a simple acid test, have been mixed up.

The count sheets show that metal quantities have increased, on average, by a third since last year; the quantity of aluminum, however, is shown to be three times more. There is no suitably qualified metallurgical expert to value inventory in the region in which Indigo operates.

The chief accountant disappeared on 1 December, taking the cash book and cash from three days' sales with him. The cash book was last posted to the general ledger as at 31 October 2007. The managing director has made an allegation of fraud against the chief accountant to the police.

The auditor's report on the financial statements for the year ended 31 December 2006 was unmodified.

Required

(a)   Describe the principal audit procedures to be carried out on the opening balances of the financial statements of Indigo Co for the year ending 31 December 2007.   **(6 marks)**

(b)   Using the information provided, state the financial statement risks arising and justify an appropriate audit approach for Indigo Co for the year ending 31 December 2007.   **(14 marks)**

(c)   Comment on the matters to be considered in seeking to determine the extent of Indigo Co's financial loss resulting from the alleged fraud.   **(6 marks)**

Note. Assume it is 11 December 2007.   **(Total = 26 marks)**

25 Phoenix (AAS Pilot paper)   36 mins

You are the manager responsible for the audit of Phoenix, a private limited liability company, which manufactures super alloys from imported zinc and aluminium. The company operates three similar foundries at different sites under the direction of Troy Pitz, the chief executive. The draft accounts for the year ended 30 September 2007 show profit before taxation of $1.7m (2006 – $1.5m).

The auditor senior has produced a schedule of 'Points for the Attention of the Audit Manager' as follows:

(a)   A trade investment in 60,000 $1 ordinary shares of Pegasus, one of the company's major shipping contractors, is included in the balance sheet at a cost of $80,000. In November 2007, the published financial statements of Pegasus as at 31 March 2007 show only a small surplus of net assets. A recent press report now suggests that Pegasus is insolvent and has ceased to trade. Although dividends declared by Pegasus in respect of earlier years have not yet been paid, Phoenix has included $15,000 of dividends receivable in its draft accounts as at 30 September 2007.   **(6 marks)**

(b)   Current liabilities include a $500,000 provision for future maintenance. This represents the estimated cost of overhauling the blast furnaces and other foundry equipment. The overhaul is planned for February 2008 when all foundry workers take two weeks annual leave.   **(7 marks)**

(c)   All industrial waste from the furnaces ('clinker') is purchased by Cleanaway, a government–approved disposal company, under a five-year contract that is due for renewal later this year. A recent newspaper article states that 'substantial fines have been levied on Cleanaway for illegal dumping'. Troy Pitz is the majority shareholder of Cleanaway.   **(7 marks)**

Required

For each of the above points:

(i)   Comment on the matters that you would consider, and

(ii)   State the audit evidence that you would expect to find, in undertaking your review of the audit working papers and financial statements of Phoenix.

Note. Assume that it is 11 December 2007.   **(Total = 20 marks)**

26 Aspersion (AAS 12/01)   36 mins

You are the manager responsible for the audit of Aspersion, a limited liability company, which mainly provides national cargo services with a small fleet of aircraft. The draft accounts for the year ended 30 September 2007 show profit before taxation of $2.7 million (2006 – $2.2 million) and total assets of $10.4 million (2006 – $9.8 million).

The following issues are outstanding and have been left for your attention.

(a)   The sale of a cargo carrier to Abra, a private limited company, during the year resulted in a loss on disposal of $400,000. The aircraft cost $1.2 million when it was purchased in September 1998 and was being depreciated on a straight-line basis over 20 years. The minutes of the board meeting at which the sale was approved record that Aspersion's finance director, Iain Jolteon, has a 30% equity interest in Abra. **(7 marks)**

(b)   As well as cargo carriers, Aspersion owns two light aircraft which were purchased in 2004 to provide business passenger flights to a small island under a three year service contract. It is now known that the contract will not be renewed when it expires at the end of March 2008. The aircraft, which cost $450,000 each, are being depreciated over fifteen years.   **(7 marks)**

(c)   Deferred tax amounting to $570,000 as at 30 September 2007 has been calculated relating to accelerated capital allowances at a tax rate of 30% under the full provision method (IAS 12 *Income taxes*). In a budget statement in October 2007, the government announced an increase in the corporation tax rate to 34%. The directors are proposing to adjust the draft accounts for the further liability arising.   **(6 marks)**

Required

For each of the above points:

(i)   Comment on the matters that you should consider; and

(ii)   State the audit evidence that you should expect to find in undertaking your review of the audit working papers and financial statements of Aspersion.

                                                                                                          (Total = 20 marks)

Note. The mark allocation is shown against each of the three issues. Assume that it is 11 December 2007.

27 Visean (AAS 6/02)

36 mins

You are the manager responsible for the audit of Visean, a limited liability company, which manufactures health and beauty products and distributes them through a chain of 72 retail pharmacies. The draft accounts for the year ended 30 June 2007 show operating profit before taxation of $1.83 million (2006 – $1.24 million) and total assets $18.4 million (2006 – $12.7 million).

The following issues are outstanding and have been left for your attention:

(a)   Visean owns nine brand names of fragrances used for ranges of products (eg perfumes, bath oils, soaps, etc), four of which were purchased and five self-created. Purchased brands are recognised as an intangible asset at cost amounting to $589,000 and amortised on a straight-line basis over 10 years. The costs of generating self-created brands and maintaining existing ones are recognised as an expense when incurred. Demand for products of one of the purchased fragrances, 'Ulexite', fell significantly in July 2007 after a marketing campaign in June caused offence to customers.   **(8 marks)**

(b)   In June 2007 the directors announced plans to discontinue the range of medical consumables supplied to hospital pharmacies. The factory manufacturing these products closed in July 2007. A provision of $800,000 has been made as at 30 June 2007 for the compensation of redundant employees and a further $450,000 for the three years unexpired lease term on the factory premises.   **(7 marks)**

(c)   Historically the company's cash flow statement has reported net cash flows from operating activities under the 'indirect method'. However, the cash flow statement for the year ended 30 June 2007 reports net cash flows under the 'direct method' and the corresponding figures have been restated.   **(5 marks)**

Required

For each of the above issues:

(i)   Comment on the matters that you should consider
(ii)   State the audit evidence that you should expect to find

in undertaking your review of the audit working papers and financial statements of Visean.

Note. The mark allocation is shown against each of the three issues. Assume it is 11 December 2007.

(Total = 20 marks)

28 Siegler (AAS 12/02)

36 mins

You are the manager responsible for the audit of Siegler, a limited liability company. Siegler develops products and technologies for the life sciences industry. The draft accounts for the year ended 30 June 2007 show profit before taxation of $4.6 million (2006 – $4.2 million) and total assets $46.3 million (2006 – $41.7 million).

The following issues are outstanding and have been left for your attention:

(a)   A government grant of $800,000 was received in May 2007 to assist in operating a new pilot plant that will use Siegler's patented bio-technology. The amount of the grant has been deducted from bio-technology development costs that are included in intangible assets with a carrying value of $4.5 million. In October 2007, Siegler's order for specialist equipment, which was to have been used in the pilot plant, was cancelled. A recent board minute shows that the company's research activities are to be focused on a new 'smart-drug' technology.   **(8 marks)**

(b)   Siegler closed and demolished one of its laboratories four years ago. The land on which it stood has not been used since and is carried at a cost of $72,000. Results of tests by the local water authority published in July 2007 show that the site is contaminated with hexavalent chromium, which is known to be toxic. Although there is currently no legislation requiring Siegler to clean up the site, a provision for $1 million has been made in the financial statements for the year ended 30 June 2007.   **(6 marks)**

(c)   Siegler owns two properties as well as its laboratories, production facilities and head office. One property is a residential apartment block and the other an office block. The apartments are leased out on an annual basis and are currently fully let. However, many of the offices are vacant and available for let on monthly as well as annual terms. On 30 June 2007, the apartment block was valued at an open market value that was $3.3m in excess of its carrying amount under the benchmark treatment of IA6 16 *Property, plant and equipment* (ie at cost less accumulated depreciation). This excess has been credited to a revaluation reserve.   **(6 marks)**

Required

For each of the above issues:

(a)   Comment on the matters that you should consider

(b)   State the audit evidence that you should expect to find, in undertaking your review of the audit working papers and financial statements of Siegler   **(Total = 20 marks)**

Note. The mark allocation is shown against each of the three issues. Assume it is 11 December 2007.

29 Vema (AAS 12/03)   36 mins

You are the manager responsible for the audit of Vema, an established, limited liability company. Vema offers a national network for the distribution of wholesale goods through a fleet of heavy goods vehicles (HGVs) and has one wholly-owned subsidiary, Weddell. The draft consolidated financial statements for the year ended 30 September 2007 show revenue $125 million (2006 – $114 million), profit before taxation of $12.4 million (2006 – $10.9 million) and total assets of $110 million (2006 – $93 million).

The following issues arising during the final audit have been noted on a schedule of points for your attention:

(a)   Historically, fleet vehicles have been depreciated at $33\frac{1}{3}\%$ on a straight-line basis as it was Vema's operational policy to replace them every three years. During the year, Vema decided to change the basis of calculation to 25% reducing balance to reflect the fact that HGVs are only replaced 'as and when necessary', usually every four to seven years. Management has calculated the current year charge on the new basis as $2.9 million (former basis; $4.2 million) and $4.7 million of accumulated depreciation has been written back in the restatement of opening reserves.   **(8 marks)**

(b)   A payment of $592,000 selected in a substantive procedure has been traced to the following nominal ledger journal in December 2006:

Debit	Administrative expenses	$786,000
Credit	Other liabilities	$194,000
Credit	Bank	$592,000

The accompanying narrative reads 'Termination payment for Mr Z – not processed on any payroll'. The audit senior has documented that 'Mr Z, a former director of Vema, was made redundant in July 2006 in a regional re-organisation'.   **(6 marks)**

(c)   The financial statements of the subsidiary company, Weddell, for the year ended 30 September 2007, are audited by another firm. Profit before taxation of $0.4 million and total assets of $34.1 million have been included in the draft consolidated financial statements of Vema. The notes to Weddell's financial statements as at 30 September 2007 disclose a contingent liability for a pending legal matter estimated at $0.2 million. In November 2007, the courts found Weddell to be liable for costs and damages amounting to $1.1 million. However, Weddell's directors have refused to make a provision, for any amount, as they have lodged an appeal against the judgement.   **(6 marks)**

Required

For each of the above issues:

(i)   Comment on the matters that you should consider
(ii)   State the audit evidence that you should expect to find

in undertaking your review of the audit working papers and financial statements of Vema for the year ended 30 September 2007.

Note. The mark allocation is shown against each of the three issues. Assume it is 11 December 2007.

(Total = 20 marks)

30 Volcan (AAS 6/05)   36 mins

You are the manager responsible for the audit of Volcan, a long-established limited liability company. Volcan operates a national supermarket chain of 23 stores, five of which are in the capital city, Urvina. All the stores are managed in the same way with purchases being made through Volcan's central buying department and product pricing, marketing, advertising and human resources policies being decided centrally. The draft financial statements for the year ended 30 September 2007 show revenue of $303 million (2006 – $282 million), profit before taxation of $9.5 million (2006 – $7.3 million) and total assets of $178 million (2006 – $173 million).

The following issues arising during the final audit have been noted on a schedule of points for your attention:

(a)   On 1 November 2007, Volcan announced its intention to downsize one of the stores in Urvina from a supermarket to a 'City Metro' in response to a significant decline in the demand for supermarket-style shopping in the capital. The store will be closed throughout December, re-opening on 1 January 2008. Goodwill of $5.5 million was recognised three years ago when this store, together with two others, was bought from a national competitor. It is Volcan's policy to write off goodwill over five years.   **(7 marks)**

(b)   On 1 October 2006 Volcan introduced a 'reward scheme' for its customers. The main elements of the reward scheme include the awarding of a 'store point' to customers' loyalty cards for every $1 spent, with extra points being given for the purchase of each week's special offers. Customers who hold a loyalty card can convert their points into cash discounts against future purchases on the basis of $1 per 100 points.

(6 marks)

(c)   In April 2007, Volcan commenced the development of a site in a valley of 'outstanding natural beauty' on which to build a retail 'megastore' and warehouse in late 2008. Local government planning permission for the development, which was received in October 2007, requires that three 100-year-old trees within the valley be preserved and the surrounding valley be restored in 2008. Additions to property, plant and equipment during the year include $4.4 million for the estimated cost of site restoration. This estimate includes a provision of $0.4 million for the relocation of the 100-year-old trees.

In September 2007 the trees were chopped down to make way for a car park. A fine of $20,000 per tree was paid to the local government in November 2007.   **(7 marks)**

Required

For each of the above issues:

(i)   Comment on the matters that you should consider
(ii)   State the audit evidence that you should expect to find

in undertaking your review of the audit working papers and financial statements of Volcan for the year ended 30 September 2007.

Note. The mark allocation is shown against each of the three issues. Assume it is 11 December 2007.

(Total = 20 marks)

31 Question with analysis: Eagle Energy (AAS 6/04)   36 mins

You are the manager responsible for the audit of Eagle Energy, an energy generation company. The draft financial statements for the year ended 30 September 2007 show revenue of $287 million (2006 – $262 million), profit before taxation of $7.2 million (2006 – $23 million) and total assets of $242 million (2006 – $221 million).

The following issues arising during the final audit have been noted on a schedule of points for your attention:

(a)   During the year Eagle Energy put its technical staff through a new training program. On the basis that this expenditure has been incurred solely for the purpose of generating future economic benefits the chief executive is adamant that the costs, amounting to $4.3 million, be capitalised as an intangible asset.

(7 marks)

(b)   During the year Eagle Energy assembles a laboratory on land which had been granted to it for 25 years, by the local authority, in 1998. Under the terms of the grant the laboratory must be dismantled and the site decontaminated when the grant term expires. This is expected to cost $18 million in 2023 and an annual provision of $1.2 million is being made.

(7 marks)

(c)   Eagle Energy receives significant funding from government sources and is required to report, monthly, on its financial performance and position. Every month end a journal entry is made, 'Debit Sundry 1 account/Credit Sundry 2 account'. There is no narrative but the chief accountant explained that the journal is approved by the chief executive to ensure that reported debt ratios stay within government specified limits. The entries are then reversed at the beginning of the following month. The net movement on these accounts over the year to 30 September 2007 was $0.3 million.

(6 marks)

Required

For each of the above issues:

(i)   Comment on the matters that you should consider
(ii)   State the audit evidence that you should expect to find

in undertaking you review of the audit working papers and financial statements of Eagle Energy for the year ended 30 September 2007.   **(Total = 20 marks)**

Note. The mark allocation is shown against each of the three issues. Assume it is 11 December 2007.

31 Question with analysis: Eagle Energy (AAS 6/04)   36 mins

You are the manager responsible for the audit of Eagle Energy, an energy generation company. The draft financial statements for the year ended 30 September 2007 show revenue of $287 million (2006 – $262 million), profit before taxation of $7.2 million (2006 – $23 million) and total assets of $242 million (2006 – $221 million).

The following issues arising during the final audit have been noted on a schedule of points for your attention:

| Material to income statement | (a) | During the year Eagle Energy put its technical staff through a new training program. On the basis that this expenditure has been incurred solely for the purpose of generating future economic benefits the chief executive is adamant that the costs, amounting to **$4.3 million**, be **capitalised as an intangible asset**. ── IAS 38   **(7 marks)** |

| Material to balance sheet | (b) | During the year Eagle Energy assembles a laboratory on land which had been granted to it for 25 years, by the local authority, in 1998. Under the terms of the grant the **laboratory must be** ── IAS 16 **dismantled and the site decontaminated** when the grant term expires. This is expected to cost |

| IAS 37 should be full amount | | **$18 million** in 2023 and an **annual provision of $1.2 million** is being made.   **(7 marks)** |

  LEARNING MEDIA

Professional scepticism, fraud?

Integrity of CE

(c) Eagle Energy receives significant funding from government sources and is required to report, ISA 330 monthly, on its financial performance and position. Every month end a **journal entry** is made, 'Debit Sundry 1 account/Credit Sundry 2 account'. There is no narrative but the chief accountant explained that the journal is **approved by the chief executive to ensure that reported debt ratios stay within government specified limits**. The entries are then reversed at the beginning of the following month. The net movement on these accounts over the year to 30 September 2007 was **$0.3 million**.

(6 marks)

Not **quantitatively** material

Reperformance, analytical procedures confirmation, recalculation. Consider: Inspection, observation, inquiry

Required

For each of the above issues:

(i) Comment on the **matters that you should consider**; and

(ii) State the audit **evidence** that you should expect to find,

in undertaking you review of the audit working papers and financial statements of Eagle Energy for the year ended 30 September 2007. **(Total = 20 marks)**

Note. The mark allocation is shown against each of the three issues. Assume it is 11 December 2007.

32 Keffler (AAS 6/06)

36 mins

You are the manager responsible for the audit of Keffler Co, a private limited company engaged in the manufacture of plastic products. The draft financial statements for the year ended 30 September 2007 show revenue of $47.4 million (2006 – $43.9 million), profit before taxation of $2 million (2006 – $2.4 million) and total assets of $33.8 million (2006 – $25.7 million).

The following issues arising during the final audit have been noted on a schedule of points for your attention:

(a) In October 2006, Keffler bought the right to use a landfill site for a period of 15 years for $1.1 million. Keffler expects that the amount of waste that it will need to dump will increase annually and that the site will be completely filled after just ten years. Keffler has charged the following amounts to the income statement for the year to 30 September 2007:

- $20,000 licence amortisation calculated on a sum-of-digits basis to increase the charge over the useful life of the site; and

- $100,000 annual provision for restoring the land in 15 years' time. **(9 marks)**

(b) A sale of industrial equipment to Deakin Co in November 2006 resulted in a loss on disposal of $0.3 million that has been separately disclosed on the face of the income statement. The equipment cost $1.2 million when it was purchased in October 1997 and was being depreciated on a straight-line basis over 20 years.

(6 marks)

(c) In October 2007, Keffler was banned by the local government from emptying waste water into a river because the water did not meet minimum standards of cleanliness. Keffler has made a provision of $0.9 million for the technological upgrading of its water purifying process and included $45,000 for the penalties imposed in 'other provisions'. **(5 marks)**

Required

For each of the above issues:

(i) Comment on the matters that you should consider

(ii) State the audit evidence that you should expect to find

in undertaking your review of the audit working papers and financial statements of Keffler Co for the year ended 30 September 2007.

Note. The mark allocation is shown against each of the three issues. Assume that it is 11 December 2007.

(Total = 20 marks)

33 Harvard

36 mins

Harvard, a company listed on a stock exchange, is a pharmaceutical company based in the south east of England. The draft accounts for the year ended 30 September 2007 show profit before taxation of $5.4 million and total assets of $20.8 million. You are the audit manager and the senior on the audit has brought the following items to your attention:

(a)   During the year ended 30 September 2007 Harvard spent $800,000 on researching the relationship between two chemicals. As a result of the research, Harvard identified a new vaccine for the prevention of smallpox and has made substantial progress in the development of the vaccine. During the year ended 30 September 2007 $1.5 million has been spent on project 'Chicken Run'. The directors of Harvard have capitalised the costs of $1.5 million as an intangible non-current asset.   **(8 marks)**

(b)   On 31 August 2006 Harvard received notification from its lawyers of a claim from users of a new type of hayfever capsule. At 30 September 2006 neither the likelihood of the success of the claim nor the amount were known and as a result no provision was made in the accounts for the year ended 30 September 2006. As at 30 September 2007 the case is still in progress but the lawyers now advise Harvard that the amount of the claim is an estimated $2.0 million and that the claimants are very likely to be successful in court.   **(7 marks)**

(c)   During the year ended Harvard expanded its overseas operations and acquired a business in Brazil. The directors have not taken any measures to disclose any information about this new geographical segment.
(5 marks)

Required

For each of the above points:

(i)   Comment on the matters that you should consider
(ii)   State the audit tests that will need to be performed

prior to your meeting with the audit partner next week.

Note. the mark allocation is shown against each of the three issues. Assume it is 11 December 2007.

(Total = 20 marks)

34 Albreda (AAS 12/05)

36 mins

You are the manager responsible for the audit of Albreda Co, a limited liability company, and its subsidiaries. The group mainly operates a chain of national restaurants and provides vending and other catering services to corporate clients. All restaurants offer 'eat-in', 'take-away' and 'home delivery' services. The draft consolidated financial statements for the year ended 30 September 2007 show revenue of $42.2 million (2006 – $41.8 million), profit before taxation of $1.8 million (2006 – $2.2 million) and total assets of $30.7 million (2006 – $23.4 million).

The following issues arising during the final audit have been noted on a schedule of points for your attention:

(a)   In September 2007 the management board announced plans to cease offering 'home delivery' services from the end of the month. These sales amounted to $0.6 million for the year to 30 September 2007 (2006 – $0.8 million). A provision of $0.2 million has been made as at 30 September 2007 for the compensation of redundant employees (mainly drivers). Delivery vehicles have been classified as non-current assets held for sale as at 30 September 2007 and measured at fair value less costs to sell, $0.8 million (carrying amount, $0.5 million).   **(8 marks)**

(b)   Historically, all owned premises have been measured at cost depreciated over 10 to 50 years. The management board has decided to revalue these premises for the year ended 30 September 2007. At the balance sheet date two properties had been revalued by a total of $1.7 million. Another 15 properties have since been revalued by $5.4 million and there remain a further three properties which are expected to be revalued during 2008. A revaluation surplus of $7.1 million has been credited to equity.   **(7 marks)**

(c)   During the year Albreda paid $0.1 million (2006 – $0.3 million) in fines and penalties relating to breaches of health and safety regulations. These amounts have not been separately disclosed but included in cost of sales.   **(5 marks)**

Required

For each of the above issues:

(i)   Comment on the matters that you should consider
(ii)   State the audit evidence that you should expect to find

in undertaking your review of the audit working papers and financial statements of Albreda Co for the year ended 30 September 2007.

Note. The mark allocation is shown against each of the three issues. Assume it is 11 December 2007.

(Total = 20 marks)

35 Cuckoo Group   54 mins

You are currently auditing the consolidated financial statements of the Cuckoo Group and are scrutinising the accounting policies being used by the group for the valuation of inventory. The group has three principal subsidiaries which are Loopy, Snoopy and Drake Retail. You are not currently the auditor of Loopy as Cuckoo only recently acquired this subsidiary company. Cuckoo, the holding company, carries on business as a dealer in gold bullion and other precious metals. It purchased the three subsidiaries in order to diversify its activities. It felt that dealing in commodities was quite risky and wished to spread the operating risk. The following are the accounting policies proposed by Cuckoo Group regarding the valuation of inventory.

Cuckoo proposes to include the bullion and other precious metals in the balance sheet at the year-end market values. It does not enter into any contracts for the forward purchase or sale of precious metals. Cuckoo does not manufacture products from the precious metals but simply buys and sells the metals on the bullion markets.

Loopy manufactures domestic products such as cutlery, small electrical appliances and crockery. The inventory is valued at the lower of cost or market value applied to the total of the inventory. Cost is determined by using the last in, first out (LIFO) method of valuation. Overhead costs are allocated on the basis of normal activity and are those incurred in bringing the inventory to its present location and condition.

Snoopy manufactures similar domestic products to Loopy. The inventory is valued at the lower of cost and net realisable value for the purpose of the group balance sheet. However, inventory is further reduced to its base value for the purpose of the group income statement. This reduction is not material in the context of the group accounts. Overheads are allocated on the basis of normal activity levels and the costs incurred in bringing the inventory to its present location and condition.

Drake Retail acts as the retail outlet for approximately 60% of the combined output of Loopy and Snoopy. It values its inventory at the lower of cost and net realisable value. Inventories mainly consist of goods held for resale. Cost is computed by deducting the gross profit margin from the selling value of inventory. When computing net realisable value, an allowance is made for any future markdowns to be made on inventory.

The directors of Cuckoo Group wish the following accounting policy note to be included in the group financial statements regarding inventory. 'Inventory is stated at the lower of cost and net realisable value and comprises raw material inventory (including bullion), work in progress and finished goods.'

Required

(a) Describe the audit procedures which you would carry out before placing reliance upon the work of the auditors of Loopy. **(12 marks)**

(b) Discuss whether you feel that the current accounting policies adopted by Cuckoo and its three subsidiaries regarding inventory are acceptable to you as group auditor. **(12 marks)**

(c) Comment on the extent to which ISA 600 *Using the work of another auditor* provides guidance on the following issues in the context of a group audit:

    (i) Co-operation between auditors
    (ii) Multi-location auditors
    (iii) Joint audits **(6 marks)**

(Total = 30 marks)

36 Beeches Technologies

54 mins

You are currently planning the audit of Beeches Technologies, a listed company, and its subsidiaries for the year ending 30 September 2007. Beeches Technologies heads an international group which sells computer software and related services. Software is developed in the UK and sold throughout the world by the group's numerous overseas subsidiaries. These subsidiaries act as agents for the parent company, selling software and providing support on its behalf. They receive a commission equal to their costs plus a 5% margin.

The costs incurred by the subsidiaries typically comprise:

- Payroll costs and associated expenses for sales, technical and administrative staff
- Sales commissions
- Establishment costs for the local office
- Depreciation
- Miscellaneous expenses

At 30 September 2006, Beeches Technologies had 24 overseas subsidiaries, at which audit work was performed as follows:

	Number
Full audit by your firm	8
Limited review by your firm	5
No work	11
	24

No new subsidiaries are expected to be established before 30 September 2007.

With the exception of the two largest subsidiaries (at which your firm performs a full audit), all of the subsidiaries are of similar size. The costs of each smaller subsidiary represent approximately 0.5% of the group's total cost base. Where a full local audit is not required, the subsidiaries are visited on a rotational basis, each subsidiary being visited at least once every three years.

You called the group financial controller of Beeches Technologies in order to arrange a planning meeting. She informed you that she has just returned from investigating a fraud at the group's subsidiary in Madrid, a location where your firm performed limited review procedures two years ago and no work in the prior year.

The financial controller in Madrid misappropriated the equivalent of $150,000 over a three year period by using company cheques and bank transfers to pay his own personal expenses. These were reported as company expenses in the income statement submitted to Beeches Technologies. Whilst the amount involved is not material to the group as a whole, it is very significant to the local subsidiary.

The group financial controller told you that the group finance director has expressed concern that the audit work performed did not uncover the fraud and has asked for a meeting with the audit partner to discuss this. You have arranged a meeting for this Friday, which is 14 December.

Required

(a)   Prepare the following schedules to assist the audit partner in his preparation for Friday's meeting:

   (i)   A list of questions you believe the audit partner should ask in order to ensure that he has sufficient information about the fraud to assess its impact on the audit for the year ending 30 September 2007.

(8 marks)

   (ii)   A summary of the most important controls you would expect the group to have in place to prevent and detect the misappropriation of funds by subsidiary employees.   **(7 marks)**

   (iii) An outline audit plan for the overseas subsidiaries for the year ending 30 September 2007. Your plan should indicate the number of planned audit visits to the overseas subsidiaries (together with the timing of those visits) and the nature of any work on overseas subsidiaries which you would perform at the group headquarters.   **(5 marks)**

(b)   Using the Beeches Technologies fraud as an example, compare and contrast the responsibility of the auditor in respect of fraud with the expectations of company directors and the general public in this area.

Note. Assume it is 11 December 2007.

(10 marks)

(Total = 30 marks)

37 Pavia (AAS 12/06)   54 mins

You are the manager responsible for the audit of Pavia Co. The company's core business is the manufacture of eight models of sports cars. The company is organised on a divisional basis with factories selling parts to assembly plants.

You have obtained the following information:

Income statement for the year to 31 December

	Note	2006 Draft $m	2005 Actual $m
Revenue	(1)	645.5	606.5
Other income	(2)	15.6	14.4
Changes in inventories		3.8	(16.4)
Cost of materials		(334.1)	(286.8)
Employee benefits expense	(3)	(91.0)	(83.9)
Depreciation and amortisation		(29.8)	(23.6)
Other expenses	(4)	(116.3)	(100.6)
Interest income, net	(5)	12.3	20.9
Profit before tax		106.0	130.5
Income tax expense		(44.4)	(47.7)
Profit for the period		61.6	82.8

Balance sheet at 31 December

ASSETS		2006 Draft $m	2005 Actual $m
Non-current assets			
Intangible assets	(6)	47.8	40.5
Property, plant and equipment	(7)	124.5	102.5
		172.3	143.0
Current assets			
Inventories	(8)	30.3	27.9
Trade receivables		73.1	50.3
Cash and cash equivalents		111.4	86.0
Total assets		387.1	307.2
EQUITY AND LIABILITIES			
Equity			
Share capital		5.8	5.8
Share premium		15.3	15.3
Retained earnings		112.1	80.1
		133.2	101.2
Non-current liabilities			
Provisions	(9)	160.1	121.4
Current liabilities			
Trade payables		33.5	31.8
Tax		50.4	44.3
Other liabilities		9.9	8.5
Total equity and liabilities		387.1	307.2

Notes

(1) Revenue from business activities:

	$m	$m
Vehicles	588.0	526.0
Parts and accessories	39.6	36.8
Other	17.9	43.7
	645.5	606.5

(2) Other income includes gains on the disposals of tangible assets and income from the reversal of provisions.

(3) Average number of employees:

	2006 Draft	2005 Actual
Wage earners	484	499
Salaried employees	483	477
Apprentices and trainees	36	37
	1,003	1,013

(4) Other expenses includes costs for warranties, administration and distribution, maintenance and insurance.

(5) Interest income, net:

	2006 Draft $m	2005 Actual $m
Interest and similar income	16.8	25.1
Interest and similar expenses	(4.5)	(4.2)
	12.3	20.9

(6) Intangible assets include development costs, also franchises and industrial rights and licences. During the year $12·7 million (2005 – $6·3 million) was spent on developing a new sports model, the Fox.

(7)   Property, plant and equipment:

	Land and buildings	Equipment	Assets under construction	Total
Cost	$m	$m	$m	$m
1 January 2006	61.8	212.1	19.0	292.9
Additions	5.0	28.9	9.4	43.3
Disposals		(4.5)		(4.5)
Reclassification	3.0	8.9	(11.9)	0.0
31 December 2006	69.8	245.4	16.5	331.7
Depreciation				
Current year	1.9	18.4	–	20.3
Accumulated	28.7	178.5	–	207.2
Net book value				
31 December 2006	41.1	66.9	16.5	124.5
31 December 2005	34.9	48.6	19.0	102.5

(8)   Inventories comprise:

	2006 Draft $m	2005 Actual $m
Raw materials, consumables and supplies	8·3	7·3
Work-in progress	6·8	4·8
Finished goods	15·2	15·8
	30·3	27·9

(9)   Provisions mainly cover manufacturing warranty, product liability and litigation risks. Also, provisions have been established for deferred maintenance and IT reorganisation.

The following additional information is available:

(i)   Pavia has achieved record sales in 2006 with the delivery of 10,153 vehicles (2005 – 7,642 vehicles).

(ii)   Although some sales are direct to individual customers the majority are ordered through dealers who take new vehicles on consignment.

(iii)   Since 1 January 2006 Pavia has offered 0% finance for three years on new vehicle sales in its most competitive markets.

(iv)   The launch of the Fox has been postponed from late 2006 to early 2007 as internal trials have revealed that the doors are not sufficiently secure at high speeds.

(v)   A car part required for the Cipeta model is bought-in exclusively from an overseas manufacturer. Deliveries of supplies have been unpredictable in 2005 causing disruption to the Cipeta model assembly schedules.

Required

In respect of the financial statements audit of Pavia Co for the year ending 31 December 2006:

(a)   Identify and explain the financial statement risks to be taken into account in planning the final audit.

(14 marks)

(b)   Illustrate how you might use analytical procedures to provide audit evidence and reduce the level of detailed substantive procedures. **(7 marks)**

(c)   Briefly describe the principal audit work to be performed in respect of the carrying amount of the following items in the balance sheet.

(i)   Development expenditure on the Fox model **(3 marks)**

(ii)   Consignment inventory **(3 marks)**

(iii)   The warranty provision **(3 marks)**

(Total = 30 marks)

73

38 RBG (AAS 12/06)

36 mins

The activities of the Retail and Business Group (RBG) comprise retailing of general merchandise and luxury goods. RBG has developed an internal audit function over many years. Employee turnover in the internal audit department has risen, with high performing employees moving to other departments and less successful ones moving out. The external auditors, Grey & Co have suggested that RBG outsources its internal audit function to experienced auditors.

Your firm, York & Co, has been invited to tender for the provision of internal audit services to RBG for the three years to 31 December 2009. The appointment will include an evaluation of organisational risk, financial compliance, information technology control and systems audits, and fraud investigation. As the prospective assignment manager, you have been asked to identify the principal matters to be presented in your firm's written submission. The invitation to tender indicates that written submissions will be used as a means of shortlisting candidates to make a detailed presentation to RBG's Audit and Risk Management Committee.

You have obtained the following information from RBG:

(i)   The Audit and Risk Management Committee receives annual reports from the head of internal audit on the controls over operational, financial and compliance risks.

(ii)   RBG has a comprehensive system of budgetary control including monthly performance reviews of both financial and non-financial indicators.

(iii)   Financial extracts ($m):

	Six months to 30 June 2006 Draft	Year to 31 December 2005 Actual
Revenue	387	751
Profit before tax	46	83

(iv)   A substantial proportion of RBG's revenue is generated through retail outlets in department stores and shopping centres. Many of the rents payable for these premises are contingent on revenues earned.

Required

(a)   Briefly describe potential advantages and disadvantages to RBG of outsourcing its internal audit services.

(6 marks)

(b)   Describe the principal matters that should be included in your firm's submission to provide internal audit services to RBG.
(10 marks)

(c)   Explain the possible impact of RBG outsourcing its internal audit services on the audit of the financial statements by Grey & Co.
(4 marks)

(Total = 20 marks)

39 Seymour (AAS 12/06)

36 mins

You are the manager responsible for the audit of Seymour Co. The company offers information, proprietary foods and medical innovations designed to improve the quality of life. (Proprietary foods are marketed under and protected by registered names.) The draft consolidated financial statements for the year ended 30 September 2006 show revenue of $74·4 million (2005 – $69·2 million), profit before taxation of $13·2 million (2005 – $15·8 million) and total assets of $53·3 million (2005 – $40·5 million).

The following issues arising during the final audit have been noted on a schedule of points for your attention:

(a)   In 2001, Seymour had been awarded a 20-year patent on a new drug, Tournose, that was also approved for food use. The drug had been developed at a cost of $4 million which is being amortised over the life of the patent. The patent cost $11,600. In September 2006 a competitor announced the successful completion of preliminary trials on an alternative drug with the same beneficial properties as Tournose. The alternative drug is expected to be readily available in two years time. **(7 marks)**

(b) Seymour offers health-related information services through a wholly-owned subsidiary, Aragon Co. Goodwill of $1·8 million recognised on the purchase of Aragon in October 2004 is not amortised but included at cost in the consolidated balance sheet. At 30 September 2006 Seymour's investment in Aragon is shown at cost, $4·5 million, in its separate financial statements.

Aragon's draft financial statements for the year ended 30 September 2006 show a loss before taxation of $0·6 million (2005 – $0·5 million loss) and total assets of $4·9 million (2005 – $5·7 million). The notes to Aragon's financial statements disclose that they have been prepared on a going concern basis that assumes that Seymour will continue to provide financial support. **(7 marks)**

(c) In November 2006 Seymour announced the recall and discontinuation of a range of petcare products. The product recall was prompted by the high level of customer returns due to claims of poor quality. For the year to 30 September 2006, the product range represented $8·9 million of consolidated revenue (2005 – $9·6 million) and $1·3 million loss before tax (2005 – $0·4 million profit before tax). The results of the 'petcare' operations are disclosed separately on the face of the income statement. **(6 marks)**

Required

For each of the above issues:

(i) comment on the matters that you should consider; and

(ii) state the audit evidence that you should expect to find, in undertaking your review of the audit working papers and financial statements of Seymour Co for the year ended 30 September 2006.

Note. The mark allocation is shown against each of the three issues. **(Total = 20 marks)**

40 Bellatrix (AAS Pilot paper) 45 mins

Bellatrix, a limited liability company, is a carpet manufacturer and an audit client of your firm. Bellatrix has identified Scorpio, a company in the same business, as a target for acquisition in the current year.

As audit manager to Bellatrix and its subsidiaries for the year ended 31 December 2007, you have been asked to examine Scorpio's management accounts and budget forecasts. The chief executive of Bellatrix, Sirius Deneb, believes that despite its current cash flow difficulties, Scorpio's current trading performance is satisfactory and future prospects are good. The chief executive of Scorpio is Ursula Minor.

The findings of your examination are as follows:

Budget forecasts for Scorpio, for the current accounting year to 31 December 2007 and for the following year, reflect a rising profit trend.

Scorpio's results for the first half to 30 June 2007 reflect a $800,000 profit from the sale of a warehouse that had been carried in the books at historical cost. There are plans to sell two similar properties later in the year and outsource warehousing.

About 10% of Scorpio's sales are to Andromeda, a limited liability company. Two members of the management board of Scorpio hold minority interests in Andromeda. Selling prices negotiated between Scorpio and Andromeda appear to be on an arm's length basis.

Scorpio's management accounts for six months to 30 June 2007 have been used to support an application to the bank for an additional loan facility to refurbish the executive and administration offices. These management accounts show inventory and trade receivables' balances that exceed the figures in the accounting records by $150,000. This excess has also been reflected in the first half year's profit. Upon enquiry, you have established that allowances, to reduce inventory and account receivables to estimated realisable values, have been reduced to assist with the loan application.

Although there has been a recent downturn in trading, Ursula Minor has stated that she is very confident that the negotiations with the bank will be successful as Scorpio has met its budgeted profit for the first six months. Ursula believed that increased demand for carpets and rugs in the winter months will enable results to exceed budget.

Required

(a) Identify and comment on the implications of your findings for Bellatrix's plan to proceed with the acquisition of Scorpio. **(10 marks)**

(b) Explain what impact the acquisition will have on the conduct of your audit of Bellatrix and its subsidiaries for the year 31 December 2007. **(15 marks)**

Note. Assume it is 11 December 2007. **(Total = 25 marks)**

41 Prescott (AAS 6/06) (amended) **45 mins**

Your audit client, Prescott Co, is a national hotel group with substantial cash resources. Its accounting functions are well managed and the group accounting policies are rigorously applied. The company's financial year-end is 30 June.

Prescott has been seeking to acquire a construction company for some time in order to bring in-house the building and refurbishment of hotels and related leisure facilities (eg swimming pools, squash courts and restaurants). Prescott's management has recently identified Robson Construction Co as a potential target and has urgently requested that you undertake a limited due diligence review lasting two days next week.

Further to their preliminary talks with Robson's management, Prescott has provided you with the following brief on Robson Construction Co:

- The chief executive, managing director and finance director are all family members and major shareholders. The company name has an established reputation for quality constructions.

- Due to a recession in the building trade the company has been operating at its overdraft limit for the last 18 months and has been close to breaching debt covenants on several occasions.

- Robson's accounting policies are generally less prudent than those of Prescott (eg assets are depreciated over longer estimated useful lives).

- Contract revenue is recognised on the percentage of completion method, measured by reference to costs incurred to date. Provisions are made for loss-making contracts.

- The company's management team includes a qualified and experienced quantity surveyor. His main responsibilities include:

    - supervising quarterly physical counts at major construction sites;
    - comparing costs to date against quarterly rolling budgets; and
    - determining profits and losses by contract at each financial year end.

- Although much of the labour is provided under subcontracts all construction work is supervised by full-time site managers.

In February 2007, Robson received a claim that a site on which it built a housing development in 2003 was not properly drained and is now subsiding. Residents are demanding rectification and claiming damages. Robson has referred the matter to its lawyers and denied all liability, as the site preparation was subcontracted to Sarwar Services Co. No provisions have been made in respect of the claims, nor has any disclosure been made.

The auditor's report on Robson's financial statements for the year to 31 December 2006 was signed, without modification, in September 2007.

Required

(a) Explain what you understand by the term 'due diligence' and state some practical examples of this type of assignment. **(5 marks)**

(b) Identify and explain the specific matters to be clarified in the terms of engagement for this due diligence review of Robson Construction Co. **(6 marks)**

(c) State, with reasons, the principal additional information that should be made available for your review of Robson Construction Co. **(8 marks)**

(d) State the specific inquiries you should make of Robson Construction Co's management relevant to its accounting for construction contracts. **(6 marks)**

Note. You should assume it is 11 December 2007. **(Total = 25 marks)**

42 Plaza (AAS 6/05)   **43 mins**

Plaza, a limited liability company, is a major food retailer. Further to the success of its national supermarkets in the late 1990s it has extended its operations throughout Europe and most recently to Asia, where it is expanding rapidly.

You are a manager in Andando, a firm of Chartered Certified Accountants. You have been approached by Duncan Seymour, the chief finance officer of Plaza, to advise on a bid that Plaza is proposing to make for the purchase of MCM. You have ascertained the following from a briefing note received from Duncan.

MCM provides training in management, communications and marketing to a wide range of corporate clients, including multi-nationals. The 'MCM' name is well regarded in its areas of expertise. MCM is currently wholly-owned by Frontiers, an international publisher of textbooks, whose shares are quoted on a recognised stock exchange. MCM has a National and an International business.

The National business comprises 11 training centres. The audited financial statements show revenue of $12.5 million and profit before taxation of $1.3 million for this geographic segment for the year to 30 June 2007. Most of the National business's premises are owned or held on long leases. Trainers in the National business are mainly full-time employees.

The International business has five training centres in Europe and Asia. For these segments, revenue amounted to $6.3 million and profit before tax $2.4 million for the year to 30 June 2007. Most of the International business's premises are held on operating leases. International trade receivables at 30 June 2007 amounted to $3.7 million. Although the International centres employ some full-time trainers, the majority of trainers provide their services as freelance consultants.

Required

(a) Define 'due diligence' and describe the nature and purpose of a due diligence review. **(4 marks)**

(b) Explain the matters you should consider before accepting an engagement to conduct a due diligence review of MCM. **(10 marks)**

(c) Illustrate how:

    (i) Inquiry **(4 marks)**
    (ii) Analytical procedures **(6 marks)**

    might appropriately be used in the due diligence review of MCM.

(Total = 24 marks)

43 Ferry (AAS 6/03)

45 mins

You are a manager in Costello, a firm of Chartered Certified Accountants, which has recently adopted a business risk methodology. You have been involved in briefing clients about this 'top down approach' and promoting the risk management assurance services which Costello offers.

The following information concerns one of your clients, Ferry, a limited liability company:

In January 2004, Ferry purchased exclusive rights to operate a car and passenger ferry route until June 2013. This offers an alternative to driving an additional 150 kilometres via the nearest bridge crossing. There have been several ambitious plans to build another crossing but they have failed through lack of public support and government funds.

Ferry refurbished two 20-year old roll-on, roll-off ('Ro-Ro') boats to service the route. The boats do not yet meet the emission standards of Environmental Protection Regulations which come into force in 2009. Each boat makes three return crossings every day of the year, subject to weather conditions, and has the capacity to carry approximately 250 passengers and 40 vehicles. The ferry service carried just 70,000 vehicles in the year to 30 June 2007 (2006: 58,000; 2005: 47,000).

Hot and cold refreshments and travel booking facilities are offered on the one hour crossing. These services are provided by independent businesses on a franchise basis.

Ferry currently receives a subsidy from the local transport authority as an incentive to increase market awareness of the ferry service and its efficient and timely operation. The subsidy increases as the number of vehicles carried increases and is based on quarterly returns submitted to the authority. Ferry employs 20 full-time crew members who are trained in daily operations and customer service, as well as passenger safety in the event of personal accident, collision or breakdown.

The management of Ferry is planning to apply for a recognised Safety Management Certificate (SMC) in 2007. This will require a ship audit including the review of safety documents and evidence that activities are performed in accordance with documented procedures. A SMC valid for five years will be issued if no major nonconformities have been found.

Your firm has been asked to provide Ferry with a business risk assessment (BRA) as a management assurance service.

Required

(a) Describe what is meant by the term 'top down approach' in the context of business risk audit methodology.

(5 marks)

(b) Identify and explain the business risks facing Ferry which should be assessed. **(10 marks)**

(c) Describe the processes by which the risks identified in (b) could be managed and maintained at an acceptable level by Ferry. **(10 marks)**

(Total = 25 marks)

44 Pacific Group (AAS 12/03)

36 mins

Pacific Group (PG), a limited liability company, is a publisher of a monthly magazine 'Sea Discovery'. Approximately 70% of the magazine's revenue is derived from advertising, the remainder being subscription income.

Individual advertisements, which may be quarter, half or whole page, are priced at $750, $1,250 and $2,000, respectively. Discounts of 10% to 25% are given for repeat advertisements and to major advertising customers.

PG's management has identified the following risks relating to its advertising revenues:

(i) Loss of revenue through failure to invest in developments which keep the presentation of advertisements up to date with competitor publications (such as 'The Deep');

(ii)   Due to unsuitable credit limits being set, business is accepted from a small proportion of advertising customers who are uncreditworthy;

(iii)   Published advertisements may not be invoiced due to incomplete data transfer between the editorial and invoicing departments;

(iv)   Individual advertisements are not charged for at approved rates – either in error or due to arrangements with the advertisers. In particular, the editorial department does not notify the invoicing department of reciprocal advertisement arrangements, whereby advertising customers provide PG with other forms of advertising (such as website banners).

(v)   Individual advertisers refuse to pay for the inaccurate production of their advertisement;

(vi)   Cash received at a front desk, which is significant, may not be passed to cashiers, or be misappropriated;

(vii)   The risk of error arising from unauthorised access to the editorial and invoicing systems;

(viii) The risk that the editorial and invoicing systems are not available;

(ix)   The computerised transfer of accounting information from the invoicing system to the general ledger may be incomplete or inaccurate;

(x)   The risk that PG may be sued for advertisements which do not meet the National Standards Authority's 'Code of Advertising'.

Risks are to be screened out, as 'non-applicable', if they meet any of the following criteria:

(1)   the effect of the risk can be quantified and is less than $5,000;
(2)   the risk is mitigated by an effective risk strategy e.g. insurance;
(3)   the risk is likely to be low or its effect insignificant.

Those risks not screened out, called 'applicable risks', will require further consideration and are to be actively managed.

Required

(a)   For each of the above risks identified by management, state, with a reason, whether it should be considered an 'applicable risk'.   **(14 marks)**

(b)   Describe suitable internal controls to manage any FOUR of the applicable risks identified in (a).   **(6 marks)**

(Total = 20 marks)

45 Azure Airline (AAS 12/04)   43 mins

Azure, a limited liability company, was incorporated in Sepiana on 1 March 2007. In April, the company exercised an exclusive right granted by the government of Pewta to provide twice weekly direct flights between Lyme, the capital of Pewta, and Darke, the capital of Sepiana.

The introduction of this service has been well advertised as 'efficient and timely' in national newspapers. The journey time between Sepiana and Pewta is expected to be significantly reduced, so encouraging tourism and business development opportunities in Sepiana.

Azure operates a refurbished 35 year old aircraft which is leased from an international airline and registered with the Pewtan Aviation Administration (the PAA). The PAA requires that engines be overhauled every two years. Engine overhauls are expected to put the aircraft out of commission for several weeks.

The aircraft is configured to carry 15 First Class, 50 Business Class and 76 Economy Class passengers. The aircraft has a generous hold capacity for Sepiana's numerous horticultural growers (eg of cocoa, tea and fruit) and general cargo.

The six hour journey offers an in-flight movie, a meal, hot and cold drinks and tax-free shopping. All meals are prepared in Lyme under a contract with an airport catering company. Passengers are invited to complete a 'satisfaction' questionnaire which is included with the in-flight entertainment and shopping guide. Responses received show that passengers are generally least satisfied with the quality of the food – especially on the Darke to Lyme flight.

Azure employs 10 full-time cabin crew attendants who are trained in air-stewardship including passenger safety in the event of accident and illness. Flight personnel (the captain and co-pilots) are provided under a contract with the international airline from which the aircraft is leased. At the end of each flight the captain completes a timesheet detailing the crew and actual flight time.

Ticket sales are made by Azure and travel agents in Sepiana and Pewta. On a number of occasions Economy seating has been over-booked. Customers who have been affected by this have been accommodated in Business Class as there is much less demand for this, and even less for First Class. Ticket prices for each class depend on many factors, for example, whether the tickets are refundable/non-refundable, exchangeable/non-exchangeable, single or return, mid-week or weekend, and the time of booking.

Azure's insurance cover includes passenger liability, freight/baggage and compensation insurance. Premiums for passenger liability insurance are determined on the basis of passenger miles flown.

Required

(a)   Identify and explain the business risks facing Azure.   **(9 marks)**

(b)   Describe how the risks identified in (a) could be managed and maintained at an acceptable level by Azure.
                                                                                                         (9 marks)

(c)   Suggest four measures of operational performance and the evidence that should be available to provide assurance on their accuracy.   **(6 marks)**

Note. Assume it is 11 December 2007.   **(Total = 24 marks)**

46 Alexis Allison   54 mins

You are a senior accountant employed by Alexis Allison (AA), a firm of chartered certified accountants. One of AA's major clients is Super Retail, a limited liability company. AA provides a variety of work for Super Retail, including the annual audit.

Super Retail operates a number of departmental stores across the UK. It currently retails only to customers who physically visit the stores. However, it operates a delivery system for purchases that are too large for a customer to take home himself, for example, for the furniture department and many of the electrical goods.

Super Retail is seeking to extend sales beyond customers who visit the stores and the directors are giving consideration to starting to trade via a website, within the country Super Retail operates in. They are considering options to achieve the aim of offering e-commerce from 1 March 2008. These options are:

(1)   Engaging an internal firm of specialist to build a website and employing additional staff to operate the ordering system. They would also expand their current delivery system to deal with the additional demand.

(2)   Option two is the same as option one, except that the company would use surface mail to deliver small goods, and would outsource the additional delivery requirement.

(3)   Outsourcing the entire 'e-commerce' business (website, order processing, delivery).

(4)   Purchasing an identified family Internet retailer which has a website and an existing contract with a delivery firm.

The directors of Super Retail have asked AA to conduct a business risk analysis of the strategy to diversify into e-commerce.

The directors have also put together some profit, cash and capital expenditure projections and net present value calculations in relation to the proposed strategic options. They are keen that AA should conduct a review of the prospective financial information, which they will have to present to their bankers as part of their financing plans, and provide a degree of assurance on them.

The strategy to consider outsourcing has been suggested by a director who is fairly new to the board. The other directors have no previous experience of outsourcing, and wonder what the advantages and disadvantages of such a strategy might be in practice.

The finance director has asked AA to issue him with a report noting any points which might be specifically relevant to Super Retail in this situation, including a risk analysis of the proposed strategy, a summary of the assurance that AA will be able to give on the prospective financial information and of the work that AA would carry out on that information to arrive at their opinions, and a discussion of the advantages and disadvantages of outsourcing.

Required

(a)   As a senior accountant at Alexis Allison, draft the report for the finance director, covering all the items that he has requested.   **(22 marks)**

(b)   Comment on whether AA providing such a report to the directors of Super Retail raises any ethical issues.

(3 marks)

(c)   Assume that Super Retail chooses option 3. Comment on the implications that this option would have for the audit of Super Retail.   **(5 marks)**

Note. Assume it is 11 December 2007.   **(Total = 30 marks)**

47 Acrylics
36 mins

Acrylics, a limited liability company, was established in June 2005 to produce acrylic products which are used as display units in the retail industry. The shares are owned equally by two executive and two non-executive directors.

The company's revenue increased steadily over the first two years of trading. The results for the first year of trading indicated an operating profit margin of 15% and the management accounts for the second year of trading indicate that this has increased to 18%. The directors are currently negotiating a contract worth $600,000 to supply a major retailer which has over 100 outlets throughout the country. The company will require an increased overdraft facility to fulfill the order.

The finance director of Acrylics has prepared a business plan for submission to the company's bankers in support of a request for a larger overdraft facility. The plan includes details of the company's products, management, markets, method of operation and financial information. The financial information includes profit and cash flow forecasts for the six months ending 31 December 2007 together with details of the assumptions on which the forecasts are based and the accounting policies used in compiling the profit forecast. The company's bankers require this financial information to be reviewed and reported on by independent accountants.

Although the company's revenue was below the threshold for a statutory audit for its first year of trading, the company was required by its bankers to have an audit of its financial statements for the year ended 30 June 2006. Your firm conducted this audit in accordance with Auditing Standards and issued an unqualified report.

Required

(a)   Describe the benefits, in addition to continuance of its overdraft facility, to the company and its directors and shareholders of having an audit of its annual financial statements.   **(5 marks)**

(b)   Describe the matters you would consider and any procedures you would perform in reviewing the profit and cash flow forecast.   **(10 marks)**

(c)   Explain how and why the level of assurance provided by a report on profit and cash flow forecasts differs from the level of assurance provided by an audit report on annual financial statements.   **(5 marks)**

(Total = 20 marks)

REPORTING

Questions 48 to 58 cover Reporting, the subject of Part E of the BPP Study Text for Paper P7.

48 Delphinus (AAS Pilot paper) (amended)   36 mins

(a) Explain the importance of corresponding figures to the conduct of an audit.   **(7 marks)**

(b) Libra & Leo, a small firm of certified accountants, has provided audit services to Delphinus for many years. The company, which makes hand-crafted beds, is undergoing expansion and has recently relocated its operations. Having completed the audit of the financial statements for the year ended 31 December 2006 and issued an unmodified opinion thereon, Libra & Leo have now indicated that they do not propose to offer themselves for re-election.

The chief executive of Delphinus, Mr Pleiades, has now approached your firm to audit the financial statements for the year ended 31 December 2007. However, before inviting you to accept the nomination he has asked for your views on the following extracts from an auditors' report.

'Because we were appointed auditors of the company during 2006, we were not able to observe the counting of the physical inventories at 30 June 2006 or satisfy ourselves concerning those inventory quantities by alternative means.

'In our opinion, except for the effect on the corresponding figures for 2007 of the adjustments, if any, to the result of operations for the year ending 30 June 2007, which we might have determined to be necessary had we been able to observe beginning inventory quantities as at 30 June 2006, the financial statements give a true and fair view of the financial position of the company as of June 30, 2007, and of the results of its operations and its cash flows for the year then ended in accordance with ...'

Mr Pleiades has been led to understand that such a qualified opinion must be given on the financial statements of Delphinus for the year ended 31 December 2007, as a necessary consequence of the change in audit appointment. He is anxious to establish whether you would issue anything other than an unmodified opinion.

Required

Comment on the proposed auditors' report. Your answer should consider whether and how the chief executive's concerns can be overcome.   **(13 marks)**

(Total = 20 marks)

49 Avid (AAS 12/01) (amended)   36 mins

(a) Explain, with reasons, how a member of the Association of Chartered Certified Accountants should respond to a request to provide a 'second opinion'.   **(7 marks)**

(b) Avid, a limited liability company, is a wholly-owned subsidiary of Drago. As a result of Drago divesting its non-core activities, Avid ceased to trade in the year to 30 September 2006 when its trade and assets were sold to a competitor.

At 30 September 2006, Avid's remaining assets (including amounts due to group companies, current investments, cash and cash equivalents) were sufficient to meet Avid's provisions which totalled $9.7 million in respect of:

- Product liability
- Staff redundancies
- Claims for unfair dismissal
- Property leases
- Breach of contracts with distributors and suppliers

The audit opinion on the financial statements for the year ended 30 September 2006 was unqualified.

All known claims and liabilities have since been settled. The draft financial statements for the year ending 30 September 2007 show the balance on the provisions account to be $3.9 million.

Avid's finance director, Marek, has approached you, as a personal friend, to discuss the following extract from the draft auditors' report which he received yesterday:

'As more fully explained in note 7 an amount of $3.9m has been included in 'Provisions' in respect of general risks facing the company. The directors consider that such a provision is prudent in the light of the impending liquidation of the company. In our opinion future liabilities should be recognised in accordance with International Accounting Standards 37 'Provisions, contingent liabilities and contingent assets'. If liabilities had been so recognised, the effect would have been to increase the profits brought forward in the financial statements to 30 September 2006 by $3.9m.'

'In our opinion, because of the effects of the matters discussed above, the financial statements do not give a true and fair view of the state of the company's affairs as at 30 September 2007, and of its profit for the year then ended ... .'

Required

Comment on the suitability or otherwise of the proposed auditors' report. Your answer should discuss the appropriateness of alternative audit opinions. **(13 marks)**

(Total = 20 marks)

50 Question with student answer: Cinnabar Group (AAS 6/02)
27 mins

(a)   Explain the auditor's responsibilities for the appropriateness of the going concern assumption as a basis for the preparation of financial statements. **(5 marks)**

(b)   You are a manager in the quality control review department of Scheel, a firm of Chartered Certified Accountants. You are currently responsible for reviewing the appropriateness of your firm's proposed auditors' reports on financial statements.

The draft financial statements of Cinnabar group for the year to 30 June 2007 disclose the following:

Note 1 Significant event

During the year, Cinnabar sold a significant amount of its business and certain assets (plant and equipment and inventory) and commenced a systematic winding down of its operations. The group's remaining assets (including property, trade receivables and cash) were sufficient to meet the group's liabilities, as at 30 June 2007.

Note 2 Accounting policies

The consolidated financial statements have been prepared in accordance with the International Financial Reporting Standards (IFRS) under the historical cost convention. As described in Note 1, the group has commenced the winding down of its operations and remaining assets have been restated to their net realisable values.

There are no other disclosures relating to the going concern basis although the 'significant event' is referred to in the directors' report under the heading 'principal activities and business review'.

Cinnabar ceased to trade in October 2007. The auditors' report on Cinnabar's financial statements for the year ended 30 June 2006 was unmodified.

BPP
LEARNING MEDIA

Required

Comment on the suitability or otherwise of an unmodified auditors' report for Cinnabar for the year ended 30 June 2007. Your answer should discuss the appropriateness of alternative audit opinions. **(10 marks)**

Note. Assume it is 11 December 2007. **(Total = 15 marks)**

51 Jinack (AAS 12/05) 27 mins

(a) Explain the auditor's responsibilities in respect of subsequent events. **(5 marks)**

(b) You are the audit manager of Jinack Co, a private limited liability company. You are currently reviewing two matters that have been left for your attention on the audit working paper file for the year ended 30 September 2007:

   (i) Jinack holds an extensive range of inventory and keeps perpetual inventory records. There was no full physical inventory count at 30 September 2007 as a system of continuous inventory checking is operated by warehouse personnel under the supervision of an internal audit department.

   A major systems failure in October 2007 caused the perpetual inventory records to be corrupted before the year-end inventory position was determined. As data recovery procedures were found to be inadequate, Jinack is reconstructing the year-end quantities through a physical count and 'rollback'. The reconstruction exercise is expected to be completed in Janaury 2008. **(6 marks)**

   (ii) Audit work on after-date bank transactions identified a transfer of cash from Batik Co. The audit senior has documented that the finance director explained that Batik commenced trading on 7 October 2007, after being set up as a wholly-owned foreign subsidiary of Jinack. No other evidence has been obtained. **(4 marks)**

Required

Identify and comment on the implications of the above matters for the auditor's report on the financial statements of Jinack Co for the year ended 30 September 2007 and, where appropriate, the year ending 30 September 2008.

Note. The mark allocation is shown against each of the matters. Assume it is 11 December 2007.

(Total = 15 marks)

52 Icehouse (AAS 6/03) 27 mins

(a) Comment on the limitations that shareholders may perceive exist in the standard unmodified auditor's report as described in ISA 700 *The Independent auditor's report on a complete set of general purpose financial statements.* **(5 marks)**

(b) You are an audit manager in Fine & Young, a firm of Chartered Certified Accountants. One of your audit clients, Icehouse, is a textbook publisher. Icehouse is planning to expand through the acquisition of a number of small publishers of other media such as video tapes and CDs. The finance director of Icehouse has been reviewing the financial statements of potential targets. He has come across an auditors' report dated 19 July 2006, on financial statements for the year ended 31 March 2005, which does not have the standard wording of an unqualified report. The finance director has now approached you for an explanation of its meaning. The auditor's responsibility and opinion paragraphs are as follows:

Auditor's responsibility

Our responsibility is to express an opinion on these financial statements based on our audit. We conducted our audit in accordance with International Standards on Auditing. Those standards require that we comply with ethical requirements and plan and perform the audit to obtain reasonable assurance whether the financial statements are free from material misstatement.

An audit involves performing procedures to obtain audit evidence about the amounts and disclosures in the financial statements. The procedures selected depend on the auditor's judgement, including the assessment of the risks of material misstatement of the financial statements, whether due to fraud or error. In making those risk assessments, the auditor considers internal control relevant to the entity's preparation and fair presentation of the financial statements in order to design audit procedures that are appropriate in the circumstances, but not for the purpose of expressing an opinion on the effectiveness of the entity's internal control.

'Adjustments have been made and are disclosed in Note 22. An audit also includes evaluating the appropriateness of accounting policies used and the reasonableness of accounting estimates made by management, as well as evaluating the overall presentation of the financial statements. We believe that the audit evidence we have obtained is sufficient and appropriate to provide a basis for our audit opinion'.

Opinion

'In our opinion the financial statements give a true and fair view of the state of the company's affairs as at 31 March 2005 and its financial performance and its cash flows for the year then ended in accordance with International Financial Reporting Standards.

'The company's liabilities exceed its assets at 31 March 2005 creating an adverse situation which the directors believe is reversible over the coming twelve months. The directors further believe that the company is capable of continuing to trade for twelve months from the date of this report.

'19 July 2006'

Required

Identify and explain the shortcomings of this report.　(10 marks)

(Total = 15 marks)

53 Frazil (AAS 12/03)　27 mins

(a)　Explain the auditor's responsibilities for reporting on compliance with International Financial Reporting Standards (IFRSs) when the financial statements state that they are prepared in accordance with:

(i)　Only IFRSs

(ii)　Both IFRSs and relevant national standards or practices

(iii)　Relevant national standards or practices, but which disclose in the notes to the financial statements the extent of compliance with IFRSs.　(5 marks)

(b)　You are the engagement partner to Frazil, a private limited liability company. Frazil's financial statements for the year ended 30 September 2007, show total assets $107 million and profit before tax $8.2 million. The following matters require your consideration:

(i)　The basis of accounting note states that the financial statements have been prepared in compliance with International Financial Reporting Standards. However, the accounting policy note for development costs states that all development costs are expensed as incurred. Results of audit tests showed that of the $3.7 million development costs expensed during the year, $1.4 million should have been recognised as an asset in accordance with IAS 38 *Intangible assets*.

(ii)　The management of Frazil has just informed you that, for the first time, the annual report is to be published on the company's website.

Required

Identify and comment on the implications of the above matters for your auditors' report on the financial statements of Frazil for the year ended 30 September 2007.　(10 marks)

(Total = 15 marks)

54 Johnston and Tiltman (AAS 6/06)　　　　27 mins

(a)　The purpose of ISA 510 *Initial engagements – opening balances* is to establish standards and provide guidance regarding opening balances when the financial statements are audited for the first time or when the financial statements for the prior period were audited by another auditor.

Required

Explain the auditor's reporting responsibilities that are specific to initial engagements. 　　**(5 marks)**

(b)　You are the audit manager of Johnston Co, a private company. The draft consolidated financial statements for the year ended 30 September 2007 show profit before taxation of $10.5 million (2006 – $9.4 million) and total assets of $55.2 million (2006 – $50.7 million).

Your firm was appointed auditor of Tiltman Co when Johnston Co acquired all the shares of Tiltman Co in September 2007. Tiltman's draft financial statements for the year ended 30 September 2007 show profit before taxation of $0.7 million (2006 – $1.7 million) and total assets of $16.1 million (2006 – $16.6 million). The auditor's report on the financial statements for the year ended 30 September 2006 was unmodified.

You are currently reviewing two matters that have been left for your attention on the audit working paper files for the year ended 30 September 2007:

(i)　In June 2006 Tiltman installed a new computer system that properly quantified an overvaluation of inventory amounting to $2.7 million. This is being written off over three years.

(ii)　In November 2007, Tiltman's head office was relocated to Johnston's premises as part of a restructuring. Provisions for the resulting redundancies and non-cancellable lease payments amounting to $2.3 million have been made in the financial statements of Tiltman for the year ended 30 September 2007.

Required

Identify and comment on the implications of these two matters for your auditor's reports on the financial statements of Johnston Co and Tiltman Co for the year ended 30 September 2007. 　　**(10 marks)**

Note. Assume it is 11 December 2007. 　　**(Total = 15 marks)**

55 Hegas (AAS 6/05)　　　　27 mins

(a)　Explain the auditor's responsibilities for other information in documents containing audited financial statements. 　　**(5 marks)**

(b)　You are an audit manager with specific responsibility for reviewing other information in documents containing audited financial statements before your firm's auditors' report is signed. The financial statements of Hegas, a privately-owned civil engineering company, show total assets of $120 million, revenue of $261 million, and profit before tax of $9.2 million for the year ended 30 September 2007. Your review of the Annual Report has revealed the following:

(i)　The statement of changes in equity includes $4.5 million under a separate heading of 'miscellaneous item' which is described as 'other difference not recognised in income'. There is no further reference to this amount or 'other difference' elsewhere in the financial statements. However, the Management Report, which is required by statute, is not audited. It discloses that 'changes in shareholders' equity not recognised in income includes $4.5 million arising on the revaluation of investment properties'.

The accounting policies note to the financial statements state that the company has implemented IAS 40 *Investment Property* for the first time in the year to 30 September 2006 and also that 'the adoption of this standard did not have a significant impact on Hegas's financial position or its results of operations during 2005'.

(ii) The chairman's statement asserts 'Hegas has now achieved a position as one of the world's largest generators of hydro-electricity, with a dedicated commitment to accountable ethical professionalism'. Audit working papers show that 14% of revenue was derived from hydro-electricity (2006: 12%). Publicly available information shows that there are seven international suppliers of hydro-electricity in Africa alone, which are all at least three times the size of Hegas in terms of both annual revenue and population supplied.

Required

Identify and comment on the implications of the above matters for the auditors' report on the financial statements of Hegas for the year ended 30 September 2007. **(10 marks)**

(Total = 15 marks)

56 Question with analysis: Beige Interiors (AAS 12/04) 27 mins

(a) Compare and contrast the auditor's considerations of materiality at the planning stage and the overall review stage of an audit. **(6 marks)**

(b) You are the manager in charge of the audit of Beige Interiors, a limited liability company. Your auditors' report for the year to 30 September 2006 was signed, without modification, in January 2007.

The scope of the audit for the year to 30 September 2007 has however been limited as the former chief executive fled the country in early February 2007, taking the accounting records with him. As a training exercise you have asked one of the trainees assigned to the audit, Jade, to draft the extracts for the basis of opinion and opinion paragraphs that would not be standard wording in an unmodified auditors' report. Jade has drafted the following:

Basis of opinion (extract)

However, the evidence available to us was limited because accounting records were missing at the beginning of the period and it was not possible to completely reconstruct them.

Opinion (extract)

Because of the possible effect of the limitation in evidence available to us, we do not express an opinion on the financial statements.

Required

Discuss the suitability of Jade's draft. Your answer should identify and comment on the principal matters relevant to forming an appropriate opinion on the financial statements of Beige Interiors for the year ended 30 September 2007. **(9 marks)**

Note. You are NOT required to redraft the extracts. Assume it is 11 December 2007.

(Total = 15 marks)

56 Question with analysis: Beige Interiors (AAS 12/04) 27 mins

(a) **Compare and contrast** the auditor's considerations of **materiality** at the **planning stage** and the **overall review stage** of an audit.

Just these stages

(6 marks)

(b) You are the manager in charge of the audit of Beige Interiors, a limited liability company. Your auditors' report for the year to 30 September 2006 was signed, **without modification**, in **January 2007**.

Stolen records re last year?

Material or pervasive	The **scope** of the **audit for the year to 30 September 2007** has however been **limited** as the **former chief executive** fled the country in early **February 2007**, taking the accounting records with
Therefore appropriate	him. As a **training exercise** you have asked one of the trainees assigned to the audit, Jade, to draft the extracts for the basis of opinion and opinion paragraphs that would not be standard wording in an unmodified auditors' report. Jade has drafted the following:

Basis of opinion (extract)

However, the evidence available to us was limited because accounting records were missing at the

But some reconstruction?	beginning of the period and it was **not possible to completely reconstruct them**.

Opinion (extract)

pervasive

Because of the possible effect of the limitation in evidence available to us, we **do not express an opinion** on the financial statements.

Is opinion shown reasonable?	*Required*
Sufficient evidence, disclosures, fraud?	Discuss the **suitability** of Jade's draft. Your answer should **identify** and **comment** on the **principal matters relevant to forming an appropriate opinion** on the financial statements of Beige Interiors for the year ended 30 September 2007. **(9 marks)**
Prior year problems?	*Note.* **You are NOT required to redraft the extracts**. Assume it is 11 December 2007.

DON'T then

(Total = 15 marks)

57 AsiaSport

27 mins

(a) Describe the problems international auditors might face when auditing companies in developing countries.

(5 marks)

(b) WorldSport, a company listed on a stock exchange, recently expanded its overseas operations by entering into an agreement on 1 April 2007 with the government of a developing Asian country. The intention was to open up the market for its products of sporting goods in that part of the world. A new company called AsiaSport was set up with a share capital of $30 million owned equally by WorldSport and the government of the Asian country. WorldSport would provide finance, equipment (sold at cost to AsiaSport) and expertise; the government would provide premises, a ready supply of material and labour, and the potential market for the goods.

AsiaSport has been incorporated for an initial five year period and will operate under the local government's foreign investment laws and regeneration scheme. After this period either party can insist on the business being wound up, or its operating terms may be renegotiated. In the event of a winding up after five years, or earlier if the business is not viable, the government has a priority in the repayment of its share of the original capital. WorldSport will only receive a maximum of its original capital.

The board of AsiaSport is made up of equal numbers of directors from Worldsport and the government. The Chairperson, who has the casting vote, is rotated annually between the two parties. In the first year, WorldSport will nominate one of its representatives as the Chairperson. On this basis, the accountant of WorldSport has decided to treat AsiaSport as a subsidiary of WorldSport in the consolidated financial statements.

You are the audit partner reviewing the audit file. You find the following note from the audit senior on the report to partner file:

Treatment of AsiaSport as subsidiary

The accountant's treatment appears reasonable given the facts, so an unqualified opinion is appropriate. However, given that it is a complex investment, I suggest the following emphasis of matter paragraph in the auditors' report:

Emphasis of matter paragraph – investment in AsiaSport

In forming our opinion, we have considered the treatment of the investment in AsiaSport, details of which can be found in note 18 to the financial statements. We confirm the accountant's view that as WorldSport has a casting vote on the board of AsiaSport, it has control of the entity and it is justifiable to treat the investment as a subsidiary.

Opinion

In our opinion, the financial statements give a true and fair view...'

Required

Comment on the audit senior's proposed audit report. Your comments should include comments on the proposed audit opinion and the format of the report. **(10 marks)**

(Total = 15 marks)

58 Cleeves (AAS 12/06)   27 mins

(a) The purpose of ISA 250 *Consideration of laws and regulations in an audit of financial statements* is to establish standards and provide guidance on the auditor's responsibility to consider laws and regulations in an audit of financial statements.

Explain the auditor's responsibilities for reporting non-compliance that comes to the auditor's attention during the conduct of an audit. **(5 marks)**

(b) You are an audit manager in a firm of Chartered Certified Accountants currently assigned to the audit of Cleeves Co for the year ended 30 September 2006. During the year Cleeves acquired a 100% interest in Howard Co. Howard is material to Cleeves and audited by another firm, Parr & Co. You have just received Parr's draft auditor's report for the year ended 30 September 2006. The wording is that of an unmodified report except for the opinion paragraph which is as follows:

Audit opinion

As more fully explained in notes 11 and 15 impairment losses on non-current assets have not been recognised in profit or loss as the directors are unable to quantify the amounts. In our opinion, provision should be made for these as required by International Accounting Standard 36 (Impairment). If the provision had been so recognised the effect would have been to increase the loss before and after tax for the year and to reduce the value of tangible and intangible non-current assets. However, as the directors are unable to quantify the amounts we are unable to indicate the financial effect of such omissions.

In view of the failure to provide for the impairments referred to above, in our opinion the financial statements do not present fairly in all material respects the financial position of Howard Co as of 30 September 2006 and of its loss and its cash flows for the year then ended in accordance with International Financial Reporting Standards.

Your review of the prior year auditor's report shows that the 2005 audit opinion was worded identically.

Required

(i) Critically appraise the appropriateness of the audit opinion given by Parr & Co on the financial statements of Howard Co, for the years ended 30 September 2006 and 2005. **(7 marks)**

(ii) Briefly explain the implications of Parr & Co's audit opinion for your audit opinion on the consolidated financial statements of Cleeves Co for the year ended 30 September 2006. **(3 marks)**

(Total = 15 marks)

Answers

1 Confidentiality

Text reference. Chapter 2

Top tips. Part (a) is a nice lead in to this question. Part (b) looks for application of the knowledge from part (a). The application is more tricky, so you should not spend too long on part (a) to the detriment of part (b). In order to answer the question well, you should first be sure that you understand clearly what Rosella's requests are. Then you have to consider the matters that arise in relation to those requests. You will generally be given a mark for each valid, relevant point you make.

Easy marks. These can be obtained for a good explanation of confidentiality in part (a).

(a)   **Confidentiality**

Confidentiality is an **implied term** of an auditor's contract with the client. It is also a requirement of the ACCA's *Code of Ethics and Conduct* and IFAC's *Code of Ethics for Professional Accountants*. Confidentiality is essential to the auditor-client relationship because in order to form an opinion, the auditor must work closely with those who have prepared the financial statements and have their **trust**. If this is lacking, the client will not be open with the auditor fearing that matters may be reported to competitors, other third parties or regulatory authorities.

The duty of confidentiality owed by the auditor is not absolute. There are **circumstances** in which auditors have a **right or duty to disclose** matters to third parties without the client's knowledge or consent. Duties are mainly **legal duties** to report matters such as any suspicions of money laundering, drug trafficking or terrorist offences. A right to report matters also exists in these circumstances but the duty to report is more important. An auditor may also disclose matters to **defend himself** in disciplinary proceedings.

It is not uncommon for regulatory authorities such as the tax authorities or the police to ask 'informally' for details of confidential matters. Only when the persons requesting the information have obtained the appropriate statutory or other authorities to demand such information should the request be granted.

Auditors are under no general duty to report illegal acts (except money laundering) to the authorities, however, it is not appropriate for an auditor to continue a relationship with a client that engages in such activities, not least because the auditor may be implicated in the crime.

Confidentiality is one of the fundamental principles of professional ethics as set out in IFAC's *Code of Ethics for Professional Accountants*. This imposes an obligation on accountants to refrain from disclosing confidential information acquired as a result of professional and business relationships without proper and specific authority or unless there is a legal or professional right or duty to disclose, and from using confidential information acquired as a result of professional and business relationships to their personal advantage or the advantage of third parties.

This guidance is also reflected in ACCA's *Code of Ethics and Conduct* which was revised so that is was aligned with IFAC's ethical guidance.

(b)   **Blake Seven**

Auditors should avoid **conflicts of interest** where possible. One example of a conflict of interest is where two parties in dispute both request advice from the same firm. There is no absolute rule that says that a firm cannot act for both parties in these circumstances but there have to be stringent controls to ensure that the interests of one client do not adversely affect the interests of another, and of course permission of both parties is required, which may not be forthcoming. This can be difficult with small firms because there are often insufficient staff to have two different 'teams' acting on behalf of the parties.

Request - remuneration package

Some information on directors' remuneration packages should be available by inspection of the financial statements filed on public record, although this information will be historical rather than current. There are also requirements for companies to make details of service contracts available for inspection by members of companies, such as Rosella, although these often constitute a very incomplete picture of the total remuneration package.

It is clear that as existing auditor and advisor to Blake Seven, it would be **inappropriate** to disclose any such information to Rosella, or even to help her find the information that is available on the public record, without the **permission** of Blake Seven which is unlikely to be forthcoming.

Personal advisor

It would only be possible to act as personal advisor to Rosella if the remaining directors of Blake Seven **agreed** (which seems unlikely) because the current 'negotiations' may well turn into a dispute over the valuation of the shareholding. The existing company might well wish to understate profits and assets in order to reduce the valuation, and Rosella may wish to see the amounts increased. It may be possible to act as personal tax advisor, although there are unlikely to be complicated tax implications to the buy-out.

Auditor to Blakes Heaven

There are potentially serious problems associated with becoming auditor to the new company because it is both in competition with the existing client, and has a very similar name. Blake Seven may well have a **legal case** against Rosella and the new company for attempting to pass itself off as the existing company, and thereby damaging the existing company's goodwill. The fact that Rosella has done this, together with her request for information, which she should know is confidential (in relation to remuneration), may cast doubt on her **personal integrity** which is a further reason not to act for her.

Alternatively, if the information presented in the question is incomplete, it may be possible to take the view that the firm would prefer to act as auditor and advisor to Rosella and the new company, rather than to the existing company, particularly if the terms of the engagement are attractive. There is no specific 'rule' which prohibits this course of action, however, the requirement to behave with **integrity** in all professional and business relationships suggests that this would not be an appropriate course of action.

2 Aventura International

Text reference. Chapter 2

Top tips. You should read through the examiner's fairly extensive comments below to consider how you should approach questions of ethics. Note the examiner's feeling that candidates did not give enough detail on the action the auditor should take. Bear in mind also, that ethical guidance is **guidance** only. There are few hard and fast rules, and you need to provide your own analysis and consideration to the guidance you have learnt in the practical situations you encounter.

Easy marks. The situations outlined in parts (1) and (2) were more straightforward than (3) and therefore offered you the easier marks.

Examiner's comments. The first two parts were better answered than the third. Candidates tended to lose marks by failing to write about the action that should be taken in sufficient detail.

(1) Gifts offered to audit staff – goods at 70% discount

Many candidates did not know that modest gifts are allowed and dismissed the matter along the lines of 'this is unethical and disciplinary action must be brought against the staff' – with no consideration even of why it was unethical (eg in terms of integrity and objectivity) or whether or not the offer had been accepted.

Better candidates identified the issue about the inadvisability of inventory movements during the count, considered some 'benchmark' for what might be regarded as modest (eg whether the same discounts were available to others) and questioned management's motives for the offer.

A significant number read the question as a discount of 30% rather than 70%. Although candidates were not penalised for this misreading of the question it was perhaps harder for them to judge whether or not 30% would be modest (70% is clearly not!).

(2) Gift/Hospitality accepted by audit manager – travel by private jet

Candidates either identified that the manager should not have accepted the use of the private jet or that the expense should not be charged to the company, but not both.

Very few candidates identified the implications on the audit work of the manger's involvement (ie the need for further review, new manager, etc) and strayed into discussion about the manager being disciplined and reported to ACCA. Some candidates concentrated on Armando charging his private expense to the company (although the question clearly stated that he charged for business use), his dominant position in the company and his apparent overriding of controls, rather than the gravity of Darius' acceptance of a free flight to Florida.

Better candidates made comparisons of (2) with (1) and distinguished between acceptance/offer, gift/hospitality and the level of staff involved in their assessment of objectivity impairment.

(3) Former audit staff employed by client – close personal relationships

Many candidates quoted a non-existent ethical 'rule' about having to wait two years before going to work for a client! (Ethical guidance only covers the reverse situation where client's staff join the audit team.)

The better candidates identified the real problems of Kirsten's involvement as AIC during the current year and the prior year (when presumably a close relationship with the client existed). Exceptionally, a candidate offered sensible suggestions for the action to be taken (eg review of her work and planning an audit team to include staff who were not her close former colleagues).

The general consensus appeared to be that Kirsten should be 'severely reprimanded', reported for 'disciplinary action' or 'struck off' whilst Armando should be prevented from marrying until the audit was signed off.

Many candidates did not read the question and said that Kirsten should be removed from the audit immediately (when she had already left).

Marks

(a) Ethical issues and actions to be taken
Generally 1 mark a point
Action ideas
  – Enquire (ask)/discuss/review/inspect/accept/decline
  – Safeguards
Reason ideas
  – Ethical rules
  – Risk – actual/perceived
For each matter
Max 4 marks for issues
Max 4 marks for actions
Max 6 marks for any one matter × 3   15

Ethical situations arising in connection with the audit of Aventura International

(a) Offer of goods

At the inventory count, the auditors attending were invited to purchase inventory at 30% of RRP, that is, at a 70% discount.

ACCA's guidance on accepting goods states that such benefits should only be accepted on 'normal commercial terms' or at a 'modest benefit'. What constitutes modest benefit will be a matter of judgement for the auditor.

Benefit

It is possible that this offer does approximate to offers made to staff at Aventura, as clothes commonly retail at prices with a substantial mark up on cost. It would not be unreasonable for a clothes retailer to give staff a 'cost' benefit. The auditor should determine whether such a benefit is made available to staff. If it is not made to staff it should not be accepted by the auditor.

The term 'modest benefit' should be considered both in terms of materiality to the auditor and the company. The offer is not material to Aventura, for whom clothes retail is only one division. However, the offer of unlimited fashion at a 70% discount is extremely likely to be material to junior audit staff (who are the grade most likely to be allocated to the inventory count). In this context, the benefit is **not** clearly insignificant.

Timing

It would be inappropriate to take up the offer at the inventory count, not least because this would constitute movement of inventory during the count, which would be wrong.

Also, the junior staff members should not accept such goods without having discussed the matter with the audit partner (it is assumed in this answer that this is the first time such an offer has been made).

Lastly, if mistakes were to be made on the inventory count, the audit might be open to charges of negligence if it appeared its staff members indulged in a shopping trip when they should have been auditing.

Action to be taken

The staff members should not have taken up the offer at the inventory count.

The audit partner should discuss the matter with management, ascertain whether a similar benefit is offered to staff and decide whether he feels it is appropriate for his staff to take up the offer. It may be inappropriate as Aventura might become perceived to be a 'reward' job by audit staff. Alternatively, it might be appropriate if the audit firm imposed a financial limit to the benefits their staff could accept.

(b) **Hospitality**

An invoice to the company for business use of the Chief Executive's jet shows that the audit manager was flown to Florida and back for a stay of two weeks.

Issues arising

(a) If the invoice was ostensibly for 'business use', what was the business? (Neither the client nor the auditor have offices in Florida.)

(b) If the invoice was not for business, the Chief Executive is wrong to invoice it to the company. Is this common practice?

(c) If it was for business, the cost of the auditor's flight should not have been charged directly to the company, but the audit firm, who could then have re-charged it. Was Darius Harken working for the weeks in question, or is it recorded as holiday in the audit firm's records?

(d) Does the invoice actually represent a significant example of hospitality being accepted by the audit manager?

(e) Did the audit manager travel alone, with family, or even with the Chief Executive? Does this indicate that the audit manager has a close personal relationship with the Chief Executive?

Hospitality/close personal relationship

It is possible that points (d) and (e) above may be indicated by the invoice.

In terms of accepting hospitality, ACCA's guidance is the same as was discussed above in relation to accepting goods. It is unlikely that paying for an auditor's flight would be considered normal commercial terms, because it would be traditional for the audit firm simply to recharge the cost of a business trip. Taking steps such as these would help to reduce the suggestion that something inappropriate has occurred, if the trip was genuinely business related.

If the trip was a pleasure trip (a) it should not have been charged to the company, which raises several auditing issues in its own right and (b) it does not come within the definition of 'modest commercial benefit'.

In terms of close business or personal relationships, ACCA's guidance states that these might adversely affect, or appear to affect, the objectivity of the auditor. It seems likely that in this instance, if the Chief Executive and the audit manager have been on holiday together, or at least a business 'jolly', then as a minimum, objectivity will **appear** to be threatened.

Action to be taken

(a) The audit firm should check their personnel records and see whether Darius Harken was working or holidaying at the relevant time.

(b) If the trip was business-related, the audit partner should check why the cost has been invoiced to the company by the Chief Executive and not by the audit firm.

(c) If the trip was personal, then the audit manager appears to have threatened the objectivity of the audit, and indeed, given that the trip appears to have been taken around the time the prior year audit was taking place, that audit is also adversely affected.

(d) The prior year audit files should be subjected to a cold review and the audit manager should be replaced on this year's audit, which should also be subject to a quality control review.

(e) All invoices rendered to the company in respect of the jet should be scrutinised by the audit team, for further evidence of personal expenses being charged to the company.

(c) **The impending marriage of the Chief Executive**

The Chief Executive's assistant is the former accountant in charge of the audit of Aventura, who is likely to have been involved with the audit of the previous year-end. She has just announced her engagement to the Chief Executive.

Issues arising

(a) Current year audit – there is a risk of loss of independence as the Chief Executive's assistant is aware of audit method.

(b) Prior year audit – there is a suggestion that the accountant in charge of the audit may have been in a personal relationship with the Chief Executive which may have adversely affected her objectivity.

Movement of audit staff

ACCA does not cover the issue of audit staff moving between the employments of the audit firm and audit clients. However, it is clear that this might adversely affect objectivity, so members involved in such activity should bear in mind the general guidance on objectivity.

IFAC suggests a number of safeguards, such as:

- Considering the appropriateness of modifying the plan for the engagement
- Assigning the audit team to someone of sufficient experience in relation to the person who has left
- Involving an additional accountant not previously associated with the audit to review

Action to be taken

Although the accountant in charge was not the most senior staff member on the audit, it would have been prudent to modify the audit plan before this year's audit. However, this does not appear to have been done, and the audit is nearing completion.

Therefore, it is important that Voest implement the third bullet point above, and conduct a quality control review of this audit.

In relation to the suspicion that Ms Fennimore's objectivity may have been affected last year, it might also be a good idea to conduct a similar review of last year's audit work, evidence obtained and conclusions drawn. However, as the work should have been reviewed by an audit manager and partner after Ms Fennimore's involvement, the risk of a problem on last year's audit appears to be slight.

3 Corundum

Text references. Chapters 2 and 5

Top tips. This question looks at the issue of ethics albeit from a slightly unusual angle. The best way to approach the question is to deal with the information on a step by step basis dealing with each new relevant piece of information in turn. If you try to respond to the situation as a whole you will miss many of the key points and your answer will lack detail. Make sure you are clear on the sequence of events. Notice that the error is discovered **before** this year's accounts are issued, whilst the old auditors are still in office. This has a significant impact on the way you approach the question.

Easy marks. The easier marks in this question are available for the pure ethics comments (for example, the lack of independence demonstrated by the auditor's willingness to sign an unqualified audit report).

Examiner's comments. Answers lacked structure and were very light on detail or explanation. Worrying misunderstandings were also evident. Many candidates misinterpreted verbal assurances from the prospective auditors as oral management representations!

Marking scheme

Marks

Generally 1 mark a point up to a maximum 3 marks (say) for any one issue

Issues ideas

Re: Change in appointment

Audit firm rotation – an independence safeguard

- Inference on communication ('professional etiquette')
- Engagement letter (responsibilities)

Re: Omission of provision

- Fundamental error
- Error vs fraud
- Competence, integrity & objectivity (Skarn and Nuee)
- (IAS 8 non-compliance)
- Confidentiality (communication with Nuee)
- Duty of care/users
- Negligence/liability
- Misconduct

Re: Legal documentation, etc

- Audit scope
- Report to management
- Transfer books/papers/information
- Other services opportunity

<u>15</u>

Change of auditors

Corundum's policy to change auditors on a periodic basis is good practice. This type of rotation is seen as a safeguard to protect independence.

As Nuee Ardente has accepted nomination there were no matters brought to their attention by Skarn, or if matters were raised they have been dealt with.

Due to the current circumstances ie the directors not wishing to change the accounts and not agreeing to a modified audit report, this may be an opportunity for Nuee Ardente to remind the directors of their responsibilities for the accounts and the accounting policies adopted. If not yet finalised this could be included in the engagement letter.

Error

Impact on 2007 accounts

As the financial statements have not been issued there is an opportunity to **correct the error**. This should be done even if this means delaying the issue of the financial statements.

If the directors refuse to correct the accounts they are deliberately misleading the shareholders. (The error is so significant that the accounts are unreliable unless corrected.)

Skarn should issue an **adverse audit opinion** irrespective of the directors' willingness or otherwise to accept it as their prime responsibility is to the shareholders and not to the directors.

Impact on 2008 accounts

In the accounts for June 2008 the omission should be treated as a fundamental error in accordance with IAS 8. This would also result in the restatement of the comparatives.

Ethical considerations

The fact that the error has only been identified at this late stage calls into question the professionalism with which the audit has been conducted and the **quality of the work performed**.

The fact that Skarn is willing to sign an unmodified audit report, knowing that the accounts are materially misstated, shows a **lack of integrity**. This could result in negligence claims being made against them and disciplinary action being taken by their regulatory body.

It also demonstrates a **lack of independence** as they are clearly being influenced by the directors.

The fact that Nuee Ardente has also agreed not to restate the comparatives also shows a **lack of judgement and integrity** on their part. Their independence is being affected by both the directors and the previous auditors. It also shows a lack of appreciation of respective responsibilities as it would be the directors who would prepare the accounts.

Skarn and Nuee have obviously had discussions regarding this issue. Unless Skarn obtained permission from Corundum to communicate with the prospective auditors they will have breached **client confidentiality**.

Outsourced work

Outsourcing of legal and company secretarial work is common practice. The situation offers an opportunity to Nuee to offer additional services.

Nuee may experience difficulties in obtaining certain key documents. Even if Adam had made contingency plans it is likely that there will be some time delay in obtaining information. If the problem is significant it may constitute a limitation in scope.

Corundum does not keep copies of key documents. This should be raised in Nuee's management letter as it would be good practice to keep adequate documentation regarding outsourced activities.

It may be that Skarn has legal documents and board minutes on their audit files which would be of ongoing use to the new auditors. Once formally appointed Skarn would be expected to provide Nuee with all the books and papers in their possession free of charge. If requested to do so other information may also be provided at the request of Corundum (or Nuee's request with the agreement of Corundum). Depending on the amount of work involved a fee could be charged.

4 Isthmus

Text reference. Chapter 2

Top tips. This question deals with the familiar topic of ethics and professional issues. Note however that a good answer will not simply be confined to the ACCA's *Code of Ethics and Conduct* (or IFAC's Code of Ethics). There is more to ethics than simply independence and more to professional issues than ethics. Other relevant points include competence, confidentiality, quality control and risk assessment. Don't fall into the trap of writing every 'rule' you are aware of. At this level the examiner assumes that you are aware of the basics. You must apply your knowledge and only make points as they are relevant to the scenario.

The answer below has been based on IFAC's Code of Ethics.

Easy marks. These were available for outlining the issues in connection with the inherited shares.

Examiner's comments. Many candidates lacked the basic knowledge to answer this question which was surprising as it was at 2.6 level. Answers also tended to see situations as right or wrong and did not explore the area in between. Due diligence was largely misunderstood in part (a) with many candidates stating that the work constituted a breach of confidentiality. Parts 2 and 3 were answered better.

Marks

Generally 1 mark each ethical/other professional issue raised and 1 mark each implication for staffing the final audit

Issues ideas
(1)   Profits warning
- Increased inherent risk
- Advocacy threat
- Self-review threat
- Competence

Implications (= conclusions) eg on involvement of audit trainees
(2)   Shares inherited
- Self-interest threat
- Inadvertent violation
- Disposal vs
- Removal from team and/or firm
- Safeguard (review)

Implication/conclusion on Mercedes as assistant audit manager
(3)   Shares dealing
- Self-interest
- Insider-dealing? (Anthony vs father)
- Confidentiality

Implication/conclusion on Anthony as audit senior

$\underline{\underline{15}}$

Profits warning

Ethical and professional issues

Kloser needs to consider whether the work carried out by the Corporate Finance department was of the highest standard, assess the likelihood of any claim being made against them, who it might be made by and determine a plan of action.

If Isthmus decides to take action this could give rise to an advocacy threat.

There is a self review threat in that the comparative figures in this years accounts will have been audited shortly after the due diligence work was performed. There is a possibility that audit work in certain areas, for example the valuation of assets, may have been **restricted** due to the due diligence work being performed.

The fact that the company has issued a profits warning increases the **inherent risk** in the audit.

Implications for staffing

As a safeguard in respect of the provision of the due diligence work the audit trainees may be excluded from the audit team. If it is felt, however, that the benefits of their prior knowledge outweigh any risks, they could be involved in parts of the audit which were not the subject of the due diligence work.

More staff may be required as compared to the 2006 audit, assuming that less audit work was performed due to the due diligence.

The increased risk attached to the audit will affect the seniority of staff selected.

All work should be closely **monitored and reviewed** particularly in the light of the potential issue surrounding the due diligence.

Inherited shares

Ethical and professional issues

The ownership of shares by Mercedes affects her independence as an auditor as she now has a **financial interest** in the company. This is accentuated by the fact that she has expressed her desire to see the share price increase. There is a possibility that this may affect her professional judgement as she may be more concerned with the results showing the most favourable position rather than the true and fair view.

If Mercedes is unwilling to dispose of the shares (which seems to be the case) she should be excluded from the audit team although there is no reason why the firm should not continue to perform the audit.

The firm's procedures appear to be operating effectively in terms of staff declarations of share ownership.

The firm may wish to consider whether they want to take any further action regarding Mercedes' refusal to dispose of the shares. (In some firms employees are prohibited from owning shares in any client companies.)

Implications for staffing

Unless Mercedes disposes of the shares immediately she should not be allowed to undertake any further work on the audit. If she has inadvertently done any work whilst holding the shares this should be reviewed thoroughly for any signs of bias.

Dealing in shares

Ethical and professional issues

If Anthony (in spite of his assurances) has **knowingly** provided his father with information resulting in the sale of the shares he has committed a criminal act. This would result in immediate dismissal from the firm followed by disciplinary action by the ACCA. (Criminal proceedings may also follow.)

If he was unaware of the fact that the shares were held by his father there would have been no self interest threat. However if he provided his father with the information inadvertently, for example by mentioning the company's results, this would constitute a breach of **client confidentiality**. This should be investigated and could result in disciplinary action being taken.

Anthony's father may be guilty of **insider dealing** if he acted upon price sensitive information provided by Anthony (unknowingly or otherwise).

Implications for staffing

Assuming that Anthony's assurances are believed he has not committed any offence so there is no reason why he should not continue with the audit, particularly as his father's shares have now been sold, removing any self-interest threat.

The situation should however be reviewed for any change in circumstances. For example if Anthony's father was investigated for insider dealing Anthony should be removed from the audit team.

5 Question with analysis: Depeche

Text reference. Chapter 2

Top tips. This question looks at a number of ethical dilemmas. Care must be taken when reading the information to ensure that the key issues are identified. (Hopefully the analysis in the question helped with this.) It can be easy to become sidetracked by minor details or basic misunderstandings and end up missing the point of the question. Think carefully, in particular about the meaning of the term 'final report' used in issue 3.

Easy marks. You should be able to gain good marks for issues (1) and (2) outlining basic ethics guidance about independence.

Marking scheme

	Marks
(a) Ethical and professional issues	Max 12

Generally 1 mark each comment

Ideas

General

- 5 – 10% fees for listed co ⇒ review
- Review = a safeguard (independence & integrity)

(1) Hospitality

- Threat to objectivity
- Corrupt practice (?)
- When acceptable (social courtesy)

(2) Financial reward (= bonus)

- Manager v other staff participation
- Bribe (?)
- Audit fee (not recurring element)
- Practice management implications

(3) Client/auditor integrity

- ISA 250
- ISA 260
- reason for exclusion from final report

	Marks
(b) Appropriateness of available safeguards	Max 8

Generally 1 mark each safeguard and 1 mark each comment thereon

Ideas

- Review (policies, procedures)
- Second partner involvement
- Rotation (partner/senior staff)
- Audit committee involvement

1 mark for advice **clearly** based on adequacy of available safeguards

<u>20</u>

(a) **Ethical and professional issues**

    (i) *Provision of meals*

        The provision of meals to the auditors constitutes hospitality. The acceptance of **hospitality could impair the judgement** of the auditors **or be perceived** as having that effect. Hospitality may be accepted if it is of modest value.

The cost of providing meals is **unlikely to be significant** and in practice the chances of accepting this type of hospitality affecting key decisions made by the auditors is remote. It is unlikely that they have been offered as a bribe but merely as a **courtesy** to the audit team.

An alternative would be for the audit team to **pay for their own meals** and **recover the cost** from Depeche. This would then be recharged as part of the audit fee.

(ii) *Bonus payments*

The auditor must **be** and must be **seen to be independent.** Independence may be impaired if the auditor is to receive financial reward from a client even if it is received indirectly.

Payments of bonuses in this way are **not normal professional practice**. This may **raise suspicion** that the payments are a **bribe** or a **pay-off** for failing to report on matters that would otherwise have been noted. This calls into question the **integrity** of the audit team.

If the audit team were aware of the potential receipt of the bonus this increases the risk that they will not be seen to be independent.

The bonus does not apply to those of manager status and above. This **decreases** the risks described above. However, the fact that it has been limited to lower grade staff demonstrates that the situation is perceived to be a threat to objectivity. The rationale behind allowing the bonus to less senior staff should have been considered by the ethics partner and his conclusions documented.

The bonus forms part of the basic audit fee and should be treated as such for **disclosure** purposes. The full amount should be disclosed as the audit fee in the accounts of Duran.

The bonus could have an adverse effect on the morale of other staff at Depeche. Those not involved in the audit may feel that they have been unfairly treated as they have not been given the opportunity to earn the extra income. This could lead to **future staffing problems**.

(iii) *Illegal dumping of waste*

The attitude of Frankie Sharkey to environmental legislation calls into question the **integrity of management** and the overall manner in which the company does business. This may affect the extent to which the auditors would be prepared to rely on **management representations**.

The disregard for legislation **increases audit risk** and should have been taken into account as part of the overall risk assessment. In particular the **control environment** is affected.

The audit team should have taken into account the requirements of ISA 250 *Consideration of laws and regulations in an audit of financial statements*. Consideration should have been given to:

- The frequency of the illegal dumping and how long it had been going on for

- The potential impact of fines and penalties

- The possibility of any other type of action being taken against the company

- Whether there has been any attempt made by management to conceal information from the auditors and if so whether risk assessments need to be revised

- The need to disclose the potential consequences of the illegal action

The auditor should report to the audit committee in accordance with ISA 260 *Communication of audit matters with those charged with governance*. Matters which should be reported include:

- The potential effect of any material risks and exposures such as pending litigation. (This could arise as a result of the illegal dumping.)

- Other matters warranting attention by those charged with governance such as questions regarding management integrity.

This matter has not been referred to in the report to the audit committee. This would be of some concern unless there is a valid reason for the exclusion. For example, the audit committee may already be aware of the situation as a result of information provided by the internal audit department.

The audit file should document the reasons behind the decision to leave this information out of the final report and should state by whom the decision was made.

(b) **Available safeguards**

(i) The firm's ethics partner should review the hospitality received from Duran and ensure that it is in compliance with the firm's guidance.

(ii) The process by which the engagement partner decided to accept the bonus should be reviewed by the ethics partner to ensure that it followed the firm's procedures.

(iii) The audit staff who were involved in the audit this year and received the bonus should not be involved in the audit next year.

(iv) If the partner has had a long association with the client partner rotation may be required.

(v) A second partner review should be performed to provide an independent assessment of the conduct of the audit.

(vi) The issues of independence should be brought to the attention of the audit committee. Written representations from the audit committee that they are aware of the threats posed by the hospitality etc and that they are satisfied that Duran's safeguards are sufficient should be obtained.

Advice

Duran should continue to serve as the auditor of Depeche provided that:

(i) There are no other unresolved ethical issues (eg undue dependence on Depeche due to the size of the audit fee)

(ii) The ethics partner believes that the safeguards are adequate to reduce the risk to independence to an acceptable level

6 Bartolome

Text reference. Chapter 2

Top tips. As always think broadly about the situations described in the question and jot down any possible implications (ethical, quality, professional) you can think of. Often one leads to another. So for example, in part (b) (probably the most challenging section of this question), it is important to consider whether the auditors have obtained enough audit evidence to draw the audit opinion, and then the ethical and quality implications of their possible failure to.

Easy marks. Note that the question requires you to comment on the implications for continuing the audit. Marks for this requirement will not necessarily be easy, but the examiner has indicated by her requirement that they are available, so they would be easy marks to lose by not answering this part of the requirement.

Examiner's comments. Many candidates could have scored one more mark on each part by concluding whether or not each engagement could be properly continued. In part (a), most candidates recognised that Leon must have some relationship with the client that would be seem to impair his objectivity, and so should be moved from the assignment, and his work should be reviewed. This was enough to earn half-marks. Careless reading of the question led some candidates to suppose that Leon had already accepted the position. For part (b) there were a few good answers from those candidates who appreciated the seriousness of the situation and dealt with it. Many candidates dwelt at length on the evidence and aspects of unmodified reports for no more marks than if they had dealt with these points briefly. Weaker candidates 'denied' the facts of the question. The audit opinions should have been modified/unmodified – but they were not. That could not be 'undone'. In part (c), not a lot needed to be written for just four marks. As the situation was explained in just two sentences, candidates should have had time to read it more than once to understand it.

Marking scheme

Marks

(a)   Ethical and other professional issues

Generally 1 mark each ethical/professional issue/implication
for continuation with assignment
Ideas
(a) Senior audit staff leaving for employment with client
   - Objectivity (Lean)/self-interest threat
   - Integrity (James and/or Leon)
   - Professional courtesy
   - Implications for staffing final audit
   - Review of interim audit working paper

(b) Unqualified auditors' report
   - Meaning of – no emphasis of matter (eg re going concern)
   - Sufficiency of evidence (Ayora and Chatam)
   - Reliance on management representations (and wider implications)
   - Familiarity threat
   - Self-interest threat
   - Undue influence

(c) Threatened legal action
   - Advocacy threat
   - Integrity of Bartolome
   - Industry practice?
   - Legal obligation?
   - Terms of engagement

$$\overline{15}$$

(a)	max 5
(b)	max 6
(c)	max 4
	$\overline{15}$

(a)   **Moreno**

Independence

In being shortlisted for a position at Moreno, Leon is no longer independent with regard to the audit of Moreno. There is too great a risk that he will want to impress his potential future employer and this will affect the audit that he carries out.

Quality control procedures

The IFAC Code states that a firm should have quality control policies setting out that if a senior member of audit staff is potentially going to be employed by an audit client, then that member of staff should disclose that fact to the audit firm.

In this case, either Bartolome does not have such a policy, which is a failing in its own quality control, or, it does have such a policy and Leon has breached this policy in not telling the audit firm he had applied for a job at Moreno.

Regardless of whether Bartolome has such a policy, it is a matter of Leon's personal integrity that he should have made the disclosure, as he should have been aware that he was not sufficiently independent of Moreno to carry out the audit.

Leon should receive a warning from his employer about his conduct.

Implications for continuing the engagement

Leon should be removed from the audit immediately and a different senior appointed in his place.

Any work that Leon has already carried out, such as the planning of the audit, should be reviewed, and amended if this is felt to be necessary.

(b)   **Chatham**

Audit evidence

Auditors should obtain management representations on 'matters material to the financial statements when other sufficient appropriate audit evidence cannot reasonably be expected to exist. However, these representations cannot be a substitute for other audit evidence that the auditor could reasonably expect to be available'.

An auditor would expect there to be sources of evidence other than management opinion about whether an asset is impaired. For example, management should have carried out an impairment review of the asset, which the auditors could have used as audit evidence, carrying out verifications on the assumptions and facts used in the impairment review.

If this evidence had been available, Bartolome should not have needed to obtain written representations about the goodwill. If the evidence had not been available, this would have constituted a limitation in scope on the audit, as the auditors cannot just accept representations in lieu of audit evidence they expect to be available.

In addition, if the evidence was not available, then this should also have given rise to a disagreement about accounting treatment, because Chatham would not have been fulfilling the requirements of IFRS 3.

Fraudulent financial reporting

Given that due to persistent losses, the goodwill in Arora appears to be impaired and the requirements of IFRS 3 may not have been followed, there is a suspicion that in not recognising the impairment in Arora, there has been fraudulent financial reporting in this situation, particularly since the Chief Executive stands to benefit from the company doing well in the short term when he is likely to exercise his share options.

Lack of independence due to long association

It is possible that the auditors have overlooked the problems outlined above due to a lack of independence arising from the fact that the audit firm have had a long association with this client. Audit staff may have a personal relationship with Charles Barrington to the extent that they believe him to be honest and do not suspect any wrongdoing on his part to the point where their professional skepticism has been affected.

Implications for audit evidence

Insufficient audit evidence appears to have been obtained about the goodwill in Arora and therefore the going concern basis of the financial statements. It is possible that there is insufficient audit evidence for other areas of the audit.

Implications for continuing the engagement

This problem does not give rise to a need for the audit firm to divest this audit client, but it does suggest that it might be necessary to rotate the senior staff associated with the audit so that the danger of long association is averted. The audit opinion for 2006 should be subject to a cold review to ensure that sufficient evidence was obtained on which to base the audit opinion.

(c) **Pinzon**

Advocacy threat

An advocacy threat to independence has arisen as Pinzon is threatening legal action against Bartolome.

Lack of integrity

If the allegation is true and Bartolome has recharged excessive expenses to Pinzon, this does appear to indicate a lack of integrity on the part of Bartolome. However, it could have been a simple error, or it could be because Bartolome believes this to be accepted industry practice or it was an agreed policy in the engagement letter between the parties.

As legal proceedings are expensive and Bartolome does not appear to have acted illegally, Pinzon might be better advised to take this matter up with the ACCA disciplinary committee than in a court of law. The audit engagement partner could advise Pinzon of this, although it is unlikely that client staff will accept his advice if they believe the audit firm to be guilty.

Action to take

Bartolome should issue a credit note for the difference to attempt to solve the breach.

Implications for continuing with the assignment

Unless the dispute is settled very quickly, Bartolome is no longer independent with regard to the Pinzon audit and should resign for the audit of the year-end 31 December 2006 (assuming they had previously been elected).

7 Boleyn

Text references. Chapters 2 and 5

Top tips. You should be able to score well in part (a). In part (b), take each question in turn, noting the mark allocation for each and the fact that you need to both explain the threats to objectivity and the safeguards that should be put in place to mitigate those threats. This should make part (b) more manageable and ensure that you don't spend all your time on one specific area that you are very knowledgeable on to the detriment of the other parts of the question.

Easy marks. These are available in part (a) of the question. In part (b), you should be able to think of threats and safeguards for each of the scenarios to gain some good marks.

ACCA examiner's answer. The examiner's answer to this question is included at the back of this kit.

Marking scheme

	Marks
(a) IFAC's Code	
Generally *1 mark* each point	max 3
Ideas	
• Professional accountants = IFAC members	
... in public practice = practitioners (partners/employees/managers/firms)	
• Employed ... = in industry, commerce, etc (1/4 mark each)	
(b) FAQs	
Generally *1 mark* each comment	(i) max 5
	(ii) max 3
	(iii) max 4

Ideas

Threats to independence

- Self-interest
- Self-review (other services)
- Familiarity
- Management

Possible safeguards

- Prohibition
- Separate partners/staff
- Policies and procedures (specified)
- Disclosure (e.g. to audit committee)

<u>15</u>

(a)   'Professional accountants' are members of an IFAC member body and can be in public practice or employed persons, or may be a sole practitioner, a partnership or a corporate body.

'Professional accountants in public practice' are partners, employees in a practice that provides professional services or professional accountants in practice with management responsibilities.

'Employed professional accountants' are professional accountants employed in industry, commerce, the public sector or education.

(b)   (i)   *IT services*

Offering information technology services to an audit client could give rise to a self-review threat if the firm designed internal control IT services for the client and then reviewed this as part of the audit of the financial statements. It could also lead to a management threat if the firm starts making decisions that should really be taken by the client. Offering information technology services to an audit client could also give rise to a self-interest threat if the fees from such work are regular and make up a substantial part of the firm's fees.

The ACCA's *Code of Ethics and Conduct* suggests possible safeguards to mitigate these risks, such as ensuring that the client acknowledges its responsibility for establishing and monitoring a system of internal controls. The client could also ensure that a competent senior manager makes all management decisions in terms of designing and implementing the system. The client should also be responsible for operation of the system and the data used or produced by the system. Another safeguard would be to use staff from the firm who were not involved with the audit to be involved in IT-related work for the client so that objectivity was not impaired.

(ii)   *Entertaining and corporate hospitality*

Entertaining clients as a gesture of goodwill could give rise to a familiarity threat which could impair the objectivity and independence of audit staff for that client. It could also give rise to a self-interest threat if the provision of the goodwill, say annually, is provided in order to retain the client.

The ACCA's *Code of Ethics and Conduct* states that unless the value of the gift/hospitality is clearly insignificant, a firm or a member of an assurance team should not accept. This would also apply to the audit firm offering hospitality to a client. Safeguards involve discussing with the audit engagement partner and ethics partner as appropriate and making a judgement as to whether the hospitality would be considered significant.

(iii)   *Cross-selling other services to audit clients*

Cross-selling other services to audit clients could give rise to threats such as self-review and self-interest. A self-review threat arises because there is a risk that the firm's staff will review their own work performed in undertaking other services. A self-interest threat can arise because the firm would be relying on higher fees being generated from services other than the audit such as consultancy.

Appropriate safeguards might include ensuring that staff providing non-audit services do not take part in the audit and involving an additional professional accountant to advise on the possible impact of non-audit services on the independence of the firm and the audit team.

8 Hawk Associates

Text references. Chapters 2 and 5

Top tips. Break each section of this question into discrete parts. As noted below, some parts are easier than others and there are easy marks to be had. If you break each part down, you can ensure that you gain the one or two marks available for each little section and gain good answer coverage. For example in part (a), focus on cold calling, then on second opinions, then on free services. There are three areas for five marks, so if you comment on each, you should pass this section of the question. The answer below has been broken down into sections indicated by the subheaders. If you indicate your answer has been so broken down, then it is easier for a marker to give you marks in each section.

Easy marks. Each of these segments contains an item which has basic ACCA or IFAC guidance connected with it which you should be able to outline. For example, in (a), if you are not sure about cold calling, you should have learnt the rules about second opinions. In part (b), you might be unsure about contingent fees, but you should know the rules concerning an advert. You will gain easy marks outlining the guidance relating to each of these items.

Examiner's comments. The question called for an extension of lower level auditing knowledge on obtaining professional work in the areas of advertising, fees and firms' names. Easy marks were thrown away if candidates did not state one way or the other whether each of the proposals was suitable.

In part (a), most candidates knew little about 'cold calling'. Many homed in on second opinions, but incorrectly supposed that a free audit was being offered. Candidates should not drop jargon into their answers which they do not properly understand.

In part (b), although most candidates had some idea of the basic rules on advertising, few were able to relate them to the suggested advertisement and thereby explain why it was inappropriate. However, candidates who took time to sift through the wording for ideas earned good marks.

Few candidates observed in part (c) that offering such a wide range of services conflicted with the increasing restrictions on the provision of non-audit services set out in the opening paragraph of the scenario.

Marking scheme

Marks

Generally 1 mark each comment

Ideas
- Whether prohibited
- Permitted (ACCA)
- Commercial/competitive practice
- Fundamental principles apply
- 'Free' – when permitted
- Second opinions – discouraged

Tax planning advertisement
- Advertising restrictions
- The 'best'?
- How ensure?
- Assertion of 'all'
- Exposure to litigation
- Contingency fees

Business cards
- Where advertised
- Size of advertisement
- Use of ACCA name
- PROFESSIONAL
- Range of non-audit services
- Basis of asserting 'competitive rates'
- 'Money back'
- Cannot guarantee opinions

(a) max	5
(b) max	6
(c) max	4
	15

(a) **Cold calling and second opinions**

Cold calling

ACCA's general rule about advertising is that 'the medium used should not reflect adversely on the accountancy profession'. Cold calling is generally unpopular, but this does not necessarily make it unprofessional. However, advertisements must be in line with ACCA guidance that it should not discredit other members of the profession by claiming superiority for the member's own services, it should not be misleading and it should be legal, honest, decent, clear and truthful.

Cold calling itself is legal (in many states) and there is no reason why it should not be honest and truthful. However, it may present a problem in terms of clarity, as it is oral and therefore there is scope for misunderstanding on the part of the companies being rung, and the customer being misled. In addition, any advertising technique that results in harassment is inappropriate.

Specifically, as we shall see below, cold calling about second opinions may discredit other members of the profession.

Second opinions

A second opinion is where a company is unhappy with the audit opinion that the auditor has proposed and therefore seeks an opinion from a different firm of auditors as to whether another audit opinion might be possible.

If a client requests a second opinion from an auditor, it is generally considered acceptable to give one if certain conditions are met. These are that the second firm of auditors communicates with the first set to ensure that they have access to all the information (to ensure that the second opinion is not formed negligently) and the two firms of auditors communicate frequently during the process to ensure that the first firm are not pressurised into giving a second opinion.

However, an audit firm offering to give second opinions does not appear to be so acceptable. This immediately gives the impression that all audit opinions are negotiable, and automatically puts pressure on the first firm of auditors. If the second firm is under pressure to give a different opinion (otherwise the service they have offered is negligible) then different opinions might be formed negligently.

In addition, the service they are providing discredits other auditors as it makes the suggestion that such a service is necessary, that is, that other auditors may have drawn incorrect or inappropriate audit conclusions.

Free service

Offering a free service is not prohibited so long as the client is not misled about the potential fees for future services.

Conclusion

In general terms, cold calling potential customers is not inappropriate for an audit firm. However, if it is used, it should be done so with great care so as not to mislead potential customers. It would probably be appropriate for small services other than audit-related services. Specifically, auditors should not offer services to give second opinions as this discredits the profession.

(b) **Tax planning advert**

Tax planning

Tax planning is an important part of many accountancy firms' portfolios. People in business want to operate tax efficiently and it is a perfectly legitimate service.

Advertising

ACCA's guidance on advertising was outlined above. It must not discredit the services of other accountants, it must not be misleading and it must not fall short of the British Code of Advertising Practice, meaning that it must be legal, decent, clear, honest and truthful.

In this advert, Hawk Associates claim to give 'the best' tax planning advice, which both implies the services of others are not as good (in other words it discredits them) and also may not be a claim they can live up to, opening the firm up to liability. In addition, the advert promises to consider 'all' the tax planning options available, which is an exaggerated claim and may also open them up to liability if they do not achieve this promise. In other words, the advert exaggerates the extent of Hawk Associates' service and is therefore potentially misleading.

In addition, the advert could imply to a potential client lacking in integrity that legitimate taxes might be avoided, and while the advert does not make any illegal suggestions, it could be read to mean that taxes can be avoided by any means (ie, potentially illegally). The firm should ensure that it is seen to uphold the professional standard of integrity.

Contingent fees

The advert offers a contingent fee (that is, a charge will only be made if a tax saving is made). Contingent fees on assurance work are prohibited because the risks to independence are too great to be safeguarded against. Tax consultancy is not assurance work and there are circumstances in which IFAC would allow contingent fees for non assurance work. The firm should consider issues such as the range of fee amounts (which could be a substantial range), the degree of variability, the basis on which the fee is to be determined, whether the outcome of the work is to be reviewed by a third party (it is likely to be reviewed by tax authorities) and the effect of the transaction on any assurance engagement performed.

Given that audit clients might want to take up such an offer and that the work is likely to be scrutinised by the tax authorities, it is unlikely to be appropriate to offer contingent fees for work of this nature. If contingent fees were offered, then safeguards would need to be put into place by the firm, and the extent of these safeguards could not be explained in an advert of this size, making the advertising of the fees (or lack of them) potentially misleading.

Conclusion

The advert breaches the ACCA's guidance as it discredits other members. It is misleading as it implies a level of service which the firm cannot guarantee and therefore exposes the firm to liability. In addition, contingent fees are likely to be inappropriate as audit clients might accept this offer.

(c) **Business cards**

Use of ACCA designation

Hawk Associates are unlikely to be entitled to refer to themselves as Hawk ACCA Associates without permission from the ACCA, which is unlikely to be given. The firm is entitled to refer to itself as Hawk Associates, Chartered Certified Accountants, if 51% or more of the partners are ACCA members.

Use of the word professional

The highlighted use of the word professional appears inappropriate. Firstly it implies that other accountants are not professional, which is discrediting to the profession. In addition, the fact that Chartered Certified Accountants are professional is implied, it is not an additional selling point.

Competitive rates

There appears to be little basis for advertising that rates are competitive – with whom? for what? and it would be better to advertise that fees are reasonable and can be discussed in detail with the firm.

Money back guarantees

It is unclear in what circumstances a client would receive money back but it appears to be a claim that a firm of accountants should not make. A guarantee to give money back is akin to receiving a loan or dealing in contingent fees and it is inappropriate for a firm providing assurance services.

Location of advertisement

In principle, there is no issue in advertising in the local supermarkets and libraries where local businesses and tradesmen advertise. However, the brevity of the advert could lead to it being misleading due to the complexity of some of the services being offered, and it might be more advisable to run expanded adverts in different media.

Conclusion

The advertisements are inappropriate as they imply a discredit to the profession, they are potentially misleading and they should not offer money back guarantees.

9 Fox and Steeple

Text references. Chapters 2 and 5

Top tips. Take each scenario in turn and deal with it separately. Think about the issues in each and remember to address each part of the requirement. Make sure you present your answer well – use short, punchy paragraphs and make good use of headings by splitting your answer into three sections for each of the three scenarios and then further into sub-headings, which will give your answer more structure and coherence. Notice that the requirement is to 'compare and contrast' so you need to present your answer carefully.

Easy marks. By taking each scenario in turn and dealing with each of the three requirements, you should be able to pick up some good marks.

Examiner's comments. Candidates did well in this question, but some answers were far too long which often reduced the time available to answer questions 1 or 2 on the paper. There was a lot of evidence that some candidates were filling their answers with jargon such as low-balling, insider dealing, Chinese walls. Several candidates failed to understand at least one, if not all, of the scenarios in the question. Weaker answers discussed pre-acceptance procedures which was not relevant. This question provided evidence that candidates do not always plan their answers, especially to Section B questions. However, in this question, time spent summarising the similarities and differences between the three clients would have been very useful in producing a good 'compare and contrast' answer.

Marking scheme

Marks

Generally ½ mark each matter relevant to staffing identified and 1 mark each
comment contributing to comparison/contrast of three clients

Ideas
Ethical
- Objectivity/threats to independence
    - Self interest
    - Self-review (other services Huggins/Gray)
    - Familiarity (Huggins/Gray)
    - Intimidation (Peter/Blythe)
- Possible safeguards (some are staffing implications)
Other professional
- Risk management (of assignments)
- Quality control (direction, supervision, review)
- Client management
- Professional scepticism
Staffing implications
- Competence and due care (Qualifications/Specialisation)

$\overline{15}$

(a) **Threats to independence**

Per IFAC's *Code of ethics for professional accountants*, the threats to independence are identified as self-interest, self-review, management, advocacy, familiarity/trust and intimidation. Advocacy does not appear to be applicable in these three scenarios.

Self-interest

Self-interest is more likely to be an issue for Huggins and Gray. Huggins is a national supermarket chain and likely to provide a larger fee to the firm for its services than Blythe, which is a local manufacturer. Similarly the firm provides Gray with a number of services including audit, tax, accounting and due diligence. This could give a perception of undue fee dependence.

Self-review

Self-review is not likely to be a threat in the audit of Blythe as it is a new audit client and there is no indication that the firm will be offering other services just yet. In the case of Huggins and Gray, this could be an issue as the firm provides other services to these clients.

The firm has been asked to conduct a thorough review of the computer system in place at Huggins. Therefore appropriate safeguards need to be in place to mitigate the threat that the team is acting in a management capacity when undertaking this review.

The firm provides Gray with technical advice on accounting and tax services in addition to audit services. It has also now asked for the firm to undertake due diligence reviews on potential acquisitions. Safeguards need to be in place to reduce these risks. These include having different teams and independent reviews of work performed.

Familiarity/trust

Familiarity is unlikely to be an issue in the Blythe audit as it is a new audit client of the firm.

Familiarity will be an issue for both Huggins and Gray since the former is a long-standing client of the firm and the latter has been an audit client since 2000. In these circumstances it is necessary to implement appropriate safeguards such as rotating senior team members or having an independent review of the work carried out.

Huggins has been using the same engagement partner. The ethical guidance requires rotation of the engagement partner after seven years.

Intimidation

An intimidation threat may arise in the audit of Blythe since, although it is a new client, the Finance Director does not see much value from an audit and has put it out to tender in order to save costs by using another firm, as well as the requirement that there should not be an interim audit.

There may also be a threat of intimidation in Huggins as the senior management are looking for assurance that the annual report will not attract criticism.

(b) **Other professional and practical matters**

For Blythe, an engagement letter needs to be sent to the client, setting out the responsibilities of both parties, the fees for the audit and the timing. Given that the Finance Director does not want an interim audit and it is a new client, the timing of the audit will be a key issue to agree from the start. The terms of the due diligence reviews for Gray also need to be agreed with the client.

All these clients have the same accounting year-end so the firm needs to consider carefully how to allocate staff. Also, given that Blythe is a new audit client and Huggins is a large listed company, the firm needs to consider the need for a hot review by a second partner for these assignments.

Careful consideration should be given to ensuring that the most appropriate staff are assigned to each assignment. In the case of Huggins and Gray, as these are long-established clients of the firm, staff who have worked on these clients previously could be used as they are likely to have a good understanding of the clients and established working relationships with key client staff.

(c) **Allocating staff**

Where other services are provided (for Huggins and Gray), the firm needs to ensure that audit team members are not also involved in these other services, to maintain independence and objectivity.

Blythe is a new audit client of the firm. Given this, and the Finance Director's attitude towards the external audit, the firm should ensure that an experienced senior is allocated to the audit team. If possible, staff with experience in the manufacturing sector should be used.

The firm should ensure that the review of the computer system of Huggins is carried out using staff with appropriate experience of the system in place. The senior management of the client are expecting a thorough review to be undertaken.

10 Azure

Text reference. Chapter 5

Top tips. The practical context of this question is a tender. This may seem off putting initially as you may feel that this is something which you do not know a lot about. However if you actually look at the question you will see that the majority of the marks are in fact for part (a) which is on the familiar topic of planning issues. Also note the need to read all the information in the question. Although the requirement to part (a) specifically asks you to consider planning issues, in the body of the question you are told that this should include risk and strategy. It would therefore be sensible to include a section in your answer on both of these areas.

Part (b) then deals with the tender itself. Bear in mind that in most cases this type of requirement can be answered using a bit of common sense. Even if you had never heard of the term 'tendering' you should be able to come up with a few sensible ideas regarding the criteria a business might use to select its auditors.

Easy marks. Overall, the message with this question is not to panic. There are plenty of marks available for commenting on issues which you should be familiar with.

Examiner's comments. Part (a) was generally poorly answered with many candidates apparently being on auto-pilot, producing a general and vague answer which could apply to any planning question. Again higher level skills, which are an important element of this paper were missing, with many failing to develop points sufficiently or to consider further consequences of the points raised. Answers to part (b) were satisfactory although many did not provide sufficient detail to score good marks.

Marking scheme

	Marks

(a) Principal audit planning issues
Generally 1 mark each point contributing to a description of principal issues — Max 15
½ mark each ratio, %, etc — Max 5
Ideas – 'general'
- Risks
  - Inherent: entity, a/c balance, class of transactions
  - Control (eg strong environment)
  - Business (eg fuel costs, forex)
- Audit strategy (conclusion)
  - Audit (or business) risk model - justified
  - Reliance on internal audit (see also (2))
  - Analytical procedures (illustrated – see (3))
- Materiality (assessed/quantified)
- Logistics (multiple locations)
Ideas – 'specific'
(1) Sales & distribution
  - Retail sales ↓ as other sales ↑
  - Predict impact (for analytical procedures)
  - Health & safety
  - Potential contingent liabilities
(2) Internal financial control – use in audit (efficiency)
  - Assessment of control environment (strong)
  - Budgets etc for analytical procedures
  - Reliance on internal audit

(3)   Analytical procedures – use in audit (efficiency)
- T/o + 23.5% (expansion – see fixed asset investment)
- PBT + 6.2% (tighter margins)
- NP% 2.9% (2005 – 3.4%)
- Tangible NCA + 35.9% (see debt finance)
- Receivables + 39% (circulation 2m or 63,000 customers NOT appropriate)
- Cash etc +52% (very liquid – but see liabilities)
- New convertible debt

$\underline{15}$

(b)   Selection criteria
Generally 1 mark each criterion and comment thereon
Maximum 3 marks any one criterion $\underline{10}$
Criteria ideas
- 'Physical' – size, resources, office locations (including overseas)
- Quality of submission (timely? complete?)
- Understanding of business/experience in industry sector (client portfolio)
- Audit strategy (efficiency and effectiveness)
- Reporting timetable, deadlines, etc
- Reputation of firm (distinguished?)
- Competence of audit team (specialists needed?)
- Personal rapport ('chemistry')
- Range and quality of services provided
- Adding value (proactively?)
- Competitive fees and billing arrangements (VFM)
- 'Malleability'

$\underline{25}$

(a)   **Planning issues**

Risk

Risk is increased by the following factors:

(i)   *The nature of the business*

- The 'holiday' business is extremely competitive with increasingly cut-throat pricing policies being adopted to win market share. This has resulted in the collapse of tour operators in the past.

- The company operates from 13 holiday locations.

- The diverse geographical spread of the business gives rise to potential control issues. The business will also be subject to local laws and practices and will need to be aware of and implement these.

(ii)   *Financial issues*

- One of the most significant costs that the company will face is that of aviation fuel. This is determined by the markets and is a factor over which the company will have little control of either in terms of the price it has to pay or the amount which it uses.

- The company will be exposed to foreign exchange risk due to the nature of the business and the diversity of locations in which it operates.

(iii)   *Structure of the business*

- This is a cash-based rather than capital-based business. (For example the aircraft are leased rather than owned.) This increases liquidity risk. The company needs to maintain high levels of cash in order to make the operating lease payments and meet other liabilities.

- Control risk is likely to be low. The control environment appears to be strong with practical control procedures in place. The company has divisional planning and budgetary systems and the Board appears to take the issue seriously by reviewing the results.

(iv) *Sales methods*

- An increasing number of sales are being generated as a result of the use of call centres. These have the advantage of reducing cost to the business and convenience for the customer. However health and safety issues may arise. Call centres are often a high pressured environment in which to work and the business could be subject to claims for related health problems.

- The company is expanding into e-commerce. This gives rise to security issues. Internet sales must be made on secure websites. For example the website should have WebTrust assurance.

- The increased use of call centres and internet sales may lead to loss of business in the high street, the closure of traditional travel agents and liabilities for the company for redundancies and closure costs.

- Whilst in the long-term the development of call centres and the internet will reduce cost, in the short-term costs may increase due to duplication of costs. For example traditional travel brochures will still be required and in addition costs will be incurred in developing a web version.

Strategy

The following approach is likely to be taken:

- A risk-based approach should be adopted (audit risk or business risk model). This is on the basis that:

  - Identification of risks were part of the brief

  - Existence of risks

  - Practical difficulties in using alternative approaches eg substantive approach due to the number of locations etc

- Reliance on internal control

  From a practical point of view reliance on internal control will render the audit more efficient. This is particularly relevant as the business has a high volume of transactions and multiple locations. In order to rely on internal control the control environment would need to be strong and control procedures operating effectively. Initial indications are good as budgeting systems exist and are reviewed. Assessment would have to be made of the following however:

  - The regularity with which the budgets are reviewed

  - The actions taken as a result of the reviews. This is particularly relevant where there are large discrepancies

  Reliance would also be placed on the internal audit function if possible. The assessment would involve consideration of:

  - Its organisational status (this appears high as the audit committee review its reports)
  - Scope of functions and the actions which the audit committee takes as a result of its reviews
  - Technical competence
  - Due professional care, for example, the quality of the reports produced

- Use of analytical procedures

  These are likely to be used extensively due to the availability of disaggregated and reliable information. Divisional planning and budget documents could be used together with comparisons to actual results performed by the board.

  The nature of certain types of income and expenditure also lend themselves to analytical procedures. For example, a proof in total calculation could be performed on travel agency commissions.

Materiality

Preliminary materiality would be in the region of $4.4 million. This is an average the following assessment of materiality benchmarks and the overall assessment of risk:

½-1% turnover	= $4.7m - $9.4m
1%-2% total assets	= $2.8m - $5.5m
5%-10% PBT	= $1.4m - $2.7m

(If deemed to be very high risk materiality could be assessed to be as low as $2.9m.)

Accounting treatments

The appropriate nature of accounting treatments and policies need to be assessed particularly in the following areas:

(i) Operating leases

This raises the issue of off-balance sheet financing

(ii) Revenue recognition

Revenue and costs are currently recognised at the point that the holiday commences. Where there are a significant number of long-term holidays (ie a number of months rather than weeks) this may be an imprudent policy which could result in the overstatement of revenues and profits. Cut-off at the year-end would be particularly sensitive.

Evidence

As mentioned above analytical procedures will be used extensively as an efficient and effective means of performing the audit. An analysis of the 2005 results as compared to the 2004 results reveals the following:

Revenue has increased by 23.5%. This is likely to be due to the expansion of the direct sales market. A more detailed breakdown of revenue would clarify the extent to which this is the case.

Operating profit has increased by 6.2% representing just 2.9% of turnover. This could be due to:

- **Increased operating costs**. If these relate to the development of the direct sales the benefits of this expenditure should become apparent in future periods. Alternatively it could indicate poor cost control.

- **Reduced margins**. Due to increasing competition prices may have been cut. Special offers may also have been given to encourage customers to use the new services.

Tangible non-current assets have increased by 35.9%. The make up of these additions should be clarified although it is likely that the majority relate to the setting up of call centres. It appears that these acquisitions were financed by the issue of convertible debt.

Trade receivables have increased by 63% although the amount in absolute terms is not significant ($11.5m).

Trade receivables days have increased in 2006 from 8.7 days to 11.5 days which is of concern particularly due to the nature of the customers ie individuals from whom it may be more difficult to recover bad debts.

Cash has increased by 52%. This is largely due to the issue of the convertible debt. Cash flow for this type of business is critical In particular the business needs to consider the balance between its need to keep cash reserves and its ability to pay liabilities promptly.

In absolute terms **revenue received in advance** has increased by 13.8%. As a proportion of turnover however it has fallen from 80% to 74%.

This could be due to a reduction in advance bookings. For example internet customers may be more prone to make last minute bookings.

Practical issues

The business is made up of 13 holiday locations and 29 different outlets. Due to the number of locations involved the following approach will be adopted:

- Only the most significant locations will be visited (it is unnecessary to visit each one)
- For those not visited branch returns will be reviewed

(b) **Selection criteria**

Fee

Azure will be looking for a competitive fee. However the company will not simply be concerned about the fee in absolute terms but in terms of **value for money**.

In order to allow Azure to make this assessment, particularly in comparison to the tenders, a breakdown of the fee should be provided. This should include an analysis of the type of service provided and the number of hours involved and the relative seniority of staff.

Professionalism

This covers a number of issues including the following:

(i) *Reputation of the firm*

The choice of auditor can add increased credibility to the image of the company itself. For example if the company is to have dealings with banks or other financial institutions a nationally recognised auditor may be seen as an advantage. This has to be balanced with the fact that this type of firm can be more expensive (although this is not necessarily the case).

(ii) *Suitability of the firm*

Azure would expect the tender document to provide **background information** on the firm including details such as the number of offices and their location, the organisational structure of the firm and areas of expertise. Azure would be looking to see that the firm has the resources and the expertise to provide the required service.

(iii) *The audit team*

Azure would want to assess:

- The grade of staff being used

- The number of staff allocated (this will affect the duration of the audit)

- The structure of the team

- The experience of staff, particularly the manager and partner

- The identity of the audit partner and the amount of time he is proposing to give to the assignment

- Whether it is proposed to use any specialists and their availability eg tax advisors

(iv)   *Initial impression*

This will normally be a result of the tender process itself. Azure will be concerned that the tender document is produced according to the timetable given and that it covers any specific issues which they have requested.

They will also assess the extent to which the document shows an appreciation and understanding of the business in which they operate and an understanding of the aims and objectives of Azure specifically.

Proposed approach

Azure will be looking for an approach which meets its remit ie a well planned and risk-focused approach which shows an understanding of the business, an understanding of the audit issues and an appreciation for the importance of efficiency and cost effectiveness.

Personal service

Azure will consider the 'personal chemistry' which exists or otherwise between themselves and the key members of the audit team. This is likely to be affected by the personalities of the individuals involved but also by the auditors' ability to demonstrate an empathy with the business and its proposals for the future.

Azure will also be concerned about the auditors' ability to **add value** by providing other services. These could be tax matters and, in the case of Azure in particular, IT matters.

Azure may also consider **innovative ideas**. For example there may be beneficial tax or legal consequences of changing the way in which the business is structured.

11 Turnals

Text reference. Chapter 4

Top tips. Your answer should bring out the limited responsibility the auditors have for detecting fraud. The techniques noted in (c) all have limitations, although you should note that there are ways in which auditors can use them to best advantage.

(a)   **Conflicts of interest**

Guidance from the ACCA in the form of its *Code of Ethics and Conduct* is provided on the issue of auditor independence. Such guidance is also provided by the other accountancy bodies. The principal areas of concern are discussed below.

Provision of other services

The ACCA's rules state that objectivity may be threatened or appear to be threatened by the provision of services other than audit. One significant danger of providing non-audit services is that the product of those services may have to be judged as part of the audit. This situation is a good example of this; Garner and Company **advised** on the **design** of the system and then **tested** the system as part of the audit. Because of their involvement in the system implementation, Garner and Company may be less willing to comment adversely on the system.

One way the regulations diminish this threat is to warn against any staff of the audit firm becoming involved in **executive management** roles at the client, so that audit staff are not given responsibilities which then have to be reported on by the firm. In addition **objectivity** may be **improved** by having different partners and staff involved on the audit and non-audit work.

Undue dependence

The ACCA's guidance states that **objectivity may be threatened** or **appear to be threatened** by undue dependence on any audit client. The statement recommends that the work paid by one client should not in general exceed **15%.** Non-audit work is included within this, and whilst the guidance principally relates to recurring work, non-recurring fees such as consultancy may affect independence if they are large enough. However the question does not indicate whether the fees have breached the 15% limit.

(b)   **Auditor's responsibilities**

Fraud is an intentional act by one or more individuals among management, those charged with governance (management fraud), employees (employee fraud), or third parties involving the use of deception to obtain an unjust or illegal advantage.

Fraud is distinguished from error, which is an unintentional mistake.

Detection and reporting of fraud

The detection of fraud is the responsibility of management. It is incumbent upon management to put a strong emphasis within the company on fraud prevention. It is a by-product of an audit that auditors may discover a fraud in the course of their audit work. However, it is not a requirement of auditing standards and auditors are not under a duty to uncover fraud in this way. Fraud is concealed by the perpetrators and therefore audit tests which are likely to discover error would not necessarily uncover fraud, and uncovering fraud would not be within the scope of normal audit tests.

If the auditors uncover a fraud, or have reason to believe a fraud might exist as a result of their audit, there are several applicable requirements in ISA 240 *The auditor's responsibility to consider fraud in an audit of financial statements*:

- Auditors should **communicate** the **discovered** or **suspected fraud to management** as soon as is practicable

- If a discovered fraud involves management, employees with a significant role in internal control or the fraud has a material impact on the financial statements, the auditors must communicate these matters to **those charged with governance** without delay

- If the auditors have a **statutory duty** to **report** a fraud or suspected fraud to external regulators, they should do so, **having taken legal advice**

- If a fraud has a material impact on the financial statements, the auditors may have to **qualify their audit opinion**

Detection and reporting of error

The purpose of the audit is to state whether the financial statements give a true and fair view. In order to do this, the auditor has an expectation of discovering material errors and also assessing whether immaterial errors discovered in the course of the audit are material in aggregate. Errors are by their nature more visible than fraud, because it is unlikely that they have been concealed by the perpetrator (or they become fraud).

The auditors should keep a **record of errors discovered** in the course of the audit. They should **communicate** them to management, and should seek to have material (and material in aggregate) errors in financial statements corrected by management, or they will have to give a qualified audit opinion.

Under the terms of ISA 260 *Communication of audit matters with those charged with governance*, auditors are required to communicate to **those charged with governance**, the uncorrected misstatements aggregated by the auditor during the audit that were determined by management to be immaterial, both individually and in the aggregate, to the financial statements taken as a whole.

(c) **Audit procedures**

(i) **Evaluation of controls**

Auditors would carry out an evaluation of the system of controls by obtaining evidence about how it operates and **obtaining confirmation** by **walkthrough tests** (tracing a couple of items through the system) that the system was working as understood.

This evaluation should indicate any **faults** in the **design** of the system, and perhaps the auditors might be unwilling to identify these given their role in the design of the system.

However the faults indicated do not appear to be faults in the system design, but in other elements, which a limited review of the system may have problems identifying. The system review would show that **authorisation** by senior management does **take place**, and only a more detailed review might indicate it is not taken seriously. In addition there is **segregation of duties** within the system. Only if the auditors picked one of the weeks that the storekeeper is on holiday would they identify that segregation is not functioning fully throughout the year.

(ii) **Tests of controls**

The auditors should test that **new suppliers** were **approved** by the **purchasing manager** and are **authorised** by the **director.** The effectiveness of this test is likely to be limited for the following reasons.

(1) Only a **sample** of **suppliers** would be **selected** (this also of course applies to other tests of control that the auditor might wish to carry out such as testing purchases).

(2) It would be **difficult** for the auditor to gauge whether **authorisation** was being **taken seriously.** If defined procedures have been followed, the auditors might at best only be able to speculate that the managing director had not taken authorisation seriously, based on their knowledge of the managing director's personality.

However the auditors should be able to check that authorisation was not given without **evidence** of the **supplier's existence** (headed notepaper, address in phone book). The auditors should also confirm that laid down policies for choosing suppliers have been followed such as obtaining **references.** A clever fraudster might however be able to provide all this evidence; perhaps the only way that evidence of fictitious suppliers can then be obtained is by checks with independent third parties such as **credit agencies.**

(iii) **Analytical procedures**

Analytical procedures might have identified **unusual changes** in the profit margin and hence led to further investigation. However analytical procedures might not have been precise enough to identify questionable figures for the following reasons:

(1) Gross profit percentages may **not** have followed a **predictable** pattern in previous years.

(2) The **analytical information** required may **not** have been **available** in **sufficient detail.**

(3) Frauds such as this one tend to be spotted by reviewing changes in figures over a number of years. **Two years** is probably **insufficient time** to **identify** what appears to be an **immaterial fraud.**

(d) **Care as auditors**

The *Caparo* case indicates that the auditors have a **duty of care** to the company. However whether this duty of care means that the auditors will be liable is doubtful for the following reasons:

(i) The auditors' **terms of engagement** should have stated that the auditors carry out procedures so as to have a reasonable expectation of detecting fraud that materially impacts upon the accounts. It is questionable whether this fraud would have had a material impact.

(ii) Although the auditors did not comment on weaknesses in their management letter, they may nonetheless be able to prove that they **conducted** an **audit** that was in accordance with **auditing standards.**

(iii) The letter of engagement should also state that the directors are responsible for **safeguarding** the **assets** of the company, and for the **prevention** and **detection** of the **fraud**. The directors do not seem to have taken their duties seriously enough if approval of suppliers was just a formality.

Care as consultants

The auditors' liabilities here are uncertain. The case of *Fawkes-Underwood v Hamiltons and Hereward Philips 1997* although with different facts, indicates the possibility of liability. The court decided that the firm had held itself able to advise, but had not in fact given appropriate advice. The firm's position was undermined by the lack of a letter of engagement setting out the nature of the accountants' responsibilities. In practice then cases like this may turn on whether there is a **letter of engagement**, and whether the courts view **exclusion clauses** in the letter as **reasonable**.

In any event the company would have to prove **negligence**. The courts would clearly take into account how the company was operating the system; are its shortcomings more due to lack of care in operating the procedures rather than faults in the design.

12 TS Circuits

Text references. Chapters 3 and 4

Top tips. You should find part (a) to this question straightforward. It can be answered without reference to the information in the body of the question at all. You may find the 'user' approach we have used helpful, it certainly ties the answer into parts (b) and (c). Part (b) is in two small bits, and so should not be too daunting. Note however, that it refers to auditor liability, not director. In part (c) you will have to consider the impact of ISA 250 *Consideration of laws and regulations in an audit of financial statements*.

(a) **Small company audits**

There has always been an argument raging as to whether small companies should be subject to an audit. The EU has a maximum threshold under which an audit is not required of £5.6 million.

One of the major points against auditing the accounts of the small company is that the directors and the shareholders of the company are often (but not always) one and the same thing. If the purpose of an audit is to report to the members on the stewardship of the directors, then in such a case, it would appear that an audit is unnecessary.

However, financial statements are used by many people other than shareholders, and this fact is true in the case of small as well as large companies. The arguments for and against the small company audit are often approached from the point of view of these users, and I shall follow the same approach.

From the viewpoint of each type of user, the arguments for and against abolition are as follows.

(i) *Shareholders*

Against change — Shareholders not involved in management need the reassurance given by audited accounts. Furthermore, the existence of the audit deters the directors from treating the company's assets as their own to the detriment of minority shareholders.

Audited financial statements are invaluable in arriving at a fair valuation of the shares in an unquoted company either for taxation or other purposes.

For change — Where all the shareholders are also executive directors or closely related to them, the benefit gained from an audit may not be worth its cost.

(ii)   *Banks and other institutional lenders*

Against change   Banks rely on accounts for the purposes of making loans and reviewing the value of security.

For change   There is doubt whether banks rely on the audited accounts of companies to a greater extent than those of unincorporated associations of a similar size which have not been audited.

A review of the way in which the bank accounts of the company have been conducted and of forecasts and management accounts are at least as important to the banks as the appraisal of the audited accounts.

There is no reason why a bank should not make an audit a precondition of granting a loan.

(iii)   *Trade lenders*

Against change   Lenders and potential lenders should have the opportunity to assess the strength of their customers by examining audited financial statements either themselves or through a credit company.

For change   In practice, only limited reliance is placed on the accounts publicly available as they are usually filed so late as to be of little significance in granting short term credit.

(iv)   *Tax authorities*

Against change   Tax authorities rely on accounts for computing corporation tax and checking sales tax returns.

For change   There is little evidence to suggest that the tax authorities rely on audited accounts to a significantly greater extent than those, which, whilst being unaudited, have been prepared by an independent accountant.

(v)   *Employees*

Against change   Employees are entitled to be able to assess audited accounts when entering wage negotiations and considering the future viability of their employer.

For change   There is little evidence to suggest that, in the case of small companies, such assessments are made.

(vi)   *Management*

Against change   The audit provides management with a useful independent check on the accuracy of the accounting systems and the auditor is frequently able to recommend improvements in those systems.

For change   If the law were changed, the management of a company could, if they so desired, still elect to have an independent audit. It is likely, however, that a systems review accompanied by a management consultancy report would represent a greater benefit for a similar cost.

(b)   **Irregularities**

Effect on financial statements

Sales tax   When a sale is made, the company is liable to pay sales tax. This would become a payable until it is paid. When a credit note is raised in relation to the sale, the tax is no longer payable and is either removed from the payables balance or becomes a tax receivable to be repaid. However, as the sales were genuine, the debt is due.

Bank overdraft   As the income from the sales is being misappropriated into a private account the bank overdraft is higher than it should be, had genuine receipts been processed through it.

Auditor liability

The auditors have a duty of care to the body of the shareholders and may be found liable to them if they have been negligent. They do not owe a duty of care to third parties and cannot be liable to them.

However, as discussed below, the auditors have a duty to consider whether they should report irregularities to the authorities. If they do have such a duty and they fail to, they may be committing a statutory criminal offence. Auditors could be strongly criticised for not taking action when they were aware of fraudulent activity were it to be investigated.

(c) **Action in relation to the irregularities**

The audit partner must be mindful of his reporting requirements under ISA 250 *Consideration of laws and regulations in an audit of financial statements.* There are distinct reporting requirements if the auditor feels that the law has been broken. Tampering with cheques may also constitute fraud.

Reporting to management/persons to whom the audit report is addressed

In this case, the management and shareholders are the same people. The engagement partner should without delay discuss the irregularities with Mr and Mrs Conroy. He should explain to them that they have broken the law and invite them to correct the errors, and make full and frank disclosure to the tax authorities. This would usually result in them being more lenient in terms of penalties.

Appointment

Audit guidance on quality control requires that the auditor reassesses the ethical matters surrounding his appointment when issues such as these come to light. In this instance the integrity of the directors has been called into question and the auditor should consider resigning. If the directors refuse to make disclosure to the tax authorities, he should certainly resign.

Reporting to third parties

The auditor is restrained by his duty of confidence from disclosing errors that have arisen like this one, unless there is a statutory duty to disclose. In this instance, Mr Conroy has been perpetrating a money laundering offence (as he is in possession of the proceeds of a crime). The auditors must report this immediately to the relevant authority or they will be committing an offence themselves.

This will impact on any further disclosures they made, as they would run the risk of 'tipping off' Mr Conroy that a money laundering investigation was being carried out.

However professional guidance states that if the issue is one of public interest the auditor would not be bound by the duty of confidentiality. The auditor would seek legal advice before informing the appropriate authority.

When a situation such as this arises, an auditor should (as discussed above) try to persuade the clients to make disclosure themselves.

If the clients refuse to make the disclosure, the auditor should resign. In this instance they are permitted to appraise the tax authority of the fact that they have resigned, although not the reason why they have resigned. The tax authority are then entitled to draw their own conclusions, and investigate if they wish.

13 Benson

(a) **Requirements relating to accepting audit appointment**

Ethical requirements

The auditor is required to ensure that there is **no ethical barrier** to his accepting appointment.

Ensure **professionally qualified** to act	Consider whether disqualified on legal or ethical grounds. In terms of ethics, the following issues are relevant: • Does anyone in the audit firm own shares in Benson? • Is the nature of the relationship between the auditor and the client more personal than business? • Would the audit fee constitute too high a percentage of gross practice income? • Is there a conflict of interest with existing clients? All these issues would affect the independence of the audit firm.
Ensure **existing resources adequate**	• Consider • Available time, • Staff • Technical expertise
Obtain references	Make independent enquiries if the directors are not personally known to the audit firm.
Communicate with outgoing auditors	Enquire whether there are reasons or circumstances behind the change which the new auditors ought to know. This is also a courtesy to the outgoing auditors.

Legal requirements

The auditor must also ensure that the outgoing auditor's removal or resignation was conducted in the correct manner, once they have accepted appointment.

(b) **ABC's dealings with Benson**

ABC has had the following dealings with Benson and its directors.

• Advice given during the management buy-out

• Taxation advice (company and directors)

• Management consultancy

• Special projects, comprising:

    – Fraud investigation

    – Expansion, budgets and investigations

This has resulted in significant fee income for ABC. It mentions one statistic, that in the year of the expansion investigation, the fee income was 20% of the full office income.

ABC has now been asked to provide audit services to the company in addition to the other services it provides. It has agreed to take on the audit of the company.

Standard of conduct

Up until the point where ABC was asked to become auditors of the firm for the second time, there were no ethical issues arising.

Accountants are entitled to provide any number of services to a client, unless one of the services is an assurance service to which rules on independence apply. The services discussed above do not constitute a threat to the independence of an assurance service. A firm of accountants may take on the combined roles of tax advice, management advice, and specialist investigations, with no ethical issues.

Independence

The most recent step in the relationship between ABC and Benson is that the directors of Benson have asked the firm to provide audit services to the company.

However, audit is an assurance service and the independence of that service may be affected by the provision of other services.

The Code of ethics and conduct requires that an **auditor is, and is seen to be, independent**. The auditor must be **objective** in his dealing with audit clients. The provision of **additional services** to audit clients may result in objectivity being impaired.

The ethical guidance also states that **fee income** derived from private company audit clients should not constitute more than 15% of the firm's income. This is to protect the independence of the audit firm, who might otherwise become financially dependent on the client, to the point where they are no longer objective. In addition, fees of 10% of office income create a presumption of dependence.

Application to ABC and Benson Ltd

The fact that ABC already undertakes so much work for Benson represents a significant barrier to it being able to maintain objectivity on the audit. When asked to take on the audit, the partners should have considered whether it was appropriate to take on the audit in addition to the other work.

The question does not establish whether this has been done or not. However, the firm has clearly taken some steps to preserve some independence for the audit service. The firm has appointed a different partner to be audit engagement partner in addition to the partner who has dealt with the client previously. This indicates that they have considered the issue and decided that there is no barrier to independence.

Another key factor to consider is the level of fees that the auditors gain from the client. This is because of the specific rule that it should not exceed 15% of recurring gross practice income.

The only references to fees in the question are that the fee income from the client are high, and that in one year, when a special assignment was taken on, it represented 20% of the fee income.

This does not necessarily mean that the fee income including the audit fee will be in excess of the 15% barrier, but it certainly suggests that it is possible. As a minimum, it suggests that it may no longer be appropriate to undertake the special assignments, and that a revision of fee income will be required.

It is impossible to conclude precisely whether ABC was acting unethically in accepting the audit work. However, there is a strong indication that the firm is not independent in relation to the audit due to the high level of other services, and the fees that they bring in. This is despite efforts which have been made to preserve independence, notably appointing a different audit engagement partner.

(c) **Quality control procedures and policies**

The audit engagement partner is a key feature in quality control processes in relation to individual audits. Guidance on quality control focuses on two aspects:

- General firm-wide policies to establish quality control at a firm level
- Specific quality control requirements for individual audit assignments

Considering individual audits, It is important for the **audit engagement partner** who has been appointed to both **consider and document** his considerations of the ethical issues raised in the answer to part (b), above. He must be assured that he is **independent with regard to the audit**.

Specifically with regard to the assignment, he must ensure that the **audit work is directed, supervised and reviewed in an appropriate manner**. He may delegate much of these tasks to an audit manager, who will be responsible for undertaking planning meetings with the audit team and liaising with them on-site, perhaps undertaking an on-site review of their work.

However, the audit engagement partner cannot delegate the responsibility for drawing the audit conclusion, and must ensure that he has reviewed the audit file to ensure that he draws the correct conclusion, and that sufficient work has been undertaken to support that conclusion.

The engagement partner must consider the engagement risk attaching to the assignment, and consider the need for a **'hot review'** prior to the issue of the audit opinion. If Benson does become publicly listed, such a hot review will be essential.

The audit engagement partner is responsible in the first instance for ensuring that any **disputes** within the audit team arising over issues relating to the Benson audit are resolved appropriately. The firm should have **clear guidelines** as to how such disputes should be resolved.

Lastly, the firm should have a practice of **monitoring audits undertaken for quality**. It is likely that the audit of Benson should be monitored by the firm team this year for several reasons:

- It is the first year of a new audit
- It is a substantial client

It is a client which had significant ethical issues to consider in relation to accepting the audit, and therefore the audit risk is higher on this audit than on others.

14 Alakazam

Text reference. Chapter 6

Top tips. This question on planning an audit and considering implications of acquisitions on planning is typical of the kind of question you should expect to have to tackle in Section A of this paper. The question is tough but fair, and if you were well-prepared and well practised at identifying audit risks in scenarios, you should have been able to achieve reasonable marks on it. To tackle questions like this, you have to devise a strategy along these lines:

- Make sure you understand the requirement and answer it
- Look for key words and themes in the scenario that indicate audit risk
- Ensure you explain **why** things are audit risks and **why** you would use a particular strategy
- Do not spend too long on the question to the detriment of others

Easy marks. You should be able to score good marks on part (b) (i). There are some key things you should be able to say without necessarily relating them to the scenario. Similarly, you should automatically know several things that should go into an answer to part (b) (ii). Others may come from the scenario itself. Use the answer to part (b) below in your revision.

Examiner's comments. The major reason for low marks in this question was that candidates failed to supply enough risks in their analysis – one or two risks were not sufficient!

Part (b) (i) required consideration of a business perspective, whether a target company should be acquired. Some candidates scored an easy five marks here. There was some lack of understanding that outsourcing of a component must be to a computer service organisation.

ANSWERS

Marking scheme

		Marks
(a)	Potentially high risk areas	max 8

Generally 1 mark each risk explained (briefly)

Areas of potential risk

- Chief executive
- Growth (rapid expansion/over-trading), cashflow
- Accounting and internal control systems
- Product dependence, valuation, faults
- Trade receivables
- Warranties/contingent liabilities
- Going concern
- Intangibles

Generally 1 mark each comment relating to audit strategy   max 8

Audit process

- Obtaining information/PAF
- Recording the system
- Materiality assessment
- Test of control
- Substantive procedures ('Analytical, enquiry, inspection, observation and computation')
  - Inventory
  - Warranty provision

            max 14

(b)   (i) Principal matters

     Generally 1 mark each matter relevant to acquisition decision   max 5

     Ideas

- Acquisition → meaning? (if 100% sub → group a/cs)
- Leon → initiator?
- Held equally → same offer required?
- Stefan → worth more?/how to keep him?
- Purchase price →cash?/where from?

  (ii) Impact on conduct of audit

     Generally 1 mark each point contributing to an explanation   max 6

     Aspects of conduct of audit

- Practice management
- Neodex's auditors
- Consolidated group a/cs – goodwill vs intangible
- Planning incl materiality & y/e (non-coterminous)
- Audit strategy/systems/evidence
- Review – going concern

            25

(a) **Audit risks and strategy**

Rapid growth

Alakazam has experienced rapid growth over the previous 18 months. This raises the following audit risks.

(i) **Internal control**

The company has expanded rapidly. It has doubled its customer base, achieved near national coverage, taken on significantly more staff and moved its distribution and servicing department to

BPP)))
LEARNING MEDIA

new premises. All these factors will have required controls and systems being adapted to facilitate this change and enable the company to function. If controls and systems have not grown with the company this could pose threats to going concern, as it might adversely affect operations. In terms of audit risk, **if internal control has been inadequate** in the year, there is a significant **risk of errors** in the **financial statements**.

The implications of this for the **audit strategy** is that we should not seek **to place** heavy **reliance** on **controls**, and instead undertake more **substantive testing**.

(ii) **Financing and cash flow**

The rapid expansion may also have led to a situation where the company is **overtrading**, that is, it cannot generate enough working capital to finance its operations. This will be exacerbated by the **additional costs** that Alakazam has entered into in the year: investment in staff and premises. The audit risk arising here again is that the auditors must ensure that the company can continue to finance its operations and that the **going concern assumption** is not in doubt.

Key man

Much of the growth Alakazam has achieved appears to be attributable to the **Chief Executive**, Leon Izzardo. It may be that the man makes the company. The auditors must also be aware of this when considering going concern, bearing in mind that if Mr Izzardo was to leave before the exclusive rights were reviewed, for example, again, the going concern assumption might not be appropriate.

They should take care to review this situation carefully, reviewing Mr Izzardo's service contract, for example. It might also be a useful service to the company to advise whether his package is competitive, and to ensure the company has adequate succession plans, should they be required.

Inventory

Several issues arise in relation to inventory.

(i) **Possible obsolescence**

There appears to be a **defect** in many of the WAP phones that Alakazam distributes. This may affect the **value of inventory in-hand**, particularly if the drop in sales experienced recently is indicative of the defect being publicised.

The auditors will have to assess the extent of the problem and its impact on valuation of inventory. It is possible that Alakazam will have recourse to the manufacturer in respect of the defective inventory. It is also possible that the auditor might have to obtain an expert opinion (for example, legal) on these matters.

(ii) **Location**

The auditors should determine whether inventory at retail outlets belongs to Alakazam or to the retailer and whether this varies per retail outlet. This could raise both accounting issues (if it is consignment inventory) and audit issues (it could involve **multi-location inventory counting**).

(iii) **Returns**

If there are problems with the quality of inventory, there may be a high level of **inventory returns**, and the auditor must ensure that they are not counted in both sales and inventory.

Receivables

It appears that Alakazam are likely to have a high number of receivables, but it is possible that they may all be reasonably low value as Alakazam has a number of customers nationally. This may make receivables a difficult area to gain assurance in. The auditors will have to undertake a **substantial circularisation**.

Warranty

There appears to have been an increase in sales warranty work. This is an audit risk as it could result in a **material warranty provision**, but the auditors must ensure that any such provision confirms to the requirements of **IAS 37**.

Audit strategy-balance sheet

As many of these issues affect the balance sheet, the substantive approach to this audit (discussed above) should be directed at the balance sheet. The auditor must therefore consider issues such as which inventory counts to attend, circularising receivables and assessing whether liabilities exist in relation to warranties.

Wages and salaries

A major audit risk in the income statement is the cost of wages and salaries, particularly if controls have not been strong in the year. There has been a high number of new staff and if controls are weak, there is scope for errors and even frauds to have been perpetrated.

However, staff salaries are likely to be on a strict scale so it may be that wages and salaries can be audited by analytical review.

Audit strategy-going concern

Various issues have already been raised in relation to going concern. As there are significant indicators that going concern is an audit risk, auditors should also carry out extensive going concern procedures including:

- Reviewing cash flow statement and budgets
- Reviewing bank facilities and intentions
- Reviewing the impact a continued drop in sales could have

(b) **Proposed acquisition**

(i) **Principal matters to consider**

The directors of Alakazam should give consideration to the following matters:

Financing the purchase

As noted above, it is possible that Alakazam has cashflow difficulties at the present time. In deciding whether to purchase Neodex, the directors must consider how the purchase will be financed, whether the shareholders will want cash as shares etc.

What Alakazam is buying

The directors also need to consider what exactly they are buying. Although Neodex is a company, in effect the business is a partnership and one of its key assets is expertise/personnel. It may be that Alakazam does not have to purchase the company to get the expertise or, which they must be wary of, they do not have automatic rights to the expertise if they buy the company.

Purchase price

It may be that Alakazam is more keen to buy than Mr Koyla and Mr Neratu are to sell. This could inflate the price and make a bad investment. However, it might be important for Alakazam to buy the company so that a competitor does not, in which case, a higher price might be acceptable.

Intellectual property

Alakazam should consider matters such as the rights to the intellectual property, for example, the patent for the DINS. Is this owned by the company or the directors? Is it possible that third parties (competitors) could have access to the technology even if Alakazam were to buy the company?

Supply of the circuit board

The circuit board is a major component of the DINS. Its manufacture is currently outsourced. Alakazam should ensure that they would be able to guarantee supply of the circuit board, either by reviewing the current contract, or potentially by insourcing the manufacture.

Other matters

- Potential employment of Neodex staff
- Potential redundancy of other staff member
- Timing of acquisition (this financial year or next)

(ii)   **Implications of acquisition on audit**

(1)   **Timing**. The auditors have to consider when the acquisition takes place. If it falls after 31 March 2008, it would impact on the audit only in terms of being a post balance sheet event.

(2)   **Nature of acquisition**. The nature of the acquisition will have a significant impact on the audit:

- **Trade and assets.** There will be additional assets, including possibly purchased goodwill, to audit at the year-end.

- **Share purchase.** If Alakazam purchases the shares of Neodex, the audit will become a group audit.

(A group audit is assumed for the rest of the answer.)

(3)   **Other auditors.** The audit firm should identify whether Alakazam will want them to audit the accounts of Neodex. It is possible that Neodex was previously small enough not to be audited. If not, the auditors would have to communicate with the previous auditors, and issue an engagement letter for Neodex. If Alakazam wanted to maintain the services of any previous auditors (unlikely), the auditors might have to liase with them to conduct a group audit.

(4)   **Group audit.** It is likely that Neodex would be immaterial to the results of the Alakazam group, in which case, consolidated group accounts would not be required. However, the auditors must ensure that this is the case.

15 Meadow

Text references. Chapters 6 and 10

Top tips. This is a demanding question looking at high level planning issues. Having said that if you go back to basics this will provide you with a sensible plan of attack and a sensible structure. For example when thinking about risks you can consider the elements of audit risk (inherent risk etc). When considering other planning matters remember that these normally include materiality, accounting treatments, evidence and other practical matters. Always make sure that you read the requirement carefully. In part (a) you are asked to **identify** and **explain** the risks. You also need to note that the question refers to this as being the **final** audit. Part (b) should be more straightforward although a good understanding of some accounting issues is required.

Easy marks. These are available for identifying risks, but you must explain the risks to score well.

Examiner's comments. Part (a) was poorly answered with some candidates regurgitating the risk model. Others failed to read the requirement carefully. For example, even though the question stated that the information provided should be used many still went on to speculate, particularly in respect of control issues.

Few candidates demonstrated a knowledge of the retail method of inventory valuation, however many did make reference to materiality as an 'other matter' which was pleasing. It should be noted that it is as important to recognise a matter as not material eg receivables as it is to recognise material issues.

Answers to part (b) were disappointing with few candidates demonstrating a sound knowledge of segmental reporting.

Marking scheme

	Marks

(a) Principal audit risks/matters

Generally ½ mark each risk/matter identified and up to 1½ for a description   17

Ideas – 'general'

- Inherent risks
  - Entity (eg multiple locations)
  - A/c balances (eg non-current assets, inventory, provisions)
  - going concern
- Materiality (assessed/quantified)
- Final audit strategy ('conclusion')
  - Audit (or business) risk model – justified
  - Analytical procedures (illustrated)
- Documentation (amended)
- Logistics (multiple locations, store visits)

Ideas – 'specific'

(1)   Financial extracts

- Reliability
- Non-current assets ↓ = depreciation?
- Impairment?
- Receivables (low risk)
  - (i)   Provision for discontinuance
    - Material
    - A discontinuance? (IAS 14)
    - Recognition of restructuring provision (IAS 37)
  - (ii) Inventory valuation
    - Permitted IAS 2
    - How applied

(2)   Segment information

- IFRS 8

(3)   International restructure

- South American sale (see also (i) above)
- IAS 8 & IAS 10

(b) Audit work

Generally 1 mark each point contributing to a description to a maximum 5 marks for
each of (i) and (ii)   8

Ideas

- Procedures
- Sources of evidence
  - Internal and external
  - Oral and written
  - Auditor-generated
- PBSEs

25

(a) **Audit risks and other matters**

Risks

- The business operates in the retail industry. Transactions tend to be **high volume, low value transactions** often carried out in **cash**. (Trade receivables are therefore likely to be immaterial and therefore low risk.)

- There is a risk that it will be difficult to establish **completeness of income**. In addition there is the potential of **theft**.

- The company operates under the Vazandt brand name. **Emphasis on a single brand** increases risk as any damage to the brand name in one area/business unit could affect the other areas/business units.

- The retail industry has suffered from a **reduction in consumer spending**. This may have the following impact:

  Inventory valuation will need to be considered particularly in respect of luxury items, for example home furnishings and expensive clothes. (Food is less likely to be affected.) Inventory will be overstated if cost exceeds net realisable value. This may be the case if there are material amounts of **slow-moving inventory**. Under the retail method the gross profit margin would need to take account of any price reductions.

  Management may feel under pressure to overstate revenues and profits (and understate expenses) in order to present the results in the most favourable light. Ultimately the viability of the company could be affected although going concern does not seem to be a critical issue at this stage.

- The company operates in Africa, South America and the Far East. Inherent risk may be increased by the **diverse nature of these geographical locations**.

- The business is entering a period of **reorganisation**. This increases the risk of asset impairment, particularly in respect of the African and South American businesses.

Materiality

Preliminary materiality will be in the region of $17.7 million. This is the mid-point based on the assessment of revenue, total assets and profit before tax (see below). If this figure represents a significant change to the initial assessment, testing levels may also need to be modified.

½%-1% revenue = $12.9m-25.85m
1%-2% total assets = $16.4m-32.8m
5%-10% PBT = $6.2m-12.4m

Accounting treatments

(i) *African operations*

> **Tutorial note.** There are essentially three issues here; the provision for the loss, the discontinuance of the African operations and the potential for a restructuring provision.

The provision for the loss at $83.8m is material to the accounts (67% of operating profit).

IAS 37 *Provisions, contingent liabilities and contingent assets* prohibits the recognition of provisions for future operating losses as there is no obligation to incur losses at the balance sheet date.

The announcement on 29 September does not seem to be sufficient to give rise to a constructive obligation (which is needed if a restructuring provision is going to be included) as:

- there is no formal plan being implemented as yet
- the company has not raised a valid expectation that it will carry out the plan

If a restructuring provision is appropriate it should only include costs which are necessarily entailed by the restructuring and not associated with the ongoing activities.

In order for the results of the African operations to be disclosed as discontinued operations the IFRS 5 definition must also be applied. In this case they do seem to constitute a separate line of business or geographical area of operations and do seem to be part of a single coordinated plan. However to be classified as 'assets held for sale' management must be committed to a plan to sell the assets. The decision has not yet been finalised as it is still subject to consultation. On this basis the condition may not be met.

(ii) *Sale of South American business*

This is merely mentioned in a draft note and there does not seem to be any attempt to present the information re the South American business as a discontinued operation. As things stand this appears to be the correct treatment.

Assets should be reviewed for impairment as a consequence of the decision to sell.

(iii) *Segmental information*

This needs to comply with IFRS 8. Meadow has provided information based on geographical segments.

South America is a reportable segment on the basis that it constitutes 10% of total revenue.

Africa is a reportable segment on the basis that it constitutes more than 10% of the operating losses.

The Far East does not meet either of the above tests in 2007 but it could be argued that it is significant in that it is the only international operation which is not being sold or closed.

(iv) *Inventory valuation*

The appropriateness of the retail method as a means of establishing cost should be considered. In this case as Meadow is a retail organisation this is not uncommon.

The way in which gross profit margins are established for deduction from selling price should be assessed (see earlier point on risk).

Additional write-downs may be required as a result of the termination of the African operations.

Audit evidence

Due to the number of locations (211 stores) the auditor will have taken a risk-based approach.

Substantive procedures will have placed heavy reliance on **analytical review** due to the following factors:

- Availability of disaggregated information (trend analysis by store, by business unit, by location)

- The nature of the retail business (uniform operations, multiple locations, constant relationship between gross profit and revenue)

- The nature of the transactions (high volume, low value) making analytical procedures the most efficient

The reliability of the results depends on the accuracy of the information. The reliability of the draft financial statements should therefore be taken into account.

Practical aspects

Robert Bracco is represented by affiliated offices. The work of these will need to be coordinated in particular in respect of the attendance at inventory counts.

(b) **Audit procedures**

(i) *Segmental information*

- Check that geographical segments have been determined on a basis which is consistent with the previous year.

- Agree the segment totals to the corresponding figure in the income statement.

- Check the arithmetical accuracy of the information.

- Check that each reportable segment meets the definition in accordance with IAS 14 and that the way in which management have identified the different segments appears reasonable.

- Determine the way in which management have allocated revenues and expenses to the various segments. Test check the accuracy of these.

- If common costs have been allocated determine whether the way in which this has been done with reference for example to management accounts.

(ii) *International restructuring*

- Review board minutes approving the decision to close the African operations and to dispose of the South American operations.

- If available, obtain the detailed plan regarding the closure of the African operation. In particular the date on which the plan will be implemented will be relevant.

- Obtain copies of any press announcements made.

- Perform a post balance sheet review up to the date of the audit report to determine any progress made, for example, actual closures of African stores.

16 ABC

Text references. Chapters 6 and 9

Top tips. This three part question is based on a scenario involving contract accounting. Whilst some accounting knowledge is required to address the key issues don't fall into the trap of telling the examiner everything you know about IAS 11. The examiner is interested in the auditing issues raised. Part (a) specifically looks at the issue of risk. Think about why contract accounting is inherently risky (dependent on estimation and judgement) but also consider the information in the scenario as to the particular risks that ABC might face. Part (b) deals with the extent to which reliance can be placed on the work of the quantity surveyor. Again avoid a 'regurgitation' of ISA 620. Make sure that your answer addresses the extent to which the quantity surveyor can be relied upon rather than whether to rely on him. (The need for an expert has already been determined and we are told that he is appropriately qualified and experienced.) Part (c) is a good example of the importance of reading the question carefully. You need to ensure that you consider 'total costs to completion' as defined in the question.

Easy marks. You should have been able to pick up straightforward marks setting out audit tests in part (c).

Examiner's comments. In part (a) some answers were still too theoretical. Many did not confine their answers to the required 'audit risks' and wrote about general planning matters. Many also included audit work in part (a) in spite of this being the requirement for part (c). Marks were not awarded for repetition. A few candidates recognised the value of the recently appointed surveyor in part (a) and identified the risks associated with underabsorbed overheads. It is disappointing however to see many candidates fail to recognise correct accounting treatments. A significant number of candidates tackled part (b) as a theoretical question about ISA 620 and did not relate their comments to the scenario. Candidates must check the requirement carefully. The question clearly stated that the quantity surveyor was appropriately qualified and experienced. Rendering any speculation about this was irrelevant. In part (c) many candidates disregarded the fact that the question defined 'total costs to completion' making no reference to physical evidence (eg materials on site, hired assets etc). Audit work relating to contract revenue and billings was not asked for and earned no marks.

Marking scheme

		Marks

(a) Principal audit risks
Generally $\frac{1}{2}$ mark for identification + 1 mark each point of explanation $\qquad$ 12
Ideas
Industry
- Impact on financial statements
- Inherently uncertain outcomes
- Fixed fee contracts
- B&DD implications for WIP

Going concern
- *Less* work
- Working capital requirements

Percentage of completion method
- Subjectivity impacts on revenue, profits/losses, etc
- Judgement in projecting costs to date to completion
- % – how determined?
- IAS 11

Costs to BS date
- Materials – exist?
- Direct costs – correctly allocated?
- Overheads – appropriate apportionment?
- Consequence for foreseeable loss provision
- Cut-off – eg on subcontract labour

Estimated costs to completion
- PY qualification – high inherent risk
- Need for an expert
- Cost v contract activity
- Management bias/level of judgement

(b) Nature and extent of reliance on quantity surveyor
Generally 1 mark each point contributing to an explanation $\qquad$ 5
Ideas (ISA 620)
Nature
- Reliance v audit opinions/responsibility
- As an internal control
- As a source of audit evidence (expert)

Extent
- Results of evaluating ICs
- materiality/risk of misstatement
- Complexity of information/level of judgement
- Sufficiency of complementary evidence/alternative sources
- Expert skills

(c) Audit work on total costs to completion
Generally 1 mark each point $\qquad$ <u>8</u>
Ideas
- Actual (to date) v estimated (to completion)
- Direct materials
- Direct labour
- Other direct
- Indirect costs

<u><u>25</u></u>

(a) **Audit risks**

Nature of the business

- The company is involved in the construction industry. In order to comply with IAS 11, revenue and profits on individual contracts will be recognised as the contract progresses. Key calculations used in contract accounting are based on estimation and judgement and are therefore susceptible to error or deliberate misstatement.

- Each individual contract is likely to represent a significant part of the total business of the company. This increases the chance that errors and misstatements will be material to the financial statements as a whole.

- The company is involved in contracts which will take a significant period of time to complete (eg offices and bridges). This increases risk because the longer the contract, the more difficult it will be to assess the overall outcome at the early stages. In particular loss-making contracts may not be identified. (Expected losses should be accounted for in full at the point they are recognised.)

- It also increases the risk of bad debts as the circumstances of the customer may change between the commencement and the completion date.

- Provisions and contingencies will be a high risk area. These may result from breaches of health and safety regulations or claims due to faulty work or penalties for failing to meet deadlines.

Going concern

- The reduction in the number of government contracts being undertaken could have a significant impact on the company's ability to continue.

- If assets are sold eg specialised pieces of plant and key staff are laid off, the business may find it difficult to react quickly if there is an upturn in business in the future.

- If the company has a significant number of fixed fee contracts there is an increased risk of losses if costs are not adequately controlled.

- There is a risk of cash flow problems if stage payments are not timed correctly to meet the costs of construction. This risk may be further increased as customers include local government departments which are often slow to pay. The recent cut backs in local government expenditure may increase the chance of slow payment.

Method of recognising revenue

- The percentage completion method used is inherently risky as the calculation involves the use of estimated figures. These include revenue, costs, profit and the percentage completion. In this case risk is increased by the fact that last year's audit report was qualified on the grounds that there was insufficient evidence to support estimated costs to completion (which form part of the total expected costs).

- Costs incurred to date may not be indicative of the extent to which the contract is complete. For example cost overruns could lead to revenue and profit being inappropriately recognised.

Costs to date

- A number of direct costs are attributed to specific contracts. There is a risk that costs incurred will be attributed to the wrong contract. This risk is increased where materials and plant are transferred from one site to another.

- The costs to date figure should not include materials purchased but not used. If the accounting system and internal control are weak there is a risk that inventory could be included in this figure which would lead to an overestimation of the stage of completion.

- Costs may be misstated where security at individual sites is weak. This could lead to materials being stolen or damaged.

- Costs may be misstated if capital and revenue expenses are misclassified. In particular the nature of legal fees and the treatment of any leased assets would need to be considered.

- Site supervision costs are allocated on an apportionment basis. There is a risk that costs on individual contracts are misstated if the apportionment method used does not reflect the time actually spent.

- Cut-off will be a risk area, particularly in relation to subcontractors' invoices. Costs should include the cost of services performed to date irrespective of the point of invoicing.

- Indirect expenses will be misstated if the method of apportionment is not an accurate reflection of the extent to which the costs are related to production.

- As the 70% absorption rate is based on direct costs the reduction in the number of contracts undertaken in the year could lead to an under-absorption of indirect costs.

Estimated costs to complete

- This issue gave rise to an audit report qualification last year. If satisfactory evidence is unavailable this year the risk of a modified report remains high.

- The key risk is that estimated costs will be understated. This could lead to a contract appearing profitable when it is in fact loss making. This could have a significant impact on results as all losses should be recognised in full immediately.

- Estimated costs may be misstated due to the method by which this estimate is established. For example if it is based on costs incurred to date the accuracy of the figure will depend on the validity of the costs incurred and the assessment of the stage of completion. Risk increases where there is not a direct relationship between costs incurred and the stage of completion.

- If budgetary controls are weak and the overall control environment is poor there is an increased risk that estimated costs might be misstated.

- The auditors are likely to have to rely on information provided by the quantity surveyor as it is unlikely that the auditors will possess the expertise to determine all the information required for themselves. In particular they will need to rely on the surveyor's assessment of the percentage completion which will then have an impact on the costs to complete figure.

- Costs to complete will need to include penalties incurred for late completion of contracts. Management may not be aware that these penalties are likely to be incurred or may be reluctant to include them, particularly where negotiations are currently taking place between the company and the customer.

(b)   **Nature and extent of reliance on quantity surveyor**

Nature

In spite of the auditor's intended reliance on the work of an expert the auditor remains fully responsible for the audit opinion. This responsibility cannot be delegated and the auditor should obtain his own independent evidence to the extent that he is capable of doing so.

The precise nature of his reliance will depend upon the responsibilities given to the quantity surveyor by management. In this case the surveyor's work forms part of the control environment and more specifically he is responsible for the calculation of costs to completion by contract.

Extent

The extent of reliance will depend on:

- The auditor's assessment of the overall effectiveness of the surveyor. For example substantive procedures on year-end inventory may be reduced if the supervision of monthly physical counts has led to more accurate book inventory figures.

- The extent to which the auditor can obtain information independently. For example the auditor should have the skills and expertise to be able to find sufficient evidence to determine direct and indirect costs incurred to date. However it is less likely that he will be able to determine establish costs to completion without some reliance on the surveyor as this is an area of specialist expertise.

- The degree of risk

  Costs to complete have been identified in previous years as a key risk area. As such the auditor will need as much reliable evidence as possible so it may be inappropriate to rely solely on the surveyor. The auditor will need to balance this with the fact that this is a complex issue where the auditor will be lacking the appropriate skills. A specific issue which may affect risk which the auditor will consider here is the degree of independence that the surveyor is given. If there is evidence that the surveyor is under pressure to understate costs to complete less reliance would be placed on his work.

- The quality and quantity of work performed

  This is particularly the case in this audit as lack of evidence resulted in a qualified audit opinion. Greater reliance can be put on work which is well planned, executed and documented.

(c) **Audit work**

Direct costs incurred to date

- For a sample of material costs allocated to individual contracts vouch the expense to suppliers invoices or requisition/transfer notes

- For all material contracts visit the site and physically verify the appropriateness of costs allocated

- For a sample of labour costs allocated to individual contracts vouch the expense to payroll analysis/subcontractors' invoices

- Assess the method by which the client allocates labour to individual contracts. Reperform the client's calculations and agree a sample of hours back to source documents (eg time sheets)

- Agree significant professional fees to invoices

- For a sample of contracts agree:

  - Costs of hiring portable buildings to invoice

  - Costs of leasing plant and equipment to lease agreements ensuring that financed leased assets have not been expensed

  - Depreciation rates to accounting policy and reperform a sample of calculations

  - Transportation costs to client schedule showing how these are allocated between contracts

  - Insurance premiums to policies and ensure that the company has adequate insurance particularly in respect of accident claims

Attributable overheads

- Obtain a schedule of head office costs analysed between production and non-production related costs. Check that the analysis has been performed correctly and that non-production overheads have not been misclassified.

- Compare the value of the actual production-related head office costs with the figure based on 70% of direct costs. If the difference is material an adjustment will be required to contract costs.

Estimated costs to completion

- On a contract by contract basis select a sample of estimated materials cost. Compare with budgeted figures and with actual usage to date obtaining explanations from management for any significant discrepancies.

- On site visits estimate the stage of completion in order to determine what proportion of materials costs is still to be incurred.

- Obtain a breakdown of estimated labour costs showing the estimated number of hours for each major contract and the pay rates applied.

- Compare estimated hours to hours spent on work completed to date and budgeted figures. Any significant variations should be discussed with management.

- Compare pay rates with current payroll details. Check the basis of any changes to pay rates eg. budgeted pay rises.

- Perform analytical review. For example comparisons could be made on a contract by contract basis of actual monthly labour and subcontractors' fees with the quantity surveyors estimates of costs to be incurred in future. Any significant discrepancies should be followed up with management.

- For other direct costs establish the basis on which the estimated costs have been calculated. Assess whether the method is reasonable and takes account of the differing nature of costs incurred as the project progresses.

- Obtain a schedule showing how the surveyor has estimated future attributable overheads. Determine whether this has taken into account that there is a reduction in contract activity. (As attributable overheads are allocated on the basis of a percentage of contract costs a reduction in contract activity could lead to an under-absorption of overheads.)

Other procedures

- Discuss the progress of all major contracts with management and the quantity surveyor. In particular for any contracts identified as loss making discuss the reasons behind the situation.

- Perform a review of events after the balance sheet date. For contracts completed after the year-end compare actual costs with estimated total costs to determine the accuracy of the quantity surveyor's estimates.

- Review board minutes and events after the balance sheet date for evidence of issues which might give rise to additional costs eg fines, legal proceedings etc.

17 Question with analysis: Hydrasports

Text references. Chapters 6 and 15

Top tips. When identifying business and audit risks in part (a), have in your mind the lists of categories of risk you are looking for to get you going. For example, business risk is split into operational, financial and compliance. So if you are struggling, focus on operational risk. What does this leisure facility need to operate? Possible answer: staff. As staff are fickle, this is therefore an operational risk. Then go through financial (eg cash flow) and compliance (eg licence) risks in the same way. However, there is no need to give detail about these components in your answer. When trying to think of associated financial statements risk, try and consider how the matter might affect financial statements. Licences can be capitalised as assets. Humans can't. How does the staff problem affect the financial statements? Incidental expenses of having staff. In part (b), you may not have revised specific audit procedures for a hydrotherapy pool, so break it down a little. What is the pool actually, in terms of the financial statements? It is an asset, currently being constructed. Think of general tests for assets to get you started. Part (c) might seem terrifying on initial reading, because you haven't learnt any social and environmental performance measures for a leisure facility. What does it actually mean? It means how can management assess their impact on society and the environment? Example: By having members of the public join and use the facilities. So membership numbers is a performance measure. Are they rising or falling, for example? You can think of others.

Easy marks. In part (a), easy marks are obtained by identifying risks (shown in bold in the answer below). The harder marks are obtained by explaining those risks and identifying associated financial statement risks. In part (b) listing simple audit tests, such as verify costs to invoices, will gain you easy marks. In part (c), easy marks can be obtained by using your imagination and identifying performance measures. What criteria do you judge your gym/local leisure facilities by?

Examiner's comments. In part (a), candidates must not introduce their answers with the underlying theory (eg of components of business risks) (unless specifically asked for). In part (a)(i) when asked to 'identify', candidates must be brief. In part (a)(ii), only a minority of candidates understood that financial statement risk means the risk of misstatement in the financial statements. So not 'costs will increase', 'profit will go down', etc, but rather 'assets may not be written down for impairment', 'contingent liabilities may not be disclosed', 'provisions for liabilities may be unrecorded'. Many candidates showed a lack of understanding of linkage between commercial reality and financial statements. For example many thought, incorrectly, that a change in the basis of insurance cover necessitated a change in measurement basis in the financial statements.

In part (b), many candidates wasted time introducing audit work with 'matters to consider'. Better candidates identified cut-off tests and analytical procedures as relevant to deferred income. Too many candidates suggested inappropriate audit work – IAS 11 would be relevant to the accounts of the building contractor – not Hydrasports, for whom the pool was an asset in the course of construction. The audit of depreciation was also irrelevant. Better candidates recognised the need for an impairment review and that interest could be capitalised in this instance.

In part (c), candidates who understood what performance indicators are (eg 'Proportion of renewed memberships', 'Number of accident-free days') scored well.

Marks

(a)   (i) **Business risks**

Generally ½ mark for identification + 1 mark each point of explanation   8

Ideas

Operations risks

- Standard design
- Licences
- Alternative facilities/competition
- Customer satisfaction/poor service levels (eg staff lateness)
- Human resources

Empowerment risks

- Centralised control

Information for decision-making risks

- Business reporting risks

Financial risks

- Advance payments
- Loss of revenue
- Cash flow

Compliance risks

- Rights to operate
- Safety management (lifeguards, crèche facilities)

(a)   (ii) **Financial statement risk**

Generally 1 mark each point   8

Ideas

Assets

- Impairment/overstatement (licences, tangibles and GCUs)
- Useful lives
- Existence assurance

Liabilities

- Understatement/non-disclosure (contingent and actual)

Income statement

- Revenue (overstatement/non-compliance IAS 18)
- Staff cost overstatement

Controls

- Control risk
- Fraud/illegal acts

Inherent risks

- 'Branch' accounting

Disclosure risk

- Going concern (IAS 1)
- Contingent liabilities/assets
- Capital commitments

(b)   **Principal audit work**

Generally 1 mark each area of **principal** audit work *maximum 3 marks* each (i) and (ii)   6

Ideas

Deferred income

- Accounting estimate
- Cutoff/accrual basis/matching
- 'Test in total'

Hydrotherapy pool
- Initial measurement/cost
- Reliance on an expert (ISA 620)
- Finance costs (IAS 23)
- Impairment (IAS 36) vs depreciation (IAS 16)

(c) **Performance indicators**

Generally ½ mark for each measure suggested   <u>8</u>

½ – 1 mark each source of evidence

Ideas

Performance measures
- Types of performance measure (eg efficiency, capacity)
- Numbers/proportions/%s
  - Facilities (available vs closed)
  - Members (lapsed, renewed, introduced)
  - Accidents (personal, chemical)

Audit evidence
- Oral vs written
- Internal vs external
- Auditor generated
- Procedures ('AEIOU')

<u>30</u>

(a) **Risks**

(i) *Business risks*

(1) **Licences.** The renewable licences represent a compliance risk as, if they are not renewed, Hydrasports would be unable to continue legally in operation.

(2) **Customer dissatisfaction.** Customer dissatisfaction, over both timely opening in the morning and matters such as childcare, is another operational risk, because if Hydrasports does not get it right it risks losing customers to competitors.

(3) **Childcare.** The problems with childcare are also a compliance risk as there are strict legal requirements associated with the professional care of children which the company runs the risk of breaching.

(4) **Staff turnover and training costs.** The high staff turnover is an operational risk because the company cannot operate all its services without staff. This is exacerbated by high training costs and the need for training at all, as staff cannot simply be replaced quickly, new staff have to be appropriately trained.

(5) **Cash flow problems.** The cash flow problems are a finance risk as the company may not have sufficient cash available to respond to its business needs, which could ultimately lead to failure.

(6) **Hydrotherapy pool.** This is an operational risk as the pool cannot operate until it is finished. It being finished is threatened by cash flow problems.

(7) **Insurance.** If the rise in insurance premiums reflects the number of claims being made, this represents an operational risk as ultimately large numbers of claims may result in business closure, either because claiming customers have stopped using the facilities, or because the company will become uninsurable, in which case it cannot operate.

(8) **Management structure.** The centralised control of management policy leads to operational risk as local managers cannot respond in a timely way to local needs. Monthly accounting returns are also an operational risk as they restrict the managers' ability to do the rest of their job and ensure the local centre operates efficiently.

(9) **Payments in advance.** These add to financial risk as there is a risk that cash will not be available for the company to finance services already paid for by customers.

(10) **Refund policy.** Although fees are non-refundable, if some services are not available (such as the sauna) then the company might be legally required to make refunds or partial refunds. This is a finance risk, as the cash may not be available to meet this requirement.

(ii) *Associated financial statement risks*

(1) Financial statement risks associated with the licences are that these might be wrongly treated as expenses in financial statements, when in fact they should be capitalised as an intangible asset. As an intangible asset, there are also the risks that amortisation will not be carried out correctly and that impairment reviews will not be carried out or will be carried out wrongly and the asset will be carried at an inappropriately high value.

(2) The associated financial statement risk relating to customer dissatisfaction is going concern - that the business might be failing and the financial statements therefore prepared on the wrong basis (disclosure risk).

(3) The associated risk is that Hydrasport's failure to provide proper childcare might open the company up to legal claims resulting in large fines or compensations and possibly also threaten going concern.

(4) Training costs must be correctly accounted for as expenses.

(5) Cash flow problems ultimately can result in going concern problems, which again creates disclosure risk if the financial statements are not prepared on the correct basis.

(6) The value of the asset being constructed may be impaired and there is a risk that it is being carried at an overvalue.

(7) If the company is experiencing a large number of claims, this affects contingent liabilities and there is a risk that disclosures in the financial statements are inappropriate.

(8) There is increased control risk that systems are weak due to the possibility of local staff circumventing company policy. There is also a risk that monthly reporting is inaccurate if it is rushed.

(9) Advanced payments should be accounted for correctly, there is a possibility that revenue and liabilities for advanced payments have been misstated.

(10) Provisions may be understated if such refunds are likely.

(b) **Audit work**

(i) *Deferred income*

(1) Agree Hydrasports' analysis of fees (joining, peak and off-peak) to joining documents on a sample basis.

(2) Ensure joining fees have been excluded from deferred income (these should be recognised when received).

(3) Reconciling membership income to fees paid (if it is possible for membership to be renewed without payment being made immediately, this income should not be deferred unless a receivable is also recognised).

(4) Recalculating the deferred income from fees paid in the three months prior to the year-end.

(5)   Analytical review of the year-end balance with the prior year and investigation of any significant differences.

(ii)   *Hydrotherapy pool*

(1)   Verify cost by reviewing the contract with the builder, billings to date and stage payments.

(2)   (Assuming Hydrasports has taken advice from an expert quantity surveyor) review the expert's report concerning stage of completion at the balance sheet date and estimated costs of completion.

(3)   Inspect the asset at the year-end to assess the stage of completion and confirm reasonableness of expert's report.

(4)   Agree finance costs to the terms of the finance contract and the payments made. Recalculate capitalised amounts to ensure accuracy.

(5)   Ensure the basis of capitalisation agrees with IAS 16.

(6)   Assess whether value in use on completion is lower than current value due to delay and appraise management's consideration of impairment.

(c)   **Social and environmental responsibility**

(i)   *Performance indicators*

(1)   Members

–   Number of people on waiting lists to join centres
–   Number of recommendations by existing members
–   Proportion of renewed memberships
–   % of capacity of membership fulfilled
–   Proportion of members requesting refunds/quarter
–   Proportion of membership lapsing

(2)   Staff

–   Average number of staff employed per month
–   Numbers of starters/leavers per month
–   Average duration of employment
–   Number of courses per staff member each year
–   Average wages (per hour, per week, per year)

(3)   Customer and local needs met

–   Number of late openings
–   Number of days facilities closed per month/year
–   Local community involvement (for schools and clubs)
–   Special events for babies, disabled, pensioners
–   Participation in wider community (sponsoring events etc)

(4)   Safety

–   Number of accident-free days
–   Incident reports

(5)   Environment

–   Number of incidents of non-compliance with legislation
–   Energy efficiency
–   Environmental incentives such as recycling, secure bike parking, money off bus fares

(ii) *Evidence related to above*

The following might be sources of information which could provide evidence about the sort of measures outlined above:

–   Membership lists
–   Payroll and staff timesheets
–   Staff training records
–   Facility timetables (for example, pool and gym)
–   Safety drill reports and procedures manuals
–   Accident report register
–   Energy saving equipment
–   Correspondence with local authority
–   Any local authority reports on the centre
–   Details of insurance claims

18 Yates

Text references. Chapters 6 and 8

Top tips. This is a time-pressured question worth 30 marks in total. The best way to approach the question is to take each part in turn and deal with it, making sure you don't run out of time on each part. In part (a), it is not sufficient just to produce some calculations – you must justify your assessment of materiality as required by the question. In part (b) take each line of the accounts in turn and deal with it rather than using a scattergun approach – this is far more logical and ensures your answer contains a structured approach. In part (d), remember to describe the audit work rather than just produce a list.

Easy marks. This question is broken down into several parts which are each relatively straightforward. For example, in part (a) you should be very comfortable with calculating planning materiality as it's a topic you would have covered in detail in your earlier studies. In part (b) you should be able to pick out the key risks from the information given in the question scenario. In part (d), which is split into two parts for three marks each, you should be able to gain the majority of marks for describing the audit work on trade receivables and vehicles.

Examiner's comments. Many answers regurgitated textbook knowledge on materiality, analytical procedures and risk, which was not required and did not score any marks.

In part (a) candidates were required to calculate planning materiality and justify their assessment of materiality. Marks were not awarded for defining materiality or explaining the concept of items that are material by nature. Easy marks were available for justifying the calculations and assessment.

In part (b), on financial statement risks, marks were not awarded for considering business risk and discussing control weaknesses that could result in fraudulent transactions. Another weakness in many answers was the inability to apply knowledge to the particular scenario in the question. Many scripts also made incorrect or irrelevant statements about financial reporting requirements.

In part (c) the requirement was to discuss the extent to which analytical procedures could be relied upon as audit evidence, however many candidates discussed the use of them in audit planning and review as well, which was not required and did not score marks.

In part (d) the requirement was to describe the audit work to be performed in respect of the carrying amount but many candidates wrote any audit work (eg concerning ownership) rather than audit work that was most relevant to carrying amount.

Marks

Generally 1 mark each area of principal audit work. Max 3 marks each (i) and (ii)

(a) Preliminary materiality

For 'rule of thumb' calculations	Max 2
For appropriate degree of precision (not more than $0.1)	1
For suitable conclusion	1
Generally 1 mark each comment in justification of assessment	Max 4

Max 6

Ideas
- Suitable range(s)
- Unsuitable PBT-based assessment
- Risk of over/under auditing income statement/balance sheet
- Draft financial statements
- New audit

(b) Financial statement risks

Generally ½ mark for identification + 1 mark each point explanation
Ideas

Max 12

- Revenue/receivables – potential overstatement (rebates)
- Materials expense – overstated vs
- Depreciation/amortisation/other – understated?
- Intangibles – potential overstatement (internally-generated criteria not met/impaired)
- Tangible assets
  - potential overstatement (unrecorded disposals/impairment)
  - potential understatement (finance leases omitted)
- Receivables – overstated? (impairment allowance)
- Restructuring provision – potential overstatement (underutilised?)
- Finance lease liabilities – potential understatement/disclosure risk (IAS 17)
- Trade payables – understatement/unrecorded liabilities
- Employee liabilities – potential understatement

(c) Extent of reliance on analytical procedures (as audit evidence)

Generally 1 mark each point explanation
Ideas

Max 6

- Caveat – first audit
- Material items requiring 100% testing
- Immaterial items (eg inventory)
- Suitability of SAPs – large volume transactions (revenue, materials expense, staff costs)
- Expectation of relationships
- 'Proof in total' – staff costs, depreciation, finance
- Relevance of available information
- Efficiency and effectiveness of alternative procedures

(d) Principal audit work

Generally 1 mark each area of principal audit work max 3 marks each (i) and (ii)
Ideals

Max 6

(i) Trade receivables
- Agreements – volume rebate terms
- Direct confirmation
- After-date cash
- After-date credit notes
- Credit risk analysis/impairment assessment

(ii) Vehicles
- Opening balances (non-current asset register)
- Physical inspection (existence/condition/milometer)
- Additions to purchase invoices
- New lease contracts
- Rapir and maintenance accounts

30

(a) **Calculation of preliminary materiality**

Preliminary materiality can be calculated using the draft figures for the current year and the actual figures for the prior year and taking an average. Normally materiality will be calculated on 0.5-1% of revenue, 5-10% of profit before tax, and 1-2% of total assets:

	2007 (draft)	2006 (actual)
Revenue (0.5-1%)		
	$	$
– 0.5%	808,000	722,000
– 1%	1,615,000	1,444,000
Profit before tax (5-10%)		
– 5%	95,000	N/A
– 10%	190,000	N/A
Total assets (1-2%)		
– 1%	1,038,000	1,060,000
– 2%	2,076,000	2,120,000

Based on the above figures, a suitable range for preliminary materiality would be in the range of $1.0-1.5m.

The planning materiality should not be based on the profit before tax figure as this is small and will result in larger sample sizes and hence over-auditing. A materiality of greater than $1.6m would be material to the income statement (1% of revenue) whereas less than $800k would not be material (0.5% of revenue) so it should be based between these two values. The range for the balance sheet lies within $1-2m. The lower figure represents 0.6% of revenue and the higher figure represents 1.2% of revenue. In the case of this audit, Yates is a new client so materiality should be set lower than if it had been a recurring audit. In addition the financial statements for the year are still in draft form and there could be further changes to the figures. It would therefore be more prudent to set planning materiality at the lower end of the range calculated.

(b) **Financial statement risks**

New audit client

This is a new audit client of the firm and therefore the auditors will lack knowledge and experience of this company which may result in misstatements not being detected in the financial statements.

Revenue

Revenue has increased in the current year by 12% compared to the previous year without the same percentage increase in costs. There may be a risk that revenue has been recognised incorrectly by not taking into account all rebates due to customers.

Materials expense

The materials expense has increased by 18% which is significantly more than the increase in revenue in the year. There may be a risk that expenditure has been misclassified as materials rather than other expenses (which have fallen by 16%) or that items that should have been capitalised have incorrectly been included here.

Depreciation and amortisation

These costs have fallen by 11% compared to the prior year. Although this may be a valid decrease, there is a risk that the charge for the year is misstated if assets have been depreciated at the incorrect rates for example or impairment losses have not been recognised in the year.

Other expenses

Other expenses have fallen by 16%. There is a risk that items have incorrectly been classified as materials expense which has increased by 18% compared to the prior year.

Intangible assets

Internally generated intangible assets should only be capitalised if they meet the recognition criteria set out in IAS 38 *Intangible assets*. The balance has increased by 16% compared to the prior year. There may be a risk that intangible assets are overstated if they are being capitalised or amortised incorrectly or if they are impaired but this has not been recognised.

Tangible non-current assets

There is a risk that where vehicles have been leased, the lease has been incorrectly accounted for as an operating lease rather than as a finance lease. Other misstatements may occur if assets have been incorrectly depreciated or disposals have not been accounted for.

Trade receivables

Trade receivables have increased by 2% whereas total sales have increased by 12%. There is a risk that receivables are understated because of incorrect cut-off being applied to cash receipts. There is a risk that receivables are overstated if allowances for impairment have not been applied to year-end balances.

Provision for restructuring

The provision has fallen by 10% compared to the prior year. If the provision is no longer required it should be written back to the income statement.

Trade payables

This balance has increased by 5% compared to the previous year whereas material expense and other expenses have increased in total by 10%. There is a risk that the balance may be understated as a result of accruals not being included at the year-end.

Employee liabilities

Employee liabilities have increased by 8% but staff costs for the year have increased by 14%. There is a risk that the year-end liabilities may be understated if amounts outstanding at year-end have not been calculated correctly.

(c) **Analytical procedures**

The extent to which analytical procedures can be used as audit evidence depends on a number of factors. These include the plausibility and predictability of the relationships identified for comparison and evaluation. In the case of Yates, where materials expense has risen because of an increase in the level of business we would expect to see a similar increase in revenue.

Where analytical procedures are intended to be used for audit evidence, they are more suited to large volume transactions such as sales and staff costs. However, in this case, the auditor would also need to consider testing the controls because if these are effective, more reliance can be placed on the information and therefore on the results of analytical procedures.

Materiality also needs to be considered when using analytical procedures as audit evidence. Analytical procedures would be used for those items that are not material to the financial statements such as inventory in this case, which represents only 0.6% of total assets and which has increased by 20% compared to the prior year. It would not be suitable to use analytical procedures on items that are material and require 100% testing, such as additions to and disposals of buildings.

Analytical procedures can be used to perform proofs in total for specific figures in the accounts, such as staff costs and depreciation. In this case, the auditor needs to consider the source and reliability of information available. It may not be appropriate to perform a proof in total on the depreciation charge for the year given that for each category of non-current asset there is a range of useful lives.

Analytical procedures can be used to provide additional evidence for specific financial statement assertions, together with other audit procedures. For example, a review of after-date cash receipts can be used together with analytical procedures undertaken on an aged profile of customer accounts.

(d) **Principal audit work**

(i) Trade receivables

- A sample of receivables will be selected to check for after-date receipts in the cash book and bank statement to verify recoverability of year-end amounts

- A sample of trade receivables will be selected for circularisation to confirm amounts outstanding at the year-end

- A review of after-date credit notes will be undertaken to confirm that adequate allowance has been made for discounts earned in the year

- A sample of customer agreements will be reviewed to check the terms of rebates allowed on sales

(ii) Vehicles

- A sample of assets will be selected from the non-current assets register to check that they physically exist and to examine their condition

- A sample of assets will be selected by physical inspection and traced back to the non-current assets register to verify completeness

- The depreciation charge for the year will be recalculated using the depreciation policy for vehicles to confirm its reasonableness in the financial statements

- The disposals will be tested by reviewing board minutes authorising disposal and confirming any proceeds to cash book and bank statement and recalculating any profit or loss on disposal

- Opening balances on cost and depreciation will be checked to the non-current assets register to ensure the comparative figures are correct

- Documentation relating to any leased vehicles will be examined to ensure that leases have been capitalised correctly if they are finance leases

- A sample of additions in the year will be traced back to supporting invoices to confirm ownership and cost

19 Harrier Motors

Text references. Chapters 6 and 8

Top tips. It is a good idea before taking this exam not only to review past exam-standard questions and answers, also to look at past marking schemes. This will give you a feel for how many points you need to make to get maximum marks for an answer. For example, part (a) of this question is for 12 marks. The marking scheme indicates that ½ a mark is available for identifying a risk and one mark is available for explaining that risk. That means you need to identify eight risks to give yourself access to the 12 marks available for this part of the question. Remember when trying to identify risks to look under the headings of different categories of risk, that is, inherent, control and detection.

Easy marks. There are some easy marks to obtain in part (b) of this question which focuses on matters to consider at the inventory count. **Some** points are straightforward that you should be able to have answered from your earlier auditing knowledge, but you do also need to apply higher skills.

Examiner's comments. Candidates should not introduce their answers with underlying theory, eg the audit risk model. When asked to 'identify' - candidates must be brief. Accounting aspects were not dealt with well. There was a lack of understanding of a legal 'right'. To suppose that it meant 'obligation' and therefore that failure to return unsold cars was 'illegal' was to completely miss the substance over form issue on consignment inventory. Mr Joop was heavily criticised but rarely for any audit risk he might present. Part (b) was not a question about the auditor's instructions. Many answers gave wholly inappropriate lower level detail. The majority ignored the perpetual inventory system and that a full physical count of parts would not be necessary or appropriate. Part (c) was answered poorly with the majority of scripts addressing cost/valuation as though it had been acquired during the current financial year. Candidates must be able to audit an estimate made by management without resorting to management representations and the inevitable expert. It was encouraging that some candidates recognised the need for an impairment review.

Marks

(a) **Audit risk**

Generally ½ mark for identification +
1 mark each point of explanation

Ideas

Inherent – financial statements level

- Business expansion/going concern
- Multi-location
- Cash

Inherent – financial statements level

- Consignment inventory/substance over form
- Contingent liabilities (IAS 37) – warranty/guarantee
- Inventory valuation (used/trade-in car, ex-demo models)
- Related party disclosures (IAS 24)
- WIP
- Intangible assets (IAS 38) – non amortisation

Control

- Internal audit
- Continuous inventory checking

12

(b) **Principle matters – year-end physical inventory counting**
Generally ½ mark each **principal** matter identified +   6
1 mark each point contributing to an explanation
Ideas
- Internal audit – supervisory role
- Multi-site operations ('cyclical compliance' not appropriate)
- High value items (new cars) existence – 100%
- Parts – continuous inventory checking – sample basis
- Cut off – not material for WIP
- Restrictions on movement
- Used cards – condition
- Consignment inventory – age, ex-demo model identification

(c) **Audit work**
Generally ½ – 1 mark each appropriate suggestion of audit work +   <u>7</u>
½ – 1 mark for relevance of brand name and/or Harrier
Ideas
- Prior year working papers
- Brand history
- Marketing/advertising expenditure
- Industry comparatives
- Budgeted future expenditure
- Impairment test (IAS 36)

<u>25</u>

(a) **Audit risks**

(i) *Consignment inventory*

Consignment inventory is inventory **held by one party** (the dealer) but **legally owned by another** (the manufacturer). In this case, Harrier pays for the entire consignment (together with a finance charge of 3%) after three months. Although Harrier has a legal right to do so, it never returns unsold cars at the end of the three month period.

The inventory is high risk because it is a complex accounting issue, and, if included within the financial statements, is going to have a material impact on them.

Items should be accounted for according to the **substance of the transaction**, rather than according to their **legal form**. Here, although legally Harrier does not own the inventory until three months after it has been delivered to it, it never returns inventory and the sales director is allowed to take any car for his own use out of each consignment, and it appears that the commercial reality is that the consignment is a purchase from the date of delivery. There is a risk that both inventories and liabilities are understated.

(ii) *Expansion/going concern*

The company has carried out **significant expansion** in the year, opening three new operations to make a total of eight. Such expansion increases the company's financial commitments and makes going concern an increased risk for the audit. The auditor must ensure that the company is not overcommitted and that there is no indication of going concern problems.

(iii) *Cash sales*

The company has a **high proportion of cash sales** which increases the inherent risk of the audit. Cash sales are inherently more risky than credit sales as there is more scope for the misappropriation of cash and the understatement of income.

(iv) *Warranties*

Many of Harrier's sales have warranties attached. This is another area which involves **complex accounting**. IAS 37 requires that a company set up **provision** where there is a present obligation as a result of a past event from which it is probable that a transfer of economic benefits will be required to settle the obligation and a reliable estimate of the amount of the obligation can be made.

IAS 37 gives warranties as an example of an instance when it is likely that a provision will be required. The auditors will need to ensure that any such provision has been appropriately calculated.

(v) *Inventory valuation*

In addition to the issue of whether to recognise the consignment inventory discussed above, there are a number of lines held by Harrier that increase the risk of inventory valuation. The auditors will have to ensure that **older inventory**, **part exchange models** and **ex-demonstration models** are correctly valued and have not become **obsolete**. In the case of the older inventory, it will be particularly important to scrutinise the net realisable value of the cars, as old but previously unowned cars lose face value fast.

(vi) *Related party transactions*

Mr Joop is a **related party**. He uses an item of inventory as a company car, and although he does not pay money for it, this constitutes a related party transaction under the provisions of IAS 24. The auditors will need to ensure that all the correct related party disclosures are made. They should also be aware that this might not be the only instance of a company benefit being a related party transaction and they should be open to the possibility that more might exist which have not been disclosed to the auditor. They should make enquiries about whether other arrangements such as this exist, or whether staff and directors are entitled to discounts and such like, and whether there have been any other transactions with related parties.

(vii) *Brand name*

Harrier's directors believe that the useful life of the brand name 'Uni-fit' is indefinite and should therefore not be amortised. The auditors need to ensure that this is **reasonable**. They should test the assumptions in the directors' analysis resulting in this conclusion. The auditors should ensure that the brand is **being invested in** to ensure that it does have an indefinite useful life and it has not been impaired. IAS 36 requires management to test the brand for **impairment** where there is an indication of impairment.

(viii) *Multi-locations*

The fact that the company operates in **several locations** is risky for the auditor. It increases the chances of errors being made, for example, if items of inventory pass between sites, there is opportunity for items to be double-counted, or accounting records might get lost in being transferred from one site to another. It also means there are more locations for the auditor to visit to gain audit information, for example, at inventory counts or in order to verify fixed assets.

(b) **Inventory count matters**

The following matters should be considered:

(i) *High value items*

The auditor should focus tests on high value items, which in this case will be the new cars.

(ii) *Spare parts*

As the spare parts are maintained in a perpetual counting system, it will be unnecessary for the company to count all of this inventory and only a **sample** should be counted. The auditor should test a small sample only.

(iii) *Multi-locations*

As the inventory is based in eight different locations, audit staff will have to **attend more than one location** to check the count. If counts have previously been carried out efficiently and the auditors believe the controls over the count are good, it is not necessary to attend all the counts. However, auditors should attend the counts at all the new sites and at least one other. If there have been control problems with counts in the past, then the auditor should attend all the counts.

(iv) *Part exchange inventory*

The auditors must **assess the condition** of the part exchange inventory and ensure that any items needing to be provided against are noted.

(v) *Work in progress*

As servicing and body repairs are usually carried out within one day, there will be **negligible WIP**.

(vi) *Cut-off*

There should be little problem with purchase cut-off as the company is unlikely to receive a consignment on the day of the count. The auditors should ask the counters whether any **sales** have taken place in the day and copy records relating to those sales and make note also of any part exchange deals made on the day. As servicing and repairs are invoiced immediately on completion, there is unlikely to be a problem with cut-off relating to that day as well, but the auditor should note down any relevant invoice numbers to be sure.

(vii) *New internal audit department*

The new internal audit department are likely to be involved in the count, perhaps in a supervisory role and this is likely to **reduce control risk** relating to the counts. The auditor should liase with the internal audit department to see what its role is likely to be and to coordinate count activities.

(c) **Audit of brand asset**

(i) *Valuation*

- Agree the cost of the brand to prior year audit file

(ii) *Amortisation*

- The auditors need to ensure that the estimated useful life of the asset determined by the directors is reasonable

- Review correspondence and minutes of meetings connected with the purchase of the brand to understand the company's long-term intentions with respect to the brand

- Review documents recording the directors' determination that the useful life is greater than 20 years (these may be memos or minutes of meetings) and ensure reasoning is still valid

- Consult a brand expert to obtain a third party opinion as to the longevity of the brand

- Review budgets and expenses such as advertising in the year to ensure that the company is investing in the brand to ensure its longevity

- Obtain written representations that the directors feel that their estimation of the useful life of the brand is valid

(iii) *Impairment*

According to IAS 36, the directors should test the intangible asset for impairment annually.

- Assess whether an impairment review has been undertaken
- Review the impairment test carried out by the directors

20 Shire

Text references. Chapters 6, 7, 8 and 15

Top tips. The identification and explanation of risks is likely to come up in this paper so you must be able to carry out this skill. The examiner is unlikely to give you surplus information in the question, so every piece of information you are given should be used to help you answer the question. This doesn't mean that you should waste time being anxious about information you don't understand – there are other risks for you to identify in that valuable time, but it does mean that you should read the question carefully, thinking through what each piece of information means. For example, the examiner has given you a small amount of financial information in the question, including the EPS calculation. Although profit has increased in 2006, EPS has fallen. This means one of two things. (1) EPS has been miscalculated – which is risky because it indicates a risk of error in the financial statements, or (2) shares have been issued in the year, which is risky because it is important that these have been disclosed correctly in the financial statements. Hence, from a very small piece of information in the question, and a little deduction, you have identified a risk. In part (b) it is crucial to read the requirement properly. The examiner has asked you to describe work in respect of the useful lives of the assets – tests of initial cost or fair value or depreciation will not be relevant and will not gain you marks. In part (c) you are given a number of the responsibilities that the company has, and are asked how to measure whether the company is meeting them. So use the information given in the question and your common sense. Read the model answer below to see how this is done.

Easy marks. The easier marks were available for identifying risks from the scenario. You then had to earn the harder marks by explaining what those risks actually were.

Examiner's comments. Many candidates did not spend enough time thinking about the risks specific to Shire in part (a). Including rote-learned material on the audit risk model was not required and gained no marks. Main weaknesses in this part of the question were giving business risks rather than audit risks, copying out parts of the question, inventing risks out of non-risk issues, focusing almost exclusively on going concern issues.

In part (b), the majority of answers did not answer the question requirement, ignoring 'useful lives' or 'principal audit work'.

Part (c) was answered very well by some candidates. However, most answers were inadequate and lacked relevance to the scenario.

Marking scheme

		Marks
(a)	Audit risk	Max 12

Generally ½ mark for identification of audit risk + 1 mark each point of explanation

Ideas

Inherent – financial statements level
- Listed
- Oil industry
- Multi-location
- Fall in EPS… 2nd half-year prospects

Inherent – assertion level
- Grant of licence – cost vs fair value … how estimated?
- Intangible assets (IAS 38) – amortisation
- Item replacement (IAS 16)
- Depreciation periods – rig platforms
- Decommissioning provision (IAS 16/IAS 37)
- Abandoned rig – cessation of depreciation + impairment test
- Contingent liabilities (IAS 37) – fines/penalties
- Jointly-controlled asset (IAS 31)
- Prior year modification – 'except for'

(b)   Audit work   Max 6
       Generally ½-1 mark each appropriate suggestion of audit work (ie relevant useful lives) +
       ½-1 mark for relevance to Shire's rig platforms
       Ideas
       - Review of management's annual assessment
       - Corroborative evidence – eg abandoned rig
       - Management's past experience/expertise – evidenced
       - In reply to industry comparatives
       - Actual vs budgeted maintenance costs
       - Actual vs budgeted output (oil extracted)
       - Results of impairment testing (CGU)

(c)   Performance indicators   Max 6
       Generally ½ mark each measure suggested + ½-1 mark each source of evidence
       Ideas
       Performance indicators
       - Level of investment in sports sponsorship, etc
       - Numbers/proportions/%s
         - Championship events/participating schools/students
         - Medals/trophies awarded
         - Patients treated/bed occupancy
         - Staff – starters/leavers/absenteeism/turnover
         - Breaches of health & safety/environmental regulations
         - Oil spills
         - Accidents/deaths (employees)
       Evidence
       - Actual vs budgeted investment
       - Physical evidence (eg medals/cups awarded)
       - Press coverage/reports
       - Reduction in fines paid
       - Legal – correspondence/fees
       - Insurance claims

                                                                                              24

(a)   **Audit risks**

       (i)   *Industry*. Shire operates in an **inherently risky industry**, which increases the overall audit risk
              associated with the assignment. Various items in the financial statements could be affected by this
              inherent risk.

              Oil prices are subject to substantial change due to world politics and events, so **revenue** is a risky
              balance. As discussed below, **specialist assets** are used in the business, which may be difficult to
              value. The industry is subject to public scrutiny due to its impact on the environment, as can be seen
              by the public outcry about Shire's abandoned rig in South Asia, which could ultimately lead to **going
              concern** issues.

       (ii)   *Geographical location*. The company operates from diverse geographical locations, which adds to the
              risk of the audit, both in terms of the **control risk** over **information and asset transfers** between sites
              and also the **detection risk** of the auditor needing to attend and obtain information from and about
              various sites around the world. There is also increased disclosure risk in the financial statements as
              Shire may be more exposed to economic instability, currency devaluation and inflation operating in
              so many regions, and key assumptions about such factors have to be disclosed in the financial
              statements.

(iii) *Licence*. The company has been granted a licence by the central government. There is a risk that this will not be **accounted for correctly** in the financial statements. The fair value of the licence itself is not material to the financial statements, but it might be material by its nature, as it is possible that without continuing government support of investigation of alternative sources of oil, the company might have going concern issues.

The auditors must ensure that the company is meeting any **conditions attached** to the grant of the licence before the asset can be accounted for, as it should not be recognised in the financial statements if associated conditions are not being met (and it could, in effect, be revoked).

The company intends to value this intangible asset at its **fair value**, which is appropriate, subject to certain criteria, according to IAS 38.

Intangibles may be revalued if they belong to a homogenous class where there is a market with frequent transactions. This seems unlikely in the case of a license to explore for oil in a specific region.

In addition, it may be difficult to substantiate any estimate made of the fair value of this asset as it may be unique and therefore cannot be reliably measured. If it is valued at fair value, it should be amortised over its useful life (5 years).

(iv) *Impaired asset*. The oil rig in South Asia has been impaired to the point where it is no longer operational. The value of this rig may be overstated in the financial statements.

The value of the rig should include a provision for decommissioning it. However, it appears that the company intends to leave this asset standing, although it will not be in use. This begs the question whether the provision for decommissioning was not appropriate, or whether it is now redundant and should be reversed.

(v) *Decommissioning provisions*. The issue of the abandoned rig begs the question whether the costs of decommissioning all the rigs included within the cost of the assets are in fact not appropriate and should be looked at in detail. If there is no legal or constructive obligation to dismantle the disused oil rigs, then there is no liability to be provided for.

(vi) *Contingent or actual liabilities*. There is a risk that liabilities arising are omitted or understated, if any fines or penalties arise as a result of abandoning the South Asia rig.

(vii) *Pipeline*. Shire appears to have entered into a joint venture with another party in respect of an oil pipeline. This will have to be accounted for correctly, according to the provisions of IAS 31. The auditors will have to establish the degree of control which Shire has over the asset. This asset might be a significant part of Shire's operations, but accounting for it could be subjective and it is therefore risky to the audit as accounting for the proportion recognised and its presentation will have a significant impact on the financial statements.

(viii) *Limitation on scope of audit*. In the previous year, the auditors modified their audit report on the basis of not being able to obtain sufficient evidence about oil reserves. This means that evidence that the auditors reasonably expected to be available was not available to them. This is a risk for the audit if the situation giving rise to that modification has not been resolved and there is still a limitation on the scope of the audit.

If the scope limitation does still exist, the auditors should consider whether it is appropriate for them to continue with the engagement, as they should not accept a continuing limitation on the scope of their audit. The company or its employees could be carrying out a fraud in this area, which could be why they are enforcing a limitation on the scope of the audit, and the auditors should not accept such a limitation on an ongoing basis.

The audit report for 2007 should still contain a qualification in respect of this if there is an impact on opening balances, even if there is evidence available in the current year.

(ix) *Share issue*. The earnings per share figure given in the interim accounts suggest that the company may have made a **new issue of shares** in the year. This is because profit for the half year to 30 June

2007 is higher than profit for the half year to 30 June 2006 and yet earnings per share is **considerably reduced**. The auditor needs to ensure that the correct disclosures are made concerning new share issues or that the earnings per share **calculation and disclosure is correct** if no such share issue has taken place.

(b) **Audit work on the useful lives of the rig platforms**

- Obtain copies of management's calculations/assessments of useful lives of rig platforms as at 31 December 2007

- Corroborate key factors which have led to changes in the estimation of useful lives, for example, for the abandoned rig, obtain weather reports, the incident report relating to the cyclone damage and the details of the insurance claim

- Consider management's policies and practices in respect of assessing useful lives and whether it has been successful in the past (for example, are useful lives generally estimated as short and then lengthened or vice versa)

- Review any available industry comparative figures

- Review maintenance budgets and expenditure to ensure that the asset is being invested in to ensure its useful life is going to be achieved

- Comparison of oil extracted against budget (if it is lower, this may indicate that the useful life is shorter than had been supposed, if there is less oil to extract)

- Review management's impairment tests in relation to the rigs and reperformance of value in use calculations.

(c) **Performance measures and evidence**

Measures

(i) Continue investment in health and safety and the environment

  - Amount of money invested in sports sponsorship and hospital sponsorship
  - Percentage increase/decrease investment in the same

(ii) Operate under principles of no harm to people and the environment

  - Number of injuries (or fatalities) sustained to people connected with Shire Co (staff/visitors)
  - Percentage increase/decrease in such injuries/fatalities
  - Number of oil spills

(iii) Providing extra energy in a cleaner and more socially responsible way

  - Number of Research and Development projects into new energy sources
  - Number of projects producing different energy (solar/hydro)

Evidence

Sources of evidence on the above measures could come from:

- Records of sponsorship expenditure
- Accident log records
- Press releases
- Research activity records
- External surveys carried out on Shire or industry generally
- Records of fines and penalties paid for spills or other environmental breaches
- Legal fees and correspondence
- Insurance claims

21 Cerise

Text references. Chapters 6, 7 and 8

Top tips. Read the question carefully and jot down an answer plan first. It is important to avoid certain pitfalls, the most obvious of these is stating that there is a going concern risk. There is no such risk – Cerise is not a going concern. The risk arises from the fact that the going concern risk has already been realised. Hopefully by reading the question carefully, you observed this. Once you understand that the company has stopped trading, other risks should occur to you as you read – for instance, your general business knowledge should make you think that the inventory of a company which has stopped trading might be risky. When a company stops trading, it is likely to incur liabilities (staff redundancy, litigation from affected parties). In this question various liabilities and potential liabilities were clearly signposted for you. By jotting down an answer plan you can prioritise and make sure you get marks for the easier risks rather than getting bogged down in more complicated matters such as the treatment of the various assets. In part (b) it is important to specifically contrast the use of these audit procedures with prior years rather than to just talk generally about the procedures. In part (c), again, be specific about the situation Cerise is in. A simple receivables' circularisation may not be sufficient in this complex situation.

Easy marks. This was a demanding question in which there were no easy marks as such. To ensure you gain marks when attempting this question, make sure that you try and answer each part as generally it is easier to get one or two marks for a requirement than the total number on offer.

Examiner's comments. In part (a) there was nothing to suggest a lack of integrity on the part of management or cash flow problems. Accounting aspects were not dealt with well given clear indicators of the nature of a lease (in this case operating), speculation on the appropriate accounting treatment was rendered completely irrelevant. Some candidates were so careless in reading the scenario that they supposed that Cerise was buying patented technology and manufacturing equipment from the multinational corporation. The general lack of comprehension of a 'going concern' was overwhelming. Numerous candidates stated that laying off the workforce would lead to going concern issues. Cerise was not a going concern. In part (b) candidates should not regurgitate lower level knowledge.

Marking scheme

		Marks
(a)	**Financial statement risks**	12
	Generally ½ mark for identification +	
	1 mark each point of explanation	
	(in context of planning final audit)	
	Ideas	

- Inventory – lower of cost and NRV
- Going concern – basis of presentation
- Employee liabilities
- Sale of assets – derecognition
- Remaining assets – impairment
- Accounting – errors and increased control risk
- Onerous contracts – provision
- Product warranties – provision
- Breach of contract – provision/disclosure

		Marks
(b)	**Extent of reliance on audit evidence**	10
	Generally 1 mark each point of explanation/comparison,	
	Up to maximum 5 each (i) and (ii)	
	Ideas	
	Analytical procedures – less (conclusion)	

- Material items requiring 100% testing
- Relevance of available information
- Comparability of available information (10 months)
- Efficiency and effectiveness of alternative procedures
- Proviso – still of some use

Management representations – more (conclusion)
- Matters of judgement and opinion
- Knowledge confined to management
- Proviso – limitation on possible reliance

(c) **Principal audit work**
Generally 1 mark each area of principal audit work   8
Maximum 4 marks each (i) and (ii)
Ideas
Amounts due from distributors
- Ledger account balances
- After-date cash (any?)
- Agreements – penalties accruing
- Settlement offered (any?)

Lease liabilities
- Prior period working papers – operating leases
- Onerous contract (IAS 37)
  - Early exit?
  - Continuing economic benefit?
- Prior year IAS 17 disclosure (reconciliation)

                                                                                      30

(a) **Financial statement risks**

(i) **Basis of accounting**. The company is no longer a **going concern** and therefore it would be inappropriate for the financial statements to be prepared on the going concern basis. The auditors must ensure that the financial statements have been prepared on a **break-up basis** and this fact has been **disclosed** together with the reasons for the different basis. This will mean that assets have to be reclassified from non current to current and they should be carried at their recoverable amounts.

(ii) **Sale of assets**. The company is selling **equipment** and also the **associated patents**. Given that the deal is lucrative, this is likely to be at a profit, which will be an **item requiring special presentation or disclosure** in the financial statements. The auditors must ensure that the **non-current assets have been correctly removed** from the balance sheet and that the profit on sale is correctly accounted for and disclosed in financial statements.

(iii) **Premises**. The unsold properties may meet the requirements of IFRS 5 at the balance sheet date, in which case they should be separately classified as 'held for sale' and carried at the lower of depreciated cost and fair value less estimated costs to sell. After-date losses on disposal would give evidence of impairment, but this is unlikely given that Cerise carries assets at depreciated cost.

(iv) **Inventory**. Inventory remaining at 1 May is being sold without extended warranty which may affect its realisable value, and the auditors must ensure that it is correctly accounted for at the **lower of cost or net realisable value**.

(v) **Employee liabilities and costs**. There will certainly be **liabilities outstanding** for employees not made redundant as at 31 December 2007 but there may also be liabilities in respect of redundancy payments outstanding for the employees made redundant earlier in the year. The auditor must ensure that the costs and any outstanding liabilities are correctly accounted for. There may also be claims arising from employees who feel their statutory rights have been breached which might require disclosure or provision.

(vi) **Warranties**. Although from 1 November, extended warranties are no longer being offered, it appears the standard one year warranty is still being offered and there will be outstanding one year and longer warranties from previous sales which must be provided against under IAS 37.

(vii) **Penalties arising from breach of contract**. It appears that Cerise's contracts with its distributors contained terms binding Cerise to pay penalties in the event of breach of contract. The distributors are claiming these penalties and the penalties are therefore liabilities which must be recognised in the financial statements. The contracts with the suppliers may also contain penalty clauses, and if this is the case, these penalties should be accounted for as liabilities in a similar fashion to the penalties due to distributors above.

(viii) **Leases – onerous contracts**. Although the leases are operating and therefore are usually accounted for on a rental basis, now the company has ceased operations, the unavoidable costs of meeting the contract exceed the economic benefits which Cerise can expect to obtain from the contract now, and hence a provision for the total expected costs of the operating leases must be set up. As the head office will still be used, this should continue to be accounted for on an annual basis.

(ix) **Accounts department**. Control risk may be increased as a result of the reduction of accounts staff due to the loss of experts or the increased chance of errors being made with fewer staff and non-routine transactions.

(b) **Audit approach – contrast with prior year**

(i) *Analytical procedures*

When carrying out analytical procedures, auditors compare like figures (current year to prior year) and predictable relationships. However, due to the unusual factor in the year of the company ceasing to operate, any comparison with the prior year will be meaningless. The figures for the current year are prepared on a different basis and there is no comparability in the situation of Cerise over the two years. Similarly, it is unlikely that the auditor will be able to compare to budgets, as the sale occurred late in the year and is unlikely to have been budgeted for.

The auditors will therefore be unable to use analytical procedures in the same way as they have in prior years. In addition, different materiality requirements may necessitate other substantive procedures being used so that items can be 100% verified.

However, this does not preclude the auditors from using analytical procedures looking at predicable relationships. For example, there will still be a predictable relationship between sales and warranty provision as there will have been in previous years. In addition, in this year, there is likely to be predictable relationships in respect of the redundancy payments and provision ($x for each year of service, for example).

Conclusion

There is likely to be less use of analytical procedures in the 2007 audit, although there will be scope to use analytical procedures in a different way than in previous years.

(ii) *Management representations*

The auditor is required to obtain management representations about the following matters:

- Management's responsibility for the fair presentation of financial statements

- Management's responsibility for the design and implementation of internal controls

- Management's belief that the aggregate of uncorrected financial statements is immaterial

- Matters material to the financial statements where other sufficient appropriate audit evidence cannot reasonably be expected to exist

In this respect, obtaining management representations will be similar to the previous year as these matters will also have been required then.

However, given the unusual occurrences in the year, there are likely to be more matters requiring management representations as there are more issues where facts are confined to management and that are matters of judgement (for example, provisions and contingent liabilities).

Conclusion

In many respects, management representations will be used in a similar way to the previous audit. However, there are likely to be more items requiring management representation due to the unusual events in the year.

(c)   **Audit work**

(i)   *Amounts due from distributors*

- Obtain list of balances to see individual amounts owed

- Review all after-date receipts (they will all relate to debt existing at the year-end) to see whether any debts have been recovered

- Review terms of contracts with distributors to see who is owed penalties and the related terms

- Read correspondence with distributors to ascertain if any deals are being brokered

- Discuss with management their intention towards paying penalties/recovering debts

(ii) *Lease liabilities*

- Agree opening position from prior year file and note payments in the year
- Review terms of leases to ensure that the leases have become onerous
- Visit the premises affected to ensure that there is no prospect of future economic benefit
- Recalculate the provisions
- Reconcile the provisions to disclosures about leases in the prior year financial statements

22 Geno Vesa farm

Text references. Chapters 6, 7 and 8

Top tips. Make sure that you read this question carefully, not least the requirement so that you are clear what type of risks you are trying to assess. Then work through the requirement again, highlighting or jotting down the risks highlighted in the question. Work through the risks you have identified, making sure that they are all audit risks, or, if they are business risks, assessing what the related audit risks would be, so that when you commit the risks to paper, you are sure that you are answering the question properly. Remember that for 14 marks, you should aim to identify about 9 or 10 risks – working on the assumption that the examiner usually allocates half a mark for identifying and 1 mark for explaining. In part (b), try and think in basic terms about what you are trying to prove about the assets and what evidence will therefore be relevant. Make sure you are relevant to the scenario as well. New kids will not have purchase invoices – they have been born into the business!

Easy marks. These are available are for identifying risks, but harder marks are awarded for explaining those risks.

Examiner's comments. Candidates who ignored the fact that this was an audit risk question struggled on this part. Candidates are reminded that when asked to 'identify', they should be brief. Some candidates seemed focused solely on going concern risks. There are only so many marks that can be awarded for reference to 'going concern'.

Better candidates differentiated themselves by simply recognising the impairment reversal, the sale and repurchase of maturing inventory, a current liability if the grant should be repayable. The weakest candidates who, for example, expressed concern that all the inventory was sold to one customer, clearly had no grasp of the scenario in which sales were made to retail outlets.

Part (b) consisted of three parts for 12 marks – only four points needed for each part to score 100%. Many answers did not answer the question set, most typically ignoring the reference to 'carrying amount', preferring to write an irrelevant answer point for each item on a rote-learned list of financial statement assertions.

		Marks

(a)   **Principal audit risks**

Generally ½ mark for identification + 1 mark each point of explanation   14

Ideas

Industry
- 'farming' (weather, etc)
- bad press etc

Goat herd
- goats – non current tangible assets
- kids – inventory/current assets

Rabida Red
- cost ↑, supply problems ⇒ going concern
- socio-environmental reporting

Bachas Blue
- contingent liability/going concern?
- impairment *reversal* (IAS 36)
- value in use

Cheese
- sale and repurchase/substance over form
- capitalisation of finance costs (IAS 23)
- non-compliance with legislation ⇒ provision
- compliance with legislation ⇒ discontinued operations

Grant
- reason for implementation being deferred
- repayable? ⇒ impact on cash flow

(b)   **Audit work on carrying amounts**

Generally 1 mark each point   <u>12</u>

Max 4 each balance sheet item × 3

Ideas
- FS assertions (valuation = quantity × price)
- qty exists?
- price = cost? Depreciable amount? MV?
- *procedures*
  - analytical
  - enquiry
  - inspection
  - observation
  - computation

<u>26</u>

(a)   **Audit risks**

Nature of the business

The company is a farm which produces farmhouse cheese that is sold by mail order. Farming is inherently risky as it is affected by many conditions which are outside the direct control of management. These include adverse effects of the weather and possible disease. The product sold appears to be a luxury product so sales are likely to fluctuate due to economic and seasonal factors.

Compliance

Farming and food production are heavily controlled businesses where there is a vast amount of legislation which must be complied with. There is a risk that the business will fail to meet the required standards and may be fined as a result. Any adverse publicity eg if fines relate to animal welfare issues may affect sales.

Nature of the assets

One of the key assets of the business will be the goat herd. This asset may be valued incorrectly if a clear distinction is not made between those animals which are held for sale (ie inventory) and those which are selected for herd replacement (ie tangible non current assets).

There is a risk that the balance sheet value of the production animals and charges made to the income statement (eg for depreciation and fair value adjustments) would be misstated if:

(1)   The split of animals between production and held for sale is not carried out accurately
(2)   Useful lives are not assessed in a reasonable manner
(3)   Residual values are not estimated correctly
(4)   Impairment reviews are not undertaken
(5)   Fair values cannot be estimated reliably

Completeness may be an issue as the kids are born into the herd and as such there is no documentary evidence as there would be for purchased assets. Accurate records of kids born will be required to ensure that all animals are valued. Revenue would also be understated if kids were deliberately not recorded and subsequently sold for cash.

For animals held for sale there may be difficulties in assessing cost and net realisable value. It may prove difficult to sell animals held after they have reached their optimum size and weight so NRV may fall. The cost of goats is likely to be based on an estimate of the cost of raising the animal (as it will not have a purchase price as such).

Availability of Innittu

This is an essential ingredient of Rabida Red cheese. Recent increases in the price of this raw material may affect sales if passed on to the customer or will affect profitability if borne by the company. Future supplies of this product may be further restricted. Depending on the company's ability to diversify into alternative ranges this may raise going concern issues. Any associated bad publicity regarding the exploitation of workers and the threat to the rain forest could also impact on going concern.

Bachas Blue

This product has been connected with a skin condition. There is a risk that contingent liabilities will be understated if there is any litigation against the company.

Although the effect of the bad publicity has been short lived the product is unlikely to be able to recover a second time if further health problems are proved.

The impairment loss recognised in relation to the equipment used exclusively for the manufacture of Bachas Blue may now need to be reversed if there has been a change in the estimates used to determine the asset's recoverable amount since March 2007. The recoverable amount will need to be recalculated and is likely to be based on value in use. If future cash flows are not estimated on a reasonable basis the asset and credit to the income statement will be misstated.

Sale and repurchase agreement

The sale and repurchase agreement with Abingdon is in substance a loan secured on the inventory. There is a risk that the cash received might be treated as sales revenue. GVF should continue to recognise the cheese as inventory and the proceeds recognised as a liability.

The 7% interest should be treated as borrowing costs. Under IAS 23 *Borrowing costs* the benchmark treatment is to recognise these as they are incurred. Alternatively GVF may adopt a policy of capitalisation. In this instance the interest should be included as part of the cost of the inventories (as it is incurred in bringing the product to its present location and condition).

Health and safety legislation

The new legislation came into effect in 1 January 2008 and it is unclear as to whether the company has complied. If it has not complied there is a risk of penalties and fines being incurred. Provision for these may be required in the financial statements.

If the legislation has been complied with this may have had a significant effect on the ability of the business to produce medium and strong cheese. This represents a significant part of production. If these products are no longer available the business may no longer be viable.

There is also a risk that plant and equipment is overstated. The carrying value of the old shelves would need to be written off (assuming that they have no further use) and equipment used specifically in the production of medium and strong cheese may have suffered impairment.

Grant

The decision by management to defer the plan to convert the barn may mean that the terms of the grant are no longer met. The grant may be repayable and if this is the case it should be presented as a liability in the balance sheet.

(b) **Audit work**

(i) Goat herd

- Physical inspection of the herd to confirm the existence and condition of the animals. On a test basis check for evidence of ownership eg branding stamp.

- Discuss with management the system by which they distinguish between production animals and those held for sale. Perform tests of controls on the system.

- For production animals (tangible non current assets):

  – Agree value attributed to a sample of animals to market prices

  – Compare depreciation policy with farming industry norms industry norms

  – Check depreciation policy has been applied and calculated for a sample of animals

  – Perform a 'proof in total' or reasonableness check on the depreciation charge for the herd.

- For animals held for sale (inventory):

  – Observe inventory count and assess adequacy of procedures

  – Review management calculations for costs included in the carrying value of animals and assess whether they are appropriate in nature eg feed, vets bills, housing. (As the kids will have been born into the herd there will be no invoice cost.)

  – For a sample of animals compare carrying value at 30 September 2006 with market values.

(ii) Equipment

- Check that brought forward balances for cost and accumulated depreciation agree to previous years working papers and accounts.

- Agree the cost of any new equipment purchased for the production of Bachas Blue.

- Check that the depreciation policy applied to this category of asset has been consistently and appropriately applied.

- For the previously impaired asset:

  - Check the basis of the current calculation of value in use (This should be the present value at the estimated future cash flows – IAS 36).

  - Compare the future cash flows with budgeted cash flow figures taking into account any other knowledge of the business which might result in variations eg. any information regarding other health scares associated with the product.

  - Check that sales of Bachus Blue are returning to their former level by comparing current sales levels and budgeted sales for 2007 with sales levels before the adverse publicity

  - Agree any assumptions made by discussion with management and review of board minutes.

  - Check the period over which the cash flow projections have been made (normally a maximum of five years – IAS 36).

  - Determine the basis on which the discount rate has been calculated. Reperform the calculation and check that management have considered the current assessment of the time value of money and the risks specific to this asset.

  - Calculate the assets depreciated carrying value (ie its value if the asset had not been originally impaired) and compare with the current carrying value (The reversal impairment loss cannot result in the asset being valued at an amount which exceed its depreciated carrying value – IAS 36).

(iii)   Cheese

WIP

- Attend the inventory count and determine the process by which the stage of maturity is assessed and therefore costs attributed.

- Obtain a schedule showing the breakdown of costs and check that the basis on which they have been recharged is reasonable. (For example, the milk used is produced by the herd. The cost of milk will therefore be an estimation of the cost of producing it rather than a purchase price.)

- Check the system by which the age of inventory is monitored. Confirm that cheese which is not available for sale for more than 12 months after the year-end has been disclosed as a non-current asset.

Finished goods

- Review the terms of the sale and repurchase agreement with Abingdon to confirm that it is in substance a secured loan.

- At the inventory count ensure that all cheese including that 'owned' by Abingdon is included in the count total.

- Review costing records to confirm that the 7% interest is included for every 6 months which elapses after maturity. Perform tests of control on controls over ageing of mature inventory.

- Obtain confirmation from Abingdon of the outstanding liability at 30 September 2007. This will be the difference between the value of cheese purchased by Abingdon and the amount repurchased by GVF.

- Discuss with management the need to write down the value of inventory. The net realisable value of cheeses held on the new stainless steel shelving may be less than cost

- Confirm the adequacy of disclosure. The carrying amount of inventory pledged as security should be disclosed.

23 Taurus Traders

> **Text references.** Chapters 5. 6 and 7
>
> **Top tips.** In part (a) break your answer down into elements of business risk. This will help you in the first place to identify a wide range of risks and in the second place, give structure to your answer. Parts (b) and (d) should be relatively straightforward. In part (c) remember to justify a strategy – do not just describe various strategies without directing them at the scenario. A mark will be available for a conclusion – so make sure that you draw one.

(a) **Business risks**

Environmental risks

(i) The **nature of the business**: suppliers to the building industry are subject to the same economic cycle as the building industry itself. Operators in the building industry need adequate reserves to see them through the inevitable downturns in the business.

(ii) The **position of the business within the market**: even in an economic upturn, a supplier may struggle if the market for building suppliers is saturated or highly competitive.

(iii) The **stage of the business' development** and the **proposed future developments**: Taurus Traders is experiencing a period of rapid growth, it requires additional funding and is moving into markets in which it may have little experience (builders merchants and the overseas operation). The owner-manager has very high expectations of returns that the business can provide and he does not appear to have an appropriate attitude to his professional advisors, financial controls, and compliance matters. All of these factors present additional risks that would not be present in an established business.

(iv) **Overseas exposure**: the business is already subject to fluctuations in exchange rates and the proposal to set up an overseas operation may increase those risks if they are not properly managed.

Financial risks

The company is experiencing **rapid growth** in turnover, it is **seeking substantial loan finance** which will need to be serviced, and it **exceeds its overdraft facility** which may also result in penalties. The business has clearly outgrown the company's financing structure.

Financial controls in terms of the accounting system, the production of good management accounts, the employment of a competent accountant and the reconciliation of the ledgers are all **inadequate**. Debts are probably not being collected and suppliers may be left unpaid which may result in a loss of goodwill.

Mr Aquila's intended repayment of his loan account in this context (instead of investing in the business) indicates a **lack of understanding** of the difficult financial position the company may be in. In extremes, this could amount to a **going concern risk**.

Operational risks

If the bank loan is not forthcoming, it may not be possible to continue with the new **premises** which have already been commenced. There may be serious **contractual implications** with whoever has been contracted to construct the building if financing is delayed.

The business is experiencing a **high level of returns** which may indicate problems with the company's own **suppliers**, problems with the company's inventory control systems or simply a deterioration in the market in which the company operates. If the trend continues, inventory levels will rise and profit margins will fall. This in turn has implications for the profit forecast on which the application for the bank loan is based.

Compliance risks

The company appears to have very **poor internal financial systems and controls**. The basic system, written by a relative of Mr Aquila, is probably inadequate to cope with the volume of transactions now being put through it. The foreign currency transactions are not dealt with by the computer system at all and there are unreconciled differences on the ledgers. It is not therefore surprising that the annual budget and management accounts are of poor quality. This combined with Mr Aquila's poor relationship with his current auditors means that it is possible that the financial statements have been of poor quality, produced late, and possibly qualified or modified.

In the current year, these problems have serious implications because of the apparent **intended reliance by the bank** on the **profit forecast** – it is not clear who the forecast is to be provided by or when. If the loan is made, it is likely that the bank will require sight of the management accounts or similar, as well as the financial statements, and if systems are not improved, the company could encounter real difficulties in this respect.

(b) **Factors in making a proposal**

(i) The precise **nature of the services** to be provided. Will it be the statutory audit and financial advice to the company only, or will it include financial advice to Mr Aquila personally, as seems likely, and is any work on the profit forecast required?

Any sort of work on the profit forecast seems likely to present a risk to the firm, partly because it seems likely that allowances for inventory and other adjustments may be required which will probably have the effect of reducing the profit forecast, which will not please Mr Aquila. The need for such adjustments and a thorough review of the information to be provided to the bank is even more important in the light of the fact that the bank will be taking account of the forecast as part of its lending decision.

(ii) The **risk profile** of the firm and its existing exposure to this type of business, any history of litigation between Taurus Traders and its professional advisors and an assessment of the overall integrity of Mr Aquila.

(iii) The **experience** of the firm in this sector, the independence of the firm and the availability of staff to complete the assignment(s) on time.

(iv) The **likely level of fee income**, and any expected difficulties in collecting the fees in the circumstances. Any positive response to the letter sent to the outgoing auditors asking if there are any professional reasons why the engagement should not be accepted should be carefully noted as should any statement made in the 'statement of circumstances' issued by the outgoing auditors.

(c) **Audit strategy**

(i) **Planning and risk assessment**

A **thorough review** of the prior year financial statements, accounting systems (such as they are) and the documentation available for the current year should be conducted as early as possible in order to establish whether the records are so bad as to possibly require a modified audit report (limitation in scope, lack of proper accounting records). Any such possibility must be communicated to Mr Aquila at the earliest possible stage because it is likely to affect his application for the bank loan.

The **prior year financial statements**, and any other information such as a reconciled trial balance should also give some indication of any problem areas that the firm is not already aware of.

Analytical procedures are unlikely to be as useful as they might be as a result of the growth in the business and the poor quality of the records.

Materiality should be set at a level to reflect the risks associated with this business.

(ii) **Internal control**

If there are sufficient very basic financial controls in place a wholly substantive approach will not be necessary so, at least initially, testing of systems in relation to sales, receivables, inventory and payroll should be undertaken. Tolerable deviation rates, as with materiality, should be set at a level to reflect the control risks which are likely to be high. Assuming that systems can provide some comfort, substantive testing can be reduced.

(iii) **Specific account areas**

The specific areas that are likely to require attention are **inventory**, the **foreign currency transactions**, **receivables** and **payables**, and **gross margins**.

Detailed work on the **write-down or write-off of faulty inventories** will be required and if the records are inadequate for these purposes, it may be necessary for the company, or the firm, to construct them. The year-end inventory count may help with this. Inventory will be a material item in the balance sheet and it is unlikely that additional work can be avoided in this area in the current year.

The foreign currency transactions and balances are recorded manually and computerised controls will not exist. The manual controls appear to be weak because of the unreconciled differences on the ledgers. It is likely that extensive substantive work in this area will be required because of the **involvement of Mr Aquila** in **negotiating prices** with both customers and suppliers. There is potential for significant manipulation of the records in relation to both transactions and balances because of the absence of, or weak, internal controls that can be overridden. Direct confirmation of balances with both customers and suppliers will be necessary.

(iv) **The going concern and overall review of financial statements**

It is important in the current year to aggregate errors and to review the financial statements as a whole and **assess whether there is significant concern** about the entity's ability to continue as a going concern. An **independent review** of the financial statements may be appropriate in accordance with ISA 220 as the entity may be assessed as high risk. It is unlikely that the bank will make its decision before the financial statements and the profit forecast are signed and the firm will have to therefore take a view on this.

(d) **Two procedures to improve accounting procedures and financial controls**

Improved accounting procedures would be achieved if an **integrated computer system were developed specifically for the company**, properly tested and implemented. This would improve the efficiency of transactions processing and control (particularly foreign currency transactions), the quality of the management accounts and their usefulness for decision-making purposes (including inventory control), and ultimately the quality of the financial statements.

Financial controls would be improved by the production of a **well thought out annual budget** that was **compared to the management accounts** and revised and rolled forward during the course of the year. This would provide the company and the bank with significant additional comfort on the control of the business generally.

24 Indigo

Text references. Chapter 6 and 7

Top tips. Read the whole question through in the context of the requirement. Part (a) is straightforward, so you should complete it as quickly as possible and focus on part (b) which is slightly harder. Remember when trying to justify an audit strategy to eliminate strategies with reasons and to use the information you have just obtained about risks to shape your answer. You should have identified that inventory is a key risk – so you need to bear in mind that inventory must be focused on when carrying out the audit. In part (c), think practically. Although the cash book is missing, cash should have been banked by the company on a fairly regular basis, so theoretically the accountant could only steal cash received since the last banking.

Easy marks. Part (a) of this question was a straightforward requirement, so you should expect to score highly here. In addition, you should have been able to gain some easy marks for suggesting matters to consider in respect of the extent of the alleged fraud in part (c).

Examiner's comments. Part (a) was answered well by some candidates but others produced vague answers relating to work to be done on opening balances.

In part (b), there were lots of inadequate answers that did not answer the question set. This was more evident in answers set out in a tabular format. Some answers identified financial risks rather than financial statements risks and others explained control weaknesses and suggested recommendations – this was not asked for.

In part (c), many answers were not sufficient enough as the requirement asked for comments. Lots of candidates suggested how to improve the system – this had not been asked for in the requirement.

Marking scheme

		Marks
(a)	Opening balances – principal audit work	Max 6

Generally ½-1 mark each appropriate suggestion of audit work +
½-1 mark for relevance to Indigo.
Ideas
- consistent application of appropriate accounting policies
- review of predecessor auditor's working papers (if possible)
- current period audit procedures – receipts/payments, sales
- analytical procedures
- historical accounting records

(b)   Financial statements risks and audit approach
Generally 1 mark each financial statement risk   Max 10
Ideas
- Assets
    - inventory (overstatement, measurement, existence, obsolescence)
    - tangible non-current assets (furnace parts/linings)
    - cash (completeness, existence)
- Liabilities
    - provision overstatement (furnace linings)
- Income statement
    - sales understatement (cash)
    - purchases overstatement
    - subsidy overstatement
    - repair/renewal overstatement

- Disclosure risk
  - going concern (IAS 1)
  - contingent liabilities (IAS 37)

Generally ½ march each approach identified as suitable/unsuitable +   Max 6
1 mark each point of explanation

Ideas

- Risk-based approach –why suitable
  - high inherent risk at entity and financial assertion levels
  - focus on inventory, purchases, sales cash
- Systems-based/compliance approach – why *not* suitable
  - lack of controls
  - recent appointment – no interim audit – already December
- Detailed substantive/balance sheet approach – why suitable
  - substantial assets at balance sheet
- Cyclical approach/directional testing – why *not* suitable
  - no trade payables/receivables (cash-based)
- Analytical procedures – limitations on use
  - fluctuating margins
  - lack of reliable/historic information – first year's audit

                                                                                      Max 14

(a)   **Opening balances**

The following audit procedures should be carried out:

- Agree the opening balances per Indigo's records to the financial statements for the year ended 31 December 2006

- Review accounting policies applied in 2006 and 2007 to ensure that they are consistent and appropriate

- If relevant working papers have been made available from the previous auditors, review to ensure that sufficient evidence was obtained to state that opening balances are fairly stated. (However, there is no requirement on the previous auditors to make this information available.)

- If working papers are not available, carry out other procedures where possible:

  - Verifying receivables by after-date payments
  - Verifying payables by reference to supplier statements or after-date payments
  - Verifying bank balances to bank statements or requesting the balance from the bank
  - Verifying inventory by after-date sales

- An area which might cause concern for the new auditor is opening inventory which might be difficult to verify if evidence is not available from the previous auditor. Given the risks associated with inventories this year, and the evidence of problems associated with it, it is possible that the new auditor will need to qualify the audit report due to a lack of evidence in respect of opening inventory.

- Analytical procedures month on month for the year ending 31 December 2007 may indicate problems with opening balances if the figures are distorted in the first month.

(b)   **Financial statement risks and audit strategy**

Risks

(i)   **Inventories**. There are various risks associated with the inventories balance.

  (1)   **Evidence.** It appears that there are restrictions on evidence with regard to inventory, certainly for the closing balance and possibly for the opening balance as well, if information is not available from the previous auditors. Rolling forward an inventory count is acceptable, if there

are restrictions on a count at the year-end, but not ideal, as there is greater risk of error arising. The auditors should also determine the motive behind not counting at the year-end, as this could also impact risk, if it shows that the management are careless in their attitude to getting the right figure for the year-end.

(2)   **Nature of the inventories**. Scrap metal inventory is reduced to small bricks. It is not clear what the value of a brick is, but it is likely to be low value. Thus inventories, which is likely to be the most significant balance, consists of a high number of low value small items, and a number of piles of metal, not distinguished by type of metal. Although the metals can be distinguished from each other simply, this adds complexity to the count. Given that small bricks are portable, and controls over metal inventories seem weak (aluminium sheets have been allowed to 'escape' to a nearby field) the risk of the amount and therefore value of inventories in the balance sheet not being correct appears very high.

(3)   **Obsolescence**. Some of the iron is rusty. It is unclear whether, in a scrap business, this makes it obsolescent, but it does imply a degree of obsolescence. This adds to the risk of the value of inventories being misstated.

(4)   **Value**. There is likely to be a degree of specialism involved in valuing the metal due to considerations of quality and volume having an effect on value. However, there is no local specialist available, and it is not clear whether Indigo Co intends to obtain a suitable specialist or value the metal itself. It is likely that the auditor would need specialist assistance in determining whether inventories had been valued correctly.

(ii)   **Controls**. The fact that the cash book is not posted to the general ledger promptly suggests that controls over recording could be weak, which increases the risk that the financial statements are generally misstated due to error.

(iii)   **Missing records/fraud**. The fact that a fraud has been perpetrated and records stolen from the company also increases the risk that the financial statements will be misstated, as there are no cash records for the company for November.

(iv)   **Cash transactions**. In addition to the general control problems noted, Indigo has a high number of cash transactions, both sales and purchases, and cash transactions are more inherently risky than credit transactions. There is motive to overstate cash purchases as the subsidy is calculated on the basis of cash payments. This also adds to the risk that the financial statements will contain errors.

(v)   **Opening balances**. As the auditor is new this year, there is a risk that the auditor will not be able to obtain sufficient audit evidence about the opening balances, particularly inventories as noted above.

(vi)   **Furnace linings**. It is inappropriate to have a provision for the cost of the furnace linings, which should be included in the carrying value of the asset. This is unlikely to have a material impact on the income statement (as the net impact of expense being removed but depreciation on the asset being included is likely to be immaterial). The issue is also likely to be immaterial to the balance sheet (being a small aspect of non-current assets).

(vii)   **Illegal dumping**. The company dumps metal illegally which indicates that management have a casual attitude to some laws and regulations. If this is their attitude to other laws and regulations relevant to the company, it also gives rise to the risk that the financial statements may be misstated due to the financial effects of non-compliance with legislation.

(viii) **Government subsidy**. The company receives a government subsidy which must be accounted for correctly in the financial statements. In addition, this adds to the risk of the audit generally, as the local government may be relying on the audited figures for the purposes of their subsidy grant.

Audit strategy

(i)   **Risk.** The auditors should take a risk-based approach to the audit given the risks noted above, because inherent risk is high and there is a substantial chance of material errors arising in inventory in particular.

(ii) **Controls.** It would not be appropriate to take a controls approach to the audit due to the evidence that controls are ineffective and lacking, particularly over the key areas of inventory and cash.

(iii) **Transactions.** Although it is common to take a transactions approach to an audit where controls are identified as weak, in this instance, it does not seem appropriate to take a cyclical or transactional approach, as there are missing records, and due to the high risk associated with cash and inventory which necessarily are at the heart of the cycles that would be tested. Given that the business is largely a cash business, there is an absence of third party evidence (such as supplier statements, customer remittances) in the cycles.

(iv) **Balance sheet**. In the circumstances therefore, it does seem appropriate to take a balance sheet approach to the audit, with particular emphasis on the risk area of inventory. Key audit work will include attending an inventory count (if possible), verifying bank balances with the bank and vouching the value of the subsidy by verifying the quarterly returns to the local government.

(c) **Matters to consider in determining the extent of loss from alleged fraud**

- The regularity with which cash was banked and the date of the previous banking
- The details given to the police by the managing director
- Any apparent change in lifestyle associated with the accountant before he absconded
- An estimate of the loss being based on three days of an average month's sales
- The extent to which last year's unmodified audit report suggests the fraud started in the current year
- The likelihood of the alleged fraud proceeds being recovered
- The opinions of other staff members about the activities of the accountant
- The opinion of the police on the case against the accountant

25 Phoenix

Text references. Chapters 8 and 9

Top tips. If your accounting knowledge is up to scratch, this should be a good question for you. If it isn't, make sure you brush up on it before the real exam. You could get a similar question to this and must be on top of your financial reporting knowledge.

(a) **Trade investment**

(i) **Matters to consider**

Materiality

At $80,000 the total investment is on the borderline of **materiality** to the income statement for the current period at about 4.7%. However, if dividends receivable are added to this then the amount is more clearly material at nearly 6%. The total is unlikely to be material to the balance sheet.

Accounting treatment

If the total amount has to be written off it seems likely that **separate disclosure** will be required but if not, a judgement will have to be made. IAS 10 *Events after the balance sheet date* requires that as an **adjusting event**, the amount should be written off in the accounts. There may be amounts owing to Pegasus and there may possibly be a right of set-off against amounts receivable, although this seems unlikely.

The effect on the operations of Phoenix of the **loss of the contractor** also have to be considered. Alternative arrangements will have to be made for imported metals and this may, at least in the short-term, result in increased costs if a suitable shipping contractor cannot be found quickly. Whilst this is not likely to affect the current year figures, **disclosure may be required** as a non-adjusting post balance sheet event.

Disclosure of all matters will be required in the Directors' Report.

(ii) **Audit evidence**

- Copies of all press reports

- Documentation/report from the liquidator regarding the likely level of pay-out, whether shareholders have any priority (unlikely) and details of any shareholders' meeting

- The most recent audited accounts of Pegasus to determine the extent to which market values of assets exceed book values

- Minutes of any meetings held by the shareholders of Pegasus to discuss the way forward

- Legal correspondence regarding any legal right of set-off of dividends receivable and amounts payable

- Notes of discussions with management regarding the impact of the loss of a major shipping contractor, for example plans for a replacement

- Post year-end review of negotiations for a new contractor

- Post year-end review of order books to determine the extent of any lost business as a result of the liquidation of Pegasus

(b) **Provision for future maintenance**

(i) **Matters to consider**

Materiality

$500,000 represents nearly 30% of profits and is therefore **material**.

Accounting treatment

IAS 37 *Provisions, contingent liabilities and contingent assets* states that a provision should only be recognised when there is no uncertainty about timing or amount, and where these is a liability at the balance sheet date. A liability is a present obligation arising from past events, the settlement of which is expected to result in an outflow of economic resources.

Unless a **binding legal agreement** for maintenance has been signed, **or** unless there is **no real prospect** that the **company can avoid** the **obligation** at the balance sheet date (this seems unlikely), the provision should not be recognised, as there is no **present obligation**. Whilst there seems little uncertainty as to the timing of the expenditure, or as to the amount, there is **no actual liability** at the balance sheet date.

IAS 37 was partly designed to deal with the problem of over-provisioning for the purposes of profit smoothing. This seems a possibility in this case, even when taken together with the write-off of the investment, above.

IAS 16 *Property, plant and equipment* requires that **maintenance expenditure** should be recognised when it is incurred, however, it could be argued that the lining is a separate asset and could be accounted for as a capital item, at the point at which the expense is incurred.

Prior year accounting policies in relation to this matter are relevant and a disclosure of a change in accounting policy may be required.

(ii) **Audit evidence**

- A breakdown of the individual elements of cost making up the total provision

- Prior year working papers showing previous treatment, the rationale and the nature of the replacement (whether regular or ad hoc)

- Details of contractual arrangements/quotes if work is to be sub-contracted

- Schedule of costings if work is going to be performed 'in-house'

- Notes of discussions with management regarding the quantification and treatment of the provision.

(c)   **Cleanaway**

(i)   **Matters to consider**

Accounting treatment

Cleanaway is highly likely to be a **related party** under IAS 24 *Related party disclosures* under which **disclosure** is required of the names of the related parties, the nature of the relationship and a detailed description of the transactions entered into.

Risk

There are significant **operational implications** of the alleged illegal dumping. Firstly, there is the possibility that Cleanaway will not have its **licence** renewed which means that an alternative contractor must be found. There may also be **financial implications** as Phoenix may be liable for actions of the contractors, for any associated clean-up costs, and may also be more likely to be subject to regulatory investigations.

The **integrity** of Troy Pitz is also called into question which has implications for the financial statements as a whole to the extent that he has a responsibility for them, and for the assessment of audit risk. There are also implications for the **reputation** of Phoenix which may affect customer and supplier goodwill, and any applications for renewed operating licences required by Phoenix itself.

(ii)   **Audit evidence**

- A copy of the recent newspaper article
- A copy of the contract to determine:

    – That it is due for renewal

    – Action available to Phoenix due to the illegal dumping (eg termination of contract)

    – Any responsibility Phoenix might have as a consequence of the illegal dumping (eg costs of clean-up/fines)

- Notes of discussions with management regarding

    – The nature of the allegations

    – Any direct financial consequences for Phoenix

    – Any alternative disposal companies

    – Contingency plans until alternative disposal company can be found

- Correspondence with regulators and lawyers particularly regarding implications for Troy Pitz as managing director

- Evidence concerning the identification of related party transactions:

    – Details of the company's own procedure

    – Notes of discussions with management

    – Details of related parties/related party transactions identified last year

    – Board meeting minutes

    – Conclusions drawn from the review of the statutory books and records

- Management representations concerning the completeness of information provided regarding the related party disclosures

- Management representations regarding the effect of the loss of the shipping contractor and the allegations against Cleanaway on the viability of Phoenix

26 Aspersion

Text references. Chapters 8 and 10

Top tips. When faced with a general requirement such as 'comment on matters you should consider' it is important to thoroughly record your thought processes and not to omit anything which you feel is obvious. For example, for each of the situations in this question, you need to write down your 'alarm bells', in other words, the problems you feel could exist in the situation. This will lead to you then explaining the implications of these problems for the financial statements, and therefore the things you will need to find out and confirm in discovering whether a true or fair view has been given. Remember that there are certain matters which an auditor should always consider, such as materiality. The examiner has clearly given you scope in the scenario to consider materiality, so not to do so will lose you marks.

Examiner's comments. This question was answered relatively well apart from item (3) on deferred tax – candidates were very hazy about whether an adjustment would be appropriate and some completely failed to even attempt this section. However, it should have been answered much better.

Candidates need to be able to recognise the principle accounting issues involved in this type of question. These were:

(a)   Related party transaction (IAS 24)

Relatively good marks were gained here. Candidates that did particularly well spent sufficient time identifying the audit evidence they would look for. Weaker candidates who insisted that the transaction 'must be on an arm's length basis' scored few marks.

(b)   Impairment (IAS 36)

Most candidates missed the point and got bogged down with discussion on depreciation rates when the issue was impairment. A disappointing majority of candidates suggested (incorrectly) that the carriers should have been depreciated over 3 years. That some candidates believed that the two light aircraft should have been accounted for as a construction contract under IAS 11 was very worrying.

(c)   Deferred tax (IAS 12)

The majority of candidates clearly felt so nervous about the accounting of deferred tax that they failed even to go 'back to basics' and consider whether the post balance sheet event was adjusting or non-adjusting. Advice to candidates who do not know a relevant Accounting Standard is to revert to principles (eg the change in rate does not give rise to a liability because it did not apply at the balance sheet date). Nevertheless, some marks were gained for the audit evidence part where most candidates managed to suggest that they would need a copy of the calculation and would need to re-perform casts etc.

Although it was not in the marking scheme, those exceptionally perceptive candidates who pointed out that writing down the assets in (b) for impairment would have an impact on the deferred tax provision were awarded marks.

References to any documentation supporting 'payments of deferred tax' showed a staggering lack of understanding of the concept of deferred tax.

		Marks

(i) *Matters*
Generally 1 mark each comment
Maximum 5 marks any one issues × 3   **Max 12**
Ideas
- Materiality (assessed)
- Relevant IASs (e.g. 1, 10, 12, 24, 36)
- Risk (e.g. completeness assertion)
- Implications for auditors' report (e.g. explanatory para)

(ii) *Audit evidence*
Generally 1 mark each item of audit evidence (source)
Maximum 5 marks any one issues × 3   <u>**Max 12**</u>
Ideas
- Oral vs written
- Internal vs external
- Auditor generated

• Procedures (relevant, reliable, sufficient)		Max 20
	(a)	Max 7
	(b)	Max 7
	(b)	<u>Max 6</u>
		20

(a) **Sale of cargo carrier to Abra**

(i) **Matters to consider**

A cargo carrier has been sold to a party which is potentially related to Aspersion under the requirements of IAS 24. A loss has been made on that disposal of a non current asset.

Materiality

The loss on disposal has reduced profit before tax by $400,000. This 14% reduction is material to profit.

Related party transaction?

Iain Jolteon, the finance director who approved the sale of the cargo carrier, has a substantial equity interest in Abra, the company to whom it was sold. As such, Abra appears to fall within the criteria of a related party under IAS 24.

This connection would appear stronger if Mr Jolteon owned shares in Aspersion or was a director in Abra, and if Abra was controlled by his close family members.

Implication

The transaction should be disclosed in the financial statements as a related party transaction. This disclosure should include:

- The names of the transacting related parties
- A description of the relationship between the parties
- A description of the transactions
- The amounts involved
- Any money outstanding due to the company/related party

Other related parties

The auditors should consider, and be alert for evidence of, other related parties and transactions.

 179

Reasons for the sale

The fact that a large loss has been made on the sale raises other matters for the auditor to consider:

- Whether the sale has been made at an undervalue (this may have tax implications)
- Why the machine was sold:

    - Maintenance problem
    - Reduction in operations
    - Movement in technology rendering others obsolete

- Whether the depreciation policy was incorrect (over 20 years)

These questions will lead the auditor to review the remaining non current assets to ensure that they are not impaired and that the depreciation policies are reasonable.

Disclosure of loss on sale

As this item is material it would be disclosed separately in accordance with IAS 1 *Presentation of financial statements.*

(ii) Audit evidence

The following evidence will be sought:

- A copy of the sales agreement
- A copy of any valuation report carried out on the asset
- Evidence of receipt of the proceeds through the bank
- The calculation of the loss (this should be checked for accuracy)
- Notes of discussions with management about procedures for the identification of related party transactions
- Results of reviews of board meetings, share registers and other statutory records
- Written management representations regarding the completeness of related party disclosures
- A copy of the discount note which is to be included in the financial statements.

(b) Light aircraft

(i) Matters to consider

Aspersion owns two light aircraft which are used to service a contract which will not be renewed when it comes up in six month's time.

Materiality

The total cost of the aircraft was $900,000. They have been owned in the region of 3 years, and have been depreciated over 15 years. Therefore, their carrying value is in the region of $720,000. This represents 7% of total assets and is therefore material to the balance sheet.

Impairment

The aircraft were purchased to service a contract which will not be renewed when it expires 6 months after the balance sheet date. This significant change in the market in which the assets operate indicates impairment of the asset and requires management to carry out an impairment review under IAS 36. The auditors need to establish whether this has been carried out.

Management intentions

The auditors need to discover what management's future intentions for the assets are:

- Sale
- Alternative use

These intentions will impact on the impairment review.

Impairment loss

If an impairment loss has been identified, the auditors need to discover.

- Whether it is material (≥ $100,000, say)
- Whether it has been properly disclosed in the financial statements

(ii) **Audit evidence**

- A copy of the service contract and any correspondence
- Results of inspection of the aircraft (to ascertain condition)
- Notes of enquiries of management to ascertain

   - Future intentions
   - Whenever an impairment review was carried out

- Evidence from the impairment review – for example, any draft sales agreements, cash flow projections relating to value in use, any contracts relating to new uses for the aircraft.

(c) **Deferred tax**

(i) **Matters to consider**

Deferred tax has been provided for in respect of accelerated capital allowances in accordance with IAS 12.

Materiality

The tax provision amounts to 21% of profit before tax and is therefore material. The increase in the provision, of $76,000, is not material to profit before tax.

IAS 12 – rate of tax to use

IAS 12 requires that deferred tax is calculated at a rate of tax that is 'substantively enacted' and expected to apply to the period when the deferred tax is to be settled. Substantively enacted generally means that it has been made into law, not merely suggested or announced.

In this instance, therefore, the directors are proposing to amend the provision to apply a tax rate that is not substantively enacted, but has merely been announced.

Implication

If the directors do make the provision bigger, they will no longer be complying strictly with the requirements of IAS 12. The auditors should discuss the matter with the directors and dissuade them from making such an addition to the provision.

However, the additional provision is immaterial to the financial statements, so the auditors are unlikely to conclude that the deferred tax balance does not give a true and fair view.

(ii) **Audit evidence**

- A copy of all the calculations made in relation to the tax balances

- The client's schedules relating to the tax basis used

- Agreement of tax rate to tax legislation

- Schedules of non current assets used in tax calculations agreed to non current asset register/ general ledger

- Audit programme for non current assets with evidence of verification of changes (eg additions)

- A reconciliation of the tax expense with the accounting profit

- Minutes of directors' meetings confirming details of any major additions etc in non current assets

27 Visean

Text references. Chapters 9 and 10

Top tips. For part (a) remember that matters will cover the issues of risk, materiality and accounting treatment. There is also a heavy emphasis on accounting knowledge. Make sure you deal with all aspects of the information. There is often more than one accounting problem in each part of the question.

For part (b) it is essential that you make your points as specific as possible. Generalities will score few marks.

It would be possible to present your answer in a two column format. In this case if you choose to do so you need to take care as there is not always a corresponding piece of evidence for each matter raised.

Easy marks. These are available for assessing materiality and highlighting relevant accounting standards.

Examiner's comments. Generally answers to the questions were satisfactory. Common failings however included the following:

- Failing to carry out calculations to determine whether a balance was material

- Failing to demonstrate higher skills. For example in part (a) many considered the treatment of the purchased and internally generated brands in detail even though the question made it clear that the appropriate treatment had been adopted. The main issue was in fact impairment.

- Few demonstrated any knowledge of IAS 7 in part (c), failing to appreciate that both the direct and indirect methods of cash flow preparation are allowed.

The audit evidence section was weak and in many cases unimaginative and repetitive. Comments such as 'see board minutes' will attract few marks.

Marking scheme

		Marks
(i)	**Matters** Generally 1 mark each comment Maximum 5 marks issues (1) & (2) and 4 marks issue (3) *Ideas*	Max 12

- Materiality (assessed)
- Relevant IASs (eg 2, 7, 10, 14, 35, 36, 37, 38)
- Risks (eg FS assertions)
- Responsibilities (eg directors')
- Implications for auditors' report

(ii)	**Audit evidence** Generally 1 mark each item of audit evidence (source) Maximum 5 marks issues (1) & (2) and 4 marks issue (3) *Ideas*	Max 12

- Oval vs written
- Internal vs external
- Auditor generated
- Procedures (relevant, reliable, sufficient)

		Max 20
	(1)	Max 8
	(2)	Max 7
	(3)	Max 5
		20

(a) **Brands**

Matters

(i) *Risk*

The key risk is that the Ulexite brand has suffered an **impairment** as a result of the poor advertising campaign.

(ii) *Materiality*

The cost of purchased brands represent 3.2% of total assets and 32.2% of profit before tax. Amortisation represents approximately 3.2% of profit before tax. Net book value would be a more appropriate figure to use, however based on the information available it would appear that brands overall are **material** to the accounts.

The key issue, however, is whether any adjustment required as a result of any impairment to the Ulexite brand would be material. Assuming materiality based on 5% of profit before tax any write down in excess of approximately $92,000 would be material.

(iii) *Accounting treatment*

- Whether the recognition of brands is in accordance with IAS 38

  Purchased brands including Ulexite are capitalised. Self-created brands are expensed. This satisfies the basic requirements of the accounting standard.

- The extent to which management believe the Ulexite brand to have suffered an **impairment**

  In accordance with IAS 36 an impairment occurs where the recoverable amount of the asset falls **below the carrying amount**. This is normally the result of a change in circumstances, in this case the fall in sales due to the advertising campaign.

- The amount of any impairment

  This will depend on the **recoverable amount of the asset** which is the higher of the fair value less costs to sell (not selling price), if known, and value in use. The way in which management have calculated net realisable value and value in use will need to be considered.

  (It may be difficult to calculate the fair value of the brand, unless there is a binding sale agreement to sell the asset. Value in use should be more straightforward. It is likely that each brand will be treated as an income generating unit as it should be possible to identify the income streams which it generates ie. sales independently of those generated by other brands.)

- Valuation of inventories of Ulexite products

  Information obtained in July 2007 regarding the fall in sales of Ulexite products represents an **adjusting post balance sheet event** as it provides information about the value of the inventory at the year-end date. This information suggests that the net realisable value of this inventory has fallen below cost in which case an allowance would be required.

- Valuation of other brands

  The effect of the bad publicity could have a knock-on effect on other brands and products. Customer confidence and goodwill may have been lost in which case **other brands may have suffered an impairment** and **other lines of inventory may require provisions**.

- Proposed action to be taken by management

  This might include:

  - The possibility of **suing the advertising company** responsible for the campaign. If it is probable that Visean will win the case a **contingent gain** would be disclosed.

  - Future plans for Ulexite, for example whether it might be sold or discontinued or alternatively any plans to counteract the bad publicity.

- Period over which brands are amortised

  Currently this is over 10 years on a straight line basis. In a business which is subject to fashion and the unpredictable tastes of the general public the **useful economic life of the assets may need to be reduced**.

Evidence

- Cost of Ulexite brand at 30 June 2007 agreed to prior year working papers

- Accumulated amortisation on Ulexite brand agreed to prior year working papers and current year's amortisation charge

- Schedule showing the basis for any impairment write down of the Ulexite brand. Assuming this is based on value in use this would be cash flow projections over the remaining useful life of the brand. This period would not be expected to exceed five years.

- Analytical review of after-date sales and inventory turnover by fragrance (in comparison to budget). This will show the extent to which the publicity campaign has affected the sales of Ulexite or otherwise and the impact this may be having on other fragrances

- Records and analysis of sales returns after the year-end

- Results of review of the cash book and after-date invoices to identify any expenses incurred in order to rectify the damage caused eg advertisement with apology, new advertising campaign

- The initial advert and any press/media comment to gauge the scale of the impact and the strength of feeling

- Board minutes noting any future plans for Ulexite, for example a plan to discontinue it

- Correspondence with legal advisors in respect of any claim which might be made against the advertising company

- Industry information regarding average product lives and analysis of Visean's sales trends to assess the useful economic life of the brands

(b) **Discontinued operation**

Matters

(i) *Risk*

There is a risk that results relating to the factory are disclosed incorrectly ie continuing/discontinuing. There is also a risk that costs surrounding the closure are inappropriately provided for.

(ii) *Materiality*

Although the results of the factory are not specifically provided the disclosure (or not) of this information as a discontinued activity is likely to have a material effect on the accounts.

The provisions represent 68.3% of the profit before tax and are therefore material to the accounts.

(iii) *Accounting treatment*

- Whether the plans to discontinue medical consumables constitute a discontinued operation. This depends on whether:

  – It meets the criteria to be classified as 'held for sale' in accordance with IFRS 5
  – Represents a separate major line of business
  – Is part of a single co-ordinated plan to dispose of a separate major line of business

- Assuming the plans constitute a discontinued operation whether disclosures are adequate. As a minimum the income statement should show as a single figure:

    - The post-tax profit or loss of the discontinued operation

    - The post-tax gain or loss on remeasurement of assets classified as held for sale or on disposal.

- An analysis of the above amounts should be shown as follows:

    - Revenue, expenses and pre-tax profit or loss

    - Income tax expense

    - Gain or loss recognised on the measurement to fair value less costs to sell or on the disposal of the assets

    - Net cash flows by category

- Whether related assets need to be classified as held for sale, for example the factory. These would be disclosed in aggregate as a separate line item within current assets. This will depend on whether the following criteria are met:

    - Available for immediate sale in their present condition
    - Management are committed to the plan to sell
    - An active programme to locate a buyer has been initiated
    - Assets are being actively marketed for sale at a reasonable price
    - They are expected to be sold within one year of classification
    - It is unlikely that significant changes will be made to the plan.

- Whether any assets 'held for sale' have been valued correctly.

- Non-current assets should be valued at the lower of their carrying amount and fair value less costs to sell.

- Whether provisions for redundancy costs and the unexpired lease term should be recognised.

- In accordance with IAS 37 a provision should only be recognised if a constructive obligation exists.

- The company does seem to have a detailed and formal plan and by making the announcement in December is likely to have raised a valid expectation that the restructuring will occur.

- Whether the costs provided for are allowed.

    A restructuring provision should include only those directly arising from the restructuring and not associated with ongoing activities. The redundancy costs (excluding any retraining or relocation of continuing staff) and obligations under the onerous contract appear to meet those criteria.

- Impact on Visean's relationship with hospitals.

    Visean may lose the hospitals completely as a customer if they no longer supply medical consumables. The extent of the impact will depend on the nature and amount of any other sales.

    Visean may be liable to penalties if the cessation of supply constitutes a breach of contract.

Evidence

- Board minutes approving the closure of the factory and the decision to discontinue the medical consumables range

- Copy of the announcement made to the press/employees/customers

- Segmental analysis to support the contention that medical consumables represent an identifiable market

- Schedule/accounts showing disclosure of the medical consumables operation as discontinued and assets as 'held for sale'

- Details of the values attributed to assets 'held for sale' and the basis on which those valuations have been made

- Ledger accounts/budgets and prior year accounts for comparison with separate disclosure in the current period

- Documentation supporting a detailed and formal plan for closure

- Schedule showing the calculation of the provisions including a breakdown of the nature of the costs (eg redundancy or training) and any assumptions made

- Employment contracts for agreement of redundancy terms

- Factory lease and any correspondence with the lessor for confirmation of the penalty for surrendering the lease

- Sales agreements for plant and equipment entered into post year-end to determine impairment of assets

- Contracts with hospitals and other suppliers to determine the extent of any other penalty clauses

(c) **Cash flow statement**

Matters

(i) *Accounting treatment*

Whether Visean can report net cash flows from operating activities using the **indirect method**.

Under IAS 7 operating cash flows can be shown either under the direct method or the indirect method. Although the direct method is encouraged by IAS 7 it is not a requirement. Visean can **adopt either method** therefore and the change from one method to the other does not contravene IAS 7.

(ii) *Whether the comparative figures should have been restated*

These figures are used for comparison purposes and as such they need to be prepared on a consistent basis with the current year's figures. In accordance with IAS 8, where a change in policy is voluntary it should be applied retrospectively. The auditor has a responsibility to ensure that if comparatives have been adjusted this is properly disclosed. Provided this is the case the treatment is acceptable.

(iii) *Potential impact on the audit report*

Although they form part of the financial statements the auditor does not specifically express an opinion on the comparatives. Even though in this case they have been restated, provided that this has been done correctly and disclosed adequately, no reference would be made to this in the audit report.

Evidence

- Agreement of figures in revised comparative cash flow to previous years financial statements. (Even though the presentation of cash flows from operating activities will have changed, ultimately the final result should be the same.)

- Schedule of cash received from customers agreed to receivables ledger control account

- Schedule of cash paid to suppliers agreed to payables ledger control account

- Schedule of payments to employees agreed to payroll control account

- Analysis of any other cash payments

28 Siegler

Text reference. Chapter 10

Top tips. For part (a) matters will cover the issues of risk, materiality and accounting treatment. There is a heavy emphasis on accounting knowledge. Make sure you deal with all aspects of the information. There is often more than one accounting problem in each part of the question.

For part (b) it is essential that you make your points as specific as possible. Generalities will score few marks.

It would be possible to present your answer in a two column format. In this case if you choose to do so you need to take care as there is not always a corresponding piece of evidence for each matter raised.

Examiner's comments. Mistakes were made in part (a) due to poor accounting knowledge. For example, few knew how to deal with the repayment of the grant, and many stated that a provision for clean up costs would be allowed if future legislation was expected. Part (c) was poorly answered with many concentrating on the issue of leasing even though it was clearly stated that the buildings were owned.

Audit evidence in part (b) was generally poor. Statements such as 'see board minutes', 'discuss with management' and 'perform analytical procedures' earn no marks.

Marking scheme

		Marks
(i)	**Matters**	
	Generally 1 mark each comment	
	Maximum 6 marks issues (1) 4 marks issues (2) and (3)	Max 12
	Ideas	
	• Materiality (assessed)	
	• Relevant IASs (eg 10, 16, 20, 36, 37, 38, 40)	
	• Risks (eg FS assertion)	
	• Responsibilities (eg directors' – to carry out impairment reviews)	
	• Implications for auditor's report	
(ii)	**Audit evidence**	
	Generally 1 mark each item of audit evidence (source)	Max 12
	Maximum 6 marks issue (1) 4 marks issues (2) & (3)	
	Ideas	
	• Oral vs written	
	• Internal vs external	
	• Auditor generated	
	• Procedures (relevant, reliable, sufficient)	

		Marks
		Max 20
	(1)	Max 8
	(2)	Max 6
	(3)	Max 6
		20

(a) **Matters**

Government grant

There is a risk that the grant has been accounted for incorrectly leading to an **understatement of intangible assets**. There is also a risk that the grant is repayable.

The grant is material as it represents 17.4% of profit before tax, 1.7% of total assets and 17.8% of intangible assets.

The accounting treatment of the grant

This depends on the following:

- Whether the conditions for receipt have been met
- Whether the grant relates to capital expenditure
- Whether the grant relates to revenue expenditure

Assuming that the grant conditions have been met any grant received in respect of assets may be presented as **deferred income** in the balance sheet or deducted in arriving at the carrying value of the asset. If the grant relates to income it should be recognised in the income statement.

Why the order for specialist equipment has been cancelled

This may result in **penalties** if cancelled by Siegler. Alternatively there may be a possibility of making a claim against the supplier.

Potential repayment of the grant

There is a suggestion that the new pilot plant may not continue. If this is the case the conditions for the receipt of the grant may cease to be met. Any amount repayable should be added back to the development costs (assuming it was deducted from these in the first place) and a matching liability recognised, i.e., the repayment is treated as a revision of an accounting estimate.

Impairment of intangibles

The change in focus to 'smart-drug' technology may indicate that intangibles relating to other projects may be impaired. This will be the case if the recoverable amount is below book value.

Provision

There is a risk that liabilities are overstated by $1m if a provision is recognised inappropriately.

There is a risk that tangible assets are overstated if the value of the land does not take into account the effects of the contamination.

The provision represents 21.7% of profit before tax and 2.2% of total assets. It is therefore material.

The land represents 1.6% of profit before tax and 0.15% of total assets. Therefore even if it were to be written down to zero the effect would not be material.

Recognition of the provision

A provision should only be recognised if there is a **legal or constructive obligation**. In this case there is no legal requirement to clean up the site. A constructive obligation would exist if for example the company had a widely publicised environmental policy and it had a record of honouring this policy. On the basis that nothing has been done about the contamination for the last four years this does not seem likely (assuming that management were aware of the problem).

The reasons for the closure four years ago

If it could be demonstrated that the management were aware of the contamination at this stage this would be an indicator that a constructive obligation does not exist (see above).

The basis on which the $1m has been calculated

This may be a management estimate or may be based on expert advice. The source of the information will affect its reliability.

What instigated the local water authority investigation

This may determine whether there are to be any additional consequences of the contamination, for example, the incurring of any fines.

Investment properties

There is a risk that profits are overstated if the investment properties are inappropriately accounted for.

The $3.3 million surplus represents 7.1% of total assets and 71.7% of profit before tax. On this basis it is material.

- Whether the revaluation is appropriate under IAS 16

  IAS 16 does allow items of property to be revalued and for the **revaluation surpluses to be credited to the revaluation surplus**. If this treatment is to be adopted it should be applied consistently to all assets within the same class. The issue here is the nature of the apartment block. It appears to be an investment property as it is being held in order to earn rentals. As such it should be accounted for under IAS 40. Initially the property would be held at cost. Subsequently it can be valued using the fair value model or the cost model (the benchmark treatment under IAS 16). All investment properties have to be treated on the same basis which would mean that the office block should also be revalued in spite of the fact that it is likely to have suffered an impairment.

- Under IAS 40 all gains and losses should be recognised in the net profit for the period

  It appears that this is the first year that the fair value model has been applied. If fair value information has previously been disclosed the entity should adjust the opening balance of retained earnings and restate the comparatives.

  If the entity has not previously disclosed fair value information comparatives will not be restated.

(b) **Evidence**

Government grant

- The grant application and/or the grant contract
- The terms and conditions should be reviewed to determine in particular the basis on which the money is granted and the circumstances under which any repayment would be required
- Documentation accompanying actual receipt of the $800,000 to confirm that cash was received and that the amount is correctly stated
- Paying-in documentation showing that the cash has been banked and the account into which it has been paid
- Correspondence from the government agency relating to the grant
- This might indicate the company's ongoing ability to satisfy the grant conditions and any requests for repayment
- Any legal advice on the possibility that the grant may need to be repaid
- Post year-end review of the cash book to determine whether any amounts have been paid back to the government in respect of the grant
- Correspondence between Siegler and the specialist equipment supplier to determine whether any penalties/claims are likely
- Management representations regarding the future focus of the business

Provision

- Copy of the report and conclusions of the water authority to determine that the land is in fact contaminated and the extent of the problem
- Any correspondence between Siegler and the water authority regarding any consequences of the report
- Minutes of discussions with management about their decision to close the laboratories and their knowledge or otherwise of the contamination at that time

- Documents providing evidence of historical environmental policies, for example in the annual report

- Any estimates received from contractors regarding the cost of the clean up/contracts evidencing that the clean up has actually started

- Board minutes approving the clean up

- Written representations from management confirming that the clean up will be undertaken

Investment properties

- Notes of discussions with management regarding the reason behind the decision to revalue properties

- Copy of the valuation report looking in particular at the basis of the valuations and any assumptions made

- Results of the assessment of the reliability of the report ie qualifications, experience, independence

- Confirmation of investment property status of the office block by inspection

- Details of any office lets which are due to come into force. This will assist in determining the extent of the problem regarding the office block and therefore whether it is impaired.

29 Vema

Text references. Chapters 8 and 11

Top tips. Questions like this break down in practice into six sections of three or four marks each, which makes them more straightforward than they sometimes appear. If you feel that you can't do one section, don't panic, do the other five as far as you are able. However, see the comments under easy marks below, to ensure that you should get some simple marks everytime. For each section, jot down the relevant IFRS for each accounting issue. Then, using your accounting knowledge try and work out whether the items have been accounted for correctly, and (importantly) what the implications for the auditor are if they have not. Always try and list some examples of audit evidence in part (ii) for each question, even if you are not sure about the accounting issues at stake. Use the audit evidence criteria in ISA 500 to inspire you - audit procedures such as observation, inquiry, confirmation, computations and analytical procedures. Make the audit evidence specific – and remember to describe the piece of evidence, not the test or procedure. Don't say, 'test depreciation', say 'reperformance of the depreciation calculations based on 25% of the opening position and on additions to non-current assets in the year.'

Easy marks. You can get easy marks by calculating materiality and commenting in each part (i) whether the matters are material or not to the financial statement they affect. Calculating materiality is a straightforward auditing skill that you should know from your earlier studies. Listing straightforward audit evidence (as discussed above) should also gain you easy marks.

Examiner's comments. In part (i), it is recommended that candidates do not list questions (eg 'Is the accounting treatment correct?', 'Who is Mr Z?'). These are merely the matters to consider. The question asks for comment on these matters. For part (a), many candidates wrote extensively on changes in accounting policy – however, the change in depreciation method (rate and/or method) is the classic example of a change in accounting estimate.

Part (b) was not attempted by some. Most failed to recognise that the redundancy arose in the prior year and that a liability for the termination payment should have been previously recognised. Better candidates suggested that a prior period adjustment might be required. Too many candidates incorrectly supposed that, for example:

- A journal entry amounts to fraud
- Salary deductions can only be processed through a payroll
- Charging an amount to administrative expenses and disclosing it are mutually exclusive

Part (c) was better answered, although many candidates failed to assess materiality in terms of the parent company as well as the subsidiary and did not assess the $1.1m costs and damages in relation to group profit. Many candidates did not conclude on the necessity of a provision for $1.1m, giving equal weight to the court order and the appeal and allowing the latter to render the former ineffective.

Part (ii) on audit evidence is still poorly answered. Statements such as 'check compliance with (unspecified) accounting standards', 'perform analytical procedures', 'see board minutes', 'obtain management representation', 'discuss with management' – earn no marks at this level. Many candidates continue to write that evidence would be 'evidence of...' or 'documentation on...' demonstrating no knowledge of what that evidence or documentation might be.

In part (a), many candidates wanted to inspect purchase invoices rather than the non-current assets register. 'Autopilot' considerations of ownership ('check vehicle registration documents') and existence ('inspect assets') unrelated to the main issue (subsequent measurement) earned no marks. Candidates must understand the sufficiency and appropriateness of evidence which comes from prior year working papers and that 'ask management...' is not found on a review of audit working papers.

Marking scheme

		Marks
(i)	**Matters** Generally 1 mark each comment maximum 5 marks each issue × 3 *Ideas* • Materiality (assessed) • Relevant IASs (eg 1, 8, 10, 16, 24, 37) and the framework • Risks (eg FS assertions – existence, completeness) • Responsibilities (eg for consolidated financial statements)	Max 12
(ii)	**Audit evidence** Generally 1 mark each item of audit evidence (source) maximum 5 marks each issue × 3 *Ideas* • Oral vs written • Internal vs external • Auditor generated • Procedures (analytical procedures, enquiry, inspection, observation and computation)	Max 12

	Max 20
(1)	Max 8
(2)	Max 6
(3)	Max 6
	20

(a) **Depreciation**

(i) *Matters to consider*

(1) **Materiality**. At 4.3% of total assets, the accumulated depreciation added back to assets is material. In addition, at 10% of profit before taxation, the difference between the methods of depreciation is material to the income statement.

(2) **Accounting issues**. The accounting provisions of IAS 16 *Property, plant and equipment* must be considered to ensure that the depreciation is correctly charged and any adjustments resulting from the change in method are also correctly carried out.

Depreciation is the measure of cost or revalued amount of the economic benefits of the tangible non current asset that have been consumed during the period. According to IAS 16, this should 'reflect the pattern in which the asset's future economic benefits are expected to be consumed by the entity'.

IAS 16 requires entities to review the depreciation method applied to an asset at least at every financial year end and requires a **change in method** of depreciation for a class of assets if there has been a significant change.

As Vema's operational policy with regard to replacing fleet vehicles appears to have changed from replacement every three years to replacement when necessary, it is **necessary to change** the method of depreciation. The reducing balance method more closely represents the wearing out of an asset than straight-line depreciation, and the policy is now to replace vehicles when they wear out which tends to be between 4-7 years. The **new policy** therefore appears **reasonable**.

However, such a change in depreciation **does not represent a change in accounting policy but a change in accounting estimates.** The correct treatment according to IAS 8 is to apply the new method to the carrying value at the date of change. Therefore, the fact that Vema has **added back accumulated depreciation** of $4.7 million is **incorrect** and means that the **balance sheet is overstated**. In addition, this means that the **depreciation charge** in the income statement will be **overstated**, which at 25% of $4.7 million is arguably material as well.

The adjustment relating to accumulated depreciation should be reversed and depreciation for the year charged on the carrying value at the start of the year. If this is not done, the audit opinion should be qualified, based on disagreement over IASs 8 and 16.

(ii) *Audit evidence*

- Opening position in non-current assets agreed to prior year audit files
- Minutes of directors' meetings reviewed for evidence of new policy with regard to the fleet
- A proof in total calculation on depreciation (25% of NBV at start of year + 25% of additions)
- Review of fleet vehicles sold in the year to ensure that the sales conformed with the new policy (ie the HGVs were 4-7 years old)
- Scrutiny of disposals of vehicles in previous years (if new policy is reasonable, sales should consistently have resulted in profits)

(b) **Journal adjustment**

(i) *Matters to consider*

(1) **Materiality**. At approximately 6% of profit before tax, the charge to administrative expenses is material. The balance sheet elements are not material to the balance sheet, but it is a substantial cash payment in respect of a director, so it is likely to be material by nature anyway.

(2) **Disclosures**. It is possible that compensation to a director should be disclosed in the financial statements as required by law depending on Vema's jurisdiction. However, importantly, as a former director, Mr Z is likely to be a related party to the company and this payment requires disclosure under IAS 24. In addition, due to its materiality, this payment to Mr Z is an exceptional item and requires separate disclosure in the notes for that purpose.

(3) **Use of journal**. It is not inappropriate to use a journal entry to record an unusual transaction such as this, particularly since the former director has been taken off the payroll and the usual channels for payments to staff cannot be used. It is also possible that the transaction was entered by a senior accountant and that there is a degree of secrecy involved from lower level staff. The auditor is required by ISA 330 *The auditor's procedures in response to assessed risks* requires auditors to examine material journal entries and this would certainly qualify for that examination.

(4) **Timing**. The year-end is September 2007 and the director left in July 2006. The payment was made in December 2006. If the previous year's audit had not yet been completed at that date, the payment would have been an event after the balance sheet date. The event would have given further evidence that an obligation existed as at 30 September 2006 and that a transfer of benefits was probable. A provision should have been included for it. If this was not the case, then it might be necessary to restate opening reserves as a prior period adjustment in

the financial statements for the year ended 30 September 2007 if the effect was believed to be fundamental.

(5) **Other liabilities**. It seems likely that the other liabilities comprise tax relating to the payment, in which case a payment should subsequently have been made, and a liability should not be included in the balance sheet for this amount. If a liability remains, it should be investigated to see whether it is an outstanding payment to the director (which would require further disclosure) and whether tax was paid on the compensation should be checked as this might also require a provision.

(ii) *Audit evidence*

- Copies of working papers from prior year file reviewed for details of redundancies and whether this payment was included in prior year financial statements

- Payment agreed to bank statement

- A review of other liabilities to see if the $194,000 is outstanding/check payment to tax documentation if not

- Minutes of directors meetings and notes of discussions with finance director to obtain fuller details about the payment

- A copy of Mr Z's contract to ensure that payment was reasonable/there are no further liabilities

- Written management representations that there are no other outstanding payments in respect of redundancies

(c) **Weddell**

(i) *Matters to consider*

(1) **Materiality**. Although the Weddell's profits are not material to Vema, at 31% of total assets for the group, Weddell is material to Vema's consolidated accounts. Within Weddell's accounts the provision for the costs, were it to be adjusted would not be material to the balance sheet. However, $1.1 million is material to the income statement as it would turn a profit into a loss. In consolidated financial statements, at 8.8% of profit before tax, a provision for these costs would be material to Vema.

(2) **Provision required?** IAS 37 requires a provision to be included for items when there is a present obligation as a result of a past event, in respect of which it is probable that a transfer of economic benefit will be made when there is a reliable estimate of the relevant amount. In this case, Weddell currently has a legal obligation, and although the decision is being appealed, it is therefore probable that this amount should be provided for. The fact that the decision is being appealed should be disclosed as a post balance sheet event.

(3) **Adjustment**. As Vema controls Weddell, Vema's directors could impel Weddell's directors to make an adjustment to include the provision for the costs. If the directors refuse, then the auditors of Weddell should qualify their opinion on the individual group accounts. Although Vema's auditors cannot insist that they do so, failure by the auditors to do so would cast doubt on the audit evidence provided by the auditors of Weddell and the auditors of Vema should reconsider their reliance on the audit of Weddell.

(4) **Vema's position**. If Weddell do not make an adjustment, Vema should adjust the group accounts in respect of this provision or the audit opinion for the group accounts would need to be qualified on the grounds of disagreement in respect of IAS 37.

(ii) *Audit evidence*

- Details of the legal judgement

- A copy of the appeal lodged at court

- Correspondence with legal advisors regarding the likely outcome of appeal
- The audit report on Weddell/any correspondence or conversations with Weddell's auditors on this matter/the audit questionnaire etc from Weddell's auditors

30 Volcan

Text reference. Chapter 10

Top tips. Some of the elements of this question are tricky, but it is always best to attempt all the parts. Do not read through one and leave it out. Try and boil all the information you are given down to simple accounting basics – for instance, in part (b), associated with the original sale which gives rise to store points is the fact that the company incurs a liability (to pay a future discount). The basic principal of matching means that the discount and the liability must be associated with the original sale. In terms of audit evidence, remember that the reward point system must have resulted in changed systems and procedures which the auditor will want to document and test (audit evidence). In part (a), do not get bogged down trying to explain the intricacies of IFRS 3. You have to state what you would consider, not necessarily explain all the detail of what that consideration would entail. In this answer, it is sufficient to observe that the goodwill and asset may have been impaired, without going into enormous detail about the impairment reviews that should have been carried out. In part (c), use the detail given to you about Volcan's failure to care for the trees on the site to lead your thoughts about how likely site restoration is and whether a provision is actually required.

Easy marks. You can get easy marks for calculating materiality (in a focused and relevant fashion) and by explaining the requirements of relevant auditing standards.

Marking scheme

		Marks
(i)	**Matters**	Max 12
	Generally 1 mark each comment	
	max 6 marks each issue × 3	
	Ideas	
	• materiality (assessed)	
	• relevant IASs (eg 10, 16, 18, 36, 38, IFRS 3) and 'The Framework'	
	• risks (eg FS assertions – capital vs revenue, existence)	
	• responsibilities (eg environmental)	
(ii)	**Audit evidence**	Max 12
	Generally 1 mark each item of audit evidence (source)	
	Max 6 marks each issue × 3	
	Ideas (ISA 500)	
	• oral vs written	
	• internal vs external	
	• auditor generated	
	• procedures	
		Max 20
	(a)	Max 7
	(b)	Max 6
	(c)	Max 7
		20

(a) **Store downsize**

(i) *Matters to consider*

- The decision to downsize is a non adjusting post balance sheet event which must be disclosed in the financial statements for the year-end 30 September 2007.

- The decision may be an indication of impairment in the asset of the store and also in the associated goodwill.

- The carrying value of goodwill ($2.2 million) is not material to the balance sheet, but at 23% of the profit before tax it is material to the income statement were it to be written off (NB, under IFRS 3 Volcan should no longer be amortising goodwill, but testing it for impairment at least annually).

- However, the goodwill relates to three stores. It may not be possible to attribute any part of the goodwill to any one store and the portion relating to this store may not be impaired anyway (a city metro is still benefiting from the benefits of the associated goodwill of trade name, position etc).

- It is unclear whether the asset of the store itself is material, but as the associated goodwill is material to the income statement, it is likely that any impairment to the associated store asset would be as well.

- Management should have carried out impairment tests to ascertain whether these assets are impaired.

- Management should also have considered whether any of the other stores in Urvina are affected by similar problems and are therefore impaired.

- Lastly, if the problem identified in Urvina is more widespread there could be a going concern issue for the whole company. Management should have considered if the problem is limited to this one store or even stores beyond Urvina.

(ii) *Audit evidence*

- Records of the decision to downsize Urvina (minutes of management meetings/press releases)
- Management's impairment review
- Recalculation of asset carrying values (goodwill and value in use of the store)
- Physical inspection of closed store (to verify that it is indeed closed for refurbishment)
- Management's record of their going concern review

(b) **Reward scheme**

(i) *Matters to consider*

- If the entire revenue for the year attracted reward points, the minimum cost of reward points would be $3.03 million (as additional points can be given for special offers this is likely to be higher) which is 1% of turnover and 32% of profit before tax and is therefore material.

- Due to the high impact on profit, even if reward cards have not been widely adopted by the customers of Volcan, this matter is still likely to be material.

- Volcan incurs a liability to pay a future discount at the time of the first sale, and the expense and liability should be recognised at the time of sale.

- As this discount scheme is similar to a cash discount, sales should be recorded at full price, with discounts being included as an expense in the income statement.

- At the year-end, Volcan will have a liability to pay discounts for points as yet unredeemed in relation to sales for the year. This will not be material to the balance sheet as the whole of the first year expense is not material to the balance sheet.

- Whether store points can be used for any other purpose than obtaining future discounts

- Whether there are any restrictions or time limits on claiming discounts

- The degree to which points awarded are expected not to be claimed

(ii) *Audit evidence*

- Systems documentation giving information about the reward card scheme (how cards are issued, how points are recorded at point of sale, how points are subsequently redeemed)
- Walk-through tests to confirm the system operates as outlined
- Tests of control on how information is translated from point of sale to accounting information
- Analytical review on the number of points issued by store each month (this would be expected to be approximately 1% of turnover) with explanations for differences
- Tests of detail on a sample of transactions including the issue of reward points

(c) **Site restoration**

(i) *Matters to consider*

- The total provision of $4.4 million is material to the balance sheet at 2.5% of total assets.
- There is an overprovision of $0.34 million (provision for the relocation of the trees, less the cost of the fine for destroying the trees) which individually is immaterial to the balance sheet.
- Whether, given that the company commenced work before planning permission was received and cut down trees that were protected by the council, it will consider itself bound by a council requirement to restore the site.
- Whether the council would take serious action against them if they do not (or simply charge them small fines as in the case of the trees)
- IAS 37 only allows a provision to be included if there is:
    - A present obligation as a result of a past event
    - In respect of which it is probable there will be a transfer of economic benefit
    - Which can be estimated reliably
- If the council would not take serious action, then while Volcan may have a legal obligation (to clean up) as a result of a past event (the building work), the second requirement of IAS 37 for a provision is not met, as it is improbable that there will be a transfer of economic benefits to meet that obligation.

(ii) *Audit evidence*

- A copy of the planning application and the planning permission
- A copy of correspondence setting out the penalties for the felled trees
- Recalculation of the provision of $4.4 million
- Inspection of the asset (site) at the year-end
- Any contracts or documentation which might provide evidence of management's intention with regard to site restoration (building contracts/contracts with landscape gardeners etc)

31 Question with analysis: Eagle Energy

Text references. Chapters 8 and 10

Top tips. You should focus on materiality and the relevant accounting guidance. Remember to try and state the implications for the audit report if you feel that things have not been accounted for correctly, especially, as in this question, if the question tells you something like 'the Chief Executive is adamant that this item should be accounted for as an asset' and yet you feel that the treatment is incorrect.

Easy marks. Some easy marks can be obtained in this question for identifying basic audit tests (for example, checking costs of training back to invoices).

In part (a), many candidates regurgitated irrelevant recognition criteria from IAS 38 and many candidates seemed to take the view that the auditor must find some way of agreeing with management. Only a minority exercised any degree of professional scepticism and commented that the write-off would nearly decimate profit as compared with the prior year. Better candidates demonstrated their understanding of the key issue. On the matter of evidence, some candidates did not mention the most basic source of evidence - namely invoices.

In part (b), many candidates took the word 'grant' and dealt irrelevantly with IAS 20. Most candidates failed to recognise that it was not the granting of the land which gave rise to the need for a provision but the assembly of the laboratory during the year. Many candidates agreed with the pre-IAS 37 approach to provisioning. Few candidates saw the provision as being made now for 2023 (ie in 15 years time) and there was much irrelevant discussion of overprovision being made ($25 \times 1.2 = 30m$) when the principal issue was that the full amount needed to be capitalised now.

In part (c), many candidates demonstrated little, if any, professional scepticism for these journal entries with 'hallmarks' of suspicion.

Marking scheme

		Marks
(i)	**Matters**	
	Generally 1 mark each comment maximum 5 marks each issue × 3	Max 12
	Ideas	
	• Materiality (assessed)	
	• Relevant IASs (eg 16, 37, 38) & 'The Framework'	
	• Substance of matter/management's intention	
	• Risks (eg FS assertions – existence, completeness)	
	• Adjustment required	
	• Overall conclusion	
(ii)	**Audit evidence**	
	Generally 1 mark each item of audit evidence (source) maximum 5 marks each issue × 3	Max 12
	Ideas	
	• Oral vs written	
	• Internal vs external	
	• Auditor generated	
	• Procedures (analytical procedures, enquiry, inspection, observation and computation)	
		Max 20
	(1)	Max 7
	(2)	Max 7
	(3)	Max 6
		20

(a) **Intangible asset**

(i) *Matters to consider*

- At $4.3 million, the proposed intangible asset is not material to the balance sheet, but if it were written off as an expense for the year it would be material to the income statement as it would reduce profit by 60%, to $2.9 million.

- Generally speaking, an intangible asset is an identifiable monetary non current asset without physical substance but which is identifiable and is controlled by the entity through custody or legal rights.

- IAS 38 states that an internally generated intangible asset which meets certain criteria such as control and identifiability should be capitalised.

- Eagle Energy does not have control over the supposed asset, as it is training invested in its employees, which the company does not own. Therefore, any one of these trained staff could leave Eagle Energy and take that skill to a different company.

- The training given to Eagle Energy's own employees does not have a readily ascertainable market value. It cannot, as such, be sold on to a different company unless Eagle Energy itself was sold, in which case any staff skill would be included in the value of goodwill created by the sale.

- Therefore, it is not appropriate to capitalise the expense, which should be written off through the income statement.

- However, the details of what the cost comprises should be scrutinised. It is possible that some elements of it could be capitalised (for example if it relates to manuals now owned by the company).

- If the chief executive will not amend the accounts to expense this item then the auditors would have to qualify their audit report on the grounds of disagreement over accounting treatment.

(ii) *Audit evidence*

- A breakdown of what the $4.3 million comprises

- A sample of individual costs checked back to related invoices

- An inspection of any elements of the cost which can be classified as assets (for example, manuals)

- A review of the terms of the contracts with the staff to confirm that the company does not have sufficient control over the technical knowledge

- A review of leavers to support arguments to the Chief Executive that the 'asset' is not controlled by the company

(b) **Laboratory and provision**

(i) *Matters to consider*

- According to IAS 37, where an entity has a present obligation as a result of a past event which is probable to result in the transfer of economic benefit which can be reliably estimated, then a provision should be made.

- Such a provision should be the best estimate of the expenditure required to settle the present obligation at the balance sheet date. Where the effect of the time value of money is material, the amount of this provision should be the present value of the expenditures required to settle the obligation.

- Eagle Energy should recognise the full provision of $18 million in the balance sheet, as they have a present obligation as a result of a past event (accepting the government grant that was subject to the condition of clean up).

- $18 million is material to the balance sheet.

- The effect of the time value of money is likely not to be material so it is appropriate to make provision for $18 million.

- The cost of dismantling the site is a direct cost of the asset and should be included in the value of the asset, according to the rules of IAS 16.

- Whether the company has estimated the cost themselves or it has been done by an external expert.

(ii) *Audit evidence*

- Details of the terms of the grant from the council (likely to be on the permanent audit file)
- Details of the projected cost of clean up (report by an external expert?)
- Inspection of the building to ensure it has been built, causing the present obligation

(c) **Journal entry**

(i) *Matters to consider*

- Auditors are required by ISA 330 *The auditor's procedures in response to assessed risks* to scrutinise journal entries.

- Auditors are required to exercise professional skepticism and be alert to instances of fraud.

- The net impact of the journal entry is not material.

- However, the issue might be material by nature, and should be investigated.

- The journal is made between two odd accounts and is made solely to present the figures in a better light.

- This is fraudulent financial reporting being done to deliberately mislead the government about whether Eagle Energy is meeting the debt ratio requirements.

- The fact that the journal is carried out by the Chief Executive and is fraudulent financial reporting raises questions about the integrity of the management of the company which might have wider implications for the audit.

- As a minimum, the auditors should consider whether this indicates they should not trust representations made to them by the Chief Executive during the course of the audit.

- In addition, auditors should consider the effect on the general inherent risk of the audit.

- They should consider the likelihood of any potential liability to the government if they are aware the government relies on audited accounts and the need to disclaim such liability.

(ii) *Audit evidence*

- The terms of the funding from government sources

- The management accounts

- A copy of all the journals made to assess the effect of each journal

- Recalculation of the debt ratios monthly to assess whether the requirement was met or not

- Review of prior year files to see how the matter was addressed

- Management representations that there have been no other similar transactions which have not been brought to the attention of the auditor

32 Keffler

Text references. Chapters 8 and 10

Top tips. In this question you need to comment on matters to consider and state the audit evidence you would expect to find in three situations. Take each case in turn and deal with it separately, making sure that you answer both requirements for each. For the matters to consider make sure that you discuss both materiality and accounting treatment for each scenario. Note the mark allocation for each case – (a) is worth nine marks, so that's almost half of your time allocation for this question.

Easy marks. You need to remember your financial reporting studies here but don't panic. Take each case in turn and think about the scenario before writing down everything you know. You should be able to score reasonably well if you adopt a methodical approach and relate your answer to the information in the scenario.

Examiner's comments. Tabulation is not recommended for a question of this type since there is no relationship between materiality (a matter) and audit evidence. Using a table format to answer the question results in irrelevant or vague audit evidence. In part (i) on matters to consider, candidates must begin with an assessment of materiality by calculating relevant percentages. More candidates appeared to be interpreting materiality correctly which was encouraging although there were many assessments on revenue that were not appropriate. Lists of questions are discouraged because the requirement is to comment on the matters to consider, not just to list them. In part (ii) on evidence, candidates must make sure that what they state here would be found documented in the audit working papers and financial statements – audit evidence is not the same as audit work, therefore answers stating 'discuss' and 'ask' would not score any marks since they do not answer the question set.

Marking scheme

		Marks
(i)	**Matters**	
	Generally 1 mark each comment maximum 6 marks each issue × 3	Max 14
	Ideas	
	• Materiality (appropriately assessed)	
	• Relevant IASs (eg 1, 8, 10, 16, 24, 36, 37, 38)	
	• Fundamental concepts (accruals/prudence)	
	• Risks (eg valuation/existence/disclosure)	
	• Responsibilities (eg environmental)	
(ii)	**Audit evidence**	
	Generally 1 mark each item of audit evidence (source) maximum 6 marks each issue × 3	Max 14
	Ideas (ISA 500)	
	• Oral vs written	
	• Internal vs external	
	• Auditor-generated	
	• Procedures	
		Max 20
	(a)	Max 9
	(b)	Max 6
	(c)	Max 5
		20

(a) **Landfill site**

(i) *Matters to consider*

- The purchase of the right to use the landfill site represents 3.3% of total assets and is therefore material to the balance sheet.

- The amortisation should be charged over the period during which the site will be used, i.e. 10 years rather than 15 years. The charge of $20,000 for the year has been based on 10 years (the sum of digits is 55 so the first year's charge will be $1/55 \times 1.1m = \$20k$). The charge for the year represents 1% of profit before tax and so is not material.

- The sum of digits method has been chosen on the basis that the company has estimated that the amount of waste dumped will increase each year and this method charges higher amortisation each year. IAS 38 *Intangible assets* states that the straight line method should be used if the pattern of future economic benefits of the right cannot be determined reliably. A straight line method would charge $110k of amortisation to the income statement – the difference of $90k represents 4.5% of profit before tax so is just below materiality, but the cumulative effect would be material.

- If there is no evidence to support Keffler's expectations of the amounts of waste to be dumped each year, the accounts should be qualified on the basis of disagreement.

- The annual provision for restoring the site represents 5% of profit before tax and 0.3% of total assets so is bordering on material. However annual provisioning is not permitted by IAS 37 *Provisions, contingent liabilities and contingent assets* so the provision should be based on the best estimate of the total costs required to restore the site at the balance sheet date. Therefore the present value of the total costs should have been recognised as a provision in the financial statements. This would be added to the cost of the right to use the landfill site. This will in turn affect the amortisation charge.

(ii) *Audit evidence*

- Agreement document to confirm date of purchase of right to use landfill site for 15 years and price paid and terms of the agreement

- Confirmation of amount paid to cash book and bank statements

- Calculation schedule for depreciation using sum of digits method

- Costs schedules showing estimated costs to restore the land in 15 years time

- Senior management board minutes regarding the purchase of the right

- Physical inspection of the landfill site to confirm its use to dump waste

- Schedule showing estimated waste to be dumped each year compared to pattern of sum of digits depreciation

(b) **Sale of industrial machinery**

(i) *Matters to consider*

- The machinery was being depreciated over 20 years on straight line basis (i.e. a charge of $60,000 per year assuming a full year's charge in the year of acquisition and no charge in the year of disposal) therefore its net book value at the start of the financial year would have been $660k. A loss of $0.3m means that the proceeds from the sale were $360k.

- The loss of $0.3m represents 15% of the profit before tax and 0.6% of revenue so is material to the financial statements.

- The loss has been separately disclosed on the face of the income statement. This is in accordance with IAS 16 *Property, plant and equipment* and also with IAS 1 *Presentation of financial statements* which states that material profits or losses on disposal should be presented separately either on the face of the income statement or in the notes.

- The reason for the sale needs to be established and also the reason for the loss. Originally the machinery was being depreciated over 20 years. It may be that this estimate of useful life was incorrect and there may be other similar machinery in the accounts which would result in assets being overstated because they are being depreciated over a period longer than their actual useful lives.

- If the sale has been made to a related party, this needs to be disclosed in the accounts in accordance with IAS 24 *Related party disclosures*.

- The machinery was sold two months into the financial year. It may therefore have been identified as a non-adjusting post balance sheet event in the previous financial year in accordance with IAS 10 *Events after the balance sheet date* in which case it should have been disclosed in those accounts. If it had been impaired at the end of the prior financial year, a prior period adjustment would be required in accordance with IAS 8 *Accounting policies, changes in accounting estimates and errors*. The loss would have been material in the prior year as it represents 12.5% of the profit in that year and 0.7% of revenue.

(ii) *Audit evidence*

- Authority for the sale to Deakin in senior management board minutes

- Cash receipt on sale confirmed in the bank statements and the cash book

- Sales invoice to Deakin for the asset

- Schedule to calculate the profit or loss arising on disposal

- Non-current asset register showing cost and accumulated depreciation removed on disposal

- Prior year post balance sheet events review

- Management representation letter point to confirm that Deakin is not a related party of the company

(c) **Provision**

(i) *Matters to consider*

- The provision represents 45% of profit before tax, 1.9% of revenue and 2.7% of total assets and is therefore clearly material to the financial statements.

- The provision for the penalties is not material, since it represents only 2.3% of profit before tax and 0.13% of total assets.

- According to IAS 37 *Provisions, contingent liabilities and contingent assets* a provision can only be recognised if there is a present obligation as a result of a past event, there will be a probable transfer of economic benefits and the amount can be estimated reliably.

- The penalties meet the requirements for the provision to be recognised but the provision for the water purification system does not meet the first requirement and so should not be recognised in the financial statements for the year.

- Failure to write back the $0.9m provision will result in a qualified audit opinion on the basis of a disagreement since the amount is material to the accounts.

- The need for the upgrade to the water purification system may indicate impairment with the existing system. Any impairment should be recognised in the accounts.

(ii) *Audit evidence*

- Correspondence from the local authority relating to the ban and to confirm the amount of the penalties imposed

- Newspaper and other reports relating to the ban

- After date review of cash book and bank statements to confirm payment of fines

- Estimates from suppliers confirming the cost of the upgrade

- Senior management board minutes relating to the ban and action to be taken

33 Harvard

Text references. Chapters 9 and 10

Top tips. This question looks at three accounting issues. The answer, below, is set out in a more bulleted style than previous answers in the kit. This approach would probably be acceptable. However, you must take great care when using such an approach and ensure that your answers are not so brief that you do not fully explain the matters you are considering. You might prefer to only use it as an approach for the lists of audit evidence that you would seek.

(a) **Chicken Run**

(i) *Matters to consider*

- Whether or not the expenditure incurred on project Chicken Run meets the criteria as specified in IAS 38 for the project to be capitalised as development costs

- Whether or not the expenditure incurred is $1.5 million

- Whether or not the directors have made appropriate disclosure in accordance with IAS 38

- When the vaccine will go into commercial production (that is, might it also be development costs?)

- What the estimated revenue is from the vaccine

- How long the vaccine will be on the market for

(ii) *Audit Tests*

- Obtain details of how Harvard allocates costs to individual projects

- Review the system of cost allocating to projects

- Check that adequate controls are in place to ensure that only separately identifiable costs are allocated to each project

- Obtain an analysis of the $1.5 million and check that costs relate to project Chicken Run

- Vouch materials to invoices

- Vouch labour costs to payroll

- Ascertain how the directors allocate overheads and review method for reasonableness

- Obtain details of project Chicken Run and ascertain that there is a clearly identifiable project

- Obtain details of the results of trials to date and discuss with the project manager to confirm the technical feasibility of the project

- Obtain details of the market research performed to ensure that the project is commercially viable

- Obtain cashflow forecasts and assess assumptions for reasonableness and ascertain whether future inflows will exceed costs to date and future marketing and selling costs

- Review sales forecasts and agree back to market research to confirm reasonableness

- Review the level of funding required to complete the project and discuss with the directors how they intend to meet the funding needs

- Review board minutes for details of discussions on the progress of project Chicken Run

- Obtain management representations as to the commercial viability, technical feasibility and adequacy of funding for project Chicken Run

- Confirm with management that they will meet the disclosure requirements of IAS 38

- Review progress of the project in the post year-end period and review press for any details of any similar products from competitors

(b) **Litigation**

(i) *Matters to Consider*

- Whether or not the directors intend to make a provision in the accounts for the year ended 30 September 2007

- Whether or not a provision of $2.0 million is adequate

- The basis of the calculation of $2.0 million

- Likely date of settlement

- Whether or not $2.0 million would need to be separately disclosed in accordance with IAS 1 in the accounts for the year ended 30 September 2007

- Whether or not the directors will make adequate disclosure in the financial statements

(ii) *Audit Tests*

- Obtain details of the audit work done in respect of the year ended 30 September 2007

- Obtain copies of correspondence from the lawyers on the trial and review for details of likelihood of outcome of the trial and basis of the calculation of $2.0 million

- Discuss with the directors their reaction to the lawyers assessment of outcome of the case and value of the claim

- Obtain permission from the directors to contact the lawyers

- Contact the lawyers and ask for confirmation of their assessment of the outcome and value of the claim

- Recalculate the calculation of $2.0 million

- Review the post year-end period for further correspondence in connection with this claim

- Review the post year-end cash payments to ascertain whether there have been any out of court settlements and compare to the amount provided

- Review board minutes for discussions of the claims and ascertain the directors comments

- Discuss with management if they intend to make a provision in the financial statements for the year ended 30 September 2007

- Ascertain from management the nature of disclosures they intend to make in the accounts for the year ended 30 September 2007

- Confirm that the disclosures meet the requirements of IAS 37 and IAS 1

- Discuss with management whether there are any implications for any other products manufactured by Harvard
- Carry out a post year-end review of all legal correspondence and board minutes to verify whether or not there are further claims in respect of other products

(c) **Brazil operations**

(i) *Matters to consider*

- Whether or not the revenue, results and net assets of the Brazilian entity are material to the financial statements for the year ended 30 September 2007
- If material, whether or not the acquisition meets the definition of a geographical segment as per IAS 14
- Whether or not the directors intend to make the segmental analysis in the financial statements

(ii) *Audit Tests*

- Discuss with directors whether or not they intend to comply with the requirements of IAS 14 given that they are a listed company
- Obtain details of the Brazilian entity's revenue
- Obtain analysis of revenue from external customers and revenue from the home country
- Obtain details of the Brazilian entity's profit before taxation
- Obtain details of the Brazilian entity's net assets

34 Albreda

Text references. Chapters 8 and 9

Top tips. As you are reading through the information, jot down the accounting standards you believe are relevant and note down the matters to consider that arise from them. Think if any ISAs are relevant as well. Always comment on the materiality of matters. Bear in mind the mark allocation as well. In this question, you should have more to say in parts (a) and (b) than in part (c).

Easy marks. Easy marks are available for assessing and stating the materiality of items raised.

Examiner's comments. Setting out the answer to this question in a tabular format is not recommended as there is no relationship between materiality and audit evidence.

In setting out the matters to consider, each one should start with an assessment of materiality. Generating lists of questions is not encouraged – candidates need to provide comments on the matters to consider.

In part (ii), candidates are supposed to think about what they state would be found in the audit working papers and financial statements. Audit evidence is not the same as audit work. Therefore starting the answer with 'discuss', 'ask' etc would not answer the question set.

		Marks

(i) **Matters**
Generally 1 mark each comment maximum 6 marks each issue × 3   Max 12
Ideas
- Materiality (assessed)
- Relevant IFRSs (eg IASs 1, 8, 10, 16, 36, 37 and IFRS 5) & 'The Framework'
- Risks (eg assertions – completeness, measurement)
- All items in a class (vs 'cherry picking')
- Responsibilities (eg socio-environmental)

(ii) **Audit evidence**
Generally 1 mark each item of audit evidence maximum 6 marks each issue × 3   Max 12
Ideas (ISA 500)
- Oral vs written
- Internal vs external
- Auditor generated
- Procedures*

	Max 20
(a)	Max 8
(b)	Max 7
(c)	Max 5
	20

* Inspection, Observation, Inquiry, Confirmation, Recalculation,
Reperformance, Analytical procedures

(a) **Cessation of home-delivery service**

(i) *Matters to consider*

- At 1.4% of revenue, the income from the home delivery services is material to the income statement

- If the home delivery service qualifies as a component of Albreda's business, then the it would qualify as a discontinued operation according to IFRS 5 and discontinued operations disclosures would be necessary in the financial statements (including the comparatives)

- However, in order to be a component, the operations and cash flows would have to be clearly distinguished from the rest of the entity. Operationally, the home delivery service is not clearly distinguished from the rest of operations (it is likely to be carried out by the same chefs in the same kitchens) and so this does not count as a discontinued operation

- The provision for redundancy costs of $0.2 million is material to the income statement as it represents 11.11% of profit before tax

- The auditors should consider the timings associated with the redundancy costs to ensure that the provision meets the criteria of IAS 37, but if the division has completely closed down by 30 September, then there would be a liability arising as a result of a past event, so it appears reasonable

- The provision should have been tested for understatement

- IFRS 5 states that assets should be classified as held for sale if it is highly probable that they will be sold

- Highly probable is suggested by management having a committed plan to sell the assets, which includes plans to locate buyers having been started, active marketing and the expectation that the assets will be sold in a year's time

- The standard also states that assets held for sale should be carried at the lower of the carrying amount and the fair value less costs to sell. In this instance, the company is carrying them at fair value, which is higher than the carrying value

- The difference between the carrying value and the fair value is not material to the balance sheet at just under 1% of total assets

- However, if the credit entry is to the income statement, it is material to the income statement (16.7% of profit) and should be reversed

(ii) *Audit evidence*

- Details of the decision to close the division (board minutes/press notices/communications with employees)

- Management accounts and schedules showing the amount of revenue attributed to home delivery

- Terms of the redundancy packages (contracts of employment for the drivers)

- Proof in total of the reasonableness of the redundancy provision (number of drivers x years employed x payment per year of service)

- Schedule of the delivery vehicles per the non-current asset register

- Details of agreements to market/sell the assets held for sale (sale particulars for instance)

- Any after-date sales proceeds compared to the estimated fair values

- Physical inspection of unsold vehicles (for condition/agreement to sales particulars)

- Separate disclosure of the vehicles in the balance sheet or the notes

(b) **Revaluation**

(i) *Matters to consider*

- IAS 16 states that when assets are revalued, the entire class of those assets must also be revalued

- It is permissible to carry out rolling basis revaluations, once the revaluation basis is in place, but a company should not carry assets in the same class under different valuation bases, so all assets should be revalued in the first instance

- It appears that Albreda is seeking to revalue its properties on a rolling basis and that two properties have been revalued in the year to 30 September 2007 with a further 18 being revalued in the year to 30 September 2008

- The revaluations which have been carried out subsequent to the yearend would be material to the balance sheet for 2007, as they would represent 17.5% of total assets in 2007, and as there are three other properties to be revalued, this percentage would rise

- The corresponding credit in equity will also be material to the balance sheet

- If Albreda did not revalue all the assets in the class in the financial statements to 30 September 2007, then the auditors would have to qualify the audit report on this issue

- The financial statements should also include the disclosure required by IAS 16 when a company revalues assets:

    - The date of the revaluation

    - Whether an independent valuer was involved

    - The methods and significant assumptions applied in estimating the items' fair values

    - The extent to which the fair values were determined by reference to observable prices on the open market or other techniques

207

- The carrying amount that would have been recognised under the cost model

- The revaluation surplus, indicating the change for the period and any restrictions on the distribution of the balance to the shareholders

(ii) *Audit evidence*

- The schedule of depreciated cost of owned buildings
- Calculation of the difference between depreciated cost and revaluation per property
- The valuation reports for each of the properties
- Physical inspection of the properties with the largest surpluses to confirm condition
- Sale particulars of comparable assets to verify valuation
- The disclosure in the financial statements

(c) **Disclosure of fines**

(i) *Matters to consider*

- $0.1 million is 5.5% of profit before tax and is therefore material to the income statement. The corresponding amount in the previous year was considerably more material to profit

- The nature of these fines may also make them material if they indicate continual non-compliance with law and regulations which could result in more serious action than a fine

- Disclosure should be consistent with the previous year unless change is necessary to show a fair view or to comply with a standard

- IAS 1 states that when items of income and expense are material their nature and amount shall be disclosed separately

- Therefore, these fines should probably be disclosed separately, either on the face of the income statement or by way of a note to the financial statements

- The reasons for the breaches giving rise to the fines

- Under ISA 250, the auditor has to consider whether the effect of non compliance with laws and regulations will impact the financial statements and the possible effects of that non-compliance

- The auditors should therefore consider if the non compliance with the health and safety regulations giving rise to the fines has a potential greater impact on the financial statements, perhaps in terms of going concern or greater future liability

- If the auditor believes that non compliance is intentional he should discuss it with those charged with governance

- If the breaches are intentional and for the purpose of money saving, they might be classified as a money laundering offence

(ii) *Audit evidence*

- Schedule of amounts making up the total of $0.1 million with larger amounts agreed to cash book

- Review against prior year to see if there are any obvious omissions resulting in the figure being lower this year

- Correspondence attaching to the fines, for example, penalty notices

- Details of the company's internal health and safety policies

- Review of 'other information' to ensure it is not inconsistent/materially misstated in the context of these fines

- Written management representations that there are no other penalties/fines which have not been disclosed in the financial statements

35 Cuckoo Group

Text references. Chapters 8 and 11

Top tips. The audit of groups is a topic which is likely to require quite a sophisticated approach. In this question, it is combined with inventory valuation and disclosures. You must be comfortable with the issues discussed in part (a). Part (b) is good practice at considering accounting issues.

(a) As principal auditors of the Cuckoo Group we may have **sole responsibility** for our opinion on the group accounts even if part of the group has been audited by others. Therefore we would wish to ensure that we are confident in placing reliance on the work of the auditors of Loopy (the 'other' auditors).

Law gives us the right to **require** that the **other auditors** give us such information and explanations as we may reasonably require.

As a matter of courtesy we will inform the directors of Cuckoo Group of our intention to communicate with the auditors of Loopy.

The extent of the procedures we will undertake to ensure that we can place reliance on the work of the other auditors will depend on the **materiality** of the accounts of Loopy to the group as a whole and our assessment of the **audit risk** involved. We would also need all the **relevant information** to help us complete the consolidation of Loopy into the group accounts, including details of inter-company trading, inter-company balances at the year-end, goodwill, accounting policies and post balance sheet events. We need to **liaise** with Loopy's auditors in advance to ensure this is provided.

We would then consider the **scope of the work** of Loopy's auditors. In particular:

(i) The **terms** of their **engagement** and any limitation placed on their work
(ii) The **standards** of their **work** and the nature and extent of their audit examination
(iii) Their independence

This may be dealt with by **meeting the auditors** (most appropriate in this first year), by **questionnaire** or a combination of both. If Loopy is significant to the group, we may wish to **review** the other auditors' **working papers**. In an extreme situation, where we felt we could not rely on Loopy's auditors' work, we would need to **reperform** some or all of their **work**.

(b) (i) **Cuckoo**

The valuation of the bullion and precious metals contravenes IAS 2 which requires that it should be valued at the lower of cost and net realisable value. However depending upon the rate of turnover and fluctuations in market prices, this method is recognised as an acceptable way of valuing commodities and so departure from IAS 2 needs to be stated and justified in the financial statements. The auditors would also perform tests to assess the difference between cost and market value and whether this was material.

(ii) **Loopy**

LIFO is not an **acceptable** method of valuing inventory under IAS 2. In addition the standard requires that cost or valuation is determined for **separate items** of inventory or of groups of similar items and not on a total basis.

The auditors of Loopy will need to determine whether adjustment is needed to ensure that the inventory valuation conforms to IAS 2. Audit qualifications in the company and group accounts (if no adjustment is made) will depend on materiality.

(iii) **Snoopy**

Base inventory valuation is **not acceptable**. In addition the **balance sheet** and **income statement** should **show** the **same value** for inventory.

However the immateriality of the adjustment in the group accounts may mean that it can be ignored. If it is material in the company's own accounts an **audit qualification** may be required if the directors of Snoopy wish the adjustment to stand.

(iv) **Drake Retail**

The methods used in allocating costs to inventory need to be selected with a view to providing the **fairest possible approximation** to the expenditure actually incurred in bringing the product to its present location and condition. The practice of retail outlets using selling price less normal gross profit margin is given as an example of an acceptable method of approximating to cost. **Records** must be kept of **mark-ups** and any subsequent mark-downs, to ensure that the calculation still gives an approximation to cost.

(c) (i) **Cooperation between auditors**

ISA 600 states that 'the other auditor, knowing the context in which the principal auditor will use the other auditor's work, should cooperate with the principal auditor'. However, in practice, the degree of cooperation may be limited by factors such as the other auditor not being subject to the requirements of ISAs, but of different national practice or the principal auditor not having any legal right to contact the auditors of a component of the company preparing group accounts. ISA 600 states that the principal auditor should not accept a group audit if there are restrictions on his communication with other auditors.

(ii) **Multi-location audits**

ISA 600 applies when the financial information of any component is included in the financial statements audited by the principal auditor. A component is defined as a division, branch, subsidiary, joint venture, associated company or other entity whose financial information is included in the financial statements audited by the principal auditor. Clearly any of these could be in a different location to the parent company, so ISA 600 does apply to multi-location audits.

However, there is no specific guidance in ISA 600 or other standards on how to deal with the particular problems caused by such multi-location situations. ISA 315 recognises that multi-locations might give rise to a risk but does not suggest any solutions in a group context. This is an area where additional guidance is required.

(iii) **Joint audits**

ISA 600 specifically excludes the situation where two or more auditors are appointed as joint auditors.

Joint audits are rare because they are often costly, as both sets of auditors are responsible for the audit opinion and therefore work can be replicated. However, they are used in some countries, for example, France. In addition, in the wake of the Enron scandal joint audits have been proposed as a potential solution to such problems occurring again.

Given this, joint audits are an area which requires guidance to be produced by IFAC and IAASB.

36 Beeches Technologies

Text references. Chapters 3 and 11

Top tips. This question falls into two distinct parts. Part (a) is a scenario case study question set in a group audit situation where a fraud has been uncovered. Part (b) is a discussion question on the role of the auditor with regard to fraud. This question is therefore excellent practice for your exam, as completing it will give you good practice as two distinct exam skills: analysing and commenting on a case study scenario and also discussing a topical issue in more of an essay format.

Fraud is a difficult area for auditors. By its nature it is concealed and therefore it is very difficult to uncover in the course of audit work. However, its existence may significantly affect the financial statements and the public appear to have an expectation that financial statements that have been audited should be free from fraud.

Notice that this question gives indications of the way that it should be answered. The requirement in (a) (i) is to 'list', and the requirement in (a) (ii) is to give a 'summary'. This indicates that a bullet-point approach will be appropriate in these sections. In part (b), however, where there is a compare and contrast, discussion approach required, such bullet pointing would not be appropriate.

(a) **Schedules for Friday's meeting**

(i) **Questions re fraud**

- How was the fraud discovered?
- What has the group done to discover the full extent of the fraud?
- What breakdowns in control made the fraud possible?
- Who authorised the payments made?
- Were there any previous concerns about the behaviour of the individual?
- Were references obtained for the individual when he was recruited?
- How was the fraud perpetrated?
- How were the fraudulent transactions hidden?
- Is any action being taken to recover the money from the individual?
- Is the company insured against fraud?
- Why was the fraud not identified by a review of the subsidiary's results?
- What action has been taken to identify/prevent other frauds in the group?
- Are there any other subsidiaries where the company has concerns?
- Have you considered whether there was collusion in the fraud?
- Do you have any specific concerns about our audit procedures?
- Do you have any specific concerns about our prior year audit?
- What are your expectations of our visits to overseas subsidiaries?

(ii) **Controls which should be in place**

(1) *Authorisation of expenditure*

- Group authorisation for significant/unusual expenditure
- More than one cheque signatory for large cheques
- Review of supporting documentation by cheque signatories
- Appropriate authorisation of electronic funds transfer
- Password protection of electronic transfers
- Controlled access to bank account details on supplier file
- Review of changes to supplier file

- Segregation of duties between invoice posting and payment posting (to avoid payments being authorised on fictitious invoices)

- Proper bank reconciliations

(2) Controls over access to payroll data

(3) Review and authorisation of employee's expenses claims

(4) Review of costs against budget, which is sufficiently detailed to pick up inappropriate expenditure, including obtaining explanations for variances and comparisons to other subsidiaries

(5) Involvement of personnel department: to ensure that staff take holidays, to encourage staff rotation around subsidiaries and to ensure that adequate references are obtained on recruitment

(iii) **Outline plan for subsidiary audits**

Work at head office

- Review the controls exercised by the group over the overseas subsidiaries.

- Conduct analytical review of the subsidiaries activities in comparison to each other/past performance.

- Investigate any unusual items.

Two largest overseas subsidiaries

These should be subject to a full audit, which should be completed before the subsidiary is 'signed off' to the group audit team.

Other subsidiaries with full audit requirement (six sites)

- A full audit should be completed before the subsidiary is 'signed off' to the group audit team.
- The sites subject to a full audit should be rotated.

Other subsidiaries

- The rotational approach should be continued.

- Work should concentrate on the key controls and may be performed at interim audit.

- However, in light of the fraud perpetrated in Madrid, may increase the number of subsidiary visits we make this year.

Factors to take into account on audit

- Client's expectations
- Any internal audit reports available
- Quality of the controls established by the group
- Efficiency

If the controls at subsidiaries are found to be weak, we may do additional substantive testing this year.

(b) **Expectations re fraud**

Auditor's responsibility

The auditor is engaged to give an opinion as to whether the financial statements give a **true and fair view**. This means that he is aiming to **detect material misstatements** in the financial statements.

In the case of Beeches Technologies, the fraud caused a misstatement in financial statements, as personal expenses (fraudulently appropriated from the company) were classified as business expenses. However, in this case, the **fraud was not material to the financial statements** that the auditors were giving their opinion on.

The question of whether fraud causes a material misstatement is a difficult one. This is discussed below in the context of **public expectations**.

Auditors do not have a duty to detect fraud, therefore, merely a duty to report whether the financial statements show a true and fair view, that is, they are not affected by material misstatements. This is sometimes encapsulated in the phrase that auditors are '**watchdogs, not blood-hounds**'. They do not have a duty to seek out immaterial fraud. However, if they do discover indications of an immaterial fraud, they should alert management to their suspicions. They also have no duty to prevent fraud. This is a duty of the directors.

Public expectations

There is a **general perception from the public**, which is perhaps often shared by directors in some companies, **that an audit will uncover fraud**. Indeed, some might (wrongly) claim that the primary purpose of an audit was to uncover such irregularities.

There is therefore an implicit assumption when a fraud is uncovered that the auditor has been negligent that that the fault for the fraud lies with him.

'**Materiality**', a concept that is intrinsic to the meaning of 'truth and fairness in financial statements' is a concept **misunderstood by the general public**. An auditor's understanding of materiality is that materiality is an expression of the relative significance or importance of a particular matter in the context of financial statements as a whole. A matter is material if its omission would **reasonably influence the decisions of an addressee of the auditors' report**; likewise a misstatement is material if it would have a similar influence.

In the context of the public expectations discussed above, it can be seen that, in relation to fraud, this understanding of materiality is problematical, as **fraud is a matter that does reasonably affect the addressees of the audit report**, if you see shareholders as a microcosm of the general public.

Alternatively, shareholders may be directors of a company in a family business. However, as noted above, such directors may be less financially aware than other directors and may not fully understand the role of the auditor in relation to fraud. It is a responsibility of the auditor to ensure that his clients do understand his responsibility towards fraud.

Directors' expectations

The **expectations of directors** with regard to auditors and fraud will, as discussed above, **vary considerably**. No director should be under a misapprehension that an auditor has a duty to detect fraud, as auditors should seek to disabuse their clients of that notion.

However, directors may expect a **value added audit**, particularly if their auditor promotes himself in those terms. Their expectations of what the audit represents may become too high, and directors may rely on the audit to cover work and monitoring that they should do themselves.

The **audit** can be used as a **deterrent to fraud**, but the directors must also take action against fraud in their own company, as part of their risk management and controls activities.

Beeches Technologies

In this instance, the fraud was **not material to the group financial statements**. There was no requirement for the auditors to have designed procedures capable of uncovering it. **The local entity did not require an audit**.

The cost of the auditors visiting all subsidiaries and undertaking detailed controls work would probably have been more than the group were prepared to pay. This is work that the company should have carried out itself, particularly when an audit visit had not been made to a subsidiary in a particular year.

The company should review past reports of controls weakness issued by the auditors and review whether they could have made improvements to the controls at the relevant subsidiary so that they were better protected against such frauds being perpetrated.

Conclusion

There continues to be a **significant gap** between the actual responsibilities of the auditor with regard to fraud and the public's expectation of what those responsibilities are and should be. The expectations of directors will vary. Some will share the public expectations with regard to fraud, others will be more educated as to what an audit is. No director whose company receives an audit should be under a misapprehension about the auditor's role, as auditors should make their role clear to their clients.

37 Pavia

Text references. Chapters 6, 8 and 10

Top tips. This is a 30 mark question split into three parts. One of the most important points to note when attempting this question is to make sure that you don't run over the time allocation, both for the individual parts and for the question as a whole. In part (a), use the information in the question to generate ideas for your answer and make sure you identify financial statement risks as opposed to audit risks – a key area of confusion for many students. Take each line of the financial statements in turn and deal with it. Don't get bogged down in all the information that's provided in the question. In part (c), take each item in turn and deal with it – this makes this part of the question more manageable but make sure the audit work you suggest is specific – a vague answer will not score well.

Easy marks. Easy marks are available in part (b) of this question on analytical procedures – you should be very familiar with the use of these as a substantive test from your paper 2.6 knowledge. In part (a) you should be able to pick up good marks by using the information in the question scenario but make sure the risks you identify are well explained in order to score well.

ACCA examiner's answer. The examiner's answer to this question is included at the back of this kit.

Marking scheme

		Marks
(a)	Financial statement risks	
	Generally *1/2 mark* for identification +*1 mark* each point of explanation	Max 14
	Ideas	

- Revenue/Receivables – potential over/under/misstatement (consignment inventory, cutoff, 0% finance)
- Other income – overstated? (reversal of provisions)
- Cost of materials – overstated?/inventory understated?
- Employee benefits – overstated?
- Depreciation/amortisation – overstated?
- Interest income – understated?
- Intangibles – potential overstatement (development impaired?)
- P, P & E – potential overstatement (unrecorded disposals)
- Inventories – understated? (consignment)
- Receivables – overstated? (no year-end allowance)
- Provisions – potential overstatement?
- Trade payables – understatement/unrecorded liabilities
- Going concern – disruption to assembly schedules/fall in profits

		Marks
(b)	Illustration of analytical procedures (as audit evidence)	
	Generally *1 mark* each point	Max 7
	Ideas	

- Revenue – testing for understatement
- 'Proof in total'/reasonableness tests – employee costs, depreciation, investment/interest income
- Immaterial items – may be sufficient
- Ratio analysis – asset turnover, average collection/payment periods

(c)   Principal audit work
       Generally *1 mark* each area of principal audit work, *max 3* each balance sheet item   9
       Ideas
       (i) Development expenditure
           • Opening balance
           • Physical inspection (Fox model)
           • Additions to purchase/sub-contractor's invoices
           • Payroll records/analysis
           • Overhead absorption
           • Internal trial (test drive) results
           • Impairment test
           • Key assumptions
       (ii) Consignment inventory
           • Agreements – terms of 'sale' to dealers
           • Proforma invoices
           • Direct confirmation
           • Physical inspection – vehicle returns
       (iii) Warranty provision
           • Agreements – terms of warranty
           • Management's assumptions
           • After-date repairs (parts and labour)
           • Current year warranty costs *v* prior year provision
           • Recourse to suppliers (e.g. faulty parts)

30

(a)   **Financial statement risks**

Revenue and other income

Revenue has increased from this year compared to the prior year by 6.4%. There is a risk that income has been included in the wrong financial year due to incorrect cut-off. In the case of revenue from vehicles, this has increased by almost 12% compared to the prior year.

Revenue from other activities has fallen by 59% and may not be complete (the accounts comprise draft figures) as there may be gains or losses from disposals of non-current assets not yet accounted for or revenue has been recognised before sales have been completed in substance. Other income also includes reversals of provisions not used – these should be accounted for as a reversal to the expense where the original provision was first debited to the income statement.

Wages and salaries

The wages and salaries expense has increased by 8.5% compared to the prior year, although the average number of employees in the year has fallen by 10 compared to last year. The charge for the year could therefore be overstated.

Depreciation and amortisation

The charge for the year has increased by 26% compared to the previous year. This could be reasonable given the increases in both intangible and tangible non-current assets over the year, or indicate that the incorrect rates have been applied to some assets in error.

Other expenses

These have increased by 15.6% compared to the prior year. It does not seem that there could be any misallocation of expenses between other expenses and cost of sales as both have increased in the year. However this should be investigated further and the trend re-examined after any adjustments have been made to the treatment of the reversals of provisions.

Intangible assets

Intangible assets have increased by 18% compared to the previous year and include development costs for the Fox model. There is a risk that costs that do not meet the criteria for deferral under IAS 38 *Intangible assets* have been incorrectly capitalised as assets when they should be written-off to the income statement instead. There is also a risk that any impairment in the year to intangibles has not been written-off to the income statement.

Tangible assets

These have increased by 21.4% compared to the previous period. There is a risk of misstatement if amounts have been incorrectly capitalised when they should have been expensed in the year to the income statement. There may also be a chance that some depreciation has not yet been accounted for, for example, if depreciation is calculated on a monthly basis and the charge for December is still outstanding. Again there may be impairments to these assets that have not been recognised.

Inventory

Inventory has increased by 8.6% compared to the prior period. This may be due to incorrect cut-off being applied or the valuation of some items of inventory being overstated if any items are likely to have to be sold at significant discounts in the competitive market conditions.

Trade receivables

Trade receivables have increased substantially compared to the prior year, by 45%. This may be due to the allowance for bad and doubtful debts not yet having been made or processed through the ledger.

Trade payables

Trade payables have slightly increased (by 5%). There is a risk of understatement if year-end accruals have still to be adjusted for in the accounts.

Provisions

The provision has increased substantially by 32% compared to the previous year. New provisions have been established for deferred maintenance and IT reorganisation but the provision will be overstated if these charges do not meet the criteria for recognising a provision in IAS 37 *Provisions, contingent liabilities and contingent assets*.

(b) Analytical procedures can be used as substantive tests during audit fieldwork to provide sufficient appropriate audit evidence in a number of ways.

Proof in total tests can be used to assess the reasonableness of items in the income statement such as depreciation and the wages and salaries charge.

For depreciation and amortisation, the expected charge for the year can be calculated by applying the depreciation policy for each class of asset to the opening balances and factoring in the additions and disposals in the year.

For wages and salaries, the average number of employees can be taken and multiplied by the average salary for the year to get an estimate of the salary charge for the year. Any pay rise in the year should also be factored in to the calculation.

The reasonableness of the revenue from vehicles in the year can be assessed because we know the number of cars sold in the year and this can be multiplied by the average sale price using the prior year figures. This gives an indication as to the completeness and accuracy of the figure in the year-end accounts.

Comparisons of current year figures to prior year figures can be made for immaterial items to form an assessment about the reasonableness of these figures. Comparisons can also be made to budgeted figures for the year. Large variances should be investigated and may result in more detailed substantive testing being required.

Accounting ratios can be used as analytical procedures to provide audit evidence. They should be calculated for previous periods and for comparable companies. Important ratios in this company would include gross profit margin, inventory turnover ratio, receivables and payables ratios for example. Relationships between related items are also important to examine such as receivables and sales, inventory and cost of sales, payables and purchases, fixed assets and depreciation/amortisation.

(c)   (i)   **Development expenditure on the Fox model**

- Inspect the accounting records and invoices, orders and other documentation to confirm the $12.7 m spent on developing the Fox model.

- Discuss with management the reasons and criteria used for capitalising the expenditure spent on developing the Fox model.

- Obtain a management representation point on the feasibility of the Fox model, particularly in light of the launch postponement due to issues over the security of the doors at high speeds.

- Review the results of the internal trials of the Fox model.

- Confirm viability and feasibility of the development costs by examining feasibility studies, budgets and forecasts.

- Review calculations of future cash flows to ensure resources exist to complete the model.

- Review management's impairment test of development costs.

(ii)   **Consignment inventory**

- Review the agreement with the manufacturer to confirm who bears the risks and rewards and whether the substance of the transaction is that of an asset held by the dealer with a corresponding liability to the manufacturer or whether the asset is held by the manufacturer.

- Review the transfer price of the inventory charged by the manufacturer – if it is based on the manufacturer's list price at the date of delivery, this would indicate the inventory is an asset of the dealer. If it is based on the manufacturer's list price at the date the legal title passes to the dealer, this indicates it is an asset of the manufacturer.

- Obtain direct confirmations from dealers of the number of vehicles unsold at the year-end.

- Perform cut-off tests at the year-end to check that sales and inventory are recorded in the correct financial year.

(iii)   **Warranty provision**

- Review the calculation of the provision and agree it to the amount disclosed in the financial statements.

- Discuss with management how the warranty provision has been calculated and the assumptions used, to confirm it is a *bona fide* provision in accordance with IAS 37 *Provisions, contingent liabilities and contingent assets*, by reference to the contracts for sale.

- Review the disclosures made in the notes to the accounts to ensure that all information required in accordance with IAS 37 has been disclosed.

- Compare the prior year provision for warranties with the actual costs of repairs under warranty to assess the reliability of management's estimate this year.

- Assess reasonableness of management's estimate by reviewing actual cost of post year-end repairs against the provision made.

- Obtain management representation letter from the client in respect of all provisions and any contingent liabilities.

38 RBG

Text references. Chapters 11 and 16

Top tips. This is a fairly straightforward question on the outsourcing of the internal audit function of a company. You should be able to score well in part (a) on the advantages and disadvantages of outsourcing. Part (c) is also straightforward but note the requirement to explain the impact of outsourcing – make sure you do and that you provide a full enough answer to warrant the four marks. Part (b) is trickier but use the information in the question scenario to generate ideas for your answer and don't panic – try to plan a structured, well thought out answer and you should be able to pick up some marks in this part of the question.

Easy marks. Easy marks are available in part (a) of this question on the advantages and disadvantages of outsourcing. You should also be able to score well in part (c) of this question for four marks on the impact of outsourcing from the point of view of the external auditors.

ACCA examiner's answer. The examiner's answer to this question is included at the back of this kit.

Marking scheme

Marks

(a) Advantages and disadvantages of outsourcing
Generally *1 mark* each suggestion from RBG's perspective   Max 6
Ideas
Advantages
- Cost saving
- Continuity
- Expertise
- Availability/flexibility
- Independent evaluation
- Better recommendations/improved quality
Disadvantages
- Costlier in long run
- Less effective
- Less integrated
- Lack of availability
- Loss of management training

(b) Principal matters to be included in submission
Generally *1/2 mark* each matter identified up to max 5 and up to *1 mark* for description   Max 10
Ideas
- Introduction/background
- Services
- Identification of client issues
- Methodologies
- Resources
- Experience
- Insurance
- Work ethics
- Standards to be followed
- Sample work (reports)
- Potential conflicts
- Invoicing and payment
- Performance targets

(c)   Possible impact on audit of financial statements
Generally *1 mark* each point of explanation   Max 4
Ideas
- Organisational risk assessment
- Internal control assessment
- Reduction in substantive procedures
- Fraud and error risk assessment

20

(a)   **Advantages of outsourcing internal audit**

- Outsourcing may reduce costs for RBG because the company will pay on the basis of amount of time spent on each internal audit project. Cost savings in the areas of salary, tax, pensions, training etc could be significant.

- Outsourcing could lead to greater cost control over the internal audit function. This could lead to improved budgeting and cost control.

- Outsourcing the internal audit function to a specialist firm would ensure that high calibre staff who are technically competent are used. Staff from the specialist firm may bring a greater variety of ideas, gained from other assignments, to RBG's business.

- The service organisation used to provide internal audit services may provide indemnity in the event of problems arising. This would not be the case if the function was in-house.

- Obtaining the service through a contract could assist with cash flow as the contract will represent a flat fee, whereas the cost of providing the service in-house might lead to fluctuating costs.

- Using an outsourced internal audit department could increase the reliance that the external auditors could place on internal audit's work and this could lead to a reduced external audit fee.

- Staff turnover may not be as high as in the in-house internal audit function of RBG although it is inevitable that some staff may change from year to year.

- If the internal audit function is outsourced, this may result in the function appearing more independent and objective than if the function was in-house.

Disadvantages of outsourcing internal audit

- The company will lose control over the internal audit function by outsourcing it, although cost control will not be lost.

- The initial cost of outsourcing may be substantial if the company closes its current department, such as the cost of potential redundancies.

- The contract with the service organisation has to be managed to ensure that the service being provided is appropriate and in accordance with the contract, which could be quite time-consuming.

- The contract with the service organisation might limit the liability of the contractor, leading to problems if the contract is not performed well. In extreme cases, this could lead to court action being required.

- The contracted internal audit firm might not understand the nature of the company's business as well as an in-house function, where staff may have experience of a range of operational areas of the company.

(b)   Principal matters to be included in the submission to provide internal audit services to RBG.

- York & Co's assessment of the main risks facing RBG and how these would be addressed.

- Details of audit methodology to be used and description of how work is documented and what systems and programs are used by York & Co.

- The qualifications and experience of the staff of York & Co who would be involved in undertaking the internal audit work at RBG.

- Other clients that RBG provides internal audit services to and details for references if these are required.

- Details of previous experience of similar retail clients to RBG and examples of value added to these clients.

- Details of fees for each staff member and travel expenses and the likely fee developments over the course of the contract with RBG.

- An outline of the resources required to perform the internal audit function and the dates of availability of staff for work.

- Details of indemnity insurance.

- Additional services which could be offered to RBG, such as consultancy, tax services.

- Other information about York & Co, such as other services provided, location of offices, date when the contract would begin.

(c)   The outsourcing of the internal audit function of RBG could have a positive impact on the audit of the financial statements because Grey & Co could place a lot of reliance on the work performed and this would lead to reduced audit work. However, this might lead to a reduced fee being charged for the external audit if less detailed substantive testing was required.

The appointment of an outsourced internal audit function would include an evaluation of organisational risk, financial compliance, information technology control and systems audits and fraud investigation. All this work will provide valuable planning information for Grey & Co and assist them in directing their audit approach, for example, whether to take a controls-based or fully substantive-based approach.

39 Seymour

Text reference. Chapter 10

Top tips. The best way to approach this question is to take each part in turn and consider the issues, remembering not to go over the time allocation for any one part. In this question, around seven marks are available for each issue so you should be aiming to generate three or four points for matters to consider and the same for the audit evidence you expect to find. Don't spend too long on one particular issue because you won't be able to score marks on the other issues if you take this approach. Think about the information in the question scenario and apply your knowledge to it. Always consider materiality in this type of question.

Easy marks. You can pick up straightforward marks in this question by making an assessment of materiality for each of the issues, using the figures in the question scenario.

ACCA examiner's answer. The examiner's answer to this question is included at the back of this kit.

		Marks

(i) **Matters**
Generally *1 mark* each comment *max 6* marks each issue × 3   Max 12
Ideas
- Materiality (appropriately assessed)
- Relevant IFRSs (e.g. IAS 2, 8, 10, 36, 37, 38 & IFRS 3)
- Fundamental concepts (accruals/prudence)
- Risks (e.g. valuation (impairment)/disclosure)

(ii) **Audit evidence**
Generally *1 mark* each item of audit evidence (source) *max 6* marks each issue × 3   Max 12
Ideas (ISA 500)
- Documented on WP file – current vs PY
- Internal (e.g. CF forecasts) vs external (e.g. press release)
- Auditor generated (analytical procedure)
- Results of procedures by which obtained (e.g. physical inspection
  of inventory returns/credit notes raised)

Max 20

(a)	Max 7
(b)	Max 7
(c)	Max 6
	20

(a) **Drug patent**

(i) *Matters to consider*

- The carrying value of the development costs at the start of the year will be $3m (assuming that amortisation is charged over 20 years, i.e. $200k per year) which represents 5.6% of total assets – this is material to the balance sheet.

- Management must consider whether the drug is still likely to go on sale given that a competitor has announced the successful completion of preliminary trials on an alternative drug with the same properties as Tournose.

- The announcement by the competitor may indicate impairment of the capitalised development costs of Tournose. If this is the case, the costs must be written back to the profit and loss account.

- The management of Seymour Co should examine the unamortised balance of development expenditure on this project to ensure that it still fulfils the criteria in IAS 38 *Intangible assets* for capitalising development costs.

(ii) Audit evidence

- Patent agreement for Tournose to confirm length, cost and approval.

- Documentation to support the development costs of $4m.

- Press announcement of competitor drug.

- Written management representation point on key assumptions for the future regarding development costs of Tournose.

- Management's projections of future cashflows from Tournose for evidence of useful life of development costs.

221

(b) **Goodwill**

   (i) *Matters to consider*

- The goodwill on acquisition of Aragon is material to accounts – it represents 3.4% of total assets in the consolidated accounts.

- The goodwill should be subject to annual impairment reviews in accordance with IAS 36 *Impairment of assets*.

- The results of Aragon indicate that the investment in Aragon is also impaired.

- The investment is also material to Seymour Co's individual accounts and should be tested for impairment

   (ii) *Audit evidence*

- Purchase documentation to confirm purchase price of Aragon Co and value of purchased goodwill.

- Prior year and current year financial statements of Aragon Co to confirm balance sheet and income statement figures.

- Impairment reviews carried out by the directors of Seymour Co for both the investment and the goodwill.

- 'Comfort letter' from Seymour referring to continued financial support of Aragon.

(c) **Discontinuation**

   (i) *Matters to consider*

- The revenue from the petcare operations represent 12% of total revenue and is therefore material to the accounts.

- The high level of customer returns may prompt lots of claims against the company and it should consider setting up a provision if the criteria in IAS 37 *Provisions, contingent liabilities and contingent assets* are met. Contingent liabilities may also need to be recognised.

- Inventory returned to the company will have to be written down to net realisable value.

- The announcement of the recall and discontinuation of the range of petcare products occurred after the year-end. This is an example of a non-adjusting event after the balance sheet date in accordance with IAS 10 *Events after the balance sheet date* so should be disclosed in the accounts. As there is no indication that management are committed to selling the business as at the balance sheet date, it does not meet the definition of a discontinued operation per IFRS 5 *Non-current assets held for sale and discontinued operations* so should be classed as continuing in the income statement.

- If the directors continue to disclose it separately as a discontinued operation it may be necessary to qualify the audit opinion on the grounds of disagreement.

   (ii) *Audit evidence*

- A copy of the announcement of the recall and discontinuation of the petcare products.

- Customer correspondence on returns to assess the level of likely claims against the company.

- Correspondence from the company's legal advisors regarding any claims and the potential pay-outs.

- Assessment of value of returned inventory.

- Calculation of any provision made in regard to returns from customers.

40 Bellatrix

> **Text reference.** Chapter 11
>
> **Top tips.** Do not spend too long on any one issue in this question that you do not write a balanced answer.

(a) **Implications of findings for acquisition of Scorpio**

Cash flow, profits and purchase price

The combination of **poor cash flow** and **apparent rising profits** is not good as it implies **poor quality profits**. In this case, the main apparent reasons for the increased profit appear to be the profit on the sale of the warehouse and the reduction in the allowances for inventory and bad debts.

The basis on which the purchase price is negotiated should not include the non-recurring profit on the sale that has been made (or on the sales that are planned) and the reduction in provisions should be justifiable on the basis of previous experience of over-provisioning. If it is not, the provisions should be written back.

If the purchase price is also based on asset values, Bellatrix should consider the **financial and operational implications of the disposals of the properties**, as well as the efficiency of **outsourcing warehousing**. There may be **economies of scale** to be had by combining the warehousing capabilities of the two companies and given that there appears to be no contract of sale for the remaining properties, as yet, these plans may be altered as part of the purchase agreement.

Cash flow, as well as profits, has been improved by the sale of the properties and Bellatrix should consider the **future funding needs** of Scorpio and the possibility of consolidating bank borrowings. The cash flow issues in relation to the bank loan and refurbishment discussed below are relevant here.

Sale of warehouse, outsourcing warehousing, operational issues

Bellatrix should consider the operational issues arising from the sales of warehouses and the adequacy of detailed plans for outsourcing of warehousing, as noted above. Outsourcing is not necessarily the least expensive or the most efficient method of dealing with the issues and there may be some attempt to manipulate the management accounts by moving the costs of warehousing from the capital budget to the revenue budget. There are also implications for calculations of the return on assets.

Application for bank loan and refurbishment of offices

Given the **cash flow difficulties**, it seems, on the face of it, to be difficult to justify the **refurbishment of offices**, particularly if they are to be financed by a bank loan, because it is **unlikely to generate significant additional revenues or profits** at this point. It would be useful to establish the bank's likely position on this loan and it is very important to ascertain whether the reductions in the allowances for inventory and bad debts have been properly disclosed to the bank in the management accounts provided to them. The bank may well want to take charges over the company's assets as security for the loan which may have implications for the rights which Bellatrix has over the assets of Scorpio once it has been purchased.

Andromeda

It will be important to establish the effect of the purchase on the **future relationship** with Andromeda. If the relationship can continue as before, and if the sales are genuinely at arms length, there should be no problem but if this relationship is likely to change, there are implications for both cash flows and profits.

General

The reasons for the proposed purchase should be established, particularly given the poor cash flows, poor quality profits and the possible lack of integrity of the management of Scorpio if the reductions in provisions have not been disclosed to the bank or are not justified. The belief that profits (and presumably revenues) will increase because of the coming winter season should be investigated by Bellatrix with reference to the past performance of Scorpio.

(b) **Implications of the acquisition for the Bellatrix Audit**

Purchase of Scorpio

Assuming that the sale goes ahead in the current year, the purchase will need to be **audited by reference to the purchase agreement**, the associated **legal documentation**, any **valuations** performed as part of the purchase agreement, and the transfer of the purchase **consideration** whether this is in cash, shares, other assets or some combination of these.

The firm will also need to ensure that the appropriate company secretarial matters have been properly dealt with by the inspection of documentation sent to the Registrar of Companies and entries in the statutory books of both companies (changes in share ownership, changes in directors, etc.)

Accounting for the purchase

There is no indication in the question that the purchase is anything other than an **acquisition**. In the consolidated accounts, profits will therefore need to be split into the pre- and post-acquisition elements and accounted for either in the goodwill calculation or the income statement. The assets to be incorporated on a line by line basis should be included at fair value and in this case, this is likely to involve reliance on the work of experts because assets appear to be recorded in Scorpio's books at historical cost. Goodwill needs to be calculated as the excess of the **fair value** of the purchase consideration over the fair value of the assets acquired. The **relationship with Andromeda** and the transactions with it need to be **disclosed** (as well as details of the acquisition) in accordance with IAS 24 *Related party disclosures* in both the consolidated accounts and in Scorpio's individual accounts. If the year-ends to the two companies are not coterminous, further work may be required on Scorpio's accounts in order to perform the consolidation.

In the individual accounts of Bellatrix, it will be necessary to include the investment as an addition with the appropriate disclosure of the amount and nature of the purchase consideration. Any charges over the assets of Scorpio need to be disclosed in the accounts of both Scorpio and in the consolidated accounts.

Group audit arrangements

On the assumption that Scorpio has other auditors for the current year, appropriate arrangements need to be made in order that the information needed by the firm for the audit of the consolidated accounts is provided on a timely basis. If the firm is already auditor to Scorpio, this problem will not arise, but if the firm is to be appointed in the current year, further work will be needed to audit the opening balances of Scorpio for the current year and the co-operation of the previous auditors may be sought. All of the normal first year work in terms of the assessment of risk and the documentation of accounting systems and internal controls will also need to be performed before the consolidation is signed off.

Audit administration

Good quality control procedures suggest that a **second partner review** is required as this is a high risk audit and in the public interest. The acquisition would appear to increase inherent **risk** and the review should therefore be built into the audit plan. Additional work is likely to be required for the consolidation (and for the audit of Scorpio if the firm is to be appointed for the first time) and the audit fee needs to be negotiated as early as possible on this basis.

Audit strategy

In the accounts of Scorpio, particular attention needs to be paid to several areas. These matters will be dealt with either by the firm, if appointed, or by Scorpio's auditors in the group audit instructions. The allowances for inventory and bad debts will need to be examined carefully with reference to trading patterns and changes in them, the overall levels of inventory and receivables, and the company's previous experience of accurate provisioning, for example. The valuation of non current assets and the disclosure of profits on sales, probably as an exceptional item, should be examined and if, as seems likely, they are material to the consolidated accounts they should be disclosed in the same way.

There may be group tax implications to consider in the accounts of both companies, and the consolidated accounts.

41 Prescott

Text references. Chapters 9 and 12

Top tips. Remember to stick to the time allocation for each part of this question. In part (a), don't just produce a list – read the question requirement carefully before launching into your answer. In part (b), use the information in the scenario and think what additional information would be useful. In part (c), you are asked to state the inquiries you would make so you could produce a list of bullet point questions to ask.

Easy marks. Part (b) should be straightforward but make sure you identify and explain the issues rather than just produce a list. Part (d) should also be straightforward and draws upon your knowledge of construction contracts from your financial reporting studies.

Examiner's comments. In part (c), many candidates did not give reasons why the information they suggested should be provided – this was specifically requested in the requirement to this part of the question. Many candidates tended to list work they wanted to do that was mainly detailed and substantive – this would not have been appropriate for a two day review. Some candidates answered this part in part (b) and the repeated their answers in part (c). This shows a lack of planning and thought.

In part (d), the requirement was to state the specific inquiries to make of management and could have been answered with a questioning style. However, some answers were indistinguishable from part (c) and therefore led to repetition. This part of the question also demonstrated that many candidates have a lack of understanding of basic accounting and double-entry.

Marking scheme

		Marks
(a)	**Due diligence**	
	3 marks for defining and explaining term	Max 5
	2 marks for examples	
(b)	**Terms of engagement – specific matters to be clarified**	
	Generally ½ mark each matter identified (max 4 marks) and up to 1½ marks for explanation	Max 6
	Ideas (ISRE 2400*)	
	• Objectives/purpose of the assignment	
	• Managements responsibility	
	• Nature/scope of review (Investigation = enquiry + analytical procedures)	
	• Level of assurance – negative (Not an audit/no audit option)	
	• Timeframe	
	• Unrestricted access to information requested	
	• Disclaimer	
(c)	**Principal additional information**	
	Generally ½ mark point each principal item identified (max 3 marks)	
	and up to 1 mark a point explaining its relevance	Max 8
	Ideas	
	• Prior period financial statements (accounting policies)	
	• Management accounts/cash flow forecasts	
	• Signed bank (overdraft facility) and other agreements with lenders	
	• Standard contract terms (guarantees/disclaimers etc)	
	• Legal/correspondence file (Sarwar contract)	
	• Quantity surveyor's working papers (last quarterly count/rolling budgets)	
	• Type and frequency of constructions undertaken	

(d) **Specific inquiries – accounting for construction contracts**
Generally ½-1 mark each enquiry
Ideas

- Concerning
  - loss-making contracts
  - contingent liabilities/outcome on Sarwar
  - claims history/effectiveness of penalty clauses
  - useful lives of assets used in construction
  - nature of losses (eg theft of building supplies)

Max 6

25

* ISRE 'Engagements to Review Financial Statements' (formerly ISA 910).
ISA 210 'Terms of Audit Engagement' could also provide a suitable 'ideas list'.

(a) **Due diligence** reviews are a specific type of review engagement. A typical due diligence engagement is where an advisor (often an audit firm) is engaged by one company planning to take over another to perform an assessment of the material risks associated with the transaction (including validating the assumptions underlying the purchase), to ensure that the acquirer has all the necessary facts. This is important when determining purchase price. Similarly, due diligence can also be requested by sellers.

Practical examples include the following:

- **Financial due diligence** (a review of the financial position and obligations of a target to identify such matters as covenants and contingent obligations)

- **Operational and IT due diligence** (extent of operational and IT risks, including quality of systems, associated with a target business)

- **People due diligence** (key staff positions under the new structure, contract termination costs and cost of integration)

- **Regulatory due diligence** (review of the target's level of compliance with relevant regulation)

- **Environmental due diligence** (environmental, health and safety and social issues in a target)

(b) Matters to be clarified in engagement letter

- The nature of the opinion must be agreed. On this assignment it is likely to be expressed as negative assurance, saying 'nothing has come to our attention to indicate that the information is not free from material misstatement'. This is a normal form of words used to express a moderate level of assurance.

- The time-scale of the review should be set out. Prescott has requested a limited review over two days. The deadline for reporting should also be set.

- A liability disclaimer should be included to confirm that the engagement should not be relied upon to disclose errors or other irregularities.

- The terms of reference of the review should be set out, ie its aims and objectives. It should also state that the investigation will be mainly in the form of inquiry and analytical procedures.

- The letter should state that any decision made on whether to go ahead with the acquisition will be the responsibility of Prescott's management.

- The engagement letter should contain the fee for the engagement and details of the team undertaking the review.

(c) Additional information

- Prior years' financial statements should be obtained for details of the accounting policies used by Robson, any provisions/contingent liabilities made in the accounts, and the assumptions made in estimating completion of construction contracts.

- Recent management accounts and cash flow forecasts are required to assess the quality of management information. Robson has been operating at its overdraft limit for the last 18 months so the accuracy of this information will be critical to decision-making.

- The loan agreement with the bank and other lenders should be obtained so that details of the overdraft limit and other debt covenants are understood. The terms should be reviewed closely to determine whether any penalties or similar would be triggered by a takeover of Robson.

- Any legal correspondence regarding the claim on the site on which Robson built a housing development in 2003 should be obtained, together with any other claims or disputes that the company is involved with.

- The quantity surveyor's working papers for the last count he supervised and the latest quarterly rolling budgets should be obtained. His assessment of profits/losses/degree of completion of recent contracts will need to be reviewed.

- Information on the types of building work that Robson does is important. Prescott wants to acquire the company to undertake the building of hotels and other leisure facilities such as swimming pools.

- Details of current contract agreements with customers are required to get information on any guarantees, penalties etc that may be incurred.

(d) Specific inquiries

- Are there any losses foreseen on any contracts that are currently in progress?

- Has full provision been made for any loss-making contracts in accordance with IAS 11 *Construction contracts*?

- Are signed contracts in place for all building work currently being undertaken?

- How are ascertainable revenue and profit calculated and assessed on current contracts?

- What are management's judgements and views on the outcome of the claim relating to the housing development that was sub-contracted to Sarwar?

- Have there been any similar claims in the past or other cases on-going? If so, what has been the outcome of these claims?

- What are the actual useful lives of assets used in construction?

42 Plaza

Text references. Chapters 5 and 12

Top tips. This is an example of an exam question where an assurance service the candidate may not be familiar with is examined. In such a situation, some might panic and earn no marks. Make sure that you apply the basic principles of assurance provision that you have learnt and your common sense and business knowledge and be one of the candidates who gives an 'excellent' answer (see examiner's comments below). Make sure you read all parts of the question. In this case, even if parts (a) and (b) put you off, any business advisor who had not studied for this paper should have been able to gain marks in parts (b) and (c).

Easy marks. Easy marks were available in part (c) of this question which was basically a comprehension exercise. In (i) you had to write down questions which might have occurred to you from reading the scenario, and in (ii) you could produce some simple analysis from data given in the question. There were also easy marks available in part (b) for basic considerations about accepting an engagement.

Examiner's comments. Answers ranged from excellent to non-existent/irrelevant. However, some candidates, who were quite weak on other questions, kept their heads on this one and gained easy marks (on part (b) in particular).

Part (a): Many candidates described 'due care' (ie a 'fundamental principle') or 'customer due diligence'. Some candidates looked to the remainder of the requirement and took the mark for stating that a review would take the form of inquiry and analytical procedures.

Part (b): Anticipating this requirement is one thing, but candidates must be able to 'tailor' their answer points to the specifics of the question. This was **not** an audit assignment – rendering consideration of legal requirements and recurring fee percentages (for example) were completely irrelevant. As a clear example of not reading the question carefully, a large number of candidates made points relating to MCM's shares being quoted on a stock exchange. This was not the case – MCM was wholly-owned by Frontiers. Weaker candidates lost focus and explained matters that should not have been considered until after the engagement was made.

In part (c) many candidates defined these procedures, most usually in the context of an audit. 'Inquiry' is the process of asking questions. Although the overall appreciation of what constitutes analytical procedures has improved, many candidates are still reading 'analytical' as 'audit' and writing wholly irrelevant comments on walk-through checks, tests of control and detailed substantive procedures, obtaining management representation, etc. Candidates who calculated profit percentages for the national and international businesses, and the average collection period for the international receivables, scored easy marks.

Marking scheme

Marks

(a) **Due diligence review**
Generally up to 2 marks for each of meaning, nature and purpose   4
Ideas
- Meaning – definition/usage of term
- Nature – review = investigation + disclosure
- Purpose – fact finding
- Investigation = enquiry + analytical procedures

(b) **Matters to be considered**   10

Generally ½ mark each matter identified (max 4 marks)
and up to 1½ marks a point explaining its relevance

General Ideas

- Purpose of the review/associated risk
- Scope of the assignment
- Competence and experience
- Resources available
- Reason for acquisition
- Timescale
- Confidentiality
- Other service opportunities

Ideas specific to Plaza

- Who is Duncan Seymour?
- Why has auditor not been engaged for assignment?
- Any relationship between Plaza and MCM

(c) **Due diligence review**

(i) Generally ½ – 1 mark each enquiry   4

Ideas

Concerning

- off balance sheet finance
- contingent liabilities
- commitments/contracts
- knowledge confined to management

(ii) Generally ½-1 mark each analytical procedure   6

Ideas

Level of procedure

- MCM as a whole
- National/international business
- Centres therein

Concerning

- Income statement items (revenue/costs/profit)
- Trade receivables
- Financial ratios
- KPIs
- Cash flow

$$\overline{\underline{24}}$$

(a) **Due diligence**

Due diligence is a term most often found in connection with a prospective business purchase. It refers to work commissioned by a client involving inquiries into agreed aspects of the accounts, systems and activities of the target company.

The accountant performs an investigation such that there is a reasonable expectation that all information which might have a bearing on the acquisition is reported to the potential investor.

The accountant will rely more heavily on procedures such as inquiry and analytical review. This is because:

- A lower level of assurance is being sought as compared to an audit. In some instances no assurance may be given with the report simply highlighting issues arising.

- These techniques provide indicators to direct work to risk areas. This increases efficiency, an important factor in this type of assignment where timescales are tight.

- Due diligence normally involves the work of accountants but may also involve surveyors, actuaries, lawyers and other professionals.

(b) **Matters to consider**

- Whether there are any ethical reasons why the work cannot be undertaken.

    For example if there is a close relationship between Duncan and any of the partners of Andando objectivity would be impaired.

- Whether there are any conflicts of interest.

    This would be the case if Andando was already acting on behalf of another client also interested in acquiring MCM.

- Whether Andando has the relevant expertise in this type of work and this type of industry.

    Availability of resources and timing of deadlines would also need to be considered, particularly if work will need to be carried out on the international businesses in Europe and Asia.

- Size of the fee and the ability to obtain additional work as a result of this review.

- Why Andando has been approached to perform the work.

    Often in this case it would be the company's auditors who are asked to perform the due diligence review on the target company.

- Status of Duncan Seymour.

    As chief finance officer it is not clear if he is acting with the authority of the main board.

- The nature of the assignment.

    Duncan has asked Andando to 'advise' on a bid. Whilst Andando can provide relevant information about factors affecting the bid it would not be appropriate for the firm to take executive decisions. Ultimately the decision to purchase MCM must be taken by the board.

- The scope of the assignment.

    The precise terms of the due diligence review would need to be clarified. It is currently unclear as to whether the scope would cover just the national business or both the national and international businesses.

- The purpose behind the transaction.

    Andando would want to establish what Plaza is hoping to achieve from the acquisition of MCM. For example it may be that Plaza intends to use MCM to provide its in-house training. This knowledge would assist the team in determining the key issues in relation to the achievement of these goals.

- Availability of information.

    This will depend on the access that Andando will be given to the records and personnel of MCM. The degree of secrecy surrounding the negotiations will also affect availability of information. For example if the deal will result in redundancies Andando's access to some members of MCM staff may be restricted.

- Relationship with MCM's auditors.

    Andando should be free to communicate with the auditors of Plaza to inform them of their intention to carry out the due diligence work and to ask them to confirm whether there are any reasons why they should not accept the assignment.

(c)   (i)   **Inquiry**

- The extent to which the good name and past performance of MCM is dependent upon its relationship with Frontiers.

- Whether the change in ownership result in a loss of business. For example some contracts may have been awarded to MCM in the past on the basis that the tuition is based on material produced by Frontiers.

- Whether the purchase of MCM will lead to any 'economies of scale' in the group as a whole eg staffing, overheads.

- Whether there are any terms in the employment contracts of directors or senior employees which would result in substantial payments being made to these individuals if the acquisition went ahead.

- Whether freelance consultants would be entitled to any redundancy payments.

- Whether there are any terms in the operating leases or long leases which would be affected by the transfer of ownership of MCM. If leases are terminated, there might be penalties to pay.

- Whether any significant events have taken place after 30 June 2007 which might have a bearing on the potential acquisition eg substantial new commitments.

- What effect the change in ownership would have on liabilities. For example there may be tax consequences or terms in loan covenants which require repayment in this event.

(ii)   **Analytical procedures**

Income statement
Review trends in

- Revenue
- Gross profit
- Net profit

in the business as a whole.

Compare actual revenues and profits for the last 3 years with projected revenues and profits.

Compare actual and budgeted figures on a centre by centre basis for the following expenses:

- Staff costs
- Training material costs
- Property costs

Calculate and make comparisons of the following ratios:

- Return on capital employed
- Earnings per share
- Gross profit margin

for the business overall and on a centre by centre basis.

Balance sheet

Calculate and make comparisons of the following ratios on a month by month basis for the National and International business:

- Accounts receivable collection period (approximately 214 days in the International business at 30 June 2006.)

- Accounts payable collection period

- Current (liquidity) ratio

Cash

Compare the actual cash balance with the budgeted cash balance for the business as a whole on a month by month basis.

Compare the overdraft facility with any actual overdrawn account balances.

Performance

Compare the total number of delegates on a centre by centre basis.

Compare the total number of training days on a centre by centre basis

Compare the revenue per delegate for the National and International businesses for the last three years.

Compare the number of contracts won/cancelled by centre.

43 Ferry

Text reference. Chapter 6

Top tips. This is a relatively straightforward question where you should expect to score well. Part (a) looks at the concept of the 'top-down' approach. You need to make sure you can explain basic audit terminology as in this case you can score five marks for pure theory. For parts (b) and (c) a tabular approach would be sensible as this will enable you to make clear the connection between the two requirements. When using a tabular approach however you must take care not to produce a note-form answer. Don't fall into the trap of answering the question from the auditor's point of view. Notice you are being asked to perform the business risk assessment as a management assurance service so you need to consider the issues from the business's perspective.

Easy marks. These can be obtained for explaining a 'top-down approach' in part (a) and for identifying risks in part (b).

Examiner's comments. Many candidates did not answer part (a) of the question. Part (b) asked candidates to identify risk. Many provided an explanation of the elements of risk. This theory was not required and did not score any marks. When asked to 'identify' candidates should be brief (eg sub-headings could be used). Many candidates read the information in the question carelessly. For example, they assumed that it was Ferry who suffered a 'lack of public support and government funds.' A lack of understanding of the real world was also evident. It was often stated that the 20 year old boats should be replaced as they were obsolete in spite of the fact that they had recently been refurbished. The question clearly made a link between parts (b) and (c) and a tabular approach would have been sensible. Those who did not adopt this approach repeated points in both parts. Another reason for poor marks on this part was not attempting it, or jotting down one or two ideas like 'new boats' and 'take out insurance' without adequate explanation.

Marking scheme

Marks

(a) **Top down approach**
Generally 1 mark each point
Ideas
- Business risk methodology
- Business focus v financial statements/audit focus
- Top = overview v bottom = detail
- In planning
- In risk assessment
- In materiality assessment
- In evaluating internal controls
- In group audits

Max 5

(b) **Business risks**

Generally $\frac{1}{2}$ mark for identification +   Max 10
1 mark each point of explanation
Ideas
Environment risks
- Competition
- Weather
- Economy
- Accident, collision, breakdown

Financial risks
- Ro-Ro costs
- Fuel prices
- Loss of subsidy

Compliance risks
- Rights to operate
- Non-compliance with environmental regulations
- Waste spills
- Safety management

Operations risks
- Poor service levels (eg catering, booking, timely operation)
- Passenger safety
- Employee-related issues (eg crew safety)

(c) **Risk management processes**

Generally 1 mark each point   Max 10
Ideas
Accept the risk
- Low impact risks
- Benchmark (or could reduce risk)

Reduce the risk
- By implementing improved internal controls
- Staff training
- Hedge against it (eg fuel prices)

Avoid unacceptable risks
- Non-compliance

Transfer the risk
- By insurance (amount/type)
- Contractual risk sharing (with franchisees)

Recovery plan
- Disaster scenario

                                                                                    25

(a) **'Top-down approach'**

The top-down approach is a term which can be used to describe the overall approach to an audit and the approach to the individual stages which make up the audit process. This approach looks at the 'big picture' by trying to mirror the risk management steps that have been taken by the directors. In this way the auditor will seek to establish that the financial statement objectives have been met, through an investigation of whether all the other business objectives have been met by the directors.

The auditor gains an understanding of management's business strategy, business processes, key performance indicators and associated risks and controls and compares his assessment of these with the position reflected in the financial statements.

In other words this approach starts at the business and its objectives and works back **down** to the financial statements, rather than working up from the financial statements which has historically been the approach to audit.

Specific examples of the impact that this will have on the audit are as follows:

- At the planning stage the auditor will start at the top by obtaining a detailed understanding of the client's business as a whole and its core business processes through discussions with management and preliminary analytical procedures. Then the auditor focuses on the details, for example risky transactions and balances.

- The audit strategy summarises the overall approach to the audit while the audit plan sets out the detailed, lower level work. Materiality is judged in relation to the financial statements as a whole and then allocated to individual balances.

- As the auditor pays greater attention to high level controls used by the directors to manage business risks, controls testing will be focused on the control environment and corporate governance as well as the detailed procedural controls tested under traditional approaches.

As this approach to the audit initially concentrates on high level issues it tends to be partner led. The term 'top-down' also applies therefore to the way in which the audit team operates.

(b) Business risks	(c) Process for managing
Rights to operate The exclusive rights to operate are only effective for another 5 ½ years . Depending on the likelihood of these rights being renegotiated this raises questions about the ongoing viability of the business. The right to operate may have been granted provided that certain conditions are met. If Ferry does not continue to satisfy these terms its operational existence may be called into question.	It is unlikely that the business is in a position to change the situation regarding the period for which the rights have been granted and therefore is a risk that the business has to accept. Management should be aware of any conditions which will affect the renewal of rights and take steps to ensure that these are complied with. Relevant staff should be made aware of any contractual conditions and their responsibility for ensuring that these are met. Compliance should be reviewed and monitored by an appropriate level of management.
Future competition Profitability could be affected by future competition. This might be the case in the advent of a new bridge being constructed or if the rights were no longer exclusive to Ferry.	Management should monitor any plans which would introduce new competition, for example the building of a new bridge. Management should also consider how it can maintain its competitive advantage by ensuring that its service meets the needs of its customers.
Age of the ferries It is likely that running costs will be higher than those for newer ships. Fuel consumption is likely to be higher as the engines will be less efficient. This is of particular concern in periods when fuel prices are volatile. Ongoing maintenance is also more likely to be required.	Running costs should be adequately budgeted for and cash flows monitored to ensure that these can be met. Price structures should be flexible to allow increased fuel costs to be passed on to the customer. Forward contracts could be used to hedge against the effect of changing oil prices.
Emission standards The company will be required to meet the emission standards which come into force in 2009. If the necessary modifications are not made the company could incur substantial penalties. Custom may be lost due to the potential disruption caused to services during the period in which the modifications are made to the ferries.	Management should familiarise themselves with the Environmental Protection Regulations. Funds should be made available and the work scheduled to ensure that the deadline for compliance is met. Plans should be made to minimise the inconvenience to the customer eg changes in the schedule should be advertised, the work should not be planned for peak periods in the year.

(b) Business risks	(c) Process for managing
Surplus capacity	Management need to be aware of the capacity required to ensure that revenue at least covers costs (ie breakeven point).This should be reviewed and monitored on a continual basis.
Franchise arrangements The quality of outsourced services are outside the direct control of Ferry. Ferry may receive complaints and ultimately lose customers if services are poor.	The performance of other businesses/franchisees should be monitored by Ferry. Franchise agreements should stipulate minimum quality standards and should include penalties/termination clauses for consistent unsatisfactory performance.
Subsidy Ferry may depend on the subsidy to continue in business. Cash flow problems could arise if the subsidy stopped (ie it may only be awarded for a given period or be dependent on certain quality standards being maintained). If sufficient controls are not in place returns may be submitted late or may include inaccurate information. Cash flow problems could result due to late or non-payment. There is a risk that details on the return might be deliberately inflated to increase the payment received.	Management should be aware of the conditions attached to the payment of the subsidy and ensure that these targets are met. If the subsidy is available for a limited period plans should be made to ensure that the business can remain viable. Good internal controls should be implemented to ensure that returns are accurate and completed on time. Internal audit may provide management with added assurance. Fraudulent completion of returns is likely to be performed with the knowledge of management. The seriousness of this risk depends largely on the integrity of the individuals involved.
Health and safety Ferry may not be awarded its Safety Management Certificate if it fails to meet the performance and documentation standards. Ferry will find it difficult to find and retain staff if working conditions do not comply with health and safety regulations.	Management should monitor activities and the completion of safety documents. This function could be performed by internal audit.
Litigation Ferry may be sued by customers for personal injury and damage to or loss of property. In the case of serious injury or death damages could be substantial.	Liability should be limited where possible (eg passengers leave valuables in unattended vehicles at their own risk). Staff training should emphasise public safety. Safety drills should be practised regularly. The company should have adequate public liability insurance.
Serious incident A catastrophic incident could lead to a loss of assets which may threaten the operations in the short and long term.	The ships should be maintained to a high standard and regular checks should be made to ensure that safety equipment is in working order eg life boats. The ships should be fitted with up to date equipment to prevent or deal with serious incidents. This equipment should be tested and maintained regularly.

(W1) 2 boats × 40 vehicles × 6 crossing × 365 days = 175,200

70,000/175,200 = 40%

44 Pacific Group

Text reference. Chapter 16

Top tips. This question might seem overwhelming, but bear in mind that the risks have already been identified, and you simply have to assess how serious they are. Make sure that you read the question properly and understand the criteria that it gives you to judge whether risks are applicable or not, then apply those criteria to each risk in the question. If you are not sure, decide whether you can say more in support of classifying it as applicable or non-applicable. You gain marks for your explanations.

Easy marks. The easiest marks in this question should be for thinking up controls to mitigate risks already identified in the question. The examiner's model answer gives examples of controls even for risks the model answer classifies as non-applicable, so even if you have got some of part (a) wrong, you could still potentially get maximum marks in part (b). As the examiner notes below, there were also easy marks available for drawing conclusions as to whether risks were applicable or not.

Examiner's comments. In part (a), the majority of candidates stated whether each of the given risks was applicable or not, but fewer provided a plausible reason for their conclusions. Too many 'sat on the fence' with a loss of easy marks. In part (b) easy marks were earned for controls over data transfer, cash, back-up measures, etc.

Marking scheme

		Marks
(a)	**Applicable risk**	
	Generally ½ mark for appropriate identification as 'applicable/non-applicable'	Max 5
	up to 1½ marks each point of explanation	Max 15
		Max 14
	Ideas (types of risk)	
	Environment	
	• Competition	
	• Regulatory	
	Process	
	• Operations	
	• Financial	
	• Empowerment	
	• Information processing	
	• Integrity	
	Information for decision-making	
	• Process/operations	
	• Business reporting	
	• Environment/strategic	
(b)	**Internal controls**	
	Generally 1 mark each point, max 2 × 4 'applicable risks'	Max 6
	Ideas	
	• Control procedures/specific controls	
	• Control environment/pervasive controls	
	• Monitoring activities (including reconciliations)	

20

(a) **Applicable risks**

(i) *Failure to invest in new developments*

Applicable risk

The majority of PG's income comes from advertising revenue and therefore it is crucial that they do keep up to the cutting edge of advertising developments, particularly when their competitors do. This could have a substantial adverse financial impact if advertisers decide to cut advertising in PG in favour of more up to date advertising techniques in competitor publications such as The Deep.

(ii) *Unsuitable credit limits*

Non-applicable risk

As credit limits (albeit unsuitable) are set, and the majority of customers are likely to be creditworthy, the effect of a small number of advertisers being uncreditworthy is unlikely to be substantial.

(iii) *Incomplete data transfer (editorial – invoicing departments)*

Applicable risk

It is crucial to cash flow and business operations that published adverts are invoiced. Only two full page adverts and a half page advert would have to be omitted from invoicing before the effect of this risk would be greater than $5,000, and if the system is failing to transfer data, there is no reason to assume that the problem should be limited to so few adverts.

(iv) *Rates charged*

Applicable risk

As seen above, given the prices of adverts, a problem with a small number of adverts can have a significant (>$5,000) impact. So, for example, if two full page and three half page adverts were given a 50% discount and the same number were given 'free' for reciprocal advertising, this could have a significant financial impact.

(v) *Individual errors*

Non-applicable risk

PG is likely to have reasonable controls over production to ensure that errors in production such as typos, colour problems and such like are likely to be isolated and no individual advertisement has a significant financial effect on PG.

(vi) *Cash misappropriation*

Applicable risk

Cash received at front desk is significant and there appear to be no controls to ensure that cash is secure and passed on to cashiers. This is a big risk to PG as they may simply lose a large amount of income in this way. Again, it only requires payment for three full page adverts to be misappropriated to have a significant impact.

(vii) *Errors due to unauthorised access*

Non-applicable risk

It is likely that PG has basic computer system controls making this risk a low risk.

(viii) *Availability of systems*

Applicable risk

This risk is applicable because if PG do not have contingency plans against systems failure, and many companies with computerised systems do not, then the financial and operational risks of delay in invoicing and processing advertising orders could be significant in terms of customer dissatisfaction and delayed payments.

(ix) *Incomplete transfer of information to nominal ledgers*

Non-applicable risk

This is potentially significant to the reported results of the company but should not affect their operational or financial strength.

(x) *Risk of litigation for inappropriate advertising*

Applicable risk

As PG carries a large amount of advertising in its publication this risk is significant. Although PG is likely to have insurance for the financial impact of such litigation, the cost in terms of loss of reputation or/and therefore customers could be significant.

(b) **Controls**

(Note: The question requirement only requires you to give controls for four of the applicable risks. All six are covered in this answer for illustration purposes only. The numbers correspond to the question.)

(i) *Failure to invest in new developments*

- Regular review of developments in competitor products (for example, each edition, or each quarter)

- Regular review of developments available so as to be ready to action them if necessary

- Regular review of actual investment costs against budget, to see if any budgetary slack could be utilised

(iii) *Incomplete data transfer (editorial - invoicing departments)*

- Reconciliations of advertisements invoiced to advertisements appearing in publications
- Serial numbering of advertisements and sequence checking by invoicers

(iv) *Rates charged*

- Authorised price list
- Authorised discounts list
- Comparison of PG's own advertising budget to actual (to identify uncharged adverts)
- Monitoring of percentage yield for advertisements per issue
- Minimum percentage yield for advertisements per issue set

(vi) *Misappropriation of cash*

- Cashiers to supervise post opening
- Front desk staff to issue pre-numbered duplicate receipts for cash to couriers
- At least two people attend cash opening
- Prelisting of receipts

(viii) *Non availability of systems*

- Contingency plan to be established to receive/process adverts/invoices if system fails
- Tests to be run to ensure disaster plans are successful/well known

(x) *Risk of litigation for inappropriate advertising*

- Staff training in National Standards Code of Advertising to reduce inappropriate adverts being run

- Editorial policy on adverts should be published to all staff

- Report system including responsible official for all advert queries

45 Azure Airline

Text references. Chapters 6 and 15

Top tips. Part (a) requires you to identify and explain six risks in order to obtain full marks (½ a mark for identifying a risk and one mark for explaining it). The answer below contains more than this for illustration. Most of the risks identified below are signalled in the question. However, it is acceptable to use your general knowledge to identify a risk not signposted in the question, such as the fact that the price of fuel can escalate, and Azure needs fuel to operate. In part (b) you are basically asked for controls for the risks, and you must think widely about how the risks could be managed. For example, think about the lease contract. It must have contingencies and protections for Azure's operation in it. It is important that you do not spend so much time on parts (a) and (b) that you do not attempt part (c), even if you feel that it is hard. Again, use your common sense to think about practical measures in the airline industry. What performance factors are important to the company? The question indicates that efficiency and timeliness are important - think about how these could be measured.

Easy marks. There are no easy marks per se in this question. The easier marks are available for identifying risks from the question in the first place. Harder marks are then available for explaining those risks and how to mitigate them.

Examiner's comments. When asked to 'identify' candidates must be brief (eg using sub-headings and not copy out chunks of text from the question. Most candidates correctly identified the major business risks (half a mark each) though fewer went on to explain them well (one mark each). Far too many answers focused irrelevantly on competition. In part (b) candidates who tabulated their answers to parts (a) and (b) generally scored more highly overall, as they produced balanced answers. Candidates attempting (a) first, in isolation, tended to overrun and marks awarded to part (a) were restricted to the maximum available (9) with not enough time being given to parts (b) and (c) or later questions. Weaker candidates did not appreciate the business reality of the situation and the need to answer within the constraints imposed. For example, suggestions to 'buy a newer plane', 'buy another plane', 'employ own captain and co-pilot', were inappropriate to an entity operating just two days a week. Candidates should take note that they are provided with information relevant to the whole question. So for example, every item of information did not need to be translated into a risk in the answer to parts (a) and (b). The reference to timesheets was a pointer to evidence requirements for part (c) – even where this part was attempted many candidates did not read, or ignored, the underlined words and failed to answer the question set.

Marking scheme

	Marks

(a) **Business risks**
Generally ½ mark for identification +
1 mark each point of explanation   9
Ideas
Environment risks
- Competition
- Weather
- Emergency

Financial risks
- Overhaul costs
- Fuel prices
- Lease obligations
- Economy
- Loss of revenue

Compliance risks
- Rights to operate
- Safety management

Operations risks
- Age of aircraft
- Poor service levels (eg catering, timely operation)
- Passenger/crew safety
- Over-bookings

(b) **Risk management processes**

Generally 1 mark each point   9

Ideas

Accept the risk
- Low impact risks
- Benchmark (or could reduce risk)

Reduce the risk
- By implementing improved internal controls
- Staff training
- Hedge against it (eg fuel prices)

Avoid unacceptable risks
- Non-compliance

Transfer the risk
- By insurance (amount/type)
- Contractual risk sharing

(c) **Operational performance measures**

Generally ½ mark each measure (eg efficiency, capacity)   Max 6
½ – 1 mark each source of evidence

Ideas

Performance measures
- Types of performance measure (eg efficiency, capacity)
- Numbers/proportions/%s
    - Fights
    - Passengers
    - Cargo (tonnes)

Audit evidence
- Oral vs written
- Internal vs external
- Auditor generated
- Procedures (relevant, reliable, sufficient)

                                                                                            24

(a) **Business risks**

(i) **Leasing of equipment and specialist staff**. As Azure leases its equipment and the most specialised of its staff from another airline, there is a risk that its equipment and/or pilots could be withdrawn leaving it unable to operate.

(ii) **Conditions of exclusive right**. The PAA requires Azure's aircraft engines be overhauled biannually. There is a risk that Azure will be unable to meet this condition, if the lessor company does not agree to regular overhaul or that it will be too expensive for Azure to meet this requirement and it could lose the right to operate, or its exclusivity, opening it up to competition. There may be other conditions which Azure has to meet, such as the two weekly flights being a minimum.

(iii) **Necessary service suspension**. As Azure is required to overhaul its engines every two years, there will be a significant period every two years where Azure will either have to incur the cost of leasing other planes (assuming this is possible) or will have to suspend services. The cost of leasing other planes might be prohibitively expensive or the disruption to service might mean that conditions relating to the right to operate might not be met. As Azure only has one plane, service would also be interrupted if there was an emergency relating to the plane, such as fire or a crash.

(iv) **Age of aircraft**. The aircraft being leased is old. This raises operational risks (it may not always be able to fly due to necessary maintenance), finance risks (it may require regular repair) and compliance risks (it may not meet environmental or safety standards, now or in the future).

(v) **High proportion of expensive seats**. The plane leased by Azure has a high proportion of unrequired expensive seats and therefore insufficient (overbooked) cheaper seats. Although Azure can appease customers by upgrading them, this means the airline is operating well below capacity.

(vi) **Cargo**. The flight route results in the airline carrying a large amount of horticultural produce. This raises various risks – that Azure might be liable to passengers if their cargo degrades in transit, that the airline might be liable for any breaches of law by its passengers (for example, if prohibited items are transferred into Pewta or Sepiana, many countries prohibit the importation of animals or meat products or plants).

(vii) **On-board services**. Customers are currently dissatisfied with the food provision on the flight and there is a risk that food prepared in Lyme may become less appealing and even dangerous when served on a Darke to Lyme flight (when it has been prepared a substantial time earlier, given a six hour flight, at least an hour's turn around time, and time for getting to the airline in the first place). If the food makes customers ill, Azure might be faced with compensation claims.

(viii) **Pricing**. There is a complex system of pricing and a large number of sales agents, and Azure is at risk of operating at a sales value less than required to cover costs (for example, if too many of the cheapest tickets are sold).

(ix) **Safety**. The airline industry has stringent safety conditions and Azure may face customer boycott or difficulty in recruiting staff if safety requirements are not met.

(x) **Fuel**. The aircraft cannot fly without fuel, which can be a scarce or high-cost resource. If fuel prices escalate due to world conditions, the company might not be able to meet the costs of operating.

(b) **Managing risks**

(i) **Lease**. Azure must ensure that the terms of the contract with the international airline ensure that aircraft and staff cannot be withdrawn without reasonable notice, and that in the event of withdrawal, substitutes will be given.

(ii) **Conditions**. Azure must ensure that all staff are aware of any conditions and the importance of meeting them. However, this risk must simply be accepted as there is little Azure can do about conditions imposed on them by the governing body of their industry.

(iii) **Service suspension**. Azure must have contingency plans for service suspension, such as ensuring their contract with the international airline ensures alternative aircraft will be made available to them in the event of maintenance or damage to the aircraft, or by making arrangements to lease from a different airline in the event of emergency. As a minimum, Azure must ensure that the airline they lease from would give them financial compensation in the event of aircraft or staff not being available so that Azure's customers could be compensated.

(iv) **Age of aircraft**. Azure should have plans in place to be able to lease/afford newer planes if required to by law. Again, this could be written into their contract with the airline. Azure should manage cash flow and borrowing facilities so as to be able to afford ongoing maintenance when required.

(v) **High proportion of expensive seats**. Azure should negotiate a reconfiguration of the plane with the lessor so that business and first class seating could be reduced and more economy seats made available. If this is not possible with the current lessor, Azure should investigate leasing differently configured planes from another company. If it is not feasible to adjust the plane seating, Azure should consider its pricing and on-board facilities policies to make business and first class seats more attractive to customers. As the seats are not being sold anyway, it is probable that a reduction in prices would increase overall revenue, although this might reduce potential profit.

(vi) **Cargo**. Azure should publish a cargo policy to ensure that customers are aware of their legal obligations. They should ensure that staff are sufficiently trained to discuss the contents of baggage with customers and are aware what items Azure should not carry. They should insure against lost and damaged cargo.

(vii) **On-board services**. Azure should consider entering into a contract with a company in Darke to provide food for the Darke to Lyme journey. Obviously they must not breach any existing contract with the Lyme company and so in the meantime should review the type of food provided. For example, it might be safer to only offer cold food, for example sandwiches and cake until a Darke contract can be set up. Even if a new contract is set up, it might still be best to offer cold food as there is less chance of health problems arising as a result of serving cold food rather than hot food.

(viii) **Pricing**. As discussed above, Azure should review the pricing policy. They should also establish limits on how many of certain types of tickets (non-refundable/single etc) can be issued for one flight and they should institute a centralised system to ensure that each agent is aware when limits have been reached. As the agents must be linked to a similar system already (to be aware of whether tickets are available for sale) this should not be too difficult to achieve.

(ix) **Safety**. The company should appoint a member of staff to be specifically responsible for safety operations (such as training, updating for legal requirements, educating passengers) and should ensure that staff are regularly appraised about safety issues.

(x) **Fuel**. The company could take out hedging contracts against the cost of fuel. Other than this, there is little they can do about this matter, and it is another risk that has to be accepted.

(c) **Measures of operational performance**

(i) **Passengers/flight**. The airline could have a target number of passengers per flight and must review actual numbers against target. Evidence of the number of passengers per flight will be easy to obtain as it will be a safety requirement that Azure maintains significant records concerning its passengers. Evidence: ticketing information, check-in records.

(ii) **Time of flight/check-in**. The airline must have target times for flight time and check-in time and review the percentage difference which occurs on a regular basis. The flight times can be obtained from the pilot's timesheet and the check-in times could be monitored by asking passengers how long they have been waiting as they check-in. Evidence: timesheets, airport records.

(iii) **Customer satisfaction**. The airline should record customer satisfaction and have a target level which it hopes to achieve and maintain. This could be measured by customers completing questionnaires which ask them to rate the service, according to pre-designed ratings (for example, poor, adequate, good, excellent). Evidence: completed questionnaires.

(iv) **Safety**. The airline should have targets for safety, for example, no accidents/number of days or staff achieving safety qualifications. Evidence: accident log books and staff certificates and training records.

46 Alexis Allison

Text references. Chapters 2, 13 and 16

Top tips. Requirement (a) of this question is quite general, although the scenario outlines in more detail what should go into your answer. This makes it a tough requirement. It is vital when answering this question, therefore to construct an answer plan, making sure that you include everything in your answer that you should do. Some of the issues you will raise in your answer are quite general issues that you will have learnt about in your Study Text which in a sense are unconnected with the scenario. The trick to answering this question is not only to include them in your answer, but also to apply them to the relevant facts in the scenario to maximise your marks.

Parts (b) and (c) of this question are more straightforward. In some ways, it might be a good idea for you to tackle them first. However, you must make sure, if doing so, that you do not reduce the time available to you to answer part (a). In fact, when approaching a question such as this, it is vital that you are very strict with your timings. It would be very easy for you to overrun considerably in time when answering part (a) of this question, and this could result in you suffering badly from a lack of time towards the end of the paper. (Of course, you do not have to attempt the questions in the order in which they appear on the paper.)

As usual, when approaching a question on risks, bear in mind the components of the risk if that will help you spot the risks in the scenario. Note particularly in this question that the finance director is interested in business risks. Although the section of the question where his requirements are outlined does not specify the type of risk assessment he wants carried out the fact that he is interested in business risks has been noted earlier in the scenario. In fact, part (a) of this question has nothing to do with audit at all, but rather focuses on business risk assessment and the review of prospective financial information. Do not get confused and start talking about auditing before it is introduced in the question.

(a)

Report

To: Finance Director, Super Retail
From: Alexis Allison
Date: December 2007
Subject: Strategy to expand into e-commerce

Terms of reference

This report has been requested in relation to Super Retail's proposed strategy to trade electronically. It covers the following matters:

- Advantages and disadvantages of outsourcing
- Business risk assessment
- Work to be performed and assurance given on prospective financial information

Outsourcing

Outsourcing is the process of purchasing key functions from an outside supplier. In other words, it is **contracting-out** certain functions.

(i) **Advantages**

A key advantage of outsourcing is that it is often **cheaper** to contract a service out than it is to conduct it in-house. It can also significantly help **cost control**, as it results in a predictable cost (the contract price), whereas costs in house could escalate due to unforeseen events. For similar reasons, outsourcing assists in planning **cash flow**, as the contract terms will make cash flow predictable.

Another advantage is that outsourcing enables the firm to employ **specialists** whereas, if the service was provided in-house, there might be a shallower learning curve.

The terms of the contract with the service provider are likely to provide **indemnity** in the event of problems arising. There would be no such comfort if a service was mishandled in-house.

Outsourcing can also provide **speed** of action. In this case, as Super Retail is keen to enter the market quickly (in three months time), outsourcing the entire operation might be the best way to set up the e-commerce operation, even if in the long-term, Super Retail plans to bring the operations in-house.

(ii) **Disadvantages**

The biggest single disadvantage of outsourcing is that the company loses direct control over that aspect of their operations.

The **initial cost** of outsourcing may be substantial. The company must also consider whether there will be any impact on the current situation in terms of staff redundancies and such like. In this instance, as the proposed operations would be new, this is unlikely to be the case.

The **outsourcing contract** will have to be **managed** by the company, which could take a disproportionate amount of time.

Business risk assessment

The company is suggesting a moderate risk strategy that involves taking essentially the same products to a different market, that is, an electronic market.

E-commerce

The strategy of trading electronically raises a number of additional business risks that the directors should consider:

(i) **Customers**. This form of expansion should in theory open up the company to entirely new customers, that is, ones who do not want to visit the stores and are happy to shop on-line. However, the company should be aware of the risk of losing current customers to the new system. If in the long-run, customers prefer to shop from home, the company might find that they cannot justify the fixed costs of their primary business, that is, retailing from the department stores.

(ii) **Competition**. Trading electronically will mean that Super Retail operate against new competitors. They should ensure that they identify whom they are and what their strengths and weaknesses are, to ensure that they do not pose a significant risk.

(iii) **Technology issues**. Moving into e-commerce raises a number of risks in connection with the technology that Super Retail will need to support the expansion. They will face problems connected with viruses, business interruption due to crashes or technical difficulties, potential over-reliance on computer experts either within or outside of the business. Of course, technical difficulties in connection with the web trading will not affect the core business of trading in the stores, but bad publicity or feeling could.

(iv) **Personnel**. There may be a need to engage staff to operate the new systems, which will represent additional fixed cost. In the case of computer experts, mentioned above, this cost could be significant.

(v) **Legislation**. The company should be aware of additional compliance risks arising from engaging in e-commerce, particularly in terms of data protection and contractual issues arising from not dealing face to face with customers.

(vi) **Fraud**. The fact that Super Retail will not be dealing with these new customers face to face increases the company's exposure to fraud.

Option 1

Risks attached to Option 1 include the fact that Super Retail will have to take on an additional fixed cost in the form of employees to run the new operations once it has been set up and also the problem that the new venture might put pressure on the current/expanded delivery system, particularly as it will be difficult to predict the required level of deliveries at the outset.

However, on the positive side, buying in external expertise reduces the risk of the system being poor quality, and the terms of the contract should give Super Retail protection against negligence or poor-quality work.

Option 2

Option 2 may reduce the risk of over or under provision for delivery discussed under Option 1 above.

However, the additional cost of the delivery under this option should be considered. The company proposes to use surface mail, which will in itself represent a significant cost. In addition, the directors must consider whether the use of surface mail is an appropriate strategy. Many of the items to be delivered will be substantial, and it may be impossible to have them delivered without using one of surface mail's more specialised delivery services or a courier service. This will substantially add to the cost of the strategy.

Option 3

If the entire operation is outsourced, the directors of Super Retail lose operational control over the division, and may find it difficult to enforce issues such as quality standards. However, they maintain strategic control and should be able to formulate a contract that contains certain minimum quality standards that must be maintained.

On the positive side, if the operation was outsourced, it would be easier to withdraw it if it proves unpopular. Also, as noted above, outsourcing a new operation like this means that the operation can be commenced more quickly and therefore option 3 could be considered as a short- or medium-term measure, with a view to bringing e-commerce operations in house in the long-term.

Option 4

Taking up Option 4 would involve significant cost at the outset and although it is not dissimilar to Option 1 in that respect, the cost of buying a family business might be inflated, and would certainly be complicated if the family wanted to be kept on in employment.

There would also be contractual issues arising, such as whether the existing delivery contract would be transferable to benefit Super Retail.

It is unlikely that investing in this company would be the ideal strategy for Super Retail, as it might leave them in a situation where they do not have total control over operations, which could impact adversely on the quality of the product and therefore corporate image.

Assurance on PFI

Super Retail is accustomed to getting reasonable assurance from work performed by Alexis Allison, that is, on the truth and fairness of financial statements as a result of an audit.

An engagement to review PFI would result in a lower level of assurance, known as limited assurance, for various reasons. Assurance on prospective financial information is usually rendered in the form of negative assurance, that is, assurance given in the absence of any reason to believe the contrary.

A review of prospective financial information is likely to rely on less detailed testing than is carried out on an audit, and a higher concentration of analytical review and enquiries of management.

Prospective information is based on significantly more assumptions that historic information. For this reason, it is impossible to give a high level of assurance.

Work to be performed on PFI

The assumptions made in the PFI will be reviewed to ensure that they are reasonable. This will be in relation to known factors, such as, the reasonableness/accuracy of past prospective information produced by the company, quotations and tenders made by suppliers in relation to the strategy, our knowledge of the industry and business and the experience of any reasonably comparable companies.

The accounting policies used in the forecasts will be reviewed to ensure that they are in line with accounting policies that Super Retail uses in its reporting and that they are reasonable.

Items in the forecasts that can be verified in any way (for example, to draft contracts, to comparable historical costs, to quotations) shall be. The mathematical accuracy of the forecasts shall be checked.

Sensitivity analysis will be carried out on the forecasts to identify any points of weakness, or vulnerability to particular factors which could render them misleading.

(b)   **Ethical issues**

Super Retail is an audit client of Alexis Allison. This means that the report above and any assurance work on the prospective financial information are 'other services' which therefore fall within the scope of ACCA's guideline that the provision of other services can reduce the firms' objectivity with regard to the audit.

Alexis Allison should review their billings for the year and ensure that they are not running the risk of breaking ACCA's guidelines about fees from single clients, that is, 15% of total income, or 10% if the company is listed or public interest. Super Retail is a public limited company, but it is not clear if it is listed. However, it is probably that such a large retail business is listed. Even if it is not, given that it makes sales directly to consumers, that is, the public, it is likely to come within the guidelines for 'public interest companies'.

Although this is a topical and controversial area, Alexis Allison may not be acting unethically if they observe various safeguards.

They should ensure that the staff members providing 'other services' are not involved in the audit of Super Retail. They should ensure that they have safeguards in place designed to prevent AA staff making management decisions. They should make disclosure of the work performed and the fees charged to those charged with governance, ideally, the audit committee.

(c)   **Implications of an outsourced division on the audit of Super Retail**

AA would need to assess the materiality of the division to the company, as this will affect the degree of work that they devote to it.

The auditors need to obtain sufficient, appropriate audit evidence in relation to the division that is managed by a service organisation.

As part of the planning of the audit, the auditors should determine whether the activities undertaken by the service organisation are relevant to the audit. In this case, they are not directly relevant (ie, they are not part of the accounting function) but they are producing revenue and expenditure that shall be reported as part of the financial statements.

The auditors should obtain a copy of the service agreement and ensure that they understand its terms. They should consider how the relevant accounting records are handled and controlled.

The auditors should assess how the outsourced activity affects the risk of the audit, and also what procedures should be carried out in respect of that activity. They should assess whether the records maintained at the user entity (Super Retail) are adequate to obtain sufficient, appropriate evidence, or whether they are likely to obtain information from the service organisation or its auditors.

47 Acrylics

Text reference. Chapter 13

Top tips. This question tackles the issue of assurance, and the relative quality of the assurance given on historic financial statements and prospective financial information. It also asks you to state what work you would carry out during a review of prospective financial information. In the exam, you might expect a question on similar lines to be worth 15 marks, as this is slightly below exam standard, but it is extremely good practice to think through the important issues raised by this question. You must be aware of the limitations that exist when providing assurance on prospective financial information. In the exam, you could be faced with a case study which involves an invitation to tender for prospective financial information, or an essay in which you are required to discuss issues relating to assurance.

(a) **Benefits of audit**

There are various benefits to Acrylics and its directors, who are also its shareholders, in having an audit of financial statements.

For the **non-executive directors**, who are not involved in the day to day running of the company, it provides assurance that their **interests are not being mismanaged**.

More generally, an audit results in **more reliable financial information**, which can result in **better quality decision making** for the company. It also usually results in the auditors giving a report on **weaknesses in the company systems**, which can then be **improved**, which in turn improves Acrylics's **management of its risk**.

Lastly, as is implied in this situation, having an audit can help a company when it seeks to **obtain credit** from other companies.

(b) **Matters to consider and procedures to perform**

General

The accountants should review the entire report and ensure that the figures in the projections are **not at odds** with the rest of the report.

They should check the **additions and calculations** in the projections to ensure that they are **accurate**. They should also obtain old projections (for example, those in the original business plan two years ago) undertaken by the same people and assess how reasonable they were in the light of intervening events.

Lastly, the accountants should carry out **sensitivity analysis** on the projections to assess the margin for error and the likelihood of bank conditions not being met.

Profit forecast

The accountants should consider the **nature of the assumptions** made in compiling the profit forecast, for example, relating to turnover and margins, and determine whether they are reasonable, particularly in the light of the previous trading of the company and other known factors.

They should ensure that the **accounting policies** used in the projections

- Are in line with policies used in previous reporting information
- Are reasonable and correctly applied

Items in the forecast should be verified to the **draft contract**, for example, **projected income** (both amounts and timing).

Any amounts included in terms of **expenditure** should be verified to comparable historical costs, or to suppliers' **quotations**.

Cash forecast

The cash forecast should be checked to ensure that it **correlates** to projections in the **profit forecast**. The **timings** should be reviewed to ensure that they are **reasonable**. Any capital **expenditure** should be verified to **quotations** or other reasonable sources, for example, suppliers' sales catalogues.

(c)   **Level of assurance**

An audit of historic financial statements gives a high degree of assurance, referred to as **reasonable assurance**. It is so called because, although it is a high level of assurance, it can never be absolute assurance due to the inherent limitations of an audit and the degree of estimation and judgement in financial statements.

A high level of assurance can be given, as the delay between the events reported and the audit means that even estimations can often be substantiated.

A review of prospective financial information can only ever result in a more moderate degree of assurance, usually rendered as limited or negative assurance. This is because prospective information is based to a significant degree on assumption and uncertainty.

48 Delphinus

Text references. Chapters 8 and 17

Top tips. Part (a) is straightforward. Part (b) is more tricky. You are required to sum up the situation and assess what audit opinion should be given. You might also be expected to appraise an audit opinion in the real exam.

(a)   **Comparatives**

Comparative figures and related disclosures are **required** in financial statements under national legislation and accounting standards. Comparatives provide a **context** for the **current year financial statements**, without which the value of the current year figures for evaluation, prediction and decision making would be much reduced. Comparatives are required for both the primary statements and the notes to the accounts.

ISA 710 *Comparatives* and ISA 510 *Initial engagement-opening balances* require that auditors obtain evidence that corresponding figures meet the requirements of the relevant financial reporting framework. This means they must be free from material misstatements and appropriately incorporated in the financial statements for the current period. Opening balances must be properly brought forward and must not contain errors that affect the current year performance or position and accounting policies must be consistent (or disclosures made if policies are changed), according to IAS 8 *Accounting policies, changes in accounting estimates and errors*.

Despite the fact that auditors do not form an opinion on the comparatives *per se,* auditors do form an opinion on the financial statements that include them.

Problems can arise when the current auditors did not audit the prior period financial statements, where the prior period financial statements were not audited, and where the prior period financial statements had a modified audit report issued on them.

These problems are not necessarily insuperable as additional work in the current period can provide comfort on the comparatives, the work of any previous auditor can, in certain circumstances, be reviewed, and the work on current year's figures can provide comfort on the accuracy of the opening position.

(b)   **Audit report**

The audit report quoted is a fairly common report that is issued where there is a change of auditors. However, the **qualification given is not always necessary** and can be avoided. **Inventory** is **likely to be material** in the financial statements of Delphinus.

The audit report is qualified – an 'except for' opinion is given on the grounds of a limitation on the scope of the work performed because the auditors were unable to obtain sufficient appropriate evidence in relation to opening inventories.

Opening inventory affects both the **comparative inventory figure** in the balance sheet and income statement, and the **profit figure for the current year**.

If the company wishes to avoid such a qualification, there are **several possibilities**. It is appropriate in any case for the firm to be appointed as early as possible and for the prior period financial statements and audit report to be examined for any qualifications or problems.

The **firm should establish what inventory records are kept** and **what control procedures** are undertaken. If **cyclical inventory counting** or **regular periodic counts are undertaken**, it may be possible to rely on the company's records provided that the records are kept up-to-date, that all inventory is counted regularly and that errors are investigated and promptly corrected. Work will need to be performed to ensure that these criteria have been met. Provided that records are adequate, analytical procedures on records of inventory levels and on gross margins (which are likely to be stable) will also assist in providing comfort on the opening position.

It may also be possible, with the co-operation and permission of both the company and the outgoing auditors, for **certain working papers** or **extracts from working papers to be examined in respect of the inventories figure**. The outgoing auditors are under no obligation to co-operate in this way however. If the relationship between the company and the outgoing auditors is not good, it is highly unlikely that they will co-operate.

Even if the outgoing auditors are not prepared to co-operate, and even if there are no regular inventory counts, provided that adequate records have been kept, **detailed substantive procedures on the opening figure may be possible by reference to purchases** and **sales records** as well as **analytical procedures**.

If the firm is appointed early enough, and only a year-end inventory count is performed, it **may be possible to perform roll-back procedures** to establish the opening position. Even if no year-end count was performed, it may be possible to perform and interim count, together with a roll-back, although if there was no year-end count and the records are not adequate, it is possible that a qualified audit report would have been issued in the prior year.

49 Avid

Text reference. Chapters 2 and 17

Top tips. It is imperative that you are not only able to draw audit conclusions, but evaluate them as well. To do so, you need a very strong accounting knowledge, which at this stage of your studies, you should of course have. Part (a) of this question was a straightforward question which you should have scored high marks on, setting you up to score well on the question as a whole if you could identify the basic issues in part (b). When approaching part (b), ensure you have a firm grasp of the timescale in the question. Here, you were given details concerning two years and the proposed audit report related to both of them. It was important that you understood what the issues were in both years to put all answers together. You must also identify the accounting issues and ensure you know enough about them to answer BEFORE you attempt part (a). If you can't answer part (b) at all, consider your other options, even if part (a) is your chosen specialised subject. Five marks is not enough!

Easy marks. These were available for explaining 'second opinions' in part (a).

Examiner's comments. This question was answered poorly, almost without exception.

In part (a), those candidates who know what was meant by a 'second opinion' and the professional protocol involved scored easy marks. Those who did not know (or guessed) and wrote about peer reviews (for example) scored no marks.

In part (b), most candidates did not recognise the nature of the qualification being given ('adverse') or understand the reason for it. Clearly the issue was about the provision and, prompted by the question, most candidates did write appropriately about the definitions, etc (IAS 37). However, most candidates did not realise or would not commit themselves to stating that the company no longer had any need for it! Candidates at this level MUST show some understanding of basic concepts – provisions are made for *de facto* liabilities and if they are no longer required for the purpose for which they were established they must be reversed.

Most candidates missed the significance of the dates involved (ie that the prior year auditor's report was not qualified in respect of the provisions having initially been set up). Candidates must pay attention to detail in reading dates and interpreting the timeframe.

Some easy marks were available to those who identified other alternative opinions, but most candidates did not attempt to explain their suitability.

Marking scheme

		Marks

(a) **Explanation of a request for a 'second opinion'**
Generally 1 mark a point   Max 7
Ideas
- Meaning (eg application of accounting standard)
- Risks arising (eg threat to objectivity of auditor)
- How to minimise/need for relevant info
- Communication with auditor
- Hypothetical situations

(b) **Proposed auditors' report**
Generally 1 mark a comment   Max 13
Ideas
- Adverse opinion
- Non-compliance IAS 37
- Change in accounting estimate
- Vs fundamental error (IAS 8)
- Sufficiency of evidence
- Materiality
- Vs pervasive
- Unqualified NOT appropriate
- Limitation NOT appropriate
- 'Except for'

                                                                                   $\underline{\underline{20}}$

(a) **Second opinion**

If an auditor is asked to comment on an issue such as an accounting treatment, or a proposed audit opinion by someone who is not a client, then it is likely that he is being asked for a second opinion and he should take care in his answer.

How to respond to the request

The auditor should ask why the opinion has been sought and then contact the person's auditor to obtain any relevant facts relating to the situation. He should then ensure that a copy of his (the second) opinion is sent to the first auditor, although he will need permission from the entity to do this.

If the auditor is told that the situation is hypothetical, when he gives his opinion, he should be very careful to point out that the opinion is based on hypothetical facts and does not relate to any specific organisation.

Why such care should be taken

The auditor is at risk of giving an inappropriate opinion if he gives an opinion without being aware of all the relevant facts.

It is also a significant possibility that giving a second opinion will put pressure on the company's auditor (who gave the first opinion) and may compromise his independence. An auditor should always, therefore, decline to give a second opinion if the client refuses permission for him to contact the company's auditor.

(b) **Avid – proposed audit opinion**

The proposed audit opinion gives an adverse opinion on the grounds of disagreement with accounting treatment. The auditor does not agree with the accounting treatment of $3.9 million of provision in current or prior year.

2007 Provision

The 2007 balance sheet shows provisions of $3.9 million. Per IAS 37, a **provision** is a **liability** that is of **uncertain timing or account**.

The question clearly states that all known liabilities and claims have been settled, so this inclusion of a provision for liabilities does appear to be inappropriate.

Contingent liabilities

The directors feel that it is prudent in the light of the fact that the company is to be liquidated to recognise a provision. This implies that they believe it is possible that there are still some existing liabilities. In which case, it might be acceptable to disclose contingent liabilities (possible obligations arising from past events whose existence will be confirmed only by the occurrence of one or more uncertain future events, not wholly within the entity's control) but this also seems unlikely, as the only future event appears to be liquidation, which is neither uncertain or out of the entity's control.

Materiality

In the context of the 2007 accounts only, this amount of $3.9 million is likely to be highly material, if not pervasive because as the company has had no assets or trading during the year, there are unlikely to be many other figures in these accounts.

2006 – provisions

The auditors gave an unqualified audit opinion last year. This means that at the time, they believed, according to evidence available to them, that the provisions showed a true and fair view.

However, the audit report for 2007 indicates a belief that the provisions did not give a true and fair view in the prior year. This is not simply because in the current year the provisions have been proved in practice to be lower than was estimated. That would simply be adjusted for in the current year. It appears that the auditor believed there was a fundamental error in the calculation of provisions that necessitates a prior period adjustment in 2007.

2006 – prior period adjustment (IAS 8)

The auditor suggests in his audit opinion that an error which would have necessitated a qualified opinion last year had he been aware of it exists and that this should be adjusted in the 2007 financial statements.

Materiality

The matter is clearly material to provisions in 2007 as it would reduce them to zero. On the basis that there is likely to be little else in the accounts for 2007 (discussed above) this is also likely to be pervasive. It is also material to the 2006 accounts at 40% of last year's provisions balance.

Alternative audit opinions

If the auditor persuaded the directors to amend the financial statements in respect of his disagreements, then it appears that an unqualified report would be appropriate as there seem to be no other problems and last year's opinion was unqualified. However, assuming the directors do not want to amend the financial statements, the disagreement is clearly material, so an unqualified report would be inappropriate.

There is no question that there has been a limitation on scope, so there is no requirement to disclaim an opinion on the financial statements.

It is therefore appropriate to qualify on the grounds of disagreement. The only question that remains is whether the opinion should be 'except for' or 'adverse.'

The issues are clearly material in both years. However, it is only acceptable to issue an adverse opinion if the matter is pervasive **to the whole of the financial statements.** In this case, the comparatives will reflect a year of trading, and while the assets had been sold, there are likely to have been other liabilities at 30 September 2006.

Therefore, while the matters appear to be pervasive to the 2007 element, they are unlikely to be pervasive to the financial statements and it would be wrong to say that the financial statements as a whole did not give a true and fair view. An 'except for' qualification would be more appropriate.

50 Question with student answer: Cinnabar Group

Text references. Chapters 8 and 17

Top tips. Part (a) to this question is relatively straightforward asking for an explanation of the auditor's responsibility in respect of going concern. This part of your answer is one of the few opportunities to score marks for rote-learned knowledge. Part (b) is much more biased towards higher skills and is therefore more difficult. It is important that you score well in part (a) to compensate for lost marks in part (b). Make sure you distinguish between auditors' and directors' responsibilities. In part (a) it is the auditors' responsibilities which are relevant.

In part (b) you need to take the information at face value. It is quite clear that the company is not a going concern so don't hedge your bets! Make sure you discuss alternative forms of the audit report which are relevant, rather than every other form of audit report that you can think of.

Easy marks. These are available in part (a) of the question. You should be able to score well in this section as this part of the requirement is knowledge-based.

Student answer. The answer addresses all the question requirements very well. In part (a), the answer could have mentioned ISA 570 *Going concern* and also the possible types of audit qualifications. In part (b), the answer gives a very good summary of the situation without going into too much detail or rambling. It also addresses very well the part of the requirement to discuss the appropriateness of alternative audit opinions. The answer is presented well with lots of space and short paragraphs, making it easy for the marker to identify relevant points, although it would also have been good to use some sub-headings to give more structure to the answer. Overall, this answer is a good pass.

Examiner's comments. Surprisingly few came close to scoring full marks in part (a). Most correctly stated the key point which was that the auditors' responsibility was to assess the appropriateness of the going concern basis being used but few went further than this basic point. Answers to part (b) were weak and showed a clear lack of focus and planning. Many did not take in the key facts in the question. For example, it was clear that the company was **not** a going concern and the two notes provided **did** relate to the same issue.

Marking scheme

Marks

(a) **Explanation of auditor's responsibilities for going concern**
Generally 1 mark each comment
Ideas (ISA 570)
Max 5

- Consider ability to continue as going concern
- Assess management's procedures
- Gather evidence
- Document concerns
- Obtain written management representation
- Assess disclosure
- Qualify auditors' report (as appropriate)

(b) **Proposed auditors' report**
Generally 1 mark a comment
Ideas
Max 10

- Meaning of unqualified/'T&F'
  - Appropriate accounting policies (IAS 1)
  - Adequate disclosure
  - In accordance with legislation
- Going concern – a pervasive concept
- Basis of preparation (going concern or other)
- Disclosure required (IAS 1/ISA 570)
- Sufficiency of evidence/limitation (NOT appropriate)
- Vs disagreement
- Materiality vs pervasive
- Unqualified (NOT appropriate)
- Adverse opinion (if going concern basis used)
- Explanatory para (if additional disclosure made)
- 'Except for'

$\underline{15}$

Student answer

(a) The auditor is responsible for giving an opinion on the truth and fairness of the financial statements. Therefore, statements which assume a company is continuing as a going concern when in fact there are grave doubts as to this, would not give a true or fair view and the auditor would have to comment on this.

[Should mention ISA 570 Going concern]

The formal responsibility for determining going concern assumption lies with the directors of the audit client. They should carry out a review and prepare their accounts in the most suitable format ie going concern (no material uncertainty), going concern (material uncertainty disclosed) or not going concern (wind up).

[Good, short, punchy paragraphs throughout this answer]

The auditor is responsible for assessing the directors assumptions in the light of the audit work carried out and commenting on any areas of disagreement. If disagreement cannot be settled the auditor should bring their doubts over going concern to the attention of users of the financial statements by means of their audit report.

[Should mention types of qualifications possible]

(b)   At 30 June 2007, Cinnabar Group could not be described as a going concern.

Therefore, for Scheel to offer an unqualified audit opinion the financial statements would have to have been prepared on a non-going concern basis and sufficient, appropriate disclosure made in notes and the director's report to the imminent ceasing of operations.

> **These paragraphs provide an excellent summary of the situation**

Notes 1 and 2 together do not constitute sufficient disclosure, regardless of the basis used for preparation. Therefore an unqualified opinion would be inappropriate.

Alternatives would be to initially encourage further disclosure by the directors in the, (if necessary re-drafted) non-going concern financial statements.

> **'Except for'**

If this was rejected and the directors wished to leave the disclosure as it stands, an adverse opinion would be the only option for Scheel. The accounts as they stand do not give a true and fair view.

> **Addresses question requirement of considering alternative audit opinions**

There is no uncertainty as to the non-going concern status of the company, the intention of the directors appears clear from their 'systematic winding down of its operations' and its closure less than five months after the year-end. Therefore, as the auditor is in possession of all the facts necessary to draw an opinion, a modified opinion on the basis of limitation on scope would be inappropriate. Similarly, a modified opinion based on uncertainty would not be appropriate.

The only appropriate opinion on the statement s as they stand is an adverse opinion. The only possibility of releasing an unqualified opinion would require the accounts to be stated as a non-going concern basis with clear disclosure of the company's imminent winding up.

> **Good use of space in answer but could consider using sub-headings as well**

BPP answer

(a)   **Auditors' responsibilities**

These are as follows:

- To consider the appropriateness of management's use of the going concern assumption in the preparation of the financial statements.

- Consider whether there are any material uncertainties about the entity's ability to continue as a going concern that need to be disclosed. The auditor should remain alert for these throughout the audit, and particularly as part of the risk assessment procedures.

- The auditor should consider the same period as that used by management in making its assessment. This should be at least twelve months from the balance sheet date.

- When events or conditions have been identified which cast significant doubt on the entity's ability to continue as a going concern the auditor should:

    - review managements plans for future action

    - gather sufficient appropriate audit evidence to confirm or dispel whether or not a material uncertainty exists

    - seek written representations from management regarding its plans for future action.

- Where the auditors consider that there is a significant level of concern about the ability of the company to continue but do not disagree with the preparation of the financial accounts on a going concern basis, an unqualified opinion should be issued provided that disclosures are adequate. The auditor would also include an emphasis of matter paragraph.

- If the disclosures are inadequate the auditor would issue a qualified or adverse opinion depending on the circumstances.

- If the auditor disagrees with the basis of preparation an adverse opinion will be issued on the basis that the financial statements are seriously misleading.

(b) **Suitability of the audit report**

Unqualified report

From the information in the disclosure notes it is apparent that the company is **not a going concern**. However it is not clear on which basis the financial statements have been prepared. They may have been prepared:

- On the going concern basis or
- On an alternative basis

An unqualified audit report means that :

- The accounts give a true and fair view
- They have been prepared in accordance with statute

If the accounts have been prepared on a going concern basis an unqualified opinion would not be appropriate as this does not reflect the true position of the company. The results would be misleading as the readers would make assumptions about the company's ability to continue which are clearly not the case. In addition to the inappropriate basis of preparation, disclosure is inadequate as the notes to the accounts do not highlight the significant problems the company is facing. In this respect they are not properly prepared.

If the accounts have been prepared on an alternative basis an unqualified opinion would still not be valid. This is due to the **inadequacy of disclosure**. The going concern assumption is a fundamental principle. **Readers of accounts assume the company is viable unless it is clearly stated otherwise**. In this case even though the basis of preparation is correct the lack of disclosure means that they are not properly prepared.

Alternative opinions

The 'except for' or disclaimer of opinion would not be appropriate irrespective of the basis of preparation as the issue is not one of uncertainty. The company has liquidated assets and we are told that the company has ceased to trade in April.

If the financial statements have been prepared on a going concern basis an **adverse opinion** should be expressed. This would be due to a disagreement with the basis of preparation. For example assets and liabilities are likely to be misclassified as non current when they should be classified as current. The opinion would be adverse as the disagreement is pervasive to the overall true and fair view.

If the accounts have been prepared on an alternative basis reflecting that the company is not a going concern, for example the break-up basis, provided that this has been applied correctly the auditor would agree with this treatment.

However a qualified '**except for**' audit report should be issued on the grounds of disagreement with the adequacy of the disclosure regarding the basis of preparation.

51 Jinack

Text references. Chapters 8 and 17

Top tips. A key aspect of this question is to note that you are required to comment on the implications for two years' worth of audit reports. Make sure that you do.

Easy marks. There were easy marks available in part (a) of this question for setting out the auditor's responsibilities for subsequent events.

Examiner's comments. In part (a) many candidates made a distinction between adjusting and non-adjusting events, though this was not necessary in explaining auditors' responsibilities covered by an auditing standard (ISA 560) and not an accounting standard as asserted by many. Some candidates gave too much detail on the accounting aspects, which was not required.

In part (b), the main weaknesses included copying out lots of information in the question, dealing with implications that had no bearings on the auditor's report, taking a scattergun approach by suggesting every possible form of audit opinion and assuming an emphasis of matter paragraph to be a universal solution.

Marking scheme

		Marks
(a)	Auditor's responsibilities for subsequent events	Max 5

Generally 1 mark each comment

Ideas (ISA 560)

- Consideration of IAS 10
- Addition to routine procedures
- Up to date of auditor's report
- Accounting and disclosure
- After ... but before financial statements are issued
- Qualified or adverse opinion
- After financial statements issued

(b) Implications for auditor's report

Generally ½ mark identification and 1 mark a comment

Ideas

(i) Corruption of perpetual inventory records

- Data loss (vs asset loss) $\Rightarrow$ limitation of scope
- Non-adjusting post balance sheet event
- Limitation imposed by circumstances
- Sufficient evidence – records vs alternative ('rollback')
- Alternative procedures – analytical procedures
- Material – not pervasive
- Potential adjustment necessary
- Material $\Rightarrow$ modified opinion ('except for')
- Immaterial $\Rightarrow$ unmodified report
- *Not* emphasis of matter
- 2006 – restate opening position/comparatives for error (if any) therefore unmodified

(ii) Wholly-owned foreign subsidiary
- Management's oral representation – insufficient evidence
- Non-adjusting post balance sheet event (?) – disclosure
- Lack of evidence ⇒ limitation of scope
- Limitation imposed by entity
- Material vs material and pervasive
- Unmodified vs modified 'except for' limitation vs disclaimer

(i)		Max 6
(ii)		Max 4
		15

(a) Auditor's responsibilities in respect of subsequent events

The auditor is required to consider the effect of subsequent events on the financial statements and therefore the auditors report. Subsequent events are events which have occurred after the balance sheet date.

Subsequent events fall into three categories, and the auditor's responsibilities are different for each category.

(i) *Between the period end and the date of the auditor's report*

In the period between the balance sheet date and the auditor's report being signed, the auditor must perform procedures to obtain appropriate audit evidence that subsequent events necessitating revision of or disclosure in the financial statements have been identified and correctly accounted for. These procedures would normally include making enquiries of management, considering whether management has suitable procedures for identifying relevant subsequent events, reading the minutes of relevant management/governance meetings and reviewing the most recently available financial information, for example, management accounts.

(ii) *After the date of the auditor's report*

The auditors do not have a duty to carry out procedures in respect of subsequent events after the audit report has been signed. Management are responsible for bringing relevant matters arising before the financial statements have been issued to members to the attention of the auditors. If the auditors become aware of an issue that necessitates revision to or disclosure in the financial statements, they should encourage the directors to amend the financial statements and then should issue a new report. If the directors do not amend the financial statements and the auditors' report has not been released to the entity, then the auditors should issue a qualified opinion. If the report has been released to the entity, the auditor should notify those charged with governance not to release the financial statements. The auditor should seek legal advice and take steps to prevent reliance on their original report.

(iii) *After the financial statements have been issued*

If the auditors become aware of an issue that would have caused them to modify the auditor's report after the financial statements have been issued, they should discuss the matter with management.

If management issues a revised set of financial statements, the auditors should issue a new audit report, including an emphasis of matter paragraph outlining the reason for the new financial statements and report.

If management does not issue a new set of financial statements, the auditors should tell those responsible for the governance of the entity that they will take steps to prevent reliance on the audit report. They should seek legal advice about what steps to take, and then take them.

(b) **Matters arising during the audit of Jinack Co**

(i) *Inventory*

There has been a breakdown in the perpetual inventory system at Jinack Co, meaning that there is currently no inventory figure for 30 September 2007. This affects the closing inventory in the financial statements for 2007 and the opening inventory in the financial statements for 2007, so could potentially affect both audit reports.

The failure of the perpetual inventory system and therefore the lack of inventory figure at the year-end date could be a limitation on the scope of the audit which would necessitate the audit report being qualified on this issue (except for).

However, it appears that Jinack is attempting to reconstruct the inventory figure, and this method may provide sufficient, appropriate audit evidence about the inventory figure so that it is not necessary to modify the audit report.

The auditors should attend the inventory count being undertaken and obtain evidence about the controls over that count. They should also seek evidence that controls over the roll back are adequate.

When the count and the roll back have been completed and audited, the auditors should assess whether they have sufficient appropriate evidence concerning the inventory figure in the financial statements, and, if they do, it will not be necessary to qualify the audit report on this issue in either 2007 or 2008.

The failure of the perpetual inventory system could in itself be a non-adjusting post balance sheet event which would require disclosure in the financial statements for 2007. If this disclosure was not made, the auditors would need to qualify the audit report for 2007 on the basis of disagreement with non disclosure.

(ii) *Subsidiary*

A wholly-owned subsidiary of Jinack has commenced trading on 7 October 2007, subsequent to Jinack's year-end. It is not clear whether the company was incorporated prior to 30 September 2007.

The auditors should obtain more information about Batik. It should be possible to obtain details about its registration from the companies' registry. If this information is unavailable, this would represent a limitation on the scope of the audit and the auditors would have to qualify their audit report in respect of it.

If the company was incorporated after 30 September 2007, it requires disclosure in the financial statements as a non-adjusting post balance sheet event. If these disclosures are not made, the auditors would have to qualify the audit report for 2007 due to disagreement over the disclosure. However, assuming the subsidiary was accounted for correctly in the 2008 financial statements, the 2007 audit report would be unaffected.

If the company was incorporated before 30 September 2007 then the subsidiary needs to be consolidated in Jinack's financial statements and the relevant disclosures have to be made. If this is not the case, then the audit report for 2007 would have to be qualified over disagreement over the accounting treatment of the subsidiary Batik. This would also result in the 2008 audit report having to be qualified over the same issue if it was not corrected, as the problem would affect the comparative financial information in the following year.

52 Icehouse

Text reference. Chapter 17

Top tips. This question tests your knowledge of the audit report. In Part (a) make sure that you can produce a critique of the basic audit report as this is an important issue.

In part (b) you need to think carefully about the context in which the question is set. The finance director has asked you for an explanation regarding the example report so it is important that you reflect this situation in the style of your answer. The examiner will be looking for your ability to communicate information clearly as well as your technical knowledge.

Easy marks. Part (a) is straightforward and you should score well.

Examiner's comments. Good answers in part (a) considered the limitations of the basic audit report from the perspective of the shareholders. In part (b) it was clear that in spite of this topic being the subject of a recent examiner's article many were not well prepared for this type of question. Too many candidates included the absence of a title and an introductory paragraph etc as being a shortcoming even though the question made clear that only extracts to the audit report were reproduced. Many candidates criticised wording which had been reproduced correctly and missed the two major issues – the omission of transactions from the prior year financial statements and going concern.

Marking scheme

		Marks

(a) **Comment on perceived limitations**
Generally 1 mark each comment   5
Ideas
- What are 'standards' (on auditing)?
- Standards referred to before an audit is explained
- Jargon ('reasonable assurance', 'matter', 'misstatement' 'test basis' 'accounting principles' 'true and fair view')
- What is 'unqualified'?
- Annual report v financial statements
- Readability
- Auditor's responsibility (not much?)
- Standard wording = no judgement

(b) **Matters to be considered (before expressing an opinion)**
Generally 1 mark a comment   <u>10</u>
Ideas
- Limitation on scope? V
- Inherent uncertainty/explanatory para?
- Lack of evidence – intentionally suppressed?
- Split description of 'an audit'
- Reference to note
- No statement that opinion not qualified
- Going concern
- Fundamental uncertainty? v
- Disagreement?
- 'Adverse'
- Timing/date

Prior period
- Cause of omission
- Prior year auditors' report qualified?
- How adjusted?
- Emphasis of matter para
- IAS 8

15

(a)   **Limitations in the standard unmodified auditor's report**

The opening paragraph of the audit report sets out which parts of the annual report are subject to the audit. This can be confusing when these form part of a much bigger annual report. Readers may be left wondering what the status of all the other information is and the extent to which they can rely on it

The report assumes that the reader is familiar with both accounting and auditing terminology. The management's responsibility section refers to 'International Financial Reporting Standards' without any explanation of what these entail or which ones might be relevant to the company in question. The report also refers to 'International standards on auditing' and 'ethical requirements' again with no explanation.

The auditor's responsibility is summed up in relatively few words as being 'to express an opinion on these financial statements based on our audit.' Whilst there is then a lot of detail about the audit process itself the auditor's responsibilities are not expanded on. This may lead to the impression that these are of minor importance.

The report uses jargon the implications of which most readers would not be aware. Examples include:

- Reasonable assurance
- Material misstatement
- Reasonableness of accounting estimates
- Sufficient and appropriate evidence
- True and fair

In all of the above terms the judgement of the auditor is critical as there is no strict definition which can be applied. No information is given as to how these decisions are made or the factors which have led the auditor to his conclusions. In many cases the reader's expectations of the degree of confidence which these imply is much greater than the auditor is actually providing. This can lead to serious misunderstandings of the nature and role of the audit report.

Some of the wording has become 'legalised' in style and can therefore be difficult to understand by the reader. This is particularly the case in the auditor's responsibility paragraph.

A standardised audit report can be argued as being too rigid in its form. Some readers may feel that they have not been given all the information and explanations which they feel they are entitled to. It may also give the impression of being the performance of a routine administrative matter which is of no real relevance therefore undermining the importance of the audit.

(b)   **Shortcomings**

Prior year transactions

Limitation on scope

The paragraph commencing 'However, the evidence....' seems to suggest that there has been a limitation in the ability of the auditor to carry out relevant procedures. In a standard report a limitation on scope would be indicated by revising the opening section of the auditor's responsibility paragraph as follows:

'Our responsibility is to express an opinion on these financial statements based on our audit. *Except as discussed in the following paragraph*, we conducted our audit....'

A standard report would also include the explanation of the limitation at the end of the auditor's responsibility section. Here it is included in the middle which is confusing.

The description of the limitation is not clear. The situation seems to relate to evidence discovered during the current year that suggests a lack of information in previous years. It is unclear however if this information should have been available to the previous auditors or if it is new information which has come to light.

Emphasis of matter

The inclusion of the explanatory paragraph and the reference to adjustments described in Note 22 suggests an emphasis of matter. The reference to Note 22 is not well drafted and does not make it clear whether this is a separate issue or relates to the previously unidentified transactions.

The paragraph is included before the opinion. Under ISA 701 *Modifications to the independent auditor's report* you would normally expect this information to be presented after the opinion. It is also preferable to state that the auditor's opinion is not qualified in this respect. This statement has not been made.

Impact of prior period transactions

The audit opinion provided is unqualified in this respect. This would be acceptable if:

- The limitation is not material (however if it is not material it should not have been referred to at all)

- The situation resulted in a modified audit report last year but the matter has now been properly resolved. (In this case an emphasis of matter paragraph may deal with the situation if it is material to the current period – see below.)

- If adjustments have been made to the prior year's financial statements or in the current period's financial statements the auditor agrees with these. (If the auditor did not agree the audit opinion would be qualified on the grounds of material disagreement.)

Going concern

The presentation of the additional paragraph regarding going concern after the audit opinion suggests that it is an emphasis of matter drawing the reader's attention to a fundamental uncertainty. If this is the case it should include:

- A reference to the note in the accounts where the situation is disclosed
- A statement explaining that the opinion is not qualified in this respect (as explained above)

If there is no reference to a disclosure note because the accounts do not include this information the audit opinion should be modified (except for) on the grounds of material disagreement with the adequacy of disclosure.

The wording of the emphasis of matter paragraph is confusing. It refers to an 'adverse situation' which could be taken as meaning an adverse opinion. It also refers to the beliefs of management whilst it is the auditor's opinion that is the critical factor. If the auditors do not believe that the business is a going concern then an adverse opinion should be issued.

Date of the report

The audit report is dated 19 July 2006 which is more than 15 months after the balance sheet date of 31 March 2005. Normally the audit report date would signify the completion of the audit and indicate that the auditor has considered the impact of events on the financial statements up to this point in time. No information is provided as to why such a delay has occurred. This could be of concern particularly if the delay was related to the concerns about the viability of the company.

Conclusions

The identification of prior period transactions seems to have been dealt with as an emphasis of matter. The information given should have been clearer and should have included a reference as to where the adjustments had been made. The paragraph should have been presented after the opinion paragraph and should have included a statement saying that the audit report was not qualified in this respect.

Even if the auditors believe that the company is a going concern and that disclosures are adequate the wording of the explanatory paragraph should be amended to emphasise the auditor's rather than the management's opinion.

53 Frazil

Text reference. Chapter 17

Top tips. Part (b) is the part of this question that requires higher skills. However, in this question, even part (b) is quite straightforward. In (i) you do not have to make a judgement about whether accounting treatment is wrong or not, as the question does this for you. You are simply asked, given that this accounting treatment is wrong, what should you do? You should be able to answer it simply. In part (ii), you are tested on your knowledge of what a company should do if their audit report is published on a website. This topic is covered in the Study Text and you should be able to reproduce this knowledge fairly easily too.

Easy marks. Part (a) represents the easiest marks in this question as it is based on a piece of auditing guidance you should be aware of and you simply have to list the facts. In part (b) remember that when you are considering the impact of items on the auditors' report, you should always calculate and comment on materiality. This should gain you easy marks.

Examiner's comments. Part (a) concerned the auditor's responsibilities for reporting on compliance with IFRS. Candidates were clearly differentiated - either they scored exceptionally well or they struggled to earn a mark. In part (b)(i), most candidates recognised that the amounts involved were material and that, unless an adjustment was made in the financial statements, a qualification ('except for') would be required. It was apparent that many candidates had not read the examiner's article 'Divided Opinion.' In part (ii), weaker candidates dismissed the matter as making 'no difference'. Others incorrectly suggested that publishing accounts on a website increases an auditor's liability. Most candidates identified a security issue and better candidates considered the problem of distinguishing 'other information' from the audited financial statements.

Marking scheme

		Marks

(a) **Auditor's responsibilities for reporting on compliance with IFRSs**
Generally 1 mark each comment   5
Ideas
- Generally/background
- New 'authority' – IAPS 1014
- IFRSs only – disagreement 'except' or 'adverse'
- Both IFRS and national – simultaneous compliance, predominant framework
- National with disclosure of IFRS compliance – assertion factually correct or misleading

(b) **Implications for auditors' report**
Generally 1 mark a comment   <u>10</u>
Ideas
(i) IAS 38 non-compliance
- 'Fair presentation'
- IAS 38 mandatory requirement
- Materiality – current year vs cumulate effect
- Conclusion on compliance
- Amendments required ⇒ unqualified opinion

LEARNING MEDIA

- If not amended ⇒ 'except for' disagreement
(ii) Reporting on the internet
  - Responsibilities on the internet
  - Extent of audited information
  - Audit procedures
  - Identification of audited information
  - Vs unaudited information

15

(a) **Reporting on compliance with International Financial Reporting Standards (IFRSs)**

Auditors are required to report on whether financial statements are prepared in accordance with an *identified* financial framework.

(i) *Accounts prepared in accordance with IFRSs only*

Auditors can only give an unqualified opinion where the financial statements comply with each applicable framework. They should be alert for indicators that this might not be the case, such as:

- A note stating that the financial statements comply but specifying certain departures
- A note identifying which IFRSs have been complied with (when this list is incomplete)
- A note indicating partial compliance

If the financial statements do not comply with all the standards, the auditor must qualify his opinion on the grounds of disagreement, or give an adverse opinion if the extent of non-compliance is extreme.

(ii) *Accounts prepared in accordance with IFRSs and relevant national standards/practices*

It is extremely unlikely that a company can fully comply with two different frameworks unless the country has adopted IFRSs in their entirety.

Therefore it is very likely that the auditor will have to qualify his report with regard to at least one of the frameworks used, and as a company is required to comply with national practice, it is likely to be the IFRSs with which the company does not comply with fully.

(iii) *Accounts prepared in accordance with national practice with a disclosure about extent of compliance with IFRSs*

If an auditor was asked to report on compliance with IFRSs in this situation, it is highly likely that he would have to qualify his report, because it is unlikely that all the IFRSs have been complied with and giving disclosure about IFRSs does not constitute complying with them. The auditor would need to consider the assertions being made in the disclosures and qualify the report if the disclosure was incorrect or misleading.

(b) **Frazil's audit report**

(i) *Development costs*

In order to comply with IAS 38, development costs which meet its criteria should be capitalised. Frazil's development costs have been treated as an expense in the income statement and therefore they do not comply.

The error is not material to the balance sheet. However, costs of $3.7million are material to the income statement, as adding back the expenses would increase profit by 45%. This is a major non-compliance with the International Financial Reporting Standard.

However, the problem of non-compliance appears to be restricted to IAS 38.

Therefore, the auditors should qualify their audit report (except for) on the grounds of a material disagreement regarding accounting for development costs.

(ii) *Annual report to be published on the website*

As the audit report is included in the annual report, the company should ask the audit firm's permission to publish the audit report on the website. The auditors might want to refer to the matter in the engagement letter between the firm and the company.

If the audit report is published on the website, the auditors should ensure that their report is worded so that it is suitable for that media. For example, it might not be appropriate to refer to page numbers indicating what items their report is in respect of, but file names or other links might be more suitable.

It is important that the audit report does not become misleading when presented in this way, so it is vital that the auditors ensure that it clearly shows what financial statements it does relate to and for which years.

The auditors are likely to want to be involved in the process of publishing the audit report and may want to test controls over how the audit report is uploaded and protected from hacking.

Once the audit report has been uploaded, the auditors should check that the audit report on the website is the same as the paper version and check that the presentation has not been distorted.

54 Johnston and Tiltman

Text references. Chapters 8 and 17

Top tips. This question is straightforward if you are comfortable with ISA 510 as part (a) is worth a third of the marks for explaining the auditor's responsibilities in initial engagements. Part (b) is trickier as you need to apply your accounting and auditing knowledge to the question. However, don't be put off by this part of the question; instead, take each issue in turn and consider materiality and accounting treatment and then the impact on the audit report. By taking a methodical approach, you should be able to score reasonably well.

Easy marks. These are available in part (a) of the question if you are familiar with ISA 510 *Initial engagements – opening balances*.

Examiner's comments. In part (a) the requirement was to explain the auditor's reporting responsibilities specific to initial engagements. However many candidates did not read the question and produced an answer that related to new engagements and pre-acceptance procedures. Where answers were answered by considering ISA 510, marks were not awarded for detailing audit work to verify the balances.

In part (b), candidates did not score marks for calculating inappropriate materiality figures. Other weaknesses included copying out information from the question, dealing with issues that had no bearing on the audit report, taking a scattergun approach and assuming that an emphasis of matter was a universal solution.

Marks

(a) **Auditor's reporting responsibilities for initial engagements**
Generally 1 mark each point of explanation   Max 5
Ideas (ISA 510)
Sufficient appropriate evidence
- Opening balances
- Prior period's closing balances
- Appropriate accounting policies
If insufficient ⇒ limitation
- Qualified opinion ('except for')
- Disclaimer
- If permitted, qualified/disclaimed on results
(unqualified on financial position)
Disagreement ⇒ qualified opinion/adverse
- Misstatement not properly accounted for
- Inconsistent accounting policies
Prior period modification
- Modify again if still relevant

(b) **Implications for auditor's reports**
Generally ½ mark each implication and 1 mark each comment   Max 10
Ideas
- Materiality of Tiltman to Johnston
    (i) Inventory overvaluation
        - Non-compliance
        - Materiality to Tiltman
        - Prior year report unmodified ⇒ auditor concurred?
        - Prior period adjustment needed
    (ii) Restructuring
        - Materiality to Tiltman
        - Constructive obligation?
        - Reverse unless employees validly expect
        - Disclose non-adjusting event
        - Risk of goodwill overstatement
        - Non-compliance
        - Not a contingent liability of Johnston
Overall
- Adjustments needed in Tiltman ⇒ unmodified Tiltman (also Johnston)
- Materiality (combined effect) to Johnston
- Adjust on consolidation ⇒ unmodified Johnston
- No adjustments ⇒ 'except for' (disagreements)

$$\overline{15}$$

(a) **Auditor's responsibilities for initial engagements**

The auditor must obtain sufficient, appropriate audit evidence that the opening balances do not contain misstatements that materially affect the current period's financial statements. The auditor must obtain evidence that the prior period's closing balances have been brought forward correctly to the current period or have been restated, if appropriate. The auditor should also obtain sufficient, appropriate audit evidence that appropriate accounting policies are consistently applied or changes in accounting policies have been properly accounted for and adequately disclosed.

If this evidence cannot be obtained, the auditor's report should include a qualified opinion (limitation on scope) or a disclaimer of opinion or, in those jurisdictions where it is permitted, a qualified opinion or disclaimer of opinion regarding the results of operations and an unqualified opinion on the financial position.

If the opening balances contain misstatements that could materially affect the current period's financial statements, the auditor should inform the client's management and the predecessor auditor. If the effect of the misstatement is not properly accounted for and disclosed, a qualified or adverse opinion will be expressed.

If the current period's accounting policies have not been consistently applied to the opening balances and the change not accounted for properly and disclosed, a qualified or adverse opinion will be expressed.

If the prior period's audit report was modified, the auditor should consider the effect of this on the current period's accounts. If the modification remains relevant and material to the current period's accounts then the current period's audit report should also be modified.

(b) (i) Inventory should be valued at the lower of cost and net realisable value in accordance with IAS 2 *Inventories*. The overvaluation of $2.7 million was identified in the year ended 30 September 2006 and should have been written off then. It should not be written off over three years.

Inventory is therefore overvalued by $0.9 million in the year ended 30 September 2006. This represents 5.6% of Tiltman's total assets and 129% of the profit before tax and is therefore clearly material. In the prior year, inventory would have been overvalued by $1.8 million, so the reported profit then should actually have been a loss.

The prior period's audit report was unqualified, implying that the previous auditor either agreed with the accounting treatment or issued an inappropriate opinion on the financial statements for the year ended 30 September 2006. A prior period adjustment is required in accordance with IAS 8 *Accounting policies, changes in accounting estimates and errors*, so the comparative figures for the preceding period should be restated in the financial statements and notes and an adjustment made to the opening balances of reserves for the cumulative effect, as well as being disclosed appropriately.

(ii) A provision for $2.3 million has been made in Tiltman's accounts for the redundancies and non-cancellable lease payments that would result from the restructuring. This represents 14% of the total assets for the year and is very material.

According to IAS 37 *Provisions, contingent liabilities and contingent assets*, a provision should only be recognised if an entity has a present obligation (legal or constructive) as a result of a past event, it is probable that a transfer of economic benefits will be required to settle the obligation and a reliable estimate can be made of the amount of the obligation.

In this case, it is unlikely that there was a present obligation at the balance sheet date, given that Tiltman was acquired sometime in September 2007 and therefore very close to the balance sheet date. Furthermore the provision for restructuring costs should only be recognised if a formal plan had been prepared and a public announcement made of the plan. If this had not happened, the provision should not have been recognised in the accounts for the year ended 30 September 2007. The restructuring should, however, be disclosed in the accounts for the year ended 30 September 2007 as a non-adjusting post balance sheet event in accordance with IAS 10 *Events after the balance sheet date*.

Effect on the audit report of Tiltman

If the adjustments required in respect of the two issues discussed above are made to the accounts, then the audit report for Tiltman should be unqualified. However if the amendments are not made, the audit report will be qualified on the grounds of a disagreement with management. This would be an 'except for' qualification as the matters are not pervasive to the accounts.

Effect on the audit report of Johnston

If the adjustments required to the accounts of Tiltman are made then the audit report of Johnston will also not be qualified. If the adjustments are not made, they could be made on consolidation of Tiltman to avoid a qualification of the accounts of Johnston. However, an 'except for' qualification would result on the financial position if these adjustments were not made upon consolidation, but the results of operations would be unqualified.

55 Hegas

Text reference. Chapter 17

Top tips. Part (a) is extremely straightforward and should present you no problems. Part (b) picks up on the two issues raised in Part (a). In this instance you are asked to generate an audit opinion rather than to critique one. Make sure you attempt both parts. Remember that the requirement is to comment on the implications for the report, so make sure that you do.

Easy marks. The marks available in Part (a) are not only straightforward in the context of this question, they are the easiest on the entire paper and you should aim to collect all five of them.

Examiner's comments. Overall, there were some encouraging answers to this question.

In Part (a) full marks were easily obtained by candidates who went into sufficient detail and distinguished between: 'inconsistency' and 'misstatements in the financial statements'.

In Part (b) candidates who wanted to treat both issues the same (qualify 'except for') should have been suspicious that they had missed the point on one of the issues. Most candidates did not see the second issue. Weaker candidates missed these issues altogether and supposed that the auditor had no awareness of the revaluation of the property before reading the other information, and had therefore been limited in the scope of his work. This part again demonstrated a lack of knowledge of simple double entry. A typical comment was 'the revaluation shouldn't be in the socie/strgl – it should be in property' (but the debit entry is in property). Part (ii) tended to be answered briefly. Most just commented that the statement should be changed, though some concluded appropriately that an emphasis of matter/explanatory paragraph would be required. Comments on materiality on this part were largely irrelevant (e.g. 14% of revenue is material', 'the 2% increase is material'). Digressions into resignation, speaking at meetings etc, were beyond the scope of the retirement of the question and earned no marks.

Marking scheme

		Marks

(a) **Auditor's responsibilities for other information**
Generally 1 mark each comment   Max 5
Ideas (ISA 720)

- To read it
- 'Material inconsistency'
- Statutory obligation (e.g. Management Report) vs
- No such obligation (e.g. chairman's statement)
- Access to other information
- Need for amendment
- Implications for audit opinion ...
- ... disagreement vs
- ... emphasis of matter
- Material misstatement of fact

(b) **Implications for auditor's report**
Generally 1 mark each comment   Max 10
Ideas
Management report vs Statement of changes in equity
- Materiality assessed (up to 2 marks)
- Conclusion (material inconsistency)
- No amendment to Management report
- If no amendment ⟶ qualified opinion
- If amended ⟶ unqualified report

Chairman's statement
- Other info not statutorily required
- Material misstatement of fact/misleading representation
- Justification (Status/activity/revenue, etc)
- Chairman's statement to be amended
- No grounds for qualification
- Emphasis of matter modification

15

(a) **Auditor's responsibilities for other information**

ISA 720 requires the auditor to **read** the other information in documents containing audited financial statements to **identify material inconsistencies** with the audited financial statements.

A **material inconsistency** is when other information **contradicts** information contained within the financial statements. It may raise doubt about audit opinions drawn from evidence previously assessed.

The auditor should **consider whether the other information or the financial statements requires adjustment** as a result of the material inconsistency.

This should be discussed with management and those charged with governance.

If the financial statements need amending and the entity refuses to make an adjustment, the auditor should **express a qualified opinion**.

A material inconsistency is distinguished from a **material misstatement of fact**, which is when information unrelated to the financial statements is incorrectly stated or presented. If the auditor becomes aware of a material misstatement of fact, he should **raise it with management**.

If the entity does not amend a material misstatement of fact, the auditor should **consider appropriate action**. This is likely to be to include an **emphasis of matter paragraph** in the audit report.

(b) **Hegas**

(i) *Management report*

- The management report contains the amount and reason for a material change in equity in the financial statements that has not been properly disclosed in the financial statements themselves

- The management report and the financial statements are materially inconsistent

- The revaluation of $4.5 million is clearly material to the financial statements, as it represents 3.75% of total assets and 48.9% of profit before tax

- It is necessary to amend the financial statements. The disclosure is incorrect because the fair value adjustment should be against the opening balance of retained earnings. The disclosure is also inadequate as it has been supplemented by an unaudited report

- The adoption of IAS 40 did not have a significant impact on the results of **operations** but the financial position has increased substantially as a result of it, and hence the financial statement note should be redrafted to make it seem less insignificant

- This would necessitate the auditors qualifying their audit report for a material disagreement, unless the directors of Hegas amend the financial statements, which they are likely to do

- As the management report contains the correct information, it does not require amendment

(ii) *Chairman's statement*

- The Chairman's statement includes two assertions which are at best exaggerated, concerning the company's provision of hydro-electricity generation and its commitment to accountable ethical professionalism

- Ironically, the first claim makes the second claim appear untrue, as it is not ethical to make exaggerated claims about the company's operations

- The claim concerning hydro-electricity is demonstrably untrue

- Hegas is not required to report in segments under IAS 14, so from the auditor's point of view, the information being exaggerated is a material misstatement of fact

- The auditors should discuss this matter with those charged with governance and recommend that the claim be reduced

- If the chairman refuses to play down his claims, the auditor should include an emphasis of matter paragraph in the auditors report to outline the correct position

- This would no constitute a qualification of the audit report

- The auditors should also consider whether this material misstatement of fact has any implications for any audit evidence obtained from the Chairman during the course of the audit

56 Question with analysis: Beige Interiors

Text references. Chapters 6, 8 and 17

Top tips. In part (b) there are many clues about what not to say in this question – such as, do not comment on the fact that a junior is drafting audit report sections – it is a training exercise – and do not comment that she has missed out certain paragraphs – she only had to draft the ones without standard wording. Focus on the question asked in both sections. In part (b) that means not focusing solely on Jade's draft, but thinking generally about the matters the auditor should consider in the circumstances outlined in the question. The requirement states 'identify and comment on the principal matters relevant to forming an appropriate opinion...'. In fact, you might have found it easier to do that before looking at Jade's draft in too much detail. Remember that when critiquing an opinion, it is often best to form your own opinion on the basis of the facts and then evaluate the original audit opinion.

Easy marks. You should be able to score well in part (a) explaining how auditors consider materiality at the planning and overall review stages.

Examiner's comments. In part (a) there were a few very good and concise answers that scored highly. Many answers started with a definition of materiality - this was not asked for. Some very long answers did not answer the question set. Poor answers dealt with planning considerations in general or discussed the use of analytical procedures at the planning and overall review stages. Candidates must read the question.

In part (b) misunderstandings of auditors' reports in general and of the scenario in particular were evident in most answers. For example, candidates supposed that 'without modification' meant 'without an opinion', thereby criticising the absence of certain paragraphs, when the question indicated 'extracts', and regurgitating the different forms of audit opinion with no linkage to the scenario. Weaker candidates sometimes expressed horror that Jade had been asked to draft the report and argued for an adverse opinion wholly inappropriate in the circumstances, often resorting to redrafting the extracts (although specifically not required). Many candidates did not recognise 'Because of the significance...' as a standard introduction to a pervasive qualification.

		Marks

(a) **Considerations of materiality**
Generally 1 mark each comment   6
Ideas (ISA 230)
- Audit objective
- Quantitative vs qualitative misstatement
- Preliminary materiality $\Rightarrow$ 'NET' of audit procedures
- Criteria (%)
- Evaluating the effect of misstatements
- Qualitative factors

(b) **Suitability of draft**
Generally 1 mark a comment   9
Ideas
- Opinion disclaimed/limitation and pervasive
Principal matters relevant to forming an appropriate opinion
- Compliance with ISAs (affected?)
- Limitation of scope (yes)
- Assessment of significant estimates and judgements (made by management)
- Adequacy of disclosure
- Sufficiency of available evidence
- Reasonable assurance – misstatement caused by fraud or error
- Possible effect (material vs pervasive)
- Implications for prior year audit opinion
- Reporting by exception (proper accounting records)

                                                                        15

(a) **Materiality considerations**

Planning stage

An audit is an exercise to give reasonable assurance that the financial statements are free from **material misstatement**.

At the planning stage of an audit, auditors **set** an acceptable materiality level to enable them to detect **quantitatively** material misstatements when carrying out their audit work. Materiality will be considered at a financial statement level and at a more specific transactions and balances level, so there may be different levels of materiality.

The acceptable level will be calculated with reference to figures available to them at the time, ideally **draft figures** for the year, or recent **management accounts**, or if no such current figures are available, **budget figures**. Prior year figures will also be taken into consideration when setting materiality, but current year materiality should not simply be based on prior year figures. If budgeted figures are used, materiality should be **reassessed** when current figures are available. It is also possible that materiality will be reassessed as a result of risk assessment procedures.

Auditors tend to use a rule of thumb when setting quantitive materiality. A materiality threshold for profit may be set between 5% and 10% of profit before tax, 1% and 2% of revenue and for balance sheet items between 2% and 5% of total assets.

Auditors should also consider **qualitative** materiality at the planning stage, and if there are any known risks, such as a history of improper descriptions of accounting policies, which would be material to financial statement users, identify these in the audit plan.

Materiality needs to be considered by auditors when planning the nature, timing and extent of procedures, so will affect the overall audit strategy and plan.

Overall review stage

Auditors consider materiality when **evaluating the effects of misstatements** on the financial statements. Auditors have to consider the implications for their report if management refuse to correct errors which auditors believe are material. This will involve consideration of whether identified matters are material or even pervasive to the accounts.

The auditor also needs to consider the **cumulative effect** of immaterial errors to see whether they are material in total to the financial statements.

Auditors should report material discovered errors to management and to those charged with governance.

(b) **Audit report for Beige Interiors**

Draft audit report extracts

- Jade has drafted a **disclaimer of opinion paragraph**, which is correct only if the effect of the limitation is **pervasive**.

- However, records stolen in August are unlikely to result in a lack of evidence about **balances** (for example receivables confirmations and inventory count can be obtained) in the balance sheet at the end of September so it is **unlikely** that the effect is **pervasive** to the whole financial statements in this way.

- It is possible it would be more appropriate to give an '**except for**' **opinion** restricted to the **income statement** for the first four months of the year.

Principal matters to consider

- Whether the auditor has been able to obtain **sufficient appropriate audit evidence**. If not, then the auditor must qualify the opinion, as Jade has correctly suggested.

- What **judgements and estimates** have been made by management in reconstructing the information stolen by the former chief executive. Evidence may not be sufficient to give an unqualified opinion.

- What **disclosure** has been made in the financial statements about the loss of the financial records and the reconstruction. This should cover **what information is missing**, **what period** it related to, **why** it is missing and **what has been reconstructed**. This information should be cross-referenced from the audit report or included in the audit report. The fact that Jade has made no cross reference suggests that this information is not given in the notes to the accounts. If this is the case, the information should be given in the audit report.

- Whether the former chief executive's actions give rise to a **suspicion of fraud**. This should not be referred to in the audit report because it is unproven, but it will affect the auditors' judgement and audit work. Because of this suspicion, the auditors are very likely to qualify, in case there has been an undiscovered fraud.

- The effect these actions have on the **appropriateness of the prior year audit report**. The auditors should consider the extent of reliance on representations from the chief executive the previous year in obtaining audit evidence. It might be necessary to qualify the current audit report with regard to the **comparatives**.

57 AsiaSport

> **Text reference.** Chapter 17
>
> **Top tips.** Part (a) of this question is a straightforward 'describe' requirement that a well-revised student should be able to score highly on. Part (b) is asking you to appraise both an audit opinion and report. The best way to do well at such a question is to practice the skills involved, so work through this question and then the answer, analysing your approach.

(a) **Problems of auditing entities from developing countries**

(i) **Accounting methodology.** The officials of this ex-Communist country are unlikely to have come across Western accounting practice much in the past. It will be necessary to consider compliance with International Financial Reporting Standards, rather than national standards, but even if Western accounting practice has been followed, government staff may have difficulty understanding the concepts involved.

(ii) **Control risk** is likely to be high. It is unlikely that the country will have sophisticated corporate governance procedures.

(iii) **Audit methodology.** Local officials may not understand the audit methodology used by the audit firm and particular difficulties may arise when the auditors attempt to obtain sufficient appropriate audit evidence from third parties such as banks or solicitors, or from the government's officials. Even with full access to accounting records, lack of co-operation by local officials could hamper the audit.

(iv) **Joint practice.** At the extreme the audit firm may be forced to set up some kind of joint practice in the country concerned, or carry out a joint audit with a local firm. If a joint audit is required, division of responsibilities and how much local auditors can be relied on will need to be considered.

(b) **Audit report format**

The audit senior has wrongfully suggested that the audit firm includes an emphasis of matter paragraph in the audit report. An **emphasis of matter paragraph** is only used when the auditor needs to highlight a particular matter in the financial statements, for example, a fundamental uncertainty affecting the financial statements.

Auditors would **not draw attention to an accounting policy they agreed with** in an emphasis of matter paragraph if there was sufficient disclosure of the policy, which is implied by the reference to a note. If there was **insufficient disclosure**, the auditor would be **qualifying** his report on **grounds of disagreement**.

Accounting treatment

The accountant of Worldsport wishes to treat AsiaSport as a subsidiary or, more accurately, believes that it is a **quasi subsidiary**. Quasi subsidiaries are those investments which, while not falling into the mainstream definition of a subsidiary undertaking, are in fact controlled by the parent entity to such an extent that the parent enjoys the same benefits from the relationships with the investments as it would do if the investments were subsidiary undertakings. The important point is **control**, which in this situation means the ability to determine the financial and operating policies of the investment with a view to gaining future economic benefit. The converse is also true: control means being able to deprive others of the same rights.

Dominant party

In the situation with AsiaSport it might at first appear that there is **no dominant party** in the joint venture. It is very rare for this to be the case, however, and it is more likely that, once the **commercial reality** of the situation is revealed, a dominant party will emerge. The accountant of Worldsport obviously believes that Worldsport is the dominant partner, presumably on the grounds that it provides finance, equipment and expertise as well as because it has a casting vote.

As auditor, however, I take the opposite view, namely that the government in Worldsport's home country is the dominant party, and this view tends to be supported by the following facts:

(i) The **casting vote** rotates between the two parties, it cannot therefore be seen as an indication of permanent control. It is not correct accounting to treat the investment differently in alternate years.

(ii) **Profits are not split 50:50** because the government rakes in extra 'taxes' levied in effect only on Worldsport, plus an extra 'repatriation tax'.

(iii) **Worldsport's rights are restricted** on liquidation/termination to its original capital. The majority of the benefits accrue to the government.

(iv) **Worldsport cannot appoint a majority** of the Board.

(v) The **future plans** of AsiaSport are **determined** by the terms of the **local government's foreign investment rules** and regeneration scheme.

(vi) Most of the **agreement** has been **imposed upon Worldsport** with little choice on policy or direction.

Worldsport, while not exerting a dominant influence may be able to exercise significant influence over the financial and operating policies of AsiaSport. Further, its interest is more than 20% and is for the long term (at least five years). Therefore the investment is an associated undertaking. The appropriate way of accounting for the investment in AsiaSport is to use equity accounting.

Correct audit report format

If the accountant does not agree to change his treatment of AsiaSport in line with the above, the auditors will disagree with the accounting treatment used and, if it is material, which is implied by the auditor drawing attention to it in the original report, qualify the accounts on these grounds.

This would be a material qualification, not an adverse opinion, as the matter is not pervasive to the accounts. No explanatory paragraph would be needed, as an explanation of the disagreement would be given in the opinion paragraph (which would be headed 'Qualified opinion arising from disagreement about accounting treatment'). The opinion would end 'except for the incorrect treatment of investments, in our opinion the financial statements give a true and fair view...'

58 Cleeves

Text references. Chapters 2 and 17

Top tips. In this question, part (a) is knowledge-based and you should be able to score well if you are familiar with ISA 250 *Consideration of laws and regulations in an audit of financial statements*. In part (b) (i), ensure you go through the audit report extract carefully as there are seven marks available here. Part (b) (ii) should be fairly straightforward for three marks so make sure your points are succinct to score well. Note that the requirement in part (b) (i) asks you to appraise the audit opinion for *both* years.

Easy marks. These should be available in part (a) of the question on ISA 250. Part (b) (ii) should also be straightforward for three marks on the impact on the audit report of the group financial statements.

ACCA examiner's answer. The examiner's answer to this question is included at the back of this kit.

Marking scheme

		Marks

(a) **Auditor's reporting responsibilities for reporting non-compliance**

Generally *1 mark* each point of explanation — Max 5

Ideas (ISA 250)

- Meaning of non-compliance

To management

- Communicate with those charged with corporate governance
- Timing
- Level of authority

To users of the auditor's report

- Material
- Not properly reflected ⇒ disagreement 'except for'/adverse
- Insufficient evidence ⇒ limitation 'except for'/disclaimer

To enforcement authorities

- Normally precluded by confidentiality
- Duty may be overridden
- Take legal advice/consider public interest

(b) **(i) Appropriateness of Parr & Co's audit opinion**

Generally *1 mark* a comment — Max 7

Ideas

- Audit opinion heading
  - What is it? ('adverse')
  - Reason
- Reference to notes giving more detail is appropriate
- Non-compliance (IAS 36) – disagreement
- 'Profit or loss' *vs* loss – inconsistency
- IAS 36 title should be in full
- Information is light on detail
  - Effects not quantified – but should be quantifiable (maximum being carrying amount of non-current assets identified as impaired)
  - Why unable to quantify? – limitation in scope?
  - Non-current assets *vs* tangible and intangible (what intangible assets?)
- Why adverse? *vs* 'except for' – not pervasive
- Prior year
  - ISA 710 *Comparatives*
  - Not new (no 'as previously reported')

(ii) Implications for audit opinion on Cleeves

Generally *1 mark* an implication/comment thereon — Max 3

- Request adjustment in subsidiary's financial statements ⇒ unqualified
- Adjust on consolidation ⇒ unqualified
- No adjustment ⇒ 'except for'
- Disclosure name of other auditor

15

(a) The auditor is not responsible for preventing non-compliance with laws and regulations. However, the auditor does have some responsibilities for reporting non-compliance to management, users of the accounts and to the regulatory and enforcement authorities.

The auditor should, as soon as practicable, either communicate with those charged with governance at the client or obtain audit evidence that they are appropriately informed regarding any cases of non-compliance. If the auditor believes the non-compliance to be intentional and material, he should communicate the findings as soon as possible. However, if the auditor suspects that senior management at the client, including the board of directors, are involved, he should report to the next higher level of authority, such as an audit committee or supervisory board. If this does not exist or the auditor believes his report will not be acted upon or is unsure who to report to, he should consider seeking legal advice. In the case of suspected money laundering, it might be more appropriate to report the matter directly to the relevant authority.

If the auditor concludes that the non-compliance has a material effect on the financial statements, and has not been properly reflected in them, he should issue a qualified or adverse opinion. If the auditor is prevented from obtaining sufficient audit evidence to assess whether non-compliance that might be material or not has occurred or is likely to have, he should express an unqualified opinion or a disclaimer on the basis of a limitation in scope. If the auditor is unable to determine whether non-compliance has occurred because of limitations imposed by circumstances rather than by the entity, he should consider the effect on his audit report.

If the auditor becomes aware of an actual or suspected non-compliance which gives rise to a statutory duty to report, he should make a report to the relevant authority without delay (subject to compliance with legislation relating to 'tipping off').

(b)   (i)   The title of the opinion section does not clarify whether the report is unqualified or qualified, and if qualified, on what basis (disagreement or limitation on scope).

The quantitative effects of the failure to recognise the impairment losses have not been set out in the report and they should be – it simply states that they would increase the loss and reduce the value of non-current assets if they had been recognised.

The wording of the opinion indicates that it is an adverse opinion but it is unlikely that this would be the case – it is more likely to be a qualified opinion rather than an adverse opinion if the reason for it is that impairment losses on non-current assets have not been recognised. Without any quantifications of the amount involved it is not clear why the auditors consider the matter to be 'pervasive'.

The title of IAS 36 *Impairment of assets* should be given in full in the report.

It is not clear from the wording of the report whether the qualification is on the grounds of disagreement with the directors or a limitation on scope. The first sentence suggests disagreement with the directors but later in the report, it states that the directors have not been able to quantify the amounts and this seems to indicate a limitation on scope.

The prior year report was qualified on the same basis so the current year report should also be qualified for the comparatives. This prior year qualification should be referred to in the current year audit report.

(ii)   Howard Co is material to Cleeves. Therefore a modified audit opinion on the financial statements of Howard Co may also affect the consolidated financial statements of Cleeves if the adjustments required in Howard Co's accounts are material to the group accounts. If they were immaterial, there would be no impact on the group audit opinion.

If the adjustments required in Howard Co's accounts are made, then there would be no implication for the audit report on the consolidated financial statements. However, if the adjustments are not made, then it is likely that the audit opinion for the consolidated financial statements of Cleeves would be 'except for'.

Mock Exams

BPP
LEARNING MEDIA

ACCA Professional Level

Paper P7

Advanced Audit and Assurance (International)

Mock Examination 1

Question Paper		
Time allowed		
Reading and Planning Writing		15 minutes 3 hours
SECTION A	TWO compulsory questions to be attempted	
SECTION B	TWO questions ONLY to be attempted	
During reading and planning time only the question paper may be annotated		

DO NOT OPEN THIS PAPER UNTIL YOU ARE READY TO START UNDER EXAMINATION CONDITIONS

Section A – BOTH questions are compulsory and MUST be attempted

Question 1

You have recently been appointed to the audit of Matthew Manufacturing (MM), a limited liability company. It is a glass business with 100 employees, manufacturing glasses, jugs and vases.

The glassware is sold predominantly to a large high street retailer, but MM also sell direct to a number of local, cheaper retailers. The glassware sold to the high street store must be designed to their specification, and cannot be sold to any one else.

The company has a small accounting function which consists of the chief accountant Mr Crow, who reports directly to the managing director and major shareholder, Mr Lofthouse, and an accounts clerk, Debbie. There is a small, PC based accounting system. Debbie enters invoices into the computer and maintains the manual cash book. Mr Crow is in charge of preparing management accounts on a monthly basis, the payroll, which is approved monthly by Mr Lofthouse, the tax affairs of the company and of Mr Lofthouse. Mr Lofthouse controls purchasing and sales, although he has an assistant who produces the paperwork and liaises with Debbie in accounts.

The previous auditors did not offer themselves for re-election due to disputes with Mr Lofthouse, but have stated that they are aware of no ethical reason which bars your firm from acting. They have passed over some relevant working papers to your firm, and have met with you to give you some background information on the audit. One of the things which they mentioned about the audit was that they have always assessed internal control as poor.

Required

(a)   Identify from the scenario given above, the key

    (i)   Audit risks   **(7 marks)**
    (ii)   Business risks   **(7 marks)**

    arising from the description of Matthew Manufacturing.

(b)   Discuss the audit strategy which you feel should be adopted in the audit of Matthew Manufacturing, stating reasons why you have chosen that strategy and reasons why you have not chosen others.   **(9 marks)**

(c)   Explain the term 'professional scepticism' and comment on its role in the detection of fraud.   **(7 marks)**

(Total = 30 marks)

Question 2

You are the senior audit officer in the newly formed internal audit department of Joosy Juice, a generally well run limited liability company which operates a chain of 30 juice bars. Details of the contribution to total revenue that these outlets make is as follows:

Stoneleigh Station	24%	Guys Station	8%
Lillington Station	13%	Maltings Shopping Centre	2%
Strathearn Station	12%	Bidbury Station	2%
Gaveston Common Station	10%	Other	19%
Harveys Cross Café	10%		

The outlets sell fruit and vegetable juices and have more recently introduced a range of smoothies onto the menu. Customers may also choose from a limited range of luxury snacks including muffins and bagels. In a number of locations purchases can be consumed on the premises but the majority operate as kiosks based in shopping centres and railway stations.

Station kiosks are in operation from 6am-12pm Monday to Saturday and from 9am-6pm on Sunday. Those in shopping centres are open from 9am-6pm Monday to Saturday. Two members of staff work each shift, one of whom is the manager with responsibility for cash and inventory. Management at Head Office are becoming concerned about the high level of staff turnover at the Gaveston kiosk which has had four new managers in the last six months.

All transactions must be paid for in cash. Takings are banked after each nine hour shift. All sales and takings are recorded by computerised tills with the information transferred to Head Office on a daily basis where all the accounting records are maintained.

Reconciliations performed at Head Office have highlighted a number of discrepancies relating to the kiosk at Princes Risborough station, a relatively new outlet which has failed to perform. There have been several instances where there has been a shortfall in cash banked as compared to takings recorded by the till. In addition, information from the till shows that even though the kiosk opens at 6 am often the first transaction is not recorded until 8 am or later.

Standard menus and price lists are used throughout the organisation with the exception of the café style bars whose prices are 10% higher to cover the additional premises cost. On the whole the launch of the smoothie range has been successful. Analysis showing a breakdown of revenue of the five major kiosks has shown the following:

	Juice	Smoothies	Other
Stoneleigh	70%	19%	11%
Strathearn	69%	21%	10%
Gaveston	73%	17%	10%
Harveys Cross	86%	2%	12%
Lillington	68%	20%	12%

All ordering and purchases are dealt with from Head Office. The manager of each outlet places an order on a daily basis. The order is processed and delivered from regional warehouses the following day. Detailed inventory records are not maintained.

On a weekly basis a physical inventory count is performed and the results returned to Head Office. Each café and kiosk has a separate storeroom with the exception of the Stoneleigh Station site where two kiosks operate and share a store. At Head Office inventory reconciliations are performed and inventory losses calculated. These reconciliations have shown significant losses at the Stoneleigh and Gaveston sites.

Required

(a)   Explain the matters you would consider in planning the internal audit work for Joosy Juice.   **(15 marks)**

(b)   The directors are considering outsourcing the IT requirement, including the accounting function, of Joosy Juice. How would this affect the internal audit approach?   **(10 marks)**

(c)   Briefly discuss the advantages and disadvantages of outsourcing the internal audit function.   **(5 marks)**

(Total = 30 marks)

Section B – TWO questions ONLY to be attempted

Question 3

You are the manager responsible for the audit of Verdi, a long-established limited liability company. Verdi manufactures, distributes and installs heavy engineering machinery (eg turbines) for the oil and gas industry. The draft financial statements for the year ended 30 September 2007 show revenue of $330 million (2006 – $228 million), profit before taxation of $15.9 million (2006 – $13.7 million) and total assets of $187 million (2006 – $159 million).

The following issues arising during the final audit have been noted on a schedule of points for your attention.

(a)   During the year technological advancement of the manufacturing process resulted in an increase in production capacity in three of the company's factory buildings. The remaining factory building became surplus to Verdi's production requirements. On 29 September 2007, Verdi contracted to sell this building for $11.5 million. The building had last been revalued in September 2004 and had a carrying amount of $9.2 million at the date of sale. The gain on disposal has been credited to revenue and the balance of the revaluation surplus relating to the building, $3.7 million, has been credited against other operating charges in the income statement.   **(8 marks)**

(b) $7 million was lent to Verdi on July 2006 for five years at $5\frac{3}{4}$%, to finance investment in manufacturing equipment. The loan became repayable on demand on 1 July 2007 when Verdi failed to pay the annual interest charge for the first year. On 17 October 2007 the lender agreed to 'roll over' the overdue interest by adding it to the principal amount due. The draft financial statements classify the loan as a non-current financial liability and the first year's interest charge is accrued in 'trade and other payables'.   **(6 marks)**

(c)   Verdi's scale of charges for installing machinery was increased by 40% with effect from 1 January 2007. This increase takes into account Verdi now giving a warranty to reinstall any item which fails to perform to specification, through an installation defect, for a period of up to three years. The notes to the financial statements disclose the following:

> 'The company guarantees all installations of equipment sold since 1 July 2006. No provision has been recognised as the amount of the obligation cannot be measured with sufficient reliability.'

Installation fees for the year to 30 September 2007 amounted to $5.2 million of which $1 million related to the three months to 31 December 2006.   **(6 marks)**

Required

For each of the above issues:

(i)   Comment on the matters that you should consider; and
(ii)   State the audit evidence that you should expect to find,

in undertaking your review of the audit working papers and financial statements of Verdi for the year ended 30 September 2007.

Note. The mark allocation is shown against each of the three issues. You should assume it is 11 December 2007.

(Total = 20 marks)

Question 4

(a) Discuss the current auditing guidance in place for auditors auditing group accounts. **(8 marks)**

(b) You are an audit manager in Moltisant, a firm of Chartered Certified Accountants, and currently assigned to the audit of Capri Group. The consolidated financial statements of Capri Group are prepared in accordance with the accounting standards and guidance issued by the International Accounting Standards Board (IASB). The draft financial statements for the year ended 30 June 2007 show profit before taxation of $6.2 million (2006 – $5.5 million) and total assets $32.5 million (2006 – $29.8 million).

One of the Group's principal subsidiaries, Capri (Overseas), is audited by another firm, Marcel. You have just received Marcel's draft auditors' report as follows:

Basis of audit opinion (extract)

'As set out in notes 4 and 5, expenditure on finance leases has not been reflected in the balance sheet but included in operating expenses and no provision has been made for deferred taxation. This is in accordance with local taxation regulations.

Opinion

'In our opinion the financial statements give a true and fair view of the financial position of the company as of 30 June 2007 and of the results of its operations and its cash flows for the year then ended in accordance with ...'

The draft financial statements of Capri (Overseas) for the year ended 30 June 2007 show profit before taxation of $1.9 million (2006 – $1.7 million) and total assets $6.5 million (2006 – $6.6 million). The relevant notes (in full) are as follows:

(4) **Leased assets**

During the year the company has incurred expenditure on leasing agreements that give rights approximating to ownership of non current assets with a fair value of $790,000. All lease payments are charged to the income statement as incurred.

(5) **Taxation**

This includes current taxes on profit and other taxes such as taxes on capital. No provision is required to be made for deferred taxation and it is impracticable to quantify the financial effect of unrecognised deferred tax liabilities.

Required

Comment on the matters you should consider before expressing an opinion on the consolidated financial statements of the Capri Group. **(12 marks)**

Note. Assume it is 11 December 2007. **(Total = 20 marks)**

Question 5

(a) Explain what the term 'lowballing' means and discuss current guidance in this area. **(5 marks)**

(b) You are an audit manager in Sepia, a firm of Chartered Certified Accountants. Your specific responsibilities include advising the senior audit partner on the acceptance of new assignments. The following matters have arisen in connection with three prospective client companies:

(i) Your firm has been nominated to act as audit to Squid, a private limited company. You have been waiting for a response to your letter of 'professional enquiry' to Squid's auditor, Krill & Co, for several weeks. Your recent attempts to call the current engagement partner, Anton Fargues, in Krill & Co have been met with the response from Anton's personal assistant that 'Mr Fargues is not available'. **(5 marks)**

(ii) Sepia has been approached by the management of Hatchet, a company listed on a recognised stock exchange, to advise on a take-over bid which they propose to make. The target company, Vitronella, is an audit client of your firm. However, Hatchet is not. **(5 marks)**

(iii) A former colleague in Sepia, Edwin Stenuit, is now employed by another firm, Keratin. Sepia and Keratin and three other firms have recently tendered for the audit of Benthos, a limited liability company. Benthos is expected to announce the successful firm next week. Yesterday, at a social gathering, Edwin confided to you that Keratin 'lowballed' on their tender for the audit as they expect to be able to provide Benthos with lucrative other services. **(5 marks)**

Required

Comment on the professional issues raised by each of the above matters and the steps, if any, that Sepia should now take.

Note. The mark allocation is shown against each of the three issues.

(Total = 20 marks)

Answers

DO NOT TURN THIS PAGE UNTIL YOU HAVE COMPLETED THE MOCK EXAM

A PLAN OF ATTACK

If this were the real Advanced Audit and Assurance exam and you had been told to turn over and begin, what would be going through your mind?

An important thing to say (while there is still time) is that it is vital to have a good breadth of knowledge of the syllabus because the question requirements for each question will relate to different areas of the P7 syllabus. However, don't panic. Below we provide guidance on how to approach the exam.

Approaching the answer

Use your 15 minutes of reading time usefully, to look through the questions, particularly Questions 1 and 2 in Section A which are compulsory, to get a feel for what is required and to become familiar with the question scenarios.

It is vital that you attempt all the questions in the paper to increase your chances of passing. The best way to do this is to make sure you stick to the time allocation for each question – both in total and for each of the question parts. The worst thing you can do is run over time in one question and then find that you don't have enough time for the remaining questions.

Section A is compulsory and consists of two long case-study style questions, totalling between 50 and 70 marks. These may contain detailed information such as extracts from financial statements and audit working papers. A range of requirements will be set for each question, covering areas from across the whole syllabus.

Question 1 is for 30 marks. The scenario is quite long so make sure you have used your reading time well to familiarise yourself with it and make some notes on key issues. The key to success in this question is to stay focussed, don't run over time and answer the questions set. In part (a), notice the requirement to distinguish between audit risks and business risks – you must explain the risks fully to score well in this part of the question. Your answer to part (b) should follow on from your answer to part (a) – make sure you explain fully your chosen audit strategy as there are nine marks available here. Part (c) is on professional scepticism and fraud so you should be able to pick us some marks here.

Question 2 is also worth 30 marks and relates to internal audit work. Part (a) is on planning and therefore you must use the clues in the scenario to help you with your answer. In part (b) make sure you relate your knowledge on outsourcing to this particular company. Part (c) should be very straightforward on the advantages and disadvantages of outsourcing the internal audit function.

Section B contains three questions, from which you must attempt two. This section will typically be worth between 30 and 50 marks and will use short scenarios.

Question 3 is on audit evidence and matters to consider in the context of three mini scenarios. Note the mark allocation in each. Your answers must be focussed and coherent if you are going to score well and your financial reporting knowledge needs to be sound as you will have to apply it in this question.

Question 4 is on the audit report in a group company context. In part (a) you need to discuss current guidance and you will be able to score well if you also mention the exposure draft of ISA 600. In part (b) 12 marks are available so your answer needs to be relatively detailed if you are going to score good marks for this part of the question.

Question 5 is on ethical and professional issues. In part (a) you have to explain lowballing and the extent of current guidance in this area. Part (b) has three short scenarios on which you have to comment. Note that the requirement also asks you what steps the firm should now take – don't overlook this part of the question.

Forget about it!

And don't worry if you found the paper difficult. More than likely other candidates will too. If this were the real thing you would need to forget the exam the minute you left the exam hall and think about the next one. Or, if it is the last one, celebrate!

Question 1

(a)   **Risks at Matthew Manufacturing**

    (i)   **Audit risks**

       Inherent risk

- The business is **overly reliant** on **one major customer** who is significantly larger than Matthew Manufacturing and therefore is likely to have more bargaining power. This will affect receivables and sales, and could impact upon going concern.

- At a balance level, **inventory** may be risky because it is by its nature fragile and this could cause a degree of **obsolescent inventory**. Much of it is **designed to specification** and may not be sold to others, so this could also cause a high level of obsolescence.

- The business is **controlled by one man**, which could impact on going concern.

       Control risk

- The controls in the business have always been assessed previously as **poor**.

- There is likely to be **little segregation of duties**, although management have a 'hands on' authorisation style.

       Detection risk

- You have recently been appointed, so this is likely to be the **first audit**. This is an inherent risk because you are not going to have all the knowledge of the business which you would have on an established audit, and risk of not detecting material misstatements is therefore higher.

    (ii)   **Business risks**

       Operational risks

- The issue noted above in inherent risk of the business supplying one customer who is significantly bigger than them. This means in effect that the **customer controls operations** and holds significantly more power over the company than would be good for the company.

       Financial risks

- The company is dominated by one man (Mr Lofthouse) and **raising capital** if required might be restricted beyond him. He his likely to have to give personal guarantees to the bank for lending, there is no other obvious method of raising finance for the business.

- Lack of segregation of duties leads to higher opportunities for **fraud** and **misappropriation of cash**

- The company deals in **portable, saleable items** at high risk of being thieved.

Compliance risks

- There are a **number of employees** so the risk arising from the need to comply with the **employment laws** is significant, as the company is unlikely to employ an expert in this area.

- **Glass** is a dangerous product to work with and this will have **health and safety implications**.

(b) **Audit strategy**

The first stage of the audit will be to understand the entity. This will include documenting and confirming the systems and internal control. However, it appears likely that the controls will be assessed as ineffective, or at best, strongly reliant on the control of the key manager. Therefore, it is extremely unlikely that a **systems and controls approach** will be taken to the audit. It is far more likely that a **substantive approach** will be taken.

Risk

Audit and business risks have been discussed above. Auditors often take a risk approach to an audit in connection with a substantive approach. This can either be a business risk approach or an audit risk approach. Usually it involves an assessment of both as the two issues are related. (ISA 315 requires the auditor to assess the risks faced by the business as a means of identifying risks of material misstatement in the financial statements.)

The **business risk approach** is often taken for large companies, who have strong controls who are accustomed to the concepts of risk management and awareness. In a smaller firm, such as Matthew Manufacturing, it is less likely that the auditor will be able to rely on the business's own ability to manage risk effectively. Concerns over the controls of the business indicate that a detailed substantive approach would be more appropriate.

There are clear audit risks in this client. It is therefore sensible to take an **audit risk approach** and focus the detailed audit tests in the areas of the business where problems are most likely to arise.

Substantive approach

The fact that a detailed substantive approach is required has been mentioned several times already. This would suggest that an **analytical approach** would not be appropriate. This is compounded by the fact that it is a first year audit and with a lack of knowledge of the business to apply to the financial information, an analytical approach would be less effective.

In terms of detailed testing then, two approaches could be taken. The audit could be conducted around the balance sheet (the **balance sheet approach**) or the transactions (the transactions, or **cycles approach**). In my opinion, the cycles approach is the more sensible approach for the following reasons:

- Controls are believed to be poor, so there is a substantial chance of transactions being misstated.

- Last year's balance sheet was not audited by our firm.

- Testing the transactions will give us a significant insight into how the business operates and increase our knowledge of the business.

Conclusion

The appropriate approach is an audit risk approach, combined with a detailed substantive cycles approach.

(c) **Professional scepticism**

IFAC's definition of professional scepticism is 'an attitude that includes a questioning mind and a critical assessment of evidence'.

ISA 240 *The auditor's responsibility to consider fraud in an audit of financial statements* requires the auditor to '**maintain an attitude of professional scepticism**' throughout the audit. The auditor should recognise that a material misstatement as a result of fraud could exist regardless of the auditor's previous experience of the client and its management and those charged with governance. This attitude is important when considering fraud, due to the concealed nature of fraud. It is possible that things might not be as they seem.

In other words, it is necessary to keep an open mind to the commercial reality of the possibility of fraud while carrying out an audit and to ensure that all audit evidence gathered is critically assessed. An auditor should not be persuaded by less-than-persuasive audit evidence as a result of the fact that in the past the management and staff of the company have appeared to be honest and trustworthy.

However, the auditor is entitled to take documents on face value unless he has reason to believe otherwise. In other words, auditors are not required routinely to check whether documents presented to them as audit evidence are authentic. If their suspicions are roused, then they would be required to make further enquiry, for example, they should attempt to obtain evidence from a third party.

Question 2

> **Text reference.** Chapter 16
>
> **Top tips.** This question deals with internal audit planning matters. It also looks at the issue of outsourcing finance and other functions, albeit from the internal auditor's perspective. Some of the planning matters you must consider in part (a) are very similar to general planning issues you would consider if external auditors were doing a systems review. Similarly, in part (b), many of the issues that the internal auditors would be faced with would be similar to those that an external auditor would face. Thinking through the provisions of ISA 402 will probably help you formulate your answer therefore, even though it is not strictly relevant to internal auditors.
>
> **Easy marks.** Easy marks are available in part (c) for discussing the advantages and disadvantages of outsourcing.

(a) **Overall approach**

Both the **compliance based** and **process based approaches** would be **appropriate** here. The business is well run on the whole and there are specific procedures put in place by management, compliance with which could be assessed. In addition however, due to the nature of the business, it is clear that management and control of cash and inventory are key. These could be the focus of a process based approach. In either case, due to the number of sites involved a risk based approach is likely to be the most effective and efficient.

Specific issues to consider

The key decision to be made is to determine **which sites must be visited** and **which areas are of particular concern**.

Financial matters

On the basis of relative significance to the business as a whole the following sites should receive a routine visit: Stoneleigh, Lillington, Strathearn, Gaveston, Harveys Cross and Guys. Together these six sites contribute 77% of the total revenue of the business.

Particular issues to be addressed include:

(i) **Cash management**

Whilst there is no information from Head Office to suggest that there is a problem in this area tests should be performed to ensure that procedures are being followed consistently and correctly. Checks should be made to ensure that each kiosk manager is maintaining the physical security of the cash by, for example, maintaining the twice daily banking of cash.

(ii) **Inventory losses**

This has been identified as a particular problem at both Stoneleigh and Gaveston. Work should be performed to try to determine the source of the problems. Possible causes could include:

(1) **Poor inventory control**: due to the short product life of the inventory consistent overordering is likely to lead to inventory losses. This is perhaps accentuated at the Stoneleigh location where two kiosks share the same store. In this situation it is likely that no one individual is taking overall responsibility for the inventory management.

(2) **Poor training**: Each product should be made to a standard recipe. Where the recipe is not being followed or where errors are being made this will result in extra inventory being utilised and wasted. The fact that the Gaveston branch has had a high level of staff turnover may suggest that staff have lacked training and that the managers have lacked experience in ordering.

(iii) **Fraud**

The possibility of **theft** needs to be considered particularly in a cash based business. The apparent inventory losses mentioned above could in fact be the result of transactions being made without being recorded with the cash received being misappropriated. The overall performance of these kiosks should be reviewed to determine whether there are any unexpected falls in revenue in comparison to previous periods.

The Princes Risborough site should receive a surprise inspection preferably at the start of the morning shift. Whilst it contributes less than 2% of the total revenue of the business matters, identified at Head Office have raised some concerns. The failure of the cash takings to reconcile to the cash bankings could be the result of poor control which should be rectified or potentially written-off due to theft.

In addition the timings of the transactions have raised suspicions and it is possible that the kiosk is not in operation for the full period of the shift even though the staff members are paid for the full nine hours.

Commercial matters

The fact that the Harveys Cross café has failed to sell the newly launched smoothie needs to be investigated. At other sites these sales constitute approximately 20% of total revenue and this launch is an important part of the management strategy. Potential reasons could include poor advertising and promotion and inadequate training on how to make the product.

Operational

A number of issues have been identified in relation to staff recruitment, retention and training. In particular at the Gaveston kiosk an investigation should take place into the reasons behind the recent loss of managerial staff. A more general review of the human resources function should take place looking particularly at the way that candidates are selected and the training process which they are offered.

(b) **Effect on the activities of internal audit**

Review of accounting and internal control systems

Often internal audit is assigned specific responsibility for reviewing the design of the systems, monitoring their operation and recommending improvements.

The key difference if the IT function is outsourced is that Joosy Juice will **lose control** over these activities thereby **limiting** the extent of the work which the internal auditor can perform directly. In some instances this can be accentuated by a **lack of access to information**. Instead it will be the internal auditors' responsibility to **manage the relationship** and **monitor the performance of the service provider**.

Exactly how the internal auditor will do this would depend on the precise nature of the contract between the two parties. The **terms of the contract** would determine for example the extent to which Joosy Juice has access to accounting records prepared by the service organisation and relevant underlying information. It may be useful, therefore, for the internal auditor to be consulted at this stage.

Once the relationship has been established the internal auditor would only have a **limited impact on the design of the system**. Provided that the end product meets Joosy Juice's requirements the way in which these results are achieved and any improvements would be the responsibility of the service organisation. Instead, however it could be the internal auditors role to monitor the performance of the service organisation and determine whether the needs of the business are being met on an ongoing basis.

In respect of **controls** the internal auditor would still have **responsibility for ensuring that the overall control environment is strong**. Where services have been outsourced the control environment will be made up of a combination of those operated by Joosy Juice's personnel and those of the service organisation. There are a number of ways in which the internal auditor could monitor controls of the service provider including:

- **Information** and **assurances** regarding the operation of internal controls provided by the service organisation

- Assessment of the use of **quality assurance services** (eg the service provider's internal audit function)

- The results of **specific testing** of information provided by the service organisation eg analytical techniques could be applied to payroll information to establish the validity of processing

- **Actual experience** of adjustments to, or errors in, reports received from the service organisation

- **Reports** from the service providers' external auditors

Examination of financial and operating information

This would normally include **specific enquiry into individual items** including detailed testing of transactions and balances.

The key issue here is the internal auditors' **access** to the relevant detailed records. In some cases the user entity may not maintain detailed records or documentation initiating transactions for example, purchase invoices. If this is the case the information would be sought from the service company. Where independent records are maintained the situation is more straightforward and the internal auditor would perform his investigations as normal.

Review of economy, efficiency and effectiveness of operations

Financial efficiency or cost saving is probably one of the main reasons why Joosy Juice is considering the outsourcing of its IT function. This may be due to the reduction in staff numbers which would result or simply due to greater cost control.

The internal auditor would have an **ongoing role** in determining whether the service provider continues to provide **good value for money** by comparing the quality of the service with the negotiated fee.

Special investigations

The internal auditors of Joosy Juice would continue to have **full responsibility for non-IT related special investigations**. Any IT related projects are likely to be the remit of the service organisation as access to their expertise will be one of the main advantages of outsourcing in the first place. The internal auditors may, however, have a role in establishing what those projects should be as they have an in-depth knowledge of the detailed operations and needs of the business.

Compliance with regulation

Under company law Joosy Juice has certain **obligations to maintain proper accounting records**. If Joosy Juice were to use a service organisation the internal audit department might be involved in ensuring that the contractual arrangements are such that company law is complied with. This would include ensuring that the company has legal ownership of the records and has access to them.

(c)   **Advantages of outsourcing internal audit**

Procuring skill

The company can procure a **high level of skill** which it might not be able to bring permanently into its business. The reasons for this are various. First, an outsourced internal auditor is likely to be involved in a number of different businesses, and this variety will add to their skills. An in-house auditor is not in a position to have such **variety** to call upon, as by his nature, he is tied to the business which employs him. The firm to which it is outsourced is likely also to use the **best techniques** as that is their business.

Another consideration with regard to procuring skill is **cost** - it might be prohibitively expensive to buy in the degree of skill required permanently (in the form of an employee), whereas it is cheaper to hire the skill for shorter periods of time.

Relationship to the company

There are two elements here. The first is that as outsourced internal auditors are not employed by the company they bring a degree of **independence** to the task which it is impossible for employees of the company to bring. This may enable them to view any issues arising more clearly. It also eliminates the possibility of such issues as internal auditors having difficulty in conducting their task due to **familiarity** and **personal relationships** with other staff.

The second advantage is that as the service has been contracted out, the company has a **degree of legal protection** over the quality of the service. The company is protected against **negligent work**, for example, to the degree that it can be **compensated** for it, which is not the case if the work is carried out by employees.

Relationship to external audit

The firm providing the service may or may not be the firm that provides external audit services to the company. However, it is likely to be a firm that also specialises in external audit and this may produce **synergies** between the work performed. This is firstly because the auditors will be aware of the work required for the external audit and may ensure that they undertake work that could be used for the external audit, and secondly, because when conducting their **evaluation of** the **quality** of the work of internal audit, the external auditors are likely to be content to rely more heavily on the work of staff of a reputable firm of accountants than might otherwise be the case.

Cost

Purchasing internal audit services means that the company can **focus** on what they want to gain from internal audit and purchase a focused service. It also means that internal audit may be used on a 'part-time' basis, for example, two days a week or four weeks a year, rather than having full-time employees.

The fact that the service is being bought from a large organisation dedicated to providing auditing services might also mean that the company will benefit from the **economies of scale** which the service provider creates.

Disadvantages of outsourcing internal audit

Procuring skill .

The industry the company is in may require that its internal auditor has **specialised** skills. If the audit is outsourced, and the provider does not have the skills which the company first thought, the cost of changing the service provider could be high, and the company may have lost staff who did possess the relevant skills.

Relationship to the company

Several negative issues may arise. Firstly the relationship will be dominated by the contract between the two parties, which will mean that the contract needs to be drafted carefully in the first place and that **a lack of flexibility** may arise in the long-term. It may not be possible, for example, under the contract to drop the current programme and conduct a specific investigation if circumstances which required that arose.

Company employees might feel threatened by being asked questions by outsiders, and the internal auditors might find it difficult to carry out their duties effectively or efficiently. Their independence might impose a sometimes **excessive formality**.

Lastly, the audit committee and directors will in practical terms have **less control** over the department than they would have done if the department consisted of employees who were required to obey them. In the event of them being unhappy with the service, they might **only have recourse to legal action** rather than simply changing the internal audit programme, and this could prove costly, and have a detrimental effect on future relations.

External audit issues

If the directors of the company wish to use the same audit firm to provide their internal and external audit functions, the audit firm may feel that this would be a threat to their **ethical requirement of independence** as auditors. If the directors then used another firm for either service, this could lead to problems with their accustomed firm.

If the firm determines that no ethical issue arises, it might still appear that the distinction between services is blurred and the **credibility** of the audit report might be affected.

Question 3

Text reference. Chapter 10

Top tips. As usual with questions of this type, you should ensure that you attempt each part of the question. This means that the question breaks down into manageable sections of three to four marks each. Use all the information given to you in the question. Scrutinise dates closely to ascertain whether things impact in the relevant year. In parts (a) and (b) of this question, timings are crucial to your answer. Remember as well to always comment on materiality but, as you should note from reading the examiner's comments below, make targeted comments about materiality. You must judge whether a matter is relevant to the income statement or the balance sheet and calculate its materiality accordingly.

Easy marks. There are no easy marks as such on this paper, but marks are always available for commenting on the materiality of things under discussion, and marks are also available for correctly identifying the relevant accounting standards. It should be straightforward to obtain marks for the audit evidence required for each item too. Please note the examiner's comments about materiality and audit evidence below however. As she observes, a 'scattergun' approach, or an unsophisticated approach to audit evidence will not gain marks.

Examiner's comments. Generally scripts were either very good or very poor. Tabulation is not recommended for this question. A small minority of candidates were careless in their calculations of materiality, for example saying 3.7 is 2.3% or 0.23% of 15.9, rather than 23%. Better candidates calculated materiality only in relation to relevant amounts. This is more impressive than the 'scattergun approach' (ie calculating every number as a % of revenue and total assets and profit). Lists of questions are discouraged (for example, 'Should the gain on disposal be credited to revenue?', or 'Should the loan be classified as non-current?'). These are indeed matters to consider, but the requirement is to comment on them. On the sale of surplus assets, many candidates picked up on the exceptional item, the need for separate disclosure and the fact that the gain should not be included in revenue. Few commented on the need for further revaluation of all buildings. There was a lot of irrelevant digression into impairment testing, ignoring the fact that the asset was sold at a profit. A minority debated management's decision to sell: this was not called for. Many candidates wanted to check the valuation, the valuer's qualification (irrelevant) and the existence of the building (sold) and did not mention the most basic sources of evidence - the contract for sale (though some referred to the 'invoice') and subsequent receipt of funds (in the bank statement). Regarding the default on loan, there were many ignorant calculations of materiality - the loan balance to profit for example - that earned no marks. Candidates must take more care not to write conflicting answer points. Weaker candidates did not appreciate that the loan was made in the prior year.

Note that if dates are given in a question it is because the timeframe needs to be understood. When considering lack of provision for an obligation, candidates must take more care not to write conflicting answer points. Time was again wasted debating whether management had made a good/bad business decision (by extending warranties) and this was not called for.

Marking scheme

		Marks
(i)	**Matters**	
	Generally 1 mark each comment maximum 6 marks each issue × 3	Max 12
	Ideas	
	• Materiality (assessed)	
	• Relevant IASs (eg 1, 10, 16, 18, 37) & 'The Framework' (eg consistency)	
	• Risks (eg FS assertions – fair presentation and disclosure, completeness, appropriate valuation)	
(ii)	**Audit evidence**	
	Generally 1 mark each item of audit evidence (source) maximum 5 marks each issue × 3	Max 12
	Ideas	
	• Oral vs written	
	• Internal vs external	
	• Auditor generated	
	• Procedures (analytical procedures, enquiry, inspection, observation, computation)	

		Max 20
	(1)	Max 8
	(2)	Max 6
	(3)	Max 6
		20

(a) **Buildings**

(i) *Matters to consider*

- The profit on disposal ($2.3 million) is 14% of profit before tax (and 0.7% of the revenue it is included in) and is therefore material to the income statement.

- The profit should not be included in revenue but disclosed separately in the income statement as an exceptional item.

- The revaluation gain (also material at 23% of profit before tax) should not be credited against operating charges in the income statement but transferred to retained earnings.

- The total gain relating to the sale of the non current asset represents 37% of profit before tax for the year and it relates to a transaction on nearly the last day of the year, so the auditor should exercise professional skepticism in relation to its timing.

- The sale should only be recognised in the year if the contract to sell is binding.

- If the contract is not binding before the year-end but is completed before the audit report is signed, it will be a non-adjusting post balance sheet event requiring disclosure in the financial statements.

- If the contract is binding but not completed at the year-end, there will be a material receivable of $11.5 million (6% of total assets).

- As the sold asset is a revalued asset, all the assets in the same class will also be revalued as required by IAS 16.

- IAS 16 requires that revalued assets are revalued with sufficient regularity that the carrying amount does not differ materially from that which would be determined using fair value at the balance sheet date. The valuation on the sold building appeared to be out of date, as it sold at 25% above the valuation, which is material, and therefore it will be necessary to ensure that the valuations on the other buildings are correct, particularly if the increase in capacity has increased their value.

- If management refuse to adjust the profit on disposal and revaluation gain, then these matters are material and will necessitate a qualified opinion.

(ii) *Audit evidence*

- Sale contract for the building - for details of whether the contract is binding, what its value is, when payment is due.

- Receipt of sale proceeds in bank statement.

- Details of carrying amount from prior year file and non-current asset register.

- Valuer's certificate for other properties.

(b) **Loan**

(i) *Matters to consider*

- $7 million is 3.7% of total assets and is therefore material.

- The interest for the first year of approximately $400,000 is not material to total assets or to profit before tax.

- The liability may have been misclassified if it was technically payable on demand at the year-end (31 March), although classifying it as non-current would be consistent with the prior year.

- In this instance the condition rendering it on demand has been waived but it was not waived at the balance sheet date.

- The waiver of the condition on 17 April is a non-adjusting post balance sheet event which should be disclosed in the financial statements.

- As the loan was technically on demand at the year-end, it should all (the original loan and the outstanding interest) be included in current liabilities.

- As the loan is material to total assets, if management do not reclassify the loan, the audit report will have to be qualified on the grounds of disagreement.

(ii) *Audit evidence*

- Details of the loan (amount, interest rate, conditions) agreed to prior year working papers.

- Confirmation of the amounts owed and details of the loan at 31 March from the lenders at the year-end.

- The correspondence to Verdi setting out the waiver of the conditions and the terms of agreement about the outstanding interest.

- Proposed disclosures in the financial statements.

(c) **Warranty provision**

(i) *Matters to consider*

- Installation fees in the period covered by the warranty are $4.2 million, and, at 1.2% of revenue, are material.

- As a result of its new warranty provision, Verdi has a present obligation (to reinstall) as a result of a past event (the original installation).

- Verdi's policy on warranties claims that no provision has been recognised as the amount of the obligation cannot be measured with sufficient reliability.

- However, IAS 37 requires that where there are a number of similar obligations (giving warranties as an example), the probability that a transfer will be required in settlement is determined by considering the class as a whole.

- Therefore, although there may only be small likelihood that each individual warranty might be taken up, there is a larger likelihood that a warranty out of all of them will be taken up.

- IAS 37 therefore determines that a provision for all the warranties should be made.

- The provision should be for the best estimate of making good all the items sold under warranty. It is unlikely that Verdi would not be able to make an estimate of these costs, particularly as they will have undertaken calculations to establish the 40% increase in the price of installations.

- Such a provision is likely to be material (the provision would have to be less than $800,000 (that is, 20% of original sales cost) to be less than 5% of profit before tax).

- Given that the provision is likely to be material, if a provision for warranties is not made in the financial statements, the auditors would have to qualify their report over this issue, on the grounds of disagreement in respect of non-compliance with IAS 37.

(ii) *Audit evidence*

- The terms of the warranty.

- The costings of the warranty which will have been used to calculate the corresponding increase in price.

- The schedule of installations undertaken in the nine months to 31 March 2007, agreed on a sample basis to invoices.

- Costs of any reinstallations already undertaken.

- Average cost of an installation (taken from job cards).

Question 4

Text references. Chapters 11 and 17

Top tips. This is a demanding question set in the context of a group audit which requires some thought and planning. The requirement for part (a) is reasonably straightforward but you need to ensure that you discuss current guidance in this area. Part (b) is more tricky and there is a danger that you can become bogged down in the detail of accounting treatments. Essentially it is an audit report question. If you can spot this from the outset you have a better chance of picking up the relevant points.

Easy marks. This is a tough question on group audits. No easy marks are available as such but a logical approach is the best for this question.

Examiner's comments. In part (b) many failed to spot that this was essentially an auditor's report question. Most candidates identified that the accounting treatments mentioned were incorrect but many did not make any reference to the audit report extract. Few identified the correct impact of the matters on the audit report ie 'except for'.

Marking scheme

		Marks
(a)	**Current guidance for auditing group accounts**	
	Generally 1-1½ marks each well-explained point to a maximum of	8
(b)	**Matters to be considered (before expressing an opinion)**	
	Generally 1 mark per comment	Max 12

Ideas
- Materiality of subsidiary
- Basis para – meaning?
- Non-compliance (IAS 12 and IAS 17)
- Marcel concurs?
- Emphasis of matter should be after opinion para
- Materiality of non-compliance(s)
- Adequacy of note disclosures
  - (4) Finance vs operating
  - (5) Reason for non-compliance?
- Prior year
  - Accounting treatment(s), materiality
  - Auditors' report
  - How resolved
- Request adjustment in subsidiary's fs ⇒ unqualified
- Adjust on consolidation ⇒ unqualified
- No adjustment ⇒ 'except for'
- Disclosure name of other auditor

20

Tutorial note. The ideas are listed in roughly the order in which the information presented in the question might be extracted for synthesis. The suggested answer groups together some of these points under headings which give the analysis of the situation a possible structure.

(a)   Current guidance on the audit of groups is provided by ISA 600 *Using the work of another auditor*. However, the IAASB is in the middle of a project to update its guidance on groups which has been running for a number of years. The most recent exposure draft of ISA 600 was issued in March 2006.

The ISA conforms to the requirements of other ISAs, for example, ISAs 220, 315 and 330, in respect of the procedures required to accept the group audit, obtaining knowledge about the group and assessing risk. The group auditor should gain an understanding of the group as a whole, and assess risks for the group as a whole and for individually significant components. The group auditor has to ensure other auditors are professionally qualified, meet quality control and ethical requirements and will allow the group auditor access to working papers or components.

The stated objective of the ISA is to enable auditors to determine whether they can accept an engagement as group auditor and obtain sufficient appropriate evidence to reduce the audit risk for the group financial statements to an acceptably low level. This will be achieved by:

- Determining what work should be carried out on the consolidation process
- Determining what work should be carried out on the components
- Establishing appropriate communication with other auditors
- Evaluating audit evidence about the consolidation process and the components

The exposure draft distinguishes between significant components and other components which are not individually significant to the group financial statements. A significant component is a component identified by the group auditor that due to the nature of, or circumstances specific to, that component or the individual financial significance of the component to the group, has been identified as likely to include significant risks of material misstatement of the group financial statements. The group auditor should be involved in the assessment of risk in relation to significant components.

If a component is financially significant to the group financial statements then the group auditor will require the other auditors to carry out a full audit of that component, based on the materiality level the other auditors have calculated for that component, or, if it is lower, a materiality level set by the group auditors.

If a component is otherwise significant due to its nature or circumstances, the group auditors will require either a full audit, an audit of specified account balances relating to identified significant risks or specified audit procedures relating to identified significant risks.

The group auditor will perform, or require the other auditors to perform, audit procedures designed to identify subsequent events that may require adjustment to or disclosure in the financial statements of significant components.

If audit work on significant components does not give the group auditor sufficient appropriate audit evidence about the group financial statements, the group auditor would request one of the three procedures outlined above or a review of other individually insignificant components of group financial statements.

Components not subject to these requirements will be subject to analytical review at a group level.

The group auditor will evaluate the appropriateness, completeness and accuracy of the adjustments and reclassifications involved in the consolidation process.

The group auditors will consider whether there are any fraud risk factors or indicators of management bias in connection with the consolidation.

(b)   **Matters**

Risk

Risk is increased by the fact that the work of the other auditor, Marcel, may prove to be unreliable. This is evidenced by the confusing nature of the draft audit report.

Materiality

Capri (Overseas) is material to the group as a whole. It constitutes 30.6% of the group's profit before tax and 20% of the group's total assets.

The accounting error in respect of leases is material to both the subsidiary's own accounts and the group accounts. The $790,000 of unrecognised assets constitute 12.2% of the total assets of Capri (Overseas) and 2.4% of the total assets of the group.

Accounting treatments

(i)   *Treatment of leased assets*

The treatment of leased assets appears to be incorrect. The disclosure note suggests that the lease agreements give rights approximating to ownership in which case they should be treated as finance leases. It is also unclear if the lease payments charged to the income statement all relate to this type of lease or if some relate to operating leases (in which case the correct treatment has been adopted for these elements).

(ii) *Treatment of deferred tax*

The treatment of deferred tax also appears to be incorrect. It is unclear why no provision has been made or why it is impractical to quantify the financial effect.

(iii) *Adequacy of disclosures*

In addition to the confusing nature of the disclosures provided, key information is also omitted. This includes details of the relevant standards from which the subsidiary has departed and any reason for the non-compliance.

In respect of deferred tax there is a suggestion that the treatment adopted is to accord with local legislation. This is referred to in the draft audit report. This is an inappropriate use of the report. This information should be provided in the disclosure notes accompanying the financial statements.

Marcel's audit report

The need for an explanatory paragraph in the basis of opinion section is confusing. If the auditor agrees with the accounting treatments and the level of disclosure as indicated by the unqualified audit opinion there is no need for this explanation.

This type of disclosure cannot be used in place of a qualification. In any case it does not make it clear whether the auditor agrees with these treatments or which of the issues are in accordance with local tax regulations. If it is an emphasis of matter it should be presented after the opinion paragraph. This is to avoid giving the impression that the audit opinion is qualified.

Effect on group audit opinion.

The management of Capri Group could request that the accounts of Capri (Overseas) be redrafted in accordance with IAS 12 and IAS 17. (As a subsidiary Capri (Overseas) is controlled by Capri Group.) The audit reports of Capri (Overseas) and Capri Group would then both be unqualified.

Adjustments for compliance with IAS 12 and IAS 17 could be made on consolidation only. Again the group audit report would be unqualified.

If no adjustments are made in the subsidiary's accounts or those of the group the group audit report would be qualified on the basis of a material disagreement (except for) with the non-compliance with IAS 12 and IAS 17. The effect of non-compliance should be quantified and disclosed.

Question 5

Text references. Chapters 2 and 5

Top tips. When trying to identify professional and ethical issues, think about general themes such as independence, integrity, objectivity and confidentiality. Try and relate relevant ethical and professional guidance that you are aware of to each situation and explain why it is relevant.

Easy marks. There are easy marks available in this question for knowledge brought forward from your earlier auditing studies, such as being able to give a definition of lowballing and knowing the etiquette with regard to professional clearance letters. Easy marks can also be obtained for coming up with simple steps to take in respect of each issue – for example, if no answer has been received in part (i), it seems logical to repeat the request.

Examiner's comments. The technical content of this question was not difficult.

In part (b)(i), many candidates made a big issue of the preliminary procedures of the professional etiquette already gone through and ended their answers with Sepia no closer to a resolution to the problem than when they started.

In part (b)(ii), nearly everyone identified a 'conflict of interest' but few stated that they would refuse the assignment. Many referred to 'Chinese walls' but did not consider how unacceptable to Vitronella the assignment would be. Those that proposed resigning the audit (of Vitronella) showed a lack of professionalism.

Part (b)(iii) was probably the worst answered part. Many candidates referred the matter to the partner for his/her decision. Weaker candidates proposed unsuitable 'solutions' (eg that Sepia withdraw their tender). Few candidates acknowledged that little could be done. Candidates who referred to 'insider dealing' clearly had no understanding of the term.

Marking scheme

		Marks
(a)	Lowballing	
	Generally 1 mark for each well-explained point	5
(b)	Generally 1 mark each comment	15
	Maximum 5 marks each of three matters	

Ideas
Professional issues raised
- Integrity (management and/or audit firm)
- Objectivity/independence
- Confidentiality
- Relevant ethical guidance – ie
  (i) Changes in professional appointment
  (ii) Corporate finance advice including take-overs
  (iii) Fees
- Meaning of 'lowballing'
Steps (ie ACTIONS)
- Obtain ... what? ... why?
- Ask/advise ... who? When?

$\underline{20}$

(a) **Lowballing** is the practice of a firm quoting a significantly lower fee level for an assurance service than would have been charged by the predecessor firm. This creates a significant self-interest threat. If the firm's tender is successful, the firm must apply safeguards such as maintaining records such that the firm is able to demonstrate that appropriate staff and time are spent on the engagement and complying with all applicable assurance standards, guidelines and quality control procedures

Current guidance in the form of ACCA's *Code of ethics and conduct* and IFAC's *Code of ethics for professional accountants* states that members can quote whatever fee is deemed appropriate.

It is not considered unethical for one firm to offer a lower fee than another, however doing so may create threats to compliance with the fundamental principles. For example, a **self-interest threat** to professional competence and due care would arise if the fee quoted was so low that it would be difficult to perform the engagement in accordance with applicable technical and professional standards.

Safeguards to mitigate such threats could include making the client aware of the terms of the engagement and the basis on which fees are charged and what services are covered by the quoted fees, and also assigning appropriate time and staff to the engagements.

The International Ethics Standards Board for Accountants of IAASB recently issued an exposure draft proposing changes to enhance the independence and objectivity of accountants performing assurance engagements with a view to strengthening the independence requirements of IFAC's *Code of ethics for professional accountants*.

(b) (i) **Squid**

Professional issues

Sepia has requested a professional clearance letter from Krill & Co in respect of the audit of Squid. Krill & Co has not responded. Krill & Co has a professional duty of confidence to Squid, and therefore should have sought permission from Squid to respond to Sepia's request.

The fact that Krill & Co has not responded could indicate that Squid has refused permission for Krill & Co to respond to Sepia. However, this seems unlikely for two reasons: firstly, that Squid nominated Sepia to act as auditors and therefore should have no objection to Krill & Co responding to them and allowing them to take up that nomination, and secondly, that if Krill & Co had simply been refused permission to give that clearance, then as a professional courtesy they should have responded to Sepia informing them that they could not give them the information they requested and why.

Therefore it is possible that Anton Fargues, on behalf of Krill & Co, is not replying because he has a concern as to the integrity of the directors of Squid that he does not wish to share with Sepia due to concerns over confidentiality issues. However, if Squid has given them permission to respond, this should not be a problem. Therefore, it appears that Anton Fargues is acting unprofessionally in not responding to Sepia's request.

Steps

The manager at Sepia should ask Squid whether the company has given Krill & Co permission to respond to Sepia, and if they confirm that permission has been given, Sepia should get this confirmed in writing.

He should send a duplicate request for professional clearance by recorded delivery so that receipt has to be acknowledged by Krill & Co and gives legal evidence that it was received.

This should include a letter stating that lack of response to his letter will be taken to mean that there are no professional issues preventing Sepia accepting appointment and that if Krill & Co fails to respond, Sepia will report Anton Fargues to his professional body for unprofessional conduct.

If a reply is received, Sepia's actions will then be directed by the contents of the reply.

If there is still no reply within reasonable time, Sepia should accept the appointment and report Anton Fargues to his professional body so that his behaviour can be investigated.

(ii) **Hatchet**

Professional issues

Sepia has been approached by Hatchet to offer a non-audit service. Sepia does not provide audit services to Hatchet, so in relation to Hatchet itself, there is no independence bar to accepting appointment.

However, the service is advice in relation to a proposed take-over of Vitronella, an audit client of Sepia. This is likely to raise a conflict of interest such that it is necessary to refuse the appointment. This depends on several factors:

- Whether Hatchet or Vitronella object to Sepia offering the services
- What the services are in detail
- Whether Sepia would be Vitronella's primary advisor in the event of a takeover

(1) The fact that Sepia are Vitronella's auditors is public information reported in the financial statements. As such, it is likely that Hatchet are aware that Sepia are Vitronella's auditors and therefore do not mind. Vitronella, the target company, will be unaware at this point that their auditors have been asked to advise a company about a proposed takeover of themselves and might mind very much. Professional advice in respect of such conflicts of interest states that the firm (Sepia) should make both parties aware of the conflict so that they can decide whether they want Sepia to be advisors.

(2)/(3) The professional guidance states that one firm should not be principal advisor to both parties involved in a takeover. Therefore, if Hatchet wants Sepia to be its principal advisor, and Sepia anticipates that as auditor, it is likely to be Vitronella's principal advisor, the partners of Sepia will have to decide which side they want to advise. Being auditor does not automatically mean they would be Vitronella's principal advisors, but there is often an advantage to a company in having its auditor advise in such situations and, providing that the combined fees do not cause a problem, there should be no bar to independence in doing so. It is possible that Vitronella would expect Sepia to act as their principal advisors.

It would not be possible for Sepia to resign from the Vitronella audit in order to be able to be Hatchet's principal advisors as this would still pose a conflict of interest as far as Vitronella was concerned.

If Sepia was not principal advisor to both parties, and both parties agreed, it could advise Hatchet and do Vitronella's audit. The best way to ensure confidentiality was maintained in this instance would be to have entirely separate engagement teams and set up strict procedures for ensuring information was kept secret, for example, having teams in different areas of the office or from different offices of a national firm.

Steps

Sepia should determine whether Hatchet requires Sepia to be their principal advisors in relation to this takeover. The partners should inform Hatchet that before they accepted any engagement of this nature they would require permission from Vitronella.

Sepia should notify Vitronella that Hatchet has asked them to be principal advisor and gauge the reaction.

Ultimately it is likely that Sepia would refuse to advise Hatchet due to the conflict of interest being so great.

(iii) **Keratin**

Professional issues

Lowballing is the practice of tendering for audits at a lower price than the audit can actually be carried out for, often with the intention of obtaining other, more profitable, work from the audit client.

Lowballing is not forbidden by professional rules, because it is seen as a reasonable marketing tactic. However, it is important that the client is aware of the scope of the work that is going to be carried out and is aware that prices might rise in the future.

Professional guidance indicates also that auditors must ensure that they do not provide a service lower than is required by   quality standards regardless of the price that it is being done for. Keratin must ensure that they do not fall into the trap of providing a poor audit service because they have tendered at an unreasonable price. They would be putting themselves at risk of being found to be negligent by a professional body or even in a court of law should problems arise.

Keratin would be within their rights to provide other services to an audit client as long as this did not affect the independence of the audit. However, given that the provision of other services to audit clients is increasingly frowned upon, for example, in the US, where audit firms are prohibited from providing other services to audit clients, Keratin should be careful of taking such an approach.

Edwin Stenuit may be in breach of a duty of confidentiality to his employer, discussing the firm's affairs in such a way at a social gathering.

Steps

Sepia can take no steps against Keratin in the matter of this tender as Benthos is entitled to choose whichever audit firm they like to do their audit.

If Keratin is successful, Sepia may have to review its own pricing policy if it is likely to be tendering against Keratin in the future.

Sepia could report Edwin Stenuit to ACCA for misconduct as a result of his breach of confidentiality to his employer, but it is unlikely that they would do so.

ACCA Professional Level

Paper P7

Advanced Audit and Assurance (International)

Mock Examination 2

Question Paper		
Time allowed		
Reading and Planning Writing		**15 minutes** **3 hours**
SECTION A	TWO compulsory questions to be attempted	
SECTION B	TWO questions ONLY to be attempted	
During reading and planning time only the question paper may be annotated		

DO NOT OPEN THIS PAPER UNTIL YOU ARE READY TO START UNDER EXAMINATION CONDITIONS

Section A – BOTH questions are compulsory and MUST be attempted

Question 1

The principal activity of Bateleur Zoo Gardens (BZG) is the conservation of animals. Approximately 80% of the zoo's income comes from admission fees, money spent in the food and retail outlets and animal sponsorship. The remainder comprises donations and investment income.

Admission fees include day visitor entrance fees ('gate') and annual membership fees. Day tickets may be pre-booked by credit card using a telephone booking 'hotline' and via the zoo's website. Reduced fees are available (eg to students, senior citizens and families).

Animal sponsorships, which last for one year, make a significant contribution to the cost of specialist diets, enclosure maintenance and veterinary care. Animal sponsors benefit from the advertisement of their names at the sponsored animal's enclosure.

BZG's management has identified the following applicable risks that require further consideration and are to be actively managed:

(i)   Reduction in admission income through failure to invest in new exhibits and breeding programmes to attract visitors;

(ii)   Animal sponsorships may not be invoiced due to incomplete data transfer between the sponsoring and invoicing departments;

(iii)   Corporate sponsorships may not be charged for at approved rates – either in error or due to arrangements with the companies. In particular, the sponsoring department may not notify the invoicing department of reciprocal arrangements, whereby sponsoring companies provide BZG with advertising (eg in company magazines and annual reports);

(iv)   Cash received at the entrance gate ticket offices ('kiosks') may not be passed to cashiers in the accounts department (eg through theft);

(v)   The ticket booking and issuing system may not be available;

(vi)   Donations of animals to the collection (eg from taxation authority seizures and rare breeds enthusiasts) may not be recorded.

Required

(a)   Describe suitable internal controls to manage each of the applicable risks identified.   **(12 marks)**

(b)   Explain the financial statement risks arising from the applicable risks.   **(6 marks)**

(c)   Comment on the factors to be considered when planning the extent of substantive analytical procedures to be performed on BZG's income.   **(7 marks)**

(d)   Comment on the respective responsibilities of management and auditors relating to the effectiveness of internal financial controls. Discuss auditing and other current guidance in this area.   **(5 marks)**

                                                                                                (Total = 30 marks)

Question 2

Imperiol, a limited liability company, manufactures and distributes electrical and telecommunications accessories, household durables (eg sink and shower units) and building systems (eg air-conditioning, solar heating, security systems). The company has undergone several business restructurings in recent years. Finance is to be sought from both a bank and a venture capitalist in order to implement the board's latest restructuring proposals.

You are a manager in Hal Falcon, a firm of Chartered Certified Accountants. You have been approached by Paulo Gandalf, the chief finance officer of Imperiol, to provide a report on the company's business plan for the year to 31 December 2008.

From a brief telephone conversation with Paulo Gandalf you have ascertained that the proposed restructuring will involve discontinuing all operations except for building systems, where the greatest opportunity for increasing product innovation is believed to lie. Imperiol's strategy is to become the market leader in providing 'total building system solutions' using new fibre optic technology to link building systems. A major benefit of the restructuring is expected to be a lower on-going cost base. As part of the restructuring it is likely that certain of the accounting functions, including internal audit, will be outsourced.

You have obtained a copy of Imperiol's Interim Report for the six months to 30 June 2007 on which the company's auditors, Discorpio, provide a conclusion giving negative assurance. The following information has been extracted from the Interim Financial Report:

(1) Chairman's statement

The economic climate is less certain than it was a few months ago and performance has been affected by a severe decline in the electrical accessories market. Management's response will be to gain market share and reduce the cost base.

(2) Balance sheet

	30 June 2007 (unaudited)	31 December 2006
	$m	$m
Intangible assets	83.5	72.6
Tangible non-current assets	69.6	63.8
Inventory	25.2	20.8
Receivables	59.9	50.2
Cash	8.3	23.8
Total assets	246.5	231.2
Issued capital	30.4	30.4
Reserves	6.0	9.1
Accumulated profits	89.1	89.0
Interest bearing borrowings.	65.4	45.7
Current liabilities	55.6	57.0
Total equity and borrowings	246.5	231.2

(3)   Continuing and discontinued operations

	Six months to 30 June 2007 (unaudited) $m	Year to 31 December 2006 $m
Revenue		
Continuing operations		
Electrical and telecommunication accessories	55.3	118.9
Household durables	37.9	77.0
Building systems	53.7	94.9
Total continuing	146.9	290.8
Discontinued	–	65.3
Total turnover	146.9	356.1
Operating profit before interest and taxation -		
Continuing operations	13.4	32.2

Required

(a)   Explain what is meant by prospective financial information, distinguishing between forecasts and projections. Comment briefly on the level of assurance provided on engagements to review prospective financial information. **(5 marks)**

(b)   Explain the matters Hal Falcon should consider before accepting the engagement to report on Imperiol's prospective financial information. **(15 marks)**

(c)   Describe the procedures that a professional accountant should undertake in order to provide a report on a profit forecast and forecast balance sheet for Imperiol for the year to 31 December 2008. **(10 marks)**

Note. Assume it is 11 December 2007. **(Total = 30 marks)**

Section B – TWO questions ONLY to be attempted

Question 3

You are the manager responsible for the audit of Dexy, a long-established limited liability company. Dexy sells furniture and home furnishings through retail stores and home catalogues (ie mail order). The draft financial statements for the year ended 30 September 2007 show profit before taxation of $3.2 million (2006 – $2.9 million) and total assets of $36.4 million (2006 – $33.0 million).

The following issues are outstanding from the audit fieldwork and have been left for your attention:

(a)   During the year Dexy took a seven year non-cancellable lease on a suite of offices on the 13th floor of a new development. The lease payments are $130,000 paid annually in advance. The present value of lease payments, calculated as $770,000, has been recognised as a lease asset and lease liability. The lease asset is being amortised on a straight line basis over seven years.   **(8 marks)**

(b)   Advertising costs have increased significantly over recent years and the annual budget is now $350,000. The majority of these costs are incurred in December and June when promotional activities include the publication and distribution of a product catalogue and the design of co-ordinated magazine and billboard advertisements for products to be sold over the next six months. Dexy's management has recently reviewed the company's policy to expense all such costs as incurred and decided that they will now be time-apportioned over the six-month periods when the related products will be sold. $125,000 has been included in the balance sheet as at 30 September 2007 within prepaid expenses. This amount includes product catalogue inventory, prepaid advertising costs and other deferred expenditure.   **(6 marks)**

(c)   Dexy owns a painting by a little known artist, Lennox, which cost $7,000 when it was purchased in 1956. Following a news report that another painting by Lennox had sold at auction for more than a million dollars, the directors had Dexy's painting revalued by an independent appraisal company. The painting is now carried in the balance sheet at its fair value of $1.35 million and the excess over cost has been credited to equity. The painting, which had previously been displayed in Dexy's reception office, has been moved to the chief executive officer's residence for safekeeping.   **(6 marks)**

Required

For each of the above issues:

(i)   Comment on the matters that you should consider; and
(ii)   State the audit evidence that you should expect to find, in undertaking your review of the audit working papers and financial statements of Dexy.

Note. The mark allocation is shown against each of the three issues. Assume it is 11 December 2007.

(Total = 20 marks)

Question 4

(a)   Explain why quality control may be difficult to implement in a smaller audit firm and illustrate how such difficulties may be overcome.   **(8 marks)**

(b)   Kite Associates is an association of small accounting practices. One of the benefits of membership is improved quality control through a peer review system. Whilst reviewing a sample of auditors' reports issued by Rook & Co, a firm only recently admitted to Kite Associates, you come across the following qualified opinion on the financial statements of Lammergeier Group:

'Qualified opinion arising from disagreement about accounting treatment relating to the non-adoption of IAS 7.'

'The management has not prepared a group cashflow statement and its associated notes. In the opinion of the management it is not practical to prepare a group cashflow statement due to the complexity involved. In our opinion the reasons for the departure from IAS 7 are sound and acceptable and adequate disclosure has been made concerning the departure from IAS 7. The departure in our opinion does not impact on the truth and fairness of the financial statements.'

'In our opinion, except for the non-preparation of the group cashflow statement and associated notes, the financial statements give a true and fair view of the state of the financial position of the company as at 30 June 2007 and of the profit of the group for the year then ended, and have been properly prepared in accordance with...'

Your review of the prior year auditors' report has revealed that the 2006 year-end audit opinion was identical.

Required

Critically appraise the appropriateness of the audit opinion given by Rook & Co on the financial statements of Lammergeier Group for the years ended 30 June 2007 and 2006. **(12 marks)**

(Total = 20 marks)

Question 5

(a) 'Quality control policies and procedures should be implemented at both the level of the audit firm and the individual audits'.

Describe the nature and explain the purpose of quality control procedures appropriate to the individual audit.
(5 marks)

(b) You are an audit manager in Ebony, a firm of Chartered Certified Accountants. Your specific responsibilities include planning the allocation of professional staff to audit assignments. The following matters have arisen in connection with the audits of three client companies:

(i)   The Finance Director of Almond, a private limited company, has requested that only certain staff are to be included on the audit team to prevent unnecessary disruption to Almond's accounting department during the conduct of the audit. In particular, that Xavier be assigned as accountant in charge (AIC) of the audit and that no new trainees be included in the audit team. Xavier has been the AIC for this client for the last two years. **(5 marks)**

(ii) Alex was one of the audit trainees assigned to the audit of Phantom, a private limited company, for the year ended 31 March 2007. Alex resigned from Ebony with effect from 30 November 2007 to pursue a career in medicine. Kurt, another AIC, has just told you that on the day Alex left he told Kurt that he had ticked schedules of audit work as having been performed when he had not actually carried out the tests. **(5 marks)**

(iii) Scooby has drafted its first 'Report to Society' which contains health, safety and environmental performance data for the year to 30 September 2007. Amy, the audit senior, has filed it with the comment that it is 'to be dealt with when all other information for inclusion in the company's annual report is available'. **(5 marks)**

Required

Comment on the ethical, quality control and other professional issues raised by each of the above matters and their implications, if any, for Ebony's staff planning.

Note. The mark allocation is shown against each of the three issues. Assume it is 11 December 2007.

(Total = 20 marks)

Answers

A PLAN OF ATTACK

If this were the real Advanced Audit and Assurance exam and you had been told to turn over and begin, what would be going through your mind?

An important thing to say (while there is still time) is that it is vital to have a good breadth of knowledge of the syllabus because the question requirements for each question will relate to different areas of the P7 syllabus. However, don't panic. Below we provide guidance on how to approach the exam.

Approaching the answer

Use your 15 minutes of reading time usefully, to look through the questions, particularly Questions 1 and 2 in Section A which are compulsory, to get a feel for what is required and to become familiar with the question scenarios.

It is vital that you attempt all the questions in the paper to increase your chances of passing. The best way to do this is to make sure you stick to the time allocation for each question – both in total and for each of the question parts. The worst thing you can do is run over time in one question and then find that you don't have enough time for the remaining questions.

Section A is compulsory and consists of two long case-study style questions totalling between 50 and 70 marks. These may contain detailed information such as extracts from financial statements and audit working papers. A range of requirements will be set for each question, covering areas from across the whole syllabus.

Question 1 is for 30 marks. The scenario is quite long so make sure you have used your reading time well to familiarise yourself with it and make some notes on key issues. The key to success in this question is to stay focussed, don't run over time and answer the questions set. In parts (a) and (b) you are asked for internal controls and financial statement risks, so you could link the answers to these two requirements. Parts (c) and (d) are reasonably straightforward but note the mark allocations and ensure your answers are well explained and sufficiently detailed to score well.

Question 2 is also worth 30 marks and relates to an engagement to review prospective financial information. Part (a) is knowledge-based and you should score well here as a result. In part (b) use the information in the scenario to help you generate ideas for your answer.

Section B contains three questions, from which you must attempt two. This section will typically be worth between 30 and 50 marks and will use short scenarios.

Question 3 is on audit evidence and matters to consider in the context of three mini scenarios. Note the mark allocation in each. Your answers must be focussed and coherent if you are going to score well and your financial reporting knowledge needs to be sound as you will have to apply it in this question.

Question 4 is on quality control and audit reports. In part (a) you need to discuss quality control issues in small firms, and this part leads into a scenario-based part (b). This is a tricky question but a logical approach together with appropriate planning of your answer will be the best way to tackle it.

Question 5 is on ethical, quality control and professional issues. In part (a) you have to discuss quality control both at a firm level and individual audit level. Part (b) has three short scenarios on which you have to comment, considering any ethical, quality control and other professional issues. Note that the requirement also asks you for the implications on the audit firm's staff planning – don't forget this part of the question.

Forget about it!

And don't worry if you found the paper difficult. More than likely other candidates will too. If this were the real thing you would need to forget the exam the minute you left the exam hall and think about the next one. Or, if it is the last one, celebrate!

Question 1

Text references. Chapters 6 and 7

Top tips. This question appears daunting because of the unusual context the question is set in. A zoo is an unusual context in which to think of internal controls and the assets such as animals are also unusual. However, the question is actually reasonably straightforward, and part (c) is particularly so. You could complete your answer to part (c), which is essentially rote learning of ISA 520 before attempting parts (a) and (b) if (a) and (b) seem tricky at first glance. However, even parts (a) and (b) are manageable. Try and think of the practical business and financial statement implications of the zoo. Animals are assets in this context, which are impaired if people don't want to come and see them. Unrecorded donations are in effect unrecorded additions to non-current assets. The risks have been identified for you, you have to focus on how those risks might be controlled. Make sure you read the question properly and answer it. For example, in part (c), you are planning to use analytical procedures as substantive procedures for income. You will not gain marks talking about analytical procedures at the planning stage or at the review stage.

Easy marks. Some of the internal controls required in part (a) are more straightforward than others. Do not panic if the first applicable risk seems complicated. Read through the question completely and identify the more straightforward ones, for example, cash misappropriation, and you can gain easy marks listing controls and financial statement risks applicable in this area, which would not be out of place in the lower level auditing paper.

Examiner's comments. In part (a), candidates mostly sought to address internal controls selected from 'compare' or other mnemonics - failing to appreciate that these are only specific control procedures. Candidates needed to consider more pervasive controls and monitoring activities also ... Regarding part (b), only a minority of candidates understand that financial statement risk is the risk of misstatement in the financial statements which is not the same as 'financial risk'. Few candidates recognised that failure to record reciprocal advertisement arrangements would result in an understatement of advertising expense (and sponsorship income). Most candidates did not read the requirement in part (c) and did not answer the question.

Marking scheme

		Marks
(a)	**Internal controls**	
	Generally 1 mark each point, max 3 any one risk	12
	Ideas	
	• Control procedures/specific controls	
	• Control environment/pervasive controls	
	• Monitoring activities (including reconciliations)	
(b)	**Financial statement risk**	
	Generally 1 mark each point	6
	Ideas	
	Assets	
	• Impairment (IAS 36)/overstatement (tangibles)	
	• Useful lives	
	• Existence assurance (tangibles, cash)	
	• Completeness (tangibles, receivables)	
	Profit and loss account	
	• Admission fees (understatement)	
	• Sponsorship income/advertising expense understatement (SIC 31)	
	Reserves	
	• Existence/disclosure	
	Disclosure risk	
	• Going concern (IAS 1)	

(c)   **Substantive analytical procedures**
      Generally ½ mark each factor + up to 1 mark a comment   7
      Ideas (ISA 520)
      • Audit objectives
      • Nature of entity
      • Degree of disaggregation of information
      • Availability of information
      • Reliability of information
      • Relevance of information
      • Source of information available
      • Comparability of information
      • Expectation of relationships
      • Materiality
      • Other audit procedures
      • Accuracy of predictions
      • Inherent and control risk assessments
      • Tests of controls
(d)   Internal control effectiveness
      Generally 1 mark each comment
      • Responsibilities of management and auditors
      • Sarbanes – Oxley Act
      • ISA 330   5
                                                                         ──
                                                                         30

	(a) Internal controls	(b) Financial statements risks
(i) *Lack of investment in new exhibits*	• Regular review of admission fees/visitor numbers/lapsed memberships and sponsorships • Regular (monthly/quarterly/ annually) review of competitors' service/assets • Annual capital expenditure budget for animals/attractions and approval of it • Annual review of additions of animals/attractions in year against budget	Existing assets (animals and non current assets such as enclosures) may be impaired if they are not generating income in use. Impairment tests in line with IAS 36 should be carried out. Ultimately, failure to invest in the assets of the zoo might lead to going concern problems. There may be disclosure risk if correct disclosures under IAS 1 are required and have not been made.
(ii) *Failure to invoice animal sponsorships*	• Regular reconciliation between sponsorships and sponsorship income • Pre-numbered sponsorship documentation • Sequence checking of sponsorship documentation by invoicing staff • Monitoring of instances of lack of data transfer • Investment in automatic computerised data transfer between sponsorship/invoicing departments	Income may not be recorded completely.

	(a) Internal controls	(b) Financial statements risks
(iii) *Rates for corporate sponsorship*	• Approved price list • Price list reviewed annually • Approved discount list • Key official to authorise discounts for new clients • Sharing of discount information with invoicing department • Review of sponsorship income v budget to identify any shortfalls • Review of advertising cost v budget to identify 'free' advertising (and associated sales)	Income and expenses may not be recorded completely if sponsorship is given in exchange for advertising. Ultimately, if sponsorship is recurringly undercharged, going concern might be affected.
(iv) *Cash misappropriation*	• CCTV in ticket booths to record cash sales • Electronic till records kept and reconciled to cash received by cashiers in accounts department • More than one officer at each gate • Reconciliation of ticket stubs with cash • Secondary gate to ensure that all visitors have been issued with a ticket/to collect ticket stubs	Income will be understated if cash is misappropriated at source (and by implication, the sale is not recorded).
(v) *Booking/ticket issuing system unavailable*	• Contingency plans (see below) required • Manual tickets kept in entrance gate ticket offices • Telephone booking system alternative to website if website unavailable • Maintenance/downtime of website at anti-social hours	Loss of sales in this manner could affect the going concern status of the company, but other than that there may be no impact on the financial statements of sales lost in this manner.
(vi) *Donations of animals not recorded*	• Animal register to be maintained • Regular reconciliations between animals in zoo and animals in register	Assets may be understated if new assets have not been valued and included in non current assets in accordance with IAS 16.

(c) **Analytical procedures (income)**

The auditor should consider the following matters:

(i) *The plausibility and predictability of the relationships identified for comparison and evaluation*

For example, the relationship between current year income and prior year income is plausible unless there have been any major changes in the year (for example, new attractions) and should be predictable even if there have been changes. For example, the impact of a new attraction should be predictable on the basis of prior new attractions. In addition, BZG's income will be seasonal, and there should be clear and predictable patterns of sales in high summer season and in school holidays.

(ii) *The objectives of the analytical procedures and the extent to which their results are reliable*

The objectives will be to give evidence about the completeness of sales income and the results are likely to be reliable, given the plausibility and predictability of sales income as outlined above. However, the risks affecting sales income discussed above ((ii) and (iii)) would merit some other substantive work being carried out in this risk area.

(iii) *The detail to which the information can be analysed*

The auditor should consider what records are available with regard to sales: monthly sales figures, daily sales figures, electronic till receipt records, prior year records in the same detail, sales budgets, in order to assess how detailed the level of analytical review he is going to be able to carry out. The types of sale (sponsorship, retail outlets, gate entry) are distinct and their records should be distinct which will allow greater detail of analysis on sales generally to be made.

(iv) *The availability of the information*

The information outlined above should be easily available to the auditor if it exists. In addition, non-financial information, such as number of visitors, should be available, giving the auditor scope to assess whether actual income is consistent with income for that number of visitors etc.

(v) *The relevance of the information*

For example, if the auditor is comparing budget to actual, he should ascertain whether the budget was realistic or a tough target. He should be able to verify this by reference to the budget setter, or to sales meeting minutes or prior year budgetary practice. Information from gates (ie number of visitors) will be more relevant if there is no other method of gaining access to the zoo.

(vi) *The comparability of the information available*

For example, if the auditor intended to compare BZG's results with those of a competitor zoo, he should bear in mind whether the zoos have comparable attractions, target markets and opening times. However, as the zoo is fairly specialised, more meaningful comparisons are likely with prior period information from BZG itself.

(vii) *The knowledge gained during previous audits*

If comparing income last year to this year, it may be that there were significant new attractions in the prior year that will impact on the comparison with this year.

(viii) *Materiality and risk*

As sales is a material balance and could potentially contain single items (large sponsorship deals) that are individually material, some additional substantive procedures are likely to be necessary, for example on sponsorship. In addition, given the control problems in connection with income, control risk is higher and additional substantive tests may be required on income completeness.

(d)   **Effectiveness of internal financial controls**

Responsibilities

Management is responsible for ensuring that internal financial controls are effective. This is often a process that management employ an internal audit department to carry out.

In the UK, auditors of listed companies are required by the Combined Code to review the company's corporate governance statement which will include a review of the Board's review of the effectiveness of internal controls.

An auditor must test the effectiveness of internal controls if seeking to rely on them for audit evidence. The auditor is not required to report to management directly on their effectiveness, unless engaged specifically to do so in an engagement other than the audit.

Current guidance

Although auditors have always had the option of testing internal control effectiveness as part of their audit, ISA 330 *The auditor's procedures in response to assessed risks* makes it more likely that they will do so than was previously the case. The standard states that 'auditors are required to perform tests of controls when the auditor's risk assessment includes an expectation of the operating effectiveness of controls or when substantive procedures alone do not provide sufficient appropriate audit evidence at the assertion level'.

This changes audit practice from testing controls if the auditor intends to rely on the effectiveness of controls as audit evidence to testing controls if the auditor believes the controls to be effective. This will result in tests of controls being performed regularly because it is likely that auditors will expect a company's internal control system to be operating effectively more often than not.

In the US, the Sarbanes-Oxley Act requires CEOs and CFOs to certify that they are responsible for internal control and have reported on their effectiveness and that all major control weaknesses and management frauds have been reported to the auditors. Auditors in the US are required to report on management's report about internal control effectiveness.

In the UK, the Combined Code has recently been revised with more emphasis being put on non-executive directors paying attention to such matters as internal control effectiveness if they are members of the non-executive audit committee.

Question 2

Text reference. Chapter 13

Top tips. This question looks at the topic of prospective financial information. Many of the points in ISAE 3400 will be relevant. For part (b) however it is critical that you do not simply produce a rote-learned list of matters. To score well you must tailor general points to the scenario ensuring that your answer does not contradict with the question. Also avoid making assumptions which are clearly not the case if you read the question carefully.

For part (c) planning your answer is essential. This will avoid repetition of points which apply to both the profit forecast and the forecast balance sheet.

Easy marks. These are available in part (a) of this question as it is knowledge-based.

Examiner's comments. There were many misunderstandings in this question demonstrating that candidates had a poor grasp of this area of the syllabus. In part (b) these included the following:

- Assuming the task was an audit
- Misinterpretation of negative assurance as something bad
- Not reading the dates carefully at the top of the financial information

In part (c) similar confusion was apparent. For example many failed to realise that the information for December 2008 was prospective ie for future periods.

Marking scheme

		Marks

(a) **Prospective financial information**

Generally 1 mark per point — Max 5
- Definition of prospective financial information
- Distinguishing between forecasts and projections
- Level of assurance provided

(b) **Matters to be considered**

Generally ½ mark each matter identified and 1 mark a point explaining its relevant — Max 15
- PFI 'general' ideas
- Form and content
- Period covered
- Intended use
- Recipients of report
- Relevance and reliability of PFI
- Report required
- Timescale
- Confidentiality
- Purpose of engagement
- Other service opportunities

Ideas specific to Imperiol
- Who is Paulo Gandalf?
- Why has auditor not been engaged for assignment?

Max 15

(c) **Procedures**

Generally 1 mark each point contributing to a description of procedures — Max 10
Ideas
- General (ie applicable to both profit forecast and forecast balance sheet)
- Specific (ie relevant to profit forecast or balance sheet)
- Arithmetic accuracy
- Assumptions, bases, etc
- Inter-relationship

25

(a) **Prospective financial information** is information based on assumptions about events that may occur in the future and possible actions by an entity.

Prospective financial information can be of two types (or a combination of both):

Forecasts are prospective financial information based on assumptions as to future events which management expects to take place and the actions management expects to take (best-estimate assumptions).

Projections are prospective financial information based on hypothetical assumptions about future events and management actions, or a mixture of best-estimate and hypothetical assumptions.

Prospective financial information is difficult to give assurance about because it is **highly subjective** and this makes it a difficult area to examine and report on. Hence the level of assurance provided is **negative**, as opposed to external audits, which examine historical financial information, and where the assurance provided is reasonable.

Guidance on reporting on it is given in ISAE 3400 *The examination of prospective financial information.* The ISAE suggests that the auditor express an opinion including:

- A statement of **negative assurance** as to whether the **assumptions** provide a reasonable basis for the prospective financial information

- An opinion as to whether the prospective financial information is **properly prepared** on the basis of the assumptions and the relevant reporting framework

- Appropriate **caveats as to the achievability** of the forecasts

(b) **Matters to be considered before acceptance**

The terms of the engagement

In particular Hal Falcon should clarify whether there will be any restrictions put in place in terms of access to information and personnel.

Status of Paulo Gandalf

There may be an issue of independence if Paulo both produces the PFI and appoints those who are responsible for reviewing it.

The nature of the business plan

This could be made up of a number of different elements including profit forecasts and cash flows. The content needs to be confirmed as the procedures which will be adopted will depend on the nature of the material covered.

The intended use of the information

In this case the information is to be used by the bank/venture capitalists as a basis for determining whether to finance the business restructuring. It is likely that this information will be a significant factor in the decision making process.

Specific requirements of the recipients

If a bank or venture capitalist has already been identified they may have specific requirements of the information in terms of content and presentation.

The nature of the assumptions

These may be best estimates or hypothetical assumptions. Ideally Hal Falcon would wish to be able to distinguish between the two.

Probable reliability of the information

This will depend on management expertise and integrity. As the business has already experienced a number of restructurings it should be possible to assess the managements ability to produce PFI by comparing forecasts and actual results based on an earlier restructuring.

The period covered by the information

The forecast information is produced to 30 June 2008. Assumptions normally become more speculative as the length of period covered increases. In this case, however, the period covered does not seem excessive. Consideration would need to be given to any specific time scale requirements set down by the bank/venture capitalist.

Form of opinion required

Normally this would be a statement of negative assurance.

Time available

Hal Falcon must ensure that they have sufficient time to perform the necessary procedures.

Experience of Hal Falcon staff

The firm should only accept the appointment if they have the necessary expertise to perform the engagement.

Knowledge of the business

Hal Falcon need to be confident that they will be able to obtain a sufficient level of knowledge of the business to be able to evaluate whether all significant assumptions required for the preparation of the prospective financial information have been identified.

Degree of secrecy required

This may go beyond the normal duty of confidentiality.

Communication with Discorpio

In particular Hal Falcon would wish to enquire if there was any reason as to why they should not accept this appointment. This may be an issue particularly as Discorpio have not been asked to perform this work.

Provision of other services

Hal Falcon may be able to offer external audit services and internal audit services as these are currently outsourced.

(c)   **Procedures**

Applicable to all PFI

- Discuss with management the way in which the PFI is prepared.

- Compare the actual results of previous restructurings with forecasts to determine overall level of accuracy of PFI.

- Determine who specifically is responsible for the preparation of the PFI and assess their experience and expertise.

- Assess the role of internal audit and other control procedures over the preparation of PFI.

- Check the accounting policies normally adopted by the company. These should have been consistently applied in the preparation of the PFI.

- Check the arithmetical accuracy of the PFI by making clerical checks such as recomputation. Internal consistency should also be assessed through the use of analytical procedures.

- Obtain written representations from management regarding the intended use of the prospective financial information, the completeness of significant management assumptions and management's acceptance of its responsibility for the prospective financial information.

Profit forecast

- Discuss with management the means by which they have predicted expected revenues/profits. For example extrapolation of historical data may be inappropriate due to the restructuring.

- Check that any assumptions made are consistent with one another. For example if revenue is expected to grow certain costs would also be expected to increase (although not necessarily in direct correlation). Assess the assertion by the business that the restructuring will result in a lower cost base.

- Compare assumptions made for forecast purposes with other internal information produced by the business. For example expected sales growth can be compared to sales and marketing plans.

- Compare budgeted expenditure on R&D with budgets and final costings on completed products. (This is particularly important as the aim of increasing market share is dependent on innovative products. R&D is likely to be a major cost.)

- Compare assumptions made with general industry data and trends particularly in respect of the building systems market.

- Compare predicted costs against actual costs incurred. Clarify the rationale behind any significant cost savings.

Forecast balance sheet

- Perform analytical review comparing key ratios including ROCE, current ratio and gearing, based on the forecast information with Dec 2006/June 2007 results.

- Determine the way in which the balance for intangible assets has been calculated. Development of new products would result in increases in intangibles. However assets related to discontinued operations would need to be written off.

- Agree proposed additions to tangible assets to capital expenditure budgets. Ensure assumptions regarding depreciation are consistent with the profit forecast. (This would also apply to intangibles.)

- Agree cash balance to other forecast information eg cash flow.

- Determine the level of provisions made in respect of discontinued activities and assess whether they seem reasonable.

- Compare predicted movements in loans to cash flow.

- Analyse movement on reserves (ie is movement on revenue reserve equal to forecast profit? If not what do the other movements represent?).

Question 3

Text references. Chapters 8 and 10

Top tips. This question looks at some tricky accounting issues but is the sort of question which you need to be prepared for. One of the aspects which makes this question tough is the fact that not all the accounting problems can be solved by simply referring to an accounting standard. Don't be put off by this. Remember that this is one of the issues that you can highlight. As an auditor if you are faced with this situation you have to be able to identify that this is the case and consider the alternative means by which you would determine whether the accounting treatment is appropriate. Typically this would be by reference to basic principles. The evidence part should be more straightforward but you can lose marks by failing to address the specifics of the situation. Avoid producing the 'bog-standard' list of audit work and ensure that your audit evidence deals with the issues identified in part (a).

Easy marks. You will always gain marks for assessing materiality.

Examiner's comments. Candidates should be encouraged to read the previous examiner's articles which explain how to tackle this style of question. Those who had clearly done so scored three or four marks for considerations of materiality. Candidates should calculate relevant percentages based on information in the question rather than using a pre-calculation of all the 'rules of thumb.'

In part (a) many wrote everything they knew about leases but failed to identify the real issue, with some treating the asset as if it were an item of equipment or a vehicle.

In part (b) the underlying technical knowledge relevant to this part of the question was lacking. Many fail candidates dismissed carrying any of the cost as being intangible and showed no understanding of a prepayment. They also failed to recognise any inventory implications.

In part (c) better candidates stated that selective revaluation of one of a class of assets is not allowed. Most however were not able to address the issue of the removal of the painting in terms that would score marks. Unsubstantiated comments such as 'the painting should not be shown on Dexy's balance sheet' without any consideration of the disposal did not earn marks. Many did not appreciate that the gain had been correctly treated. Audit evidence continues to be badly answered. Statements such as 'check compliance with (unspecified) accounting standards', 'perform analytical procedures', 'see board minutes', 'obtain management representation', 'discuss with management' continue to earn no marks at this level. The weakest candidates continue to write that evidence would be 'Evidence of...' or 'Documentation on...' with no demonstration of knowledge of what that evidence or documentation might be. Many candidates are unrealistic in their expectations. Some wanted to inspect the original invoice for the painting even though it was 50 years old. Candidates must demonstrate an understanding of the sufficiency and appropriateness of evidence which comes from prior year working papers and financial statements etc.

Marking scheme

		Marks

(i) **Matters**

Generally 1 mark each comment

Maximum 6 marks issues (a)   Max 12

4 marks issues (b) & (c)

Ideas

- Materiality (assessed)
- Relevant IASs (eg 8, 16, 17, 38, 40) and 'The framework'
- Risks (eg FS assertions – capital v revenue, ownership, existence)
- Responsibilities (eg directors' – to safeguard assets)
- Implications for auditors' report

(ii) **Audit evidence**

Generally 1 mark each item of audit evidence (source)   Max 12

maximum 6 marks issue (a)

4 marks issues (2) & (3)

Ideas

- Oral vs written
- Internal vs external
- Auditor generated
- Procedures ('Analytical, enquiry, inspection, observation and computation.')

		Max 20
	(1)	Max 8
	(2)	Max 6
	(3)	Max 6
		20

(a) **Matters**

(1) *Non-cancellable lease*

- The key risk is that the lease has been **misclassified** as a finance lease when it should have been treated as an operating lease. If this is the case the lease payments should have been expensed as incurred.

- Any circumstances specific to the company which might mean that the management would wish to capitalise the lease even if it was an operating lease.

- The capitalised asset of $770,000 represents 2.1% of total assets. If the cost has been inappropriately capitalised total assets would be materially misstated.

- Whether misclassification would lead to profits being materially misstated. The potential impact on profits is likely to be immaterial. The lease payments of $130,000 represent 4% of profit before tax which in themselves would not normally be assessed as material In addition the impact of not charging these costs is offset by amortisation of $110,000 and finance costs.

- Whether the accounting treatment is in accordance with IAS 17. This requires finance leased assets to be capitalised and a liability to be recognised. Operating leased assets should be expensed in the income statement on a straight line basis over the term of the lease.

- Whether the lease is a finance lease or an operating lease. This depends on the economic substance of the lease rather than the legal form of the agreement and is assessed by establishing the extent to which risks and rewards of ownership are transferred to Dexy.

- The terms of the lease. For example:

  - Who is responsible for rates, maintenance, repairs and insurance

  - Whether there are circumstances under which legal title will eventually transfer to Dexy

  - Whether Dexy has the right to sublet the office space

  - Whether there is an option to extend the lease such that Dexy would occupy the premises for all or a substantial part of the suite's useful economic life. (The current lease term of 7 years does would not normally constitute a major part of the suite's economic life.)

- Whether the accounting treatment has been applied correctly (assuming that the classification as a finance lease is valid):

  - Whether the amount of $770,000 initially capitalised as an asset represents the present value of the lease payments at the inception of the lease (rather than at a subsequent date)

  - Whether the interest rate implicit in the lease was used to calculate the present value of the lease payments (and if not what rate was used)

  - How the finance cost is being spread over the lease term and whether the method is acceptable under IAS 17

  - Whether the straight-line amortisation policy is in line with Dexy's policy for other assets

  - Whether the 7 year amortisation period represents the shorter of the lease term and the asset's useful life. (This would appear to be the case unless there is any indication that the lease term is to be extended.)

- The need to qualify the audit report. If the evidence shows that the lease should have been treated as an operating lease the audit opinion would be qualified 'except for' for non-compliance with IAS 17.

(2) *Advertising costs*

- There is a risk that profits will be overstated if advertising costs are inappropriately deferred as prepaid expenses.

- The reason behind the change in treatment of advertising costs. With costs rising significantly in recent years this could be an attempt to limit the impact on profit.

- $125,000 deferred expenditure represents 3.9% of profit before tax and 0.3% of total assets. As such it is unlikely to be assessed as material.

- Whether the change in treatment constitutes a change in accounting policy in which case a prior period adjustment would be required.

- How the figure of $125,000 has been calculated. On the basis that it represents half of six months expenditure the total annual spend of $500,000 is in excess of budget by $150,000.

- The specific nature of the $125,000 costs. This will determine their appropriate treatment. For example costs incurred as part of the December promotion for adverts which will go out/be published after 31 March are prepaid expenses. The cost of product catalogues produced but not distributed at the year-end should be recognised as inventory.

- Advertising costs should not be accounted for as an intangible asset because, although it may represent expense incurred to provide future economic benefits, it cannot be distinguished from internally-generated goodwill.

- Whether there is evidence to support the fact that advertising expenditure incurred in June/December has a direct impact on revenue in the following six months. If a direct correlation can be proved this would be an indication that the new treatment is reasonable.

(3) *Painting*

- The key risk is that the painting will be incorrectly classified in the financial statements due to its unusual nature.

- It represents 3.7% of total assets and is therefore material to the balance sheet.

- Whether the treatment of the painting as an asset is appropriate. On the basis that it is a resource held by Dexy arising from a past event and from which future benefit is expected to flow it would constitute an asset.

- Management's future intentions. If the intention is to retain the painting it should be treated as a non-current asset. If it is to be sold it should be treated as a current asset.

- The fact that there is no specific accounting standard that deals with assets held for their investment potential. As the asset has been removed from the business premises it does not fall under IAS 16. IAS 40 deals with investment property and whilst the painting is clearly not a property the principles adopted by this standard might reasonably be applied.

- Whether the asset should be depreciated. As it does not seem to fall under the definition of property, plant or equipment it is unlikely that depreciation would be appropriate.

- The treatment of the surplus on revaluation ie whether it has been credited to a revaluation reserve or another non-distributable reserve.

- Whether the asset is to be revalued on a regular basis. Management may decide to adopt the fair value model whereby annual gains and losses are recognised in the profit or loss for the period.

- Whether other paintings need to be revalued. Accounting standards do not allow selective revaluations. If Dexy holds any other paintings they would also need to be revalued.

- Whether the painting constitutes a benefit in kind. As the painting has been moved to the chief executive's house there may be tax implications for the individual.

(b) **Evidence**

(1) *Non-cancellable lease*

- The lease agreement in order to review the terms to establish whether the risks and rewards of ownership are substantially transferred to Dexy.

- Details of maintenance, insurance and other office related costs incurred in respect of the suite agreed to invoice (in order to assess the practical implications of the lease term and hence the economic substance).

- Confirmation of existence of the suite and use by Dexy through physical inspection.

- Recalculation of present value of minimum lease payments and agreement of payment details to the lease.

- Matching of rate implicit in the lease used by Dexy to the lease agreement (or recalculation of pre-tax cost of capital of the discount rate used if there is no rate implicit in the lease).

- Schedules show up that straight-line depreciation policy has been agreed to the accounting policy note and a recalculation of the $110,000 depreciation charge.

- Adequacy of disclosure regarding the finance liability checked:
    - $130,000 due within 1 year
    - $520,000 within 2-5 years
    - $130,000 due after 5 years

(2) *Advertising costs*

- Results of analytical review comparing budgeted costs for this year on a monthly basis with actual monthly expenditure and prior year figures. This would provide evidence of possible over-spending which may have been the reason behind the change in policy.

- A schedule showing a breakdown of advertising and promotional costs. Major individual items would then be agreed to supporting invoices.

- An analysis of the $125,000 prepayment. Based on the annual budget of $350,000 the prepayment figure would be $87,500. The reason behind the extra $37,500 expenditure should be discussed with management and validated.

- A breakdown of the inventory figure in the balance sheet. If this figure includes the cost of catalogues which are also included in the prepaid expenses figure the cost would effectively be counted twice.

(3) *Painting*

- Prior year working papers and financial statements to confirm original historic cost.

- Written representation confirming the managements future intentions regarding the painting ie. whether it is to be retained or sold.

- The report produced by the independent valuer detailing the assumptions behind the increase in value to $1.35 million.

- Correspondence with insurers, in particular details of the way in which the insurance company confirmed the new valuation eg their own independent valuation.

- The disclosure note in the financial statements to ensure that the fair value basis of measurement is adequately described.

- Physical inspection of the painting at the chief executive's home to check that the asset has been retained and has not been sold.

- Insurance documents detailing the insurance cover and any required security measures for the policy to be valid.

- Written representation from the chief executive confirming that he is responsible for the safety of the painting and that adequate security measures are in place.

Question 4

Text references. Chapters 4 and 17

Top tips. If you have not learnt specifically about the problems small companies have in implementing quality control procedures, then spend a few minutes thinking through quality control requirements and the practical implications of them. Hopefully it would soon have become clear that staff shortage is a major problem. In part (b), the audit report is presented incorrectly so you have to think both about whether the opinion is correct and whether it is correctly presented. In the answer below, we have discussed what the opinion should have been before outlining the problems in the report itself so as not to get the two issues confused. It helps to break questions down into smaller components like this, as indicated by the headers in our answer.

Easy marks. As usual in a reports question (question 4 on the exam paper) the easier marks are available in part (a) of this question which is a short question about the problems of addressing quality control issues in a smaller firm and solutions to that problem. If you had read the whole question through you would have seen that one solution is given in part (b) of the question.

Examiner's comments. Part (a) was generally better answered than part (b). However, weaker candidates did not address quality control at the level of the firm and some referred to 'lack of segregation of duties' (ie internal control procedures not quality control procedures). The requirement in part (b) to 'critically appraise...' calls for an analysis of the scenario, not a textbook explanation of forms of audit report and qualification criteria.

Marking scheme

		Marks
(a)	**Quality control in a smaller audit firm**	5

Generally 1 mark each comment contributing to an explanation of difficulties in implementation + 1 mark each illustration how overcome

Ideas

Difficulties
- Staffing
- Training
- Client involvement
- Allocation of roles

How overcome
- Sharing responsibilities
- External consultation
- Professional advisory services
- Consortium arrangements

		Marks
(b)	**Appropriateness of auditors' report**	10

Generally 1 mark a comment

Ideas
- Confusion – heading vs statement of concurrence
- IAS 7 – in full
- Directors vs auditors' opinion
- 'Truth and fairness' vs
- 'Except for'
- Disclosure note vs
- Explanatory paragraph
- IAS 7 exemption
- Prior year

15

LEARNING MEDIA

(a) **Quality control**

International Quality Control Standard 1 (ISQC 1) and ISA 220 *Quality control for audits of historical financial information* set out the requirements for audit firms in relation to quality control. The requirements are detailed. There are a number of requirements to have **monitoring procedures** in place or to have **reviews carried out by independent partners**.

Such requirements will clearly be difficult for a sole practitioner or even a small partnership to implement, because there is no one to carry out such independent reviews, and the expense of employing a specific quality control staff member would be proportionally greater for such a firm, and the work available for such a member of staff, proportionally smaller, making the idea not cost effective and punitive on small firms.

Small audit firms may have **difficulty recruiting quality staff** and in **training** them. In addition, larger firms are assisted in ensuring independence and other ethical requirements are met by the **audit committees** of the companies they are auditing. Smaller firms are likely to audit smaller companies which are **owner-managed and may not have audit committees**.

As such firms still have to meet quality requirements, there are some solutions available to them. One is to employ an independent quality consultant, or a part-time member of staff to promote quality and carry out independent reviews. However, this is still financially prohibitive.

Another solution is to join an affiliation of like firms, which provide reciprocal services such as reviews in order to keep quality control requirements without incurring a great deal of added expense.

In addition, all firms of Chartered Certified Accountants have access to the ethical and professional services provided to them by ACCA.

(b) **Rook and Co - audit opinion**

From the heading in the audit report, the opinion appears to be a qualified opinion as a result of a material disagreement over accounting treatment. However, in practice this does not appear to be the case at all, and there are some significant problems with the audit opinion.

Audit opinion

There are two key questions that have to be considered:

(1)   Have the financial statements been prepared in accordance with the applicable accounting requirements?

(2)   Do the financial statements give a true and fair view?

The report indicates that the directors have not implemented the requirements of International Accounting Standard 7 *Cash flow statements*. This means that the answer to question 1 is no, because IAS 7 is an applicable accounting requirement for group financial statements and there is no available exemption for the Lammergeier Group.

The Lammergeier Group is therefore only entitled to omit a cash flow statement if it was necessary to do so in order to give a true and fair view. If omitting a cash flow statement gives a true and fair view, it would then be necessary for there to be proper disclosure of the departure from the applicable accounting requirements in order to give a true and fair view.

However, in this case, it appears that the reason that the Group did not include a cash flow statement was that it was too complex to do so. This is not a suitable reason for departing from the requirements of accounting standards. Therefore the answer to the second question above is, no, because the departure results in a true and fair view not being given.

Thus it is appropriate to give a qualified opinion on these financial statements, due to disagreement over the omission of a cash flow statement. This disagreement is material to the financial statements, as the cash flow statement is a primary financial statement. Arguably this fact could make the omission pervasive to the financial statements as a whole. However, on the other hand, the lack of truth and fairness is restricted to the cash flow statement (or lack of it), hence a material disagreement is appropriate.

Presentation of audit opinion

Therefore, at first glance, the auditors appear to have given the correct opinion, as the title to the opinion paragraph states that the opinion is qualified due to disagreement. This title is a little more laboured than is necessary, and it would have been appropriate to label the paragraph 'Qualified opinion due to disagreement over omission of cash flow statement'.

However, the opinion paragraph itself does not appear to give a qualified opinion. The auditors state that they agree with the departure from the accounting standards and that it has been adequately disclosed. This would have been appropriate had the departure been necessary to give a true and fair view. However, if this had been the case, no qualified opinion would have been necessary.

The opinion paragraph is therefore wrong. The omission of a cash flow statement is not justified and the report should be qualified. The auditors should state that they disagree with the directors and that a cash flow should have been included.

Prior year audit opinion

The fact that the prior year audit opinion was identical indicates that the same problem existed in the previous year. If the auditors are required to qualify the audit report for the same issue two years in a row, they should make some reference to that fact in the audit report.

Question 5

Text references. Chapters 2 and 4

Top tips. Read through each of these scenarios with an open mind, jotting down all the professional, quality control and/or ethical issues that arise through them. There is not necessarily going to be an obvious ethics issue in questions such as these. 'Professional issues' is a wide term and could mean anything to do with practice management (staff issues, litigation issues, misconduct) and it is important that you do not answer these questions in a narrow fashion. As the examiner suggests, the best way to see the breadth of matters you must consider is to work through lots of old exam questions – so if you struggled with this one, don't forget to try again.

Easy marks. In some ways there are no easy marks for this question, although as shown below, candidates for this sitting must have achieved marks for it as it was the best answered question in section B. There are straightforward marks to be gained for statements of quality control or ethical principles, but you have to interpret the scenario correctly to make those statements. Therefore to gain marks, make sure that you have read the question through carefully and considered all the implications. Do not jump to inappropriate conclusions (for example, that Xavier is not independent with relation to the Almond audit).

Marking scheme

		Marks
(a)	Generally 1 mark each well explained point *Ideas* • Meaning of QC policy and procedures • Direction/audit programme • Supervision/ monitors • Review • Documentation • Independent review	Max 5
(b)	Generally 1 mark each comment *Ideas* Implications for: • Practice management • Time/fee/staff budgets • Quality control (direction, supervision, review) • Threats to independence/possible safeguards • Competence (training) • Integrity (auditor) • Other audits/clients • Audit evidence (RR & S, relevance, reliability, sufficiency) • Audit opinion/report	Maximum 5 marks each of 3 matters
		$\overline{20}$

(a) Quality control on individual audit engagements

The audit engagement partner is responsible for quality control on individual audits. This requirement breaks down into several components.

(i) *Objectivity/independence*

The audit engagement partner must consider whether adequate arrangements are in place to ensure objectivity on the audit and he must document his conclusions.

(ii)   *Direction*

The audit engagement partner is responsible for directing the audit in a way that ensures it is adequately and competently performed.

This means that ultimately, the partner is responsible for ensuring that the audit is properly planned in accordance with auditing standards, that a competent audit team is assigned to the audit, and that the audit team is briefed in matters relevant to the audit about to take place.

(iii)   *Supervision*

Similarly, the audit must be supervised so as to ensure that it is progressing as directed. Ultimately, again, this is the responsibility of the partner. On an audit team, each member will be responsible for supervising the work of more junior members of the team.

Junior members of the team should be encouraged to ask questions about the work they are doing, so as to improve overall quality. The partner should also encourage senior team members to keep him informed on audit progress.

(iv)   *Review*

Lastly, the work should be reviewed to ensure that:

- It has been conducted in accordance with the plan
- Sufficient evidence has been obtained to support conclusions drawn
- Conclusions drawn are reasonable given evidence obtained

Work will be reviewed by more senior audit team members:

- Work of audit juniors is reviewed by audit senior
- Work of audit senior is reviewed by audit supervisor

The audit manager and audit partner will review the audit file as well.

(v)   *Monitoring*

For public limited and public interest companies it is the responsibility of the audit partner to consider the need for and obtain a second partner review to monitor the quality of the file.

(b)   (i)   **Almond**

Finance director's request

The finance director of Almond has requested that the audit firm use the same accountant in charge (AIC) as in previous years and does not use new trainee auditors on the company audit. This is likely to add to the **convenience** and possibly the **cost-effectiveness** of the audit (more experienced staff are likely to work more efficiently than new staff) both of which would benefit the client.

The fact that the finance director has made this request does not in itself affect the **independence** of the audit, although as a matter of practice management, the audit firm should not encourage such requests from finance directors.

Ebony needs to consider any ethical problems, see below. In addition, however, the fact that the request has been made may indicate dissatisfaction with inefficiency in previous years (caused by senior audit staff being unfamiliar with the client and by new trainees being unsure of their job) which the audit firm should address as part of client care. Regardless of who is on the audit team for the audit, the engagement partner should ensure that the team is adequately briefed about Almond and about the jobs that they will be undertaking as part of the audit. This is also a quality requirement for an audit.

Xavier

Xavier has been associated with the audit as AIC for two years previously and may have been associated with the client in more junior roles for longer. This means he should have an excellent knowledge of the business, which is vital in assessing risk and carrying out audit procedures (especially at the overall review stage of the audit) and therefore would be an excellent staff member to have as AIC this year.

Ethical standards require that audit firms consider whether there is any threat arising to the independence of the audit as a result of senior staff having a **long association** with the client. There are requirements to **rotate** staff on listed company audits. Almond is not listed, and two to three years is not an unreasonable time to be associated with a client. The engagement partner should assess whether there are any factors causing Xavier to not be independent in relation to Almond's audit, but it is unlikely that there are any, unless there is a significant **familiarity threat**.

In which case, if it is possible to use Xavier on this audit, it will be mutually beneficial to the audit firm and the client that he be used. However, it is also important that the firm considers whether it is in Xavier's interests to be AIC on this audit, as it might be better for him to undertake different, more challenging work.

New trainees

Whether to allocate new trainees to this audit will be a matter of judgement for the engagement partner. If the audit is straightforward or if Xavier himself is used regularly to train new staff, it may be beneficial for the firm to allocate a new trainee to this audit. If this is the case, then the audit partner should discuss the matter with the finance director, so as not to annoy him, and ensure that the trainees are adequately briefed so as to inconvenience the client as little as possible.

On the other hand, if it does not inconvenience Ebony to allocate different staff to the audit, then it may benefit them in terms of maintaining good relationship with the client to allocate different staff. The engagement partner should advise the finance director that this is likely to have an impact on the cost of the audit, as new trainees are obviously the cheapest staff to use.

(ii) **Phantom**

Ebony's quality control systems should be such that Alex was given work he was capable of doing, he was supervised and his work was reviewed by someone at his level or above him in the firm.

Alex appears to have admitted to not having completed work properly, although it is possible that this was a joke. The matter should be discussed with his immediate superior on the audit to ascertain whether they noticed anything untoward during the audit.

Alex's work on Phantom should be re-reviewed to assess the risk of whether **conclusions** drawn were **unsubstantiated**. This will involve looking at the reliability and relevance and sufficiency of audit work documented.

The reviewer should also consider, while carrying out this review, whether any problems should have been identified by the original reviewer (ie if work was ticked off as being done that could not possibly have been done). If this is found to be the case, the original reviewer should be given some training in how to carry out a review, to ensure that similar problems do not arise in the future.

The work carried out by Alex on other clients prior to his leaving should also be subject to scrutiny.

Alex should be reported to ACCA because his actions, if proven, constitute misconduct. In addition, if a member of Ebony's staff has issued a reference in respect of Alex, it might be necessary to issue a revision if **misconduct** is found.

As Kurt is aware of the problem, it might be wise to assign him to audits which were done last year by Alex so that he can handle any problems arising. This would be particularly the case if Ebony did not want this issue discussed widely among its staff.

(iii)   The company has produced its first Report to Society. However, there appears to have been a lack of communication on the audit of Scooby. This is illustrated by the fact that Amy, the audit senior, has not communicated this to anyone senior to her. At the very least, this would have been a point of interest to the audit partner. It could be that it represents an opportunity to sell additional assurance services to Scooby.

There is evidence that this audit is poor from a quality control perspective. It suggests a lack of the most basic quality control policies and processes required by auditing standards. Amy's work should have been reviewed by a more senior member of the team on a regular basis. This would have picked up the fact that the company has produced its first Report to Society and the fact also that this should be scrutinised carefully, as auditors must review other information for consistency with the financial statements in accordance with ISA 720 *Other information in documents containing audited financial statements*.

ACCA Professional Level

Paper P7

Advanced Audit and Assurance (International)

Mock Examination 3

Pilot Paper

Question Paper		
Time allowed		
Reading and Planning Writing		15 minutes 3 hours
SECTION A	TWO compulsory questions to be attempted	
SECTION B	TWO questions ONLY to be attempted	
During reading and planning time only the question paper may be annotated		

DO NOT OPEN THIS PAPER UNTIL YOU ARE READY TO START UNDER EXAMINATION CONDITIONS

Section A – ALL THREE questions are compulsory and MUST be attempted

Question 1

You are an audit manager in Ribi & Co, a firm of Chartered Certified Accountants. One of your audit clients Beeski Co provides satellite broadcasting services in a rapidly growing market.

In November 2005 Beeski purchased Xstatic Co, a competitor group of companies. Significant revenue, cost and capital expenditure synergies are expected as the operations of Beeski and Xstatic are being combined into one group of companies.

The following financial and operating information consolidates the results of the enlarged Beeski group:

	Year end 30 September	
	2006	2005
	(Estimated)	(Actual)
	$m	$m
Revenue	6,827	4,404
Cost of sales	(3,109)	(1,991)
Distribution costs and administrative expenses	(2,866)	(1,700)
Research and development costs	(25)	(22)
Depreciation and amortisation	(927)	(661)
Interest expense	(266)	(202)
Loss before taxation	(366)	(172)
Customers	14·9m	7·6m
Average revenue per customer (ARPC)	$437	$556

In August 2006 Beeski purchased MTbox Co, a large cable communications provider in India, where your firm has no representation. The financial statements of MTbox for the year ending 30 September 2006 will continue to be audited by a local firm of Chartered Certified Accountants. MTbox's activities have not been reflected in the above estimated results of the group. Beeski is committed to introducing its corporate image into India.

In order to sustain growth, significant costs are expected to be incurred as operations are expanded, networks upgraded and new products and services introduced.

Required

(a) Identify and describe the principal business risks for the Beeski group. **(9 marks)**

(b) Explain what effect the acquisitions will have on the planning of Ribi & Co's audit of the consolidated financial statements of Beeski Co for the year ending 30 September 2006. **(10 marks)**

(c) Explain the role of 'support letters' (also called 'comfort letters') as evidence in the audit of financial statements. **(6 marks)**

(d) Discuss how 'horizontal groups' (ie non-consolidated entities under common control) affect the scope of an audit and the audit work undertaken. **(5 marks)**

(Total = 30 marks)

Question 2

You have been asked to carry out an investigation by the management of Xzibit Co. One of the company's subsidiaries, Efex Engineering Co, has been making losses for the past year. Xzibit's management is concerned about the accuracy of Efex Engineering's most recent quarter's management accounts.

The summarised income statements for the last three quarters are as follows:

Quarter to	30 June 2006 $000	31 March 2006 $000	31 December 2005 $000
Revenue	429	334	343
Opening inventory	180	163	203
Materials	318	251	200
Direct wages	62	54	74
	560	468	477
Less: Closing inventory	(162)	(180)	(163)
Cost of goods sold	398	288	314
Gross profit	31	46	29
Less: Overheads	(63)	(75)	(82)
Net loss	(32)	(29)	(53)
Gross profit (%)	7.2%	13.8%	8.5%
Materials (% of revenue)	78.3%	70.0%	70.0%
Labour (% of revenue)	14.5%	16.2%	21.6%

Xzibit's management board believes that the high material consumption as a percentage of revenue for the quarter to 30 June 2006 is due to one or more of the following factors:

(1)   under-counting or under-valuation of closing inventory;
(2)   excessive consumption or wastage of materials;
(3)   material being stolen by employees or other individuals.

Efex Engineering has a small number of large customers and manufactures its products to each customer's specification.

The selling price of the product is determined by:

(1)   estimating the cost of materials;
(2)   estimating the labour cost;
(3)   adding a mark-up to cover overheads and provide a normal profit.

The estimated costs are not compared with actual costs. Although it is possible to analyse purchase invoices for materials between customers' orders this analysis has not been done.

A physical inventory count is carried out at the end of each quarter. Items of inventory are entered on stocksheets and valued manually. The company does not maintain perpetual inventory records and a full physical count is to be carried out at the financial year end, 30 September 2006.

The direct labour cost included in the inventory valuation is small and should be assumed to be constant at the end of each quarter. Historically, the cost of materials consumed has been about 70% of revenue.

The management accounts to 31 March 2006 are to be assumed to be correct.

Required

(a)   Define 'forensic auditing' and describe its application to fraud investigations.   **(5 marks)**

(b)   Identify and describe the matters that you should consider and the procedures you should carry out in order to plan an investigation of Efex Engineering Co's losses.   **(10 marks)**

BPP
LEARNING MEDIA

(c) (i)   Explain the matters you should consider to determine whether closing inventory at 30 June 2006 is undervalued; and

  (ii) Describe the tests you should plan to perform to quantify the amount of any undervaluation.

(8 marks)

(d) (i)   Identify and explain the possible reasons for the apparent high materials consumption in the quarter ended 30 June 2006; and

  (ii) Describe the tests you should plan to perform to determine whether materials consumption, as shown in the management accounts, is correct. **(7 marks)**

(Total = 30 marks)

Section B – TWO questions ONLY to be attempted

Question 3

You are a manager in Ingot & Co, a firm of Chartered Certified Accountants, with specific responsibility for the quality of audits. Ingot was appointed auditor of Argenta Co, a provider of waste management services, in July 2006. You have just visited the audit team at Argenta's head office. The audit team is comprised of an accountant in charge (AIC), an audit senior and two trainees.

Argenta's draft accounts for the year ended 30 June 2006 show revenue of $11·6 million (2005 – $8·1 million) and total assets of $3·6 million (2005 – $2·5 million). During your visit, a review of the audit working papers revealed the following:

(a)   On the audit planning checklist, the audit senior has crossed through the analytical procedures section and written 'not applicable – new client'. The audit planning checklist has not been signed off as having been reviewed.   **(4 marks)**

(b)   The AIC last visited Argenta's office when the final audit commenced two weeks ago on 1 August. The senior has since completed the audit of tangible non-current assets (including property and service equipment) which amount to $0·6 million as at 30 June 2006 (2005 – $0·6 million). The AIC spends most of his time working from Ingot's office and is currently allocated to three other assignments as well as Argenta's audit.   **(4 marks)**

(c)   At 30 June 2006 trade receivables amounted to $2·1 million (2005 – $0·9 million). One of the trainees has just finished sending out first requests for direct confirmation of customers' balances as at the balance sheet date.   **(4 marks)**

(d)   The other trainee has been assigned to the audit of the consumable supplies that comprise inventory amounting to $88,000 (2005 – $53,000). The trainee has carried out tests of controls over the perpetual inventory records and confirmed the 'roll-back' of a sample of current quantities to book quantities as at the year end.   **(3 marks)**

(e)   The AIC has noted the following matter for your attention. The financial statements to 30 June 2005 disclosed, as unquantifiable, a contingent liability for pending litigation. However, the AIC has seen a letter confirming that the matter was settled out of court for $0.45 million on 14 September 2005. The auditor's report on the financial statements for the year ended 30 June 2005 was unmodified and signed on 19 September 2005. The AIC believes that Argenta's management is not aware of the error and has not brought it to their attention.   **(5 marks)**

Required

Identify and comment on the implications of these findings for Ingot & Co's quality control policies and procedures.

Note: The mark allocation is shown against each of the five issues.

(Total = 20 marks)

Question 4

You are the manager responsible for four audit clients of Axis & Co, a firm of Chartered Certified Accountants. The year end in each case is 30 June 2006.

You are currently reviewing the audit working paper files and the audit seniors' recommendations for the auditors' reports. Details are as follows:

(a)   Mantis Co is a subsidiary of Cube Co. Serious going concern problems have been noted during this year's audit. Mantis will be unable to trade for the foreseeable future unless it continues to receive financial support from the parent company. Mantis has received a letter of support ('comfort letter') from Cube Co.

The audit senior has suggested that, due to the seriousness of the situation, the audit opinion must at least be qualified 'except for'.   **(5 marks)**

(b)   Lorenze Co has changed its accounting policy for goodwill during the year from amortisation over its estimated useful life to annual impairment testing. No disclosure of this change has been given in the financial statements. The carrying amount of goodwill in the balance sheet as at 30 June 2006 is the same as at 30 June 2005 as management's impairment test show that it is not impaired.

The audit senior has concluded that a qualification is not required but suggests that attention can be drawn to the change by way of an emphasis of matter paragraph.   **(6 marks)**

(c)   The directors' report of Abrupt Co states that investment property rental forms a major part of revenue. However, a note to the financial statements shows that property rental represents only 1.6% of total revenue for the year. The audit senior is satisfied that the revenue figures are correct.

The audit senior has noted that an unqualified opinion should be given as the audit opinion does not extend to the directors' report.   **(4 marks)**

(d)   Audit work on the after-date bank transactions of Jingle Co has identified a transfer of cash from Bell Co. The audit senior assigned to the audit of Jingle has documented that Jingle's finance director explained that Bell commenced trading on 7 July 2006, after being set up as a wholly-owned foreign subsidiary of Jingle.

The audit senior has noted that although no other evidence has been obtained an unmodified opinion is appropriate because the matter does not impact on the current year's financial statements.

(5 marks)

Required

For each situation, comment on the suitability or otherwise of the audit senior's proposals for the auditors' reports. Where you disagree, indicate what audit modification (if any) should be given instead.

Note: The mark allocation is shown against each of the four issues.

(Total = 20 marks)

Question 5

(a)   Comment on the need for ethical guidance for accountants on money laundering.   **(5 marks)**

(b)   You are senior manager in Dedza & Co, a firm of Chartered Certified Accountants. Recently, you have been assigned specific responsibility for undertaking annual reviews of existing clients. The following situations have arisen in connection with three clients:

(i)   Dedza was appointed auditor and tax advisor to Kora Co last year and has recently issued an unmodified opinion on the financial statements for the year ended 31 March 2006. To your surprise, the tax authority has just launched an investigation into the affairs of Kora on suspicion of underdeclaring income.   **(7 marks)**

(ii)   The chief executive of Xalam Co, an exporter of specialist equipment, has asked for advice on the accounting treatment and disclosure of payments being made for security consultancy services. The payments, which aim to ensure that consignments are not impounded in the destination country of a major customer, may be material to the financial statements for the year ending 31 December 2006. Xalam does not treat these payments as tax deductible.   **(4 marks)**

(iii)   Your firm has provided financial advice to the Pholey family for many years and this has sometimes involved your firm in carrying out transactions on their behalf. The eldest son, Esau, is to take up a position as a senior government official to a foreign country next month.   **(4 marks)**

Required

Identify and comment on the ethical and other professional issues raised by each of these matters and state what action, if any, Dedza & Co should now take.

Note: The mark allocation is shown against each of the three situations.

(Total = 20 marks)

Answers

DO NOT TURN THIS PAGE UNTIL YOU HAVE
COMPLETED THE MOCK EXAM

A PLAN OF ATTACK

If this were the real Advanced Audit and Assurance exam and you had been told to turn over and begin, what would be going through your mind?

An important thing to say (while there is still time) is that it is vital to have a good breadth of knowledge of the syllabus because the question requirements for each question will relate to different areas of the P7 syllabus. However, don't panic. Below we provide guidance on how to approach the exam.

Approaching the answer

Use your 15 minutes of reading time usefully, to look through the questions, particularly Questions 1 and 2 in Section A which are compulsory, to get a feel for what is required and to become familiar with the question scenarios.

It is vital that you attempt all the questions in the paper to increase your chances of passing. The best way to do this is to make sure you stick to the time allocation for each question – both in total and for each of the question parts. The worst thing you can do is run over time in one question and then find that you don't have enough time for the remaining questions.

Section A is compulsory and consists of two long case-study style questions, totalling between 50 and 70 marks. These will contain detailed information such as extracts from financial statements and audit working papers. A range of requirements will be set for each question, covering areas from across the whole syllabus.

Question 1 is for 30 marks and is typical of what you are likely to find in the real exam. The scenario is quite long so make sure you have used your reading time well to familiarise yourself with it and make some notes on key issues. The key to success in this question is to stay focussed, don't run over time and answer the questions set. In part (a), notice the requirement to 'identify and describe' – you must explain why the factors you have identified are business risks. Parts (c) and (d) should be relatively straightforward but make sure that you 'explain' and 'discuss' adequately to score well.

Question 2 is also worth 30 marks and relates to a non-audit assurance engagement. Part (a) is straightforward and knowledge-based. In the remaining requirements, you must use the information in the scenario to help you with your answer. Where you are asked to describe the tests you would perform, these should be specific – vague answers wont score well.

Section B contains three questions, from which you must attempt two. This section will typically be worth between 30 and 50 marks and will use short scenarios.

Question 3 is on quality control issues and focuses on five different matters in relation to an external audit assignment. Note the mark allocation in each. Your answers must be focussed and coherent if you are going to score well.

Question 4 is on audit reports for four different audit clients. Again note the mark allocation for each part. Use the information in the scenario to help you and present your answer in a logical way that makes sense.

Question 5 is on ethical and professional issues. In part (a) you have to comment on the need for ethical guidance on money laundering. Part (b) has three short scenarios on which you have to comment. Note that the requirement also asks you what action the firm should now take – don't overlook this part of the question.

Forget about it!

And don't worry if you found the paper difficult. More than likely other candidates will too. If this were the real thing you would need to forget the exam the minute you left the exam hall and think about the next one. Or, if it is the last one, celebrate!

Question 1

Text references. Chapters 6 and 11

Top tips. This is a long 30-mark case study question, typical of the type you should expect in Section A of this paper. Therefore it is extremely important that you stick to the time allocation, not only for the question as a whole, but for each of the individual parts as well.

In part (a) you are asked to identify and explain the business risks facing the group. This means explaining fully why the factor you have identified is a risk. Use a sub-heading for each risk as in the ACCA's answer. A good, methodical way of pulling out the risks is to go through the scenario carefully, noting down potential risk factors as you do so.

Part (b) is worth 10 marks so it is very important that you try to score well. Read the requirement carefully and think back to your financial reporting studies, as well as using the clues in the question, to help you plan your answer. Make sure you consider materiality.

You should be able to score reasonably well in part (c) on support letters as this is a knowledge-based question. Six marks are available here so your answer needs to be quite detailed to score well.

In part (d), use your knowledge of companies in the real world to help you with your answer.

Easy marks. You should be able to pick up most of the business risks required in part (a) of the question and provided you explain why they are risks, you should score reasonably well. Part (c) is also relatively straightforward as it is knowledge-based.

ACCA examiner's answer. The examiner's answer to this question is included at the back of this kit.

Marking scheme

		Marks
(a)	**Principal business risks**	
	Generally ½ mark each risk identified and up to 1½ marks for a (good) description	Max 9
	Ideas	
	• technological obsolescence (communications industry)	
	• competition	
	• integration (operations, cultures)	
	• operating losses	
	• falling ARPC (key performance indicator)	
	• sustaining growth	
	• exchange rate fluctuations	
	• market regulation	

(b) **Impact on planning of audit**

Generally *1 mark* each point contributing to an explanation to a maximum 3 marks each impact   Max 10

Impact ideas

- group structure
- materiality assessment (NOT on profit)
- group (related party) transactions and balances • on analytical procedures
- MTbox on income statement • other auditors
  - ACCA/competent/independent
  - introductory/co-operation letter
- group instructions
- accounting policies (Xstatic & MTbox)
- accounting policies (Xstatic & MTbox)
- timetable
- Note: Two professional marks are included

(c) **'Support letters'**

Generally 1 mark each point contributing to an explanation of their role as audit evidence   Max 6

Ideas

- Consolidated FS vs entity FS
- Bank requirement/routine
- Going concern basis
- Support by whom?
- For how long?
- Formal confirmation of *intent*
- Approved by board
- Need for evidence of *ability*

(d) **'Horizontal groups'**

Generally 1 mark each point contributing to a discussion   Max 5

Ideas

- 'business empires'
- development (as off-balance sheet vehicles)
- increased audit risk – related party/confidentiality issues
- complex fraud risk factor
- reliance on management representation

30

(a) **Business risks**

Nature of the industry

- Beeski is involved in a fast moving high tech industry. New developments may result in older products and services becoming obsolete.

- Whilst technical developments are possible it is difficult to predict whether consumers will appreciate the benefits of these for example, 3rd generation mobile technology. It is possible that vast sums of money could be spent to secure government licences which later prove to be worthless.

- Expansion may be hindered by legislation and local planning laws restricting the location of mobile phone masts. If a link between transmissions from masts (or the phones themselves) and ill health were ever proved the company could be subject to legal claims.

- The industry has seen huge expansion over the last five years or so. There is a possibility that market saturation will restrict future growth potential and drive down prices and therefore margins.

Purchase of Xstatic

- Whilst in the long-term the benefits of synergy may be felt, in the short-term the combination of the two businesses will result in additional costs.

- Customers and key staff, particularly of Xstatic, may be lost.

- As the two companies were in direct competition previously it may be difficult to integrate staff and company culture leading to a period of instability.

Results

- Losses before tax have more than doubled. It is possible that some of the increased expenditure is a result of the integration programme and that in future the benefits accrue. If this is not the case then the business may face serious difficulties in future.

- Customer numbers have increased but revenue per customer has decreased by 8.3% for contract customers and 14.8% for prepaid customers. The company needs to investigate the cause of this. For example it could be due to reduced usage by customers or the effects of changes in charges, perhaps as a result of the purchase of Xstatic or due to competitive pressure to cut prices.

Purchase of MTbox

- Beeski has expanded into the Asian market in which the business may not have had previous experience. In particular the company may not be familiar with local legislation which is critical in this type of regulated industry.

- The business is exposed to increased foreign exchange risk. The economies of India may be volatile, accentuating the problem.

- Introducing its corporate image to MTbox may not be successful due to cultural differences. Key staff may be lost in the process who could be difficult to replace.

Planned growth

- Expansion and maintenance will be costly. The company will not be able to sustain growth unless the expenditure results in increased revenues and profits.

- The company will need to finance these activities. If the business increases its gearing considerably it may find it difficult to service the debt and to raise further funds in future.

(b) **Effect of acquisitions on planning**

Risk

Risk will be increased by the acquisition of the two new companies. The revised group structure will need to be ascertained to ensure that all the relevant entities are consolidated. Dates of acquisition will need to be carefully noted.

Risk is also increased in respect of MTbox as the individual financial statements are to be audited by a local firm and not Ribi & Co.

Materiality

The materiality of the newly acquired businesses will have to be assessed in relation to the group as a whole in order to determine the extent and nature of audit work. For the Xstatic group of companies which are audited by Ribi this will help to determine those subsidiaries which need to be visited and those where more limited procedures can be applied, for example analytical review.

MTbox is less likely to have a material impact on the income statement as the company was only purchased in August (year-end is September). However it may still be material from the balance sheet perspective.

As this company is not audited by Ribi or its affiliates the materiality of MTbox will help to determine the level of discussion which will be required between Ribi and the local auditors.

Accounting treatments

(i)   *Goodwill*

The audit plan will need to address the calculation and accounting treatment of goodwill. Goodwill must be calculated by comparing the cost of the investment with the fair value of the net assets of the subsidiaries at the acquisition dates. Methods used to calculate the fair value of assets should be assessed. For example experts may have been used to value certain types of asset.

Whether goodwill has subsequently been impaired should be assessed with any known factors being taken into account.

(ii)   *Intercompany balances*

The way in which Beeski identifies intercompany balances/transactions will need to be established together with the performance of regular reconciliations.

The audit plan should contain a list of all the companies within the group so that completeness of intercompany balances/transactions can be confirmed in the course of the audit.

(iii)   *Accounting policies*

Information regarding accounting policies should be obtained as these will need to be brought into line as part of the consolidation process. It is more likely that the policies of MTbox will be different to the rest of the group due to its location in India. The local auditors could be requested to perform a reconciliation so that the consolidation adjustment can be quantified.

Practical issues

Ribi will plan to rely on the work of the auditors of MTbox. Before doing so the independence and competence of the other auditors will need to be assessed. As they are Chartered Certified Accountants there is no reason to suspect that their work should be unsatisfactory. Information will be obtained through the use of a questionnaire.

Instructions should be issued to all the other auditors (ie those affiliated to Ribi and the local auditors) in order to co-ordinate the audit work.

These will include details such as:

- Areas requiring special attention
- Procedures for the identification of intercompany transactions
- Procedures for notifying the principal auditors of unusual circumstances
- The timetable for the completion of the audit. (This should be agreed with management as soon as possible.)
- The independence requirements
- Relevant accounting, auditing and reporting requirements

(c)   **Support letters**

In the context of group accounts, the parent and subsidiaries are seen to be a single entity, so if the group as a whole is a going concern then this is sufficient. It is sometimes the case that a subsidiary, when considered in isolation, does not appear to be a going concern. In such a case the auditor may request a support letter from the directors of the parent company. This letter states that the intention of the parent is to continue to support the subsidiary, for example, if problems regarding its viability subsequently arose. (Banks also often require this type of confirmation.)

This letter represents documentary evidence and is normally approved by the parent company board and minuted. If there is a limitation on the time for which the support is to be provided other evidence may be required that the subsidiary will be able to continue after this date.

The auditor will also need to ensure that the parent company is in a position to provide the support which it is claiming to give in the letter. This can be confirmed by the review of the group cash flow statement.

(d) **Non-consolidated entities under common control**

Horizontal groups of entities under common control have been a significant feature of corporate disasters in recent times, for example, Enron and Parmalat. They are often referred to as 'business empires' and there is a degree to which accounting standards are failing to address them.

Business empires like this increase audit risk because fraud can be disguised in complex group structures and it can be difficult for auditors to obtain information about complex groups and related parties, and they rely on management to provide them with such information.

It has been the case that such entities can be excluded from group accounts. However, steps are being taken to eliminate such anomalies from accounting.

Audit work is inevitably increased when the company is part of a complex group, particularly when it crosses borders. There are clear difficulties with identified related parties and having to rely on management representations.

Question 2

Text references. Chapters 12 and 14

Top tips. This is another 30-mark compulsory Section A question so again, as for Question 1, it is key that you stick to time for both the question in total and each of the four parts.

You should be able to score will in part (a) which is knowledge-based on forensic auditing. Make sure you answer the question requirement fully – ie describe its applications as well as define what it means.

In part (b), use the clues in the scenario to help structure your answer. When you are asked for procedures, make sure these are specific and well explained – vague answers will not score well.

In parts (c) and (d), the questions are split into two requirements. Again when describing tests, make sure they are specific and well thought out. Use sub-headings to give more structure to your answers, as well as to improve presentation.

Easy marks. Easier marks on this question are available in part (a) which is knowledge-based. Using the information in the scenario should help you score marks in the other parts of this question.

ACCA examiner's answer. The examiner's answer to this question is included at the back of this kit.

![Marking scheme]

Marks

(a) **'Forensic auditing'**

Generally 1 – ½ mark each point   Max 5
Ideas
Definition
- eg of Institut des Fraud Auditeurs de Fraude (IFA-IAF)
- audit (examination) + forensic (legal)

Application to fraud investigation
- irregular nature of fraud
- objective(s)
- reactive vs proactive (preventative)

(b) **Prior to commencing investigation**

Generally 1 mark each matter/ procedure
Ideas
Matters
- Terms of reference (obtaining is a procedure)
- Purpose/scope of investigation
  - possible understatement of inventory at 30/6
  - high material consumption in quarter to 30/6
  - to give credence to y/e amount (next quarter to 30/9)
- Scope of access to records relevant to the investigation (any restriction?)/Information to be supplied
- Staffing – level/experience/number/availability/other client commitments
- Degree of reliance to be placed on report

By whom? – insurer?
- Timeframe – before next (= annual) physical count
- Form of report required – Any caveats?

Procedures
- Discuss assignment with directors – responsibilities etc
- Obtain engagement letter (terms are a matter)
- Agree investigative fee

Note: two professional marks are included

Tutorial note: There is no maximum to be awarded for each of matters and procedures as answer points about matters may be constructed as procedures (and vice versa). Marks should be awarded for either/or (not both).

(c) **Inventory undervaluation**

Generally up to 1½ marks each matter explained 1 mark each test max 8   Max 8
Ideas
(i) Matters
- omission from count
- cut-off
- scrap/waste etc

(ii) Tests
- physical inspection
- arithmetic checks

- cut-off tests
- analytical procedures
- tests on production records/pricing

Tutorial note: Tests must address *under*statement of stock at 30 June.

(d)   **High materials consumption**

Generally up to 1½ marks each matter explained 1 mark each test   Max 7

Ideas

(i)   Matters
- cut-off
- losses
- obsolescence etc
- major contracts
- change of supplier

(ii)   Tests
- physical inspection
- arithmetic checks
- cut-off tests
- tests of control

Tutorial note: Matters must address *over*statement of materials consumption in the quarter to 30 June.

$$\underline{\underline{30}}$$

(a)   **Forensic auditing**

Forensic auditing is the process of gathering, analysing and reporting on data, in a pre-defined context, for the purpose of finding facts and/or evidence in the context of financial or legal disputes or irregularities and giving preventative advice in this area.

Forensic auditing is a rapidly growing area and demand for this has arisen in part due to the increased expectation of corporate governance codes for company directors to take very seriously their responsibilities for the prevention and detection of fraud. Fraud investigations can involve:

- Quantifying losses from theft of cash or goods

- Identifying payments or receipts of bribes

- Identifying intentional misstatements in financial information, such as overstatement of revenue and earnings and understatement of costs and expenses

- Investigating intentional misrepresentations made to auditors

Forensic accountants may also be engaged to act in an advisory capacity to assist directors in developing more effective controls to reduce the risks from fraud.

(b)   **Matters to consider in planning**

- Whether our firm has the necessary resources and experience to carry out the investigation of Efex Engineering's losses

- What reliance is to be placed on the report that we produce as a result of the investigation and whether it will be relied upon by any third parties such as lenders

- What type of report it is to be and what level of assurance will be given

- Whether any potential independence issues exist with other clients that our firm has and therefore potential conflicts of interest

- What level of detail is required in terms of the work to be undertaken

Procedures to carry out

- Review staff availability and timings to assess whether sufficient resource for the investigation exists

- Discuss with the management of Xzibit the scope of the investigation and its purpose (eg whether any third parties will be relying on it or whether it is an internal report only) and other issues such as expected timing, fees etc

- Clarify the terms of reference of this engagement in writing from the management of Xzibit

- Draft an engagement letter for this investigation and obtain agreement of terms in writing from the management of Xzibit

(c) (i) **Matters to consider re. undervaluation of inventory**

- Inventory will be undervalued if cut-off has not been appropriately applied therefore particular focus needs to be on this area of the quarter-end count.

- Inventory will be undervalued if not all inventory items have been included in the count therefore the investigation should focus on the procedures in place for the quarterly counts.

- Inventory will be undervalued if the valuation methods are incorrect. Inventory is valued manually so the investigation should examine how items of inventory, such as scrap are valued.

(ii) **Procedures to carry out**

- Obtain inventory counting instructions in place at Efex Engineering and review to make an assessment of their adequacy for the quarterly counts, together with discussion with appropriate staff at Efex Engineering

- Perform analytical procedures using figures from the quarterly management accounts, such as comparisons between 30 June and 31 March

- Discuss scrap and wastage policy with warehouse staff

- Examine details of scrap and discuss figures with appropriate staff to establish whether there are any reasons for wastage being higher in this quarter

- Test cut-off is correct by tracing the last goods delivery notes and despatch notes to the invoices

- Recast additions on stocksheets to verify accuracy

(d) (i) **Reasons for high materials consumption in quarter ended 30 June 2006**

If closing inventory has been undervalued or undercounted, this could explain a high materials consumption in this quarter. It could also be due to excessive consumption or wastage of materials.

If recorded inventory has been stolen from production areas this could be another contributory factor to a high materials consumption in this quarter.

If cut-off was incorrectly applied, then this would affect the materials consumption, ie if goods delivered after the year-end were incorrectly included as purchases in the quarter then this would give rise to a higher materials consumption. Also if revenue is understated due to incorrect cut-off, then materials consumption as a % of revenue will be overstated.

(ii)   **Procedures to carry out**

- Test cut-off of purchases and sales has been done correctly by matching purchase invoices to goods received notes and matching despatch notes to invoices raised around the quarter-end date

- Compare value of inventory identified as obsolete or damaged at the quarter-end to the previous quarter-end, discussing discrepancies with appropriate staff

- Discuss levels of scrap and wastage with warehouse managers to ascertain normal levels and understand how it arises

- Review a sample of credit notes received after the quarter-end to identify any returned materials

- Inspect scrap materials to confirm it is not suitable for manufacture and therefore is not included in inventory

Question 3

Text references. Chapters 4, 9 and 10

Top tips. This question for 20 marks on quality control is split further into five mini scenarios. You need to consider each of the scenarios carefully and their impact on the firm's quality control policies and procedures. Remember to consider materiality where possible – you are given draft figures for revenue and total assets in the introductory information so are expected to use them where relevant. Make sure that the points you make are succinct and well explained and can be related to quality control. Use a separate sub-heading for each mini scenario and consider the mark allocation against each one.

Easy marks. This is a tough question and there are no easy marks as such. Make sure your answers are coherent and logical for each mini scenario and this will help you to score marks.

ACCA examiner's answer. The examiner's answer to this question is included at the back of this kit.

Marking scheme

	Marks
(a) **Implications of findings**	
Generally up to 1½ marks each (good) implication	
Specific finding ideas	
• relevant ISAs	
(a) APs mandatory at planning stage (520)	Max 4
(e) subsequent events (560)	
• materiality (ISA 320)	
(b) non-current assets 17%	Max 4
(c) receivables 58%	Max 4
(d) inventory 2.4%	Max 3
(e) prior period error 12.5%	Max 5
• inappropriate procedures?	
inventory 'roll back' (immaterial)	
• inappropriate timing	
external confirmations (ISA 505) – too late?	

QC at audit firm level ideas/Conclusions
- professional behaviour
- skills and competence
- assignment/delegation
- consultation
- acceptance of clients
- monitoring

Max 4

20

(a) **Analytical procedures**

Analytical procedures can be used at all stages of the audit but ISA 520 *Analytical procedures* states that they must be used at the planning and review stages. At the planning stage, analytical procedures are a very useful tool as they assist in identifying areas of potential audit risk and therefore help direct the approach that the audit will take.

The audit plan should have been prepared by the audit supervisor and reviewed by the audit manager and partner. It should have been finalised before the commencement of the audit. The fact that the AIC has not signed off the planning checklists indicates that the memo might not have been finalised. This may mean the audit plan is not sufficient to ensure the audit is completed adequately and competently.

(b) **AIC's review**

The audit senior appears to have been assigned to low risk tangible non-current assets which comprise 17% of total assets. Audit work on receivables on the other hand has been assigned to a trainee – this is a more risky area of the financial statements as it comprises 58% of total assets and has doubled from the previous year.

The plan appears to be significantly flawed which is likely to result in a poor quality and perhaps even negligent audit. It is implied that the partner has not reviewed the plan which it is her duty under auditing standards to do.

It is also doubtful whether the audit is being suitably supervised since the AIC is working on three other assignments at the same time and it is unclear whether sufficient time has been spent on the audit of Argenta.

(c) **Trade receivables**

A receivables confirmation is a common method used to obtain audit evidence of the amount outstanding at the year-end of a sample of receivables. However, given that it is now several weeks after the year-end and it may take a while to obtain all the responses from the confirmation requests, the team should have considered whether other audit procedures to provide evidence of this material balance would have been more suitable in the circumstances, eg after-date cash.

There is also an indication that the trainees are not being adequately supervised and their work reviewed. This should have been done on a continuing basis throughout the final audit.

(d) **Inventory**

Inventory comprises an immaterial balance in the financial statements of Argenta (2.4% of total assets). The audit approach used – tests of controls and roll-back – is therefore unsuitable for such an immaterial and low risk balance.

Adequate planning, including preliminary analytical procedures, would have identified a far more suitable audit approach for this account balance. Also adequate review of trainees' audit work by the senior and AIC on a continuous basis would have identified areas of concern.

(e) **Events after the balance sheet date**

This is a material subsequent event (the settling of litigation) which occurred before the signing of the prior year's audit report was not picked up. This is a quality issue as it suggests that somebody did not properly complete the subsequent events procedures as required by ISA 560 *Subsequent events* before the audit report was signed. Alternatively it could be that the procedures were carried out and management deliberately or in error gave audit staff the wrong information about the litigation, or that the matter was not referred to in the management representation letter (which would be a different quality control problem, as under ISA 580, this matter should have been referred to in a management representation letter).

As this matter is material to the financial statements, this error does require adjustment in the current financial statements in accordance with IAS 8 *Accounting policies, changes in accounting estimates and errors*. The AIC should therefore appraise the client of the situation so that the financial statements can be adjusted.

If management fail to adjust the financial statements and the matter is material, this would result in Argenta having to modify the 2005 audit report, because the provision should have been recognised last year, so the current year income statement is incorrect.

If this matter was included in the letter of representation last year and was incorrect, the auditors must consider the effect this has on the quality of representations made by management in the current year's audit and must also consider whether it means that there was a lack of sufficient evidence about the prior year figures that would lead either to more work being required to substantiate the comparatives, or a modified audit opinion in respect of the comparatives. It might also lead to the need to report by exception on the fact that the auditors were not given all the information and explanations they required for their audit in respect of the comparatives.

This situation is likely to result in additional audit work being carried out (as discussed above) and therefore it is possible that the audit engagement partner will have to allocate additional staff to the audit for 2006. If the error was not a client error but a failure of the audit firms' audit quality control (ie the matter was not included in a representation letter and the correct subsequent events procedures were not carried out) it might be necessary to have a second partner review of this year's audit file before the audit report is signed, to ensure that this problem does not reoccur.

Lastly, the audit partner should ensure that the year-end 2006 audit is carried out more effectively. Attention should be paid in particular to the management representation letter and to the subsequent events review.

Question 4

Text references. Chapters 8 and 17

Top tips. This is a fairly straightforward question on audit reports, split into four mini scenarios. For each one, you need to comment on the suitability of the proposed audit report, and in any cases where you disagree, you need to state what qualification should apply instead. You should be very comfortable with the topic of audit reports having studied it in-depth in your previous auditing studies.

The best way to approach this question is to look at each scenario in turn, pulling out the relevant points and commenting on them. Your answer should conclude with an assessment of the suitability of the proposed audit report and an alternative where you disagree. Use your financial reporting knowledge to help you where possible. The mark allocation for each part will assist you with how much time to spend on each scenario – generally about eight or nine minutes on each one.

Easy marks. Since audit reports should be very familiar to you now, you should be able to score well in this question, provided your answers are logical and well presented.

ACCA examiner's answer. The examiner's answer to this question is included at the back of this kit.

Marking scheme

		Marks

Auditors' reports proposals

Generally 1 mark each comment on suitability and 1 mark each conclusion
(alternative, if any)

Ideas

(a)	Going concern (ISA 570 reporting implications)	Max 5
(b)	Change in accounting policy – inadequate disclosure	Max 6
(c)	'Other information' (ISA 720)	Max 4
(d)	Subsequent event (ISA 560)	Max 5

- Disagreement vs limitation
- Material vs pervasive
- Statutory/professional requirements
- Relevant IFRSs (IASs 1, 8, 36, IFRS 3)
- Disclosure (adequate?) ==> disagreement
- Evidence (sufficient?) ==> limitation
- Validity of senior's argument/justification
- Alternative proposal ==> Conclusion

$\underline{20}$

(a) **Mantis Co**

Since Cube has confirmed its continuing support for Mantis and this is evidenced in the letter of support, then provided that this and any other audit evidence (such as written management representations) are considered sufficient and appropriate, and this has been disclosed appropriately in the financial statements, a qualified opinion would not be required.

A qualified opinion would be suitable if a letter of support from the parent company had not been received. If the letter of support were considered insufficient then the matter would be highlighted in the audit report in an emphasis of matter paragraph.

(b) **Lorenze Co**

The company has changed its accounting policy for goodwill during the year and failed to disclose this in the financial statements. In accordance with IAS 8 *Accounting policies, changes in accounting estimates and errors*, the change in policy should be disclosed in the accounts.

An unqualified opinion on the financial statements with the inclusion of an emphasis of matter paragraph is therefore not suitable as they should be qualified on the grounds of disagreement on disclosure – depending on the materiality of the issue, the qualification would either be 'except for' (if material) or adverse (if pervasive).

(c) **Abrupt Co**

Although the auditors are not required to provide an opinion on other information in documents containing financial statements, they are required to read the other information and consider its consistency with the accounts in accordance with ISA 720 *Other information in documents containing financial statements*.

As there is a material inconsistency between what has been reported in the financial statements and what is stated in the directors' report, if the directors refuse to make any amendments to the directors' report so that it is consistent with the accounts, then although an unqualified opinion on the financial statements can be issued, an emphasis of matter paragraph should also be included to highlight this inconsistency.

(d)   **Jingle Co**

A wholly-owned subsidiary of Jingle has commenced trading on 7 July 2006, subsequent to Jingle's year-end. It is not clear whether the company was incorporated prior to 30 June 2006.

The auditors should obtain more information about Bell. It should be possible to obtain details about its registration from the companies' registry. If this information is unavailable, this would represent a limitation on the scope of the audit and the auditors would have to qualify their audit report in respect of it.

If the company was incorporated after 30 June 2006, it requires disclosure in the financial statements as a non-adjusting post balance sheet event. If these disclosures are not made, the auditors would have to qualify the audit report for 2006 due to disagreement over the disclosure. However, assuming the subsidiary was accounted for correctly in the 2007 financial statements, the 2006 audit report would be unaffected.

If the company was incorporated before 30 June 2006 then the subsidiary needs to be consolidated in Jingle's financial statements and the relevant disclosures have to be made. If this is not the case, then the audit report for 2006 would have to be qualified over disagreement over the accounting treatment of the subsidiary Bell. This would also result in the 2007 audit report having to be qualified over the same issue if it was not corrected, as the problem would affect the comparative financial information in the following year.

Question 5

> **Text references.** Chapters 1, 2 and 5
>
> **Top tips.** This question on ethical and professional issues is typical of the type of Section B question you should expect. It is split into two parts. In part (a), you need to comment on the need for ethical guidance on money laundering.
>
> In part (b), the question is split into three mini scenarios, each worth between four and seven marks. Look at the question requirement carefully – as well as identifying the issues raised, you need to state what action the firm should take. Make sure you do this – these are fairly straightforward marks to achieve.
>
> **Easy marks.** Again this is a challenging question but approaching it with your knowledge of the ethical guidance and being able to apply it will help you in part (b).
>
> **ACCA examiner's answer.** The examiner's answer to this question is included at the back of this kit.

Marks

(a) **Need for ethical guidance for accountants**
Generally 1 mark a point up to   Max 5
Ideas (illustrative)
- Legal responsibilities
- Risk of offence
- Confidentiality
- Other reporting responsibilities
- Professional etiquette
- Accountants working in other jurisdictions

(b) **Ethical and other professional issues**
Generally ½ mark each issue identified + 1 mark each comment/action
Ideas
(i) Tax investigation
- new client (relatively) – CDD
- 'professional etiquette' – change in professional appointment
- quality control eg second review
- criminal property includes proceeds of tax evasion
- money laundering offence?
- suspicion of fraud (intent) vs error in incorrect tax returns
- disclosure by Dedza vs voluntary (confidentiality)
- need for STR

(ii) Advice on payments
- not a tax issue
- corruption and bribery/extortion – designated categories of offence
- clear intent
- seriousness in context of domestic laws
- need to report to FIU?

(iii) Financial advisor
- designated non-financial profession
- customer due diligence/record keeping
- politically exposed person (PEP)
- reputational risk
- additional measures
- refusal to act $\frac{15}{20}$

(a) **Need for ethical guidance**

Accountants are in a position where they deal with other people's money and financial matters. Therefore they may unwittingly, or worse, intentionally, be drawn into other people's criminal activity in relation to money laundering.

For example, there are a number of regulations relevant to professionals such as accountants which accountants must therefore comply with relating to appointing money laundering officers and making reports of suspicions of money laundering. It is also a criminal offence to continue to act if there is a suspicion that a transaction relates to criminal proceeds.

It is also a criminal offence to prejudice a money laundering investigation by letting the person being investigated know something is happening. This offence is called 'tipping off'.

There are substantial criminal penalties for these offences and accountants are at rise in incurring these penalties.

Although there is some legal protection given, some of these requirements appear to be at odds with the accountant's duty of confidentiality to a client (particularly the requirement to report knowledge or suspicion of criminal activity).

The ACCA produced a Factsheet for members (Technical Factsheet 94) summarising the responsibilities of members. Principles that ensure compliance with the OECD's Financial Action Task Force on Money Laundering recommendations have now been included in the ACCA's Professional Conduct Regulations as of 2005. This includes guidance on:

–   Internal controls and policies relating to staff training
–   Client identification procedures
–   Record keeping (minimum 5 years)
–   Recognition of what constitutes suspicion
–   Reporting of suspicious transactions; and
–   Not tipping-off potential suspects

(b) (i) **Kora Co**

Client acceptance procedures

As Kora, a relatively new client, is being investigated for tax fraud, it is possible that Dedza's quality control and other procedures on acceptance of a client may not be as robust as would be ideal, and that they have accepted a client without obtaining sufficient knowledge and understanding.

In accepting a new client, Dedza should have completed the following:

•   Obtained references about key personnel in the company and the company

•   Obtained professional clearance from the previous auditors

•   Carried out procedures in line with Dedza's anti-money laundering policies which should include detailed client identification procedures and customer due diligence

It is possible that Dedza did not obtain appropriate references or obtain professional clearance. There is no reason why the client identification procedures would necessarily have raised any issues if Kora has previously had a clean record.

Concealed, previously undiscovered fraud?

Alternatively, given that under-declaring income is a fraud, it is possible that staff at Kora were under-declaring income and concealing the fact and that the old auditors and the new auditors were unaware of the fact that it was going on. There is not necessarily any suggestion that negligent audits were carried out.

However, Dedza is also responsible for giving tax advice to Kora, so it is possible that more blame might be attributed to Dedza in this area. It is unclear whether the investigation relates to any advice given to Kora by Dedza's tax department. The working papers of the audit and tax departments relating to Kora should be reviewed to establish whether there are any suspicious matters which were overlooked.

Confidentiality

Dedza has a duty of confidentiality to its client, and the partners and staff of Dedza must ensure that they do not breach their duty of confidentiality if asked questions by the tax authority during the course of their investigation.

This may be complicated by the fact that if Kora has been underdeclaring income, this may become an investigation into the crime of money laundering, in which case, Dedza may have legal duties of disclosure that are not subject to the duty of confidentiality.

Members are entitled to make disclosures to defend themselves and their professional reputation, and if the investigation includes members of the tax department of Dedza personally, they may need to make disclosures in their own interests.

Actions to take

Dedza should take legal advice on disclosures that they are required to make and disclosures that they are not permitted to make before they make any disclosures to the tax authorities in the course of this investigation.

Tutor's note. It is assumed in this answer that the investigation is a public investigation into tax irregularities which Kora Co is fully aware of. If it were a secret money laundering investigation, Dedza would also need to be wary of committing the offence of 'tipping off' and letting staff of Kora Co know that the company was under investigation.

(ii) **Xalam Co**

Ethical matters

In terms of carrying out future audits of Xalam Co, there are two ethical issues which are relevant here.

(i)   The auditors must ensure that they do not find themselves in a position where they are to be auditing their own work (a self-review threat)

(ii)   The auditors must not breach ACCA's general rule that they should not make management decisions on behalf of the company

Preparation of the financial statements

Given that management is responsible for the preparation and presentation of financial statements, then it is the responsibility of management to determine how items are presented in financial statements. The auditors must therefore ensure that they do not take management responsibility in determining how the items are accounted for.

However it is reasonable for a company to ask advice from its auditors on how to account for a difficult item, so it is important for the audit firm to get the balance right. In this instance, the item involved is substantial and likely to be material to the financial statements. Given that the company has a tax policy in relation to them, it appears that this is not a new expense to the company, hence the provisions of IAS 8 *Accounting policies, changes in accounting estimates and errors* become relevant. This states that a company should only change its accounting policy towards an item if required to do so by an accounting standard, or if the change in policy would give a more reliable and relevant reflection of the substance of the transaction.

Tax deductible

Whether the matters are tax deductible or not depends on the tax legislation of the jurisdiction in which Xalam operates. If there is any doubt as to whether these expenses should be tax deductible or not, Dedza should recommend that Xalam obtains tax advice. Given that the matter is material, it may or may not have a material effect on the tax charge reported in the income statement. If Dedza disagrees with the tax treatment of this matter, and the matter is material to the reported tax charge, then Xalam would have to modify its audit report over this issue.

It is possible that these 'payments' are more like bribes to various parties to ensure business runs smoothly. Bribery is illegal and the auditor should clearly advise against such payments.

Actions to take

The audit manager should clarify the nature of the chief executive's request.

If the company has requested advice as a separate engagement and intends to pay separately from the audit for this service, then it would be inappropriate to accept an engagement on those terms.

However, if this matter has been raised in the context of the audit service and it is clearly the giving of advice (for example, clarifying that under IAS 8 the accounting policy should not change unless fairer presentation would result) rather than the provision of a management service, then it may be acceptable for Dedza to give advice about the accounting issue.

If the payments amount to a bribe, then this casts serious doubts on the integrity of the directors of Xalam. The auditors should resign from their position. Xalam benefits from these payments in receiving income from the related customer. This could constitute money laundering. Dedza must therefore make an appropriate money laundering report.

(iii) **Pholey family**

Carrying out transactions on behalf of a client

Particularly in the light of the money laundering requirements incumbent on accountants and auditors, it is extremely ill-advised for auditors to carry out transactions on behalf of their clients, in case they inadvertently carry out the crime of money laundering.

In addition, being asked to carry out a transaction on behalf of a client might give rise to a suspicion of money laundering that the accountant was required to report to the appropriate authority.

Actions to take

Dedza should stop carrying out transactions for clients, however innocent they may have been in the past, so as to avoid any suspicion or any problem arising.

ACCA
Examiner's answers

Pilot Paper P7 (INT)
Advanced Audit and Assurance (International)

Answers

Tutorial note: These model answers are considerably longer and more detailed than would be expected from any candidate in the examination. They should be used as a guide to the form, style and technical standard (but not length) of answer which candidates should aim to achieve. However, these answers may not include all valid points mentioned by a candidate – credit will be given to candidates mentioning such points.

1   Beeski Co

(a)   Principal business risks

Tutorial note: The requirement to 'identify and describe' suggests that although marks will be awarded for the mere identification of risks from the scenario, those risks must be described (as illustrated below).

Communications industry
- Rapid and new technological developments in the industry, providing faster data transmission and increasingly interactive capabilities, will render certain existing products and services obsolete.
- Beeski cannot predict how emerging and future technologies (eg 'Bluetooth') will affect demand for its services.

Competition
- Although Beeski may have reduced competition in the short-term (by having acquired a competitor), the communications market is still expanding. Increasing competition from other existing and new competitors offering new technologies could:
    - affect Beeski's ability to attract and retain customers
    - reduce Beeski's share of new and existing customers
    - force Beeski to reduce prices.
- The cost (and revenue-generating capabilities) of new technologies tends to fall significantly and relatively quickly (eg mobile phone technology is available in disposable form).

Integration
- Combining two groups which have previously operated independently (and competitively against each other) is likely to result in disruption.
- Potential difficulties may be encountered in seeking to retain customers and key personnel.
- The anticipated 'significant synergies' (in revenue, cost and capital expenditure) may have been optimistic. If they do not materialise to the extent predicted, Beeski's operational activities, financial condition and future prospects are likely to be adversely affected.
- Beeski may have difficulty in adapting its corporate image to the culture of the Indian network.

Operating losses
- Loss before taxation has more than doubled (increased by 113%). If Xstatic was making significant losses before it was acquired by Beeski those losses may have been expected to continue in the short-term. Although the groups operations are being combined and synergies are expected, recurring losses will clearly threaten the new group's operational existence as a going concern.

Falling ARPC
- ARPC, a key performance indicator, has fallen by more than 20% ((437-556/556 = 21.4%). This is likely to reflect falling tariffs in a competitive market.
- Although the number of customers has nearly doubled (increased by 96%), revenue has increased by only 55%. It seems unlikely that such a growth in customer base can be maintained, therefore the reduction in tariffs could result in falling revenues.
- Some (if not all) of the growth, is due to the acquisition of Xstatic. The fall in ARPC may indicate that Xstatic's ARPC (now absorbed into the enlarged Beeski group) is substantially less than that of Beeski. If Xstatic's tariffs were lower than Beeski's because it was offering a lower level of service it may be difficult for Beeski to increase them albeit for an enhanced service.

Sustaining growth
- Growth may not be sustainable as further expansion will incur significant costs and investment which must be financed.
- The significant costs expected to be incurred in upgrading networks may not be recouped if additional revenues are insufficient. Failure to maintain existing networks is likely to result in a loss of customers and market share.
- If Beeski's financial resources are insufficient to meet the operating losses it may need to issue equity and/or increase its debt. Possible adverse consequences of increasing indebtedness include:
    - high debt-service costs;
    - operating and financial restrictions being imposed by lenders;
    - difficulty in obtaining further finance in the future;
    - being unable to take advantage of business opportunities;
    - reduction in credit ratings.

Tutorial note: Although there are relatively explicit pointers to the above business risks in the scenario, marks will also be awarded for other risks which are perhaps more implicit (as illustrated below).

Countries of operation

- Operations have been expanded from European countries to India. Beeski's inexperience of economic and legal developments in India may impair the investment in MTbox.

Foreign exchange rates

- Beeski transacts business in several countries and foreign exchange rate fluctuations could have a material adverse affect on operating results.

Highly regulated market

- Network operations could be adversely affected by changes in the laws, regulations or government policies which regulate the industry.
- Difficulties in obtaining approvals for the erection and operation of transmitters could have an adverse effect on the extent, quality and capacity of Beeski's network coverage.
- Allegations of health risks (eg associated with radio waves from transmitter masts and mobile handsets) could reduce customer demand and increase exposure to potential litigation.

Tutorial note: Candidates are not expected to have knowledge of industry-related complexities (eg of licensing, subsidies and network recharging) – however, appropriate marks would be awarded for comments on such business risks arising.

(b)   Impact of acquisition on planning

Tutorial note: Note that the context here is that of the principal auditor's planning of a group audit.

Group structure

The new group structure must be ascertained to identify the entities that should be consolidated into the group financial statements of Beeski for the year ending 30 September 2006.

Materiality assessment

Preliminary materiality will be much higher, in monetary terms, than in the prior year. For example, if a % of revenue is a determinant of preliminary materiality, it will increase by 55% (based on estimate).

Tutorial note: 'Profit' is not a suitable criterion as group is loss-making.

The materiality of each subsidiary should be assessed, in terms of the enlarged group as at the planning stage. For example, any subsidiary contributing more than 10% of the group's assets and revenue (but not result) is material and less than 5% (say) is not. This will identify, for example:

- those entities requiring an audit visit by the principal auditor; and
- those for which analytical procedures may suffice.

If MTbox is particularly material to the group, Ribi may plan (provisionally) to visit MTbox's auditors to discuss any problems shown to arise in their audit work summary (see group instructions below).

Goodwill arising

The audit plan should draw attention to the need to audit the amount of goodwill arising on the acquisitions and management's impairment test at the balance sheet date.

The assets and liabilities of Xstatic and MTbox, at fair value to the group, will be combined on a line-by-line basis and any goodwill arising recognised.

The calculation of the amount attributed to goodwill must be agreed to be the excess of the cost of the acquisition over the fair value of the identifiable assets and liabilities existing at the date of acquisition (Xstatic – November 2005, MTbox – August 2006).

Significant non-current assets such as properties are likely to have been independently valued prior to the acquisition. It may be appropriate to plan to place reliance on the work of quantity surveyors or other property valuers.

Group (related party) transactions and balances

A list of all the companies in the group (including any associated companies) should be included in group audit instructions to ensure that intra-group transactions and balances (and any unrealised profits and losses on transactions with associated companies) are identified for elimination on consolidation.

It should be confirmed at the planning stage that inter-company transactions are identified as such in the accounting systems of all Beeski companies and that inter-company balances are regularly reconciled. (Problems are likely to arise if new inter-company balances are not identified/reconciled. In particular, exchange differences are to be expected.)

On analytical procedures

Having brought in the operations of a group of companies (Xstatic) with similar activities may extend the scope of analytical procedures available. This could have the effect of increasing audit efficiency.

MTbox – on income statement

The effective date of the acquisition of MTbox may be so late in the financial year (only four to eight weeks, say, before the year end) that it is possible that its post-acquisition results are not material to the consolidated income statement.

Other auditors
Other auditors will include:
- any affiliates of Ribi in any of the countries in which Beeski (as combined with Xstatic) operates; and
- unrelated auditors (including those of MTbox).

Ribi will plan to use the work of MTbox's auditors who are Chartered Certified Accountants. Their competence and independence should be assessed (eg through information obtained from a questionnaire and evidence of their work).

A letter of introduction should be sent to the unrelated auditors, with Beeski's permission, as soon as possible (if not already done) requesting their co-operation in providing specified information within a given timescale.

Group instructions will need to be sent to affiliated and unrelated auditors containing:
- proforma statements;
- a list of group and associated companies;
- a statement of group accounting policies (see below);
- the timetable for the preparation of the group accounts (see below);
- a request for copies of management letters;
- an audit work summary questionnaire or checklist;
- contact details (of senior members of Ribi's audit team).

Accounting policies (Xstatic & MTbox)
Whilst it is likely that Xstatic has the same accounting policies as Beeski (because, as a competitor, it operates in the same jurisdictions) MTbox may have material accounting policies which do not comply with the rest of the group. Ribi may request that MTbox's auditors calculate the effect of any non-compliance with a group accounting policy for adjustment on consolidation.

Timetable
The timetable for the preparation of Beeski's consolidated financial statements should be agreed with management as soon as possible. Key dates should be planned for:
- agreement of inter-company balances and transactions;
- submission of proforma statements to Ribi;
- completion of the consolidation package;
- tax review of group accounts;
- completion of audit fieldwork by other auditors ;
- subsequent events review;
- final clearance on accounts of subsidiaries;
- Ribi's final clearance of consolidated financial statements.

Tutorial note: *The order of dates is illustrative rather than prescriptive.*

(c) 'Support letters'
Tutorial note: Although there are different types and uses of such letters (eg for registering a prospectus), the only reference to them in the P7 Syllabus and Study Guide is in the context of group audits.

Consolidated financial statements are prepared on a going concern basis when a group, as a single entity, is considered to be a going concern. However, the going concern basis may only be appropriate for certain separate legal entities (eg subsidiaries) because the parent undertaking (or a fellow subsidiary) is able and willing to provide support. Many banks routinely require a letter of reassurance from a parent company stating that the parent would financially or otherwise support a subsidiary with cashflow or other operational problems.

As audit evidence:
- Formal confirmation of the support will be sought in the form of a letter of support or 'comfort letter' confirming the parent company's intention to keep the subsidiary in operational existence (or otherwise meet its obligations as they fall due).
- The letter of support should normally be approved by a board minute of the parent company (or by an individual with authority granted by a board minute).
- The ability of the parent to support the company should also be confirmed, for example, by examining the group's cash flow forecast.
- The period of support may be limited (eg to one year from the date of the letter or until the date of disposal of the subsidiary). Sufficient other evidence concerning the appropriateness of the going concern assumption must therefore be obtained where a later repayment of material debts is foreseen.
- The fact of support and the period to which it is restricted should be noted in the financial statements of the subsidiary.

(d) 'Horizontal groups'
In general, the scope of a statutory audit should be as necessary to form an audit opinion (ie unlimited) and the nature, timing and extent of audit procedures (ie the audit work undertaken) should be as necessary to implement the overall audit plan.

Horizontal groups of entities under common control were a significant feature of the Enron and Parmalat business empires. Such business empires increase audit risk as fraud is often disguised through labyrinthine group structures. Hence auditors need to understand and confirm the economic purpose of entities within business empires (as well as special purpose entities (SPEs) and non-trading entities).

Horizontal groups fall outside the requirement for the preparation of group accounts so it is not only finance that is off-balance sheet when controlled entities are excluded from consolidated financial statements.

In the absence of consolidated financial statements, users of accounts of entities in horizontal groups have to rely on the disclosure of related party transactions and control relationships for information about transactions and arrangements with other group entities. Difficulties faced by auditors include:
- failing to detect related party transactions and control relationships;
- not understanding the substance of transactions with entities under common control;
- excessively creative tax planning;
- the implications of transfer pricing (eg failure to identify profits unrealised at the business empire level);
- a lack of access to relevant confidential information held by others;
- relying on representations made in good faith by those whom the auditors believe manage the company when control rests elsewhere.

Audit work is inevitably increased if an auditor is put upon inquiry to investigate dubious transactions and arrangements. However, the complexity of business empires across multiple jurisdictions with different auditors may deter auditors from liaising with other auditors (especially where legal or professional confidentiality considerations prevent this).

2 Efex Engineering Co

(a) 'Forensic auditing'

Definition
The process of gathering, analysing and reporting on data, in a pre-defined context, for the purpose of finding facts and/or evidence in the context of financial/legal disputes and/or irregularities and giving preventative advice in this area.

Tutorial note: Credit will be awarded for any definition that covers the key components: An 'audit' is an examination (eg of financial statements) and 'forensic' means used in connection with courts of law. Forensic auditing may be defined as 'applying auditing skills to situations that have legal consequences'.

Application to fraud investigation
As a fraud is an example of an irregularity, a fraud investigation is just one of many applications of forensic auditing, where evidence about a suspected fraud is gathered that could be presented in a court of law. The pre-defined objective of a fraud audit is:
- to prove or disprove the suspicions;
  and, if proven,
- to identify the persons involved;
- to provide evidence for appropriate action, possibly criminal proceedings.

As well as being 'reactive', forensic auditing can be 'proactive' by being preventative. That is, the techniques of forensic auditing can be used to identify risks of fraud with a view to managing those risks to an acceptable level.

(b) Prior to commencement of the investigation

Tutorial note: The phrase 'matters ... and ... procedures' is used to encourage candidates to think more widely than just 'considerations' or just 'actions. A possible structure for this answer could be under two separate headings: 'matters' and 'procedures'. However, many matters could be phrased as procedures (and vice versa). For example, a matter would be 'the terms of reference' and the procedure 'to obtain and clarify the TOR'. Candidates should note that a tabular/columnar answer is NOT appropriate as any attempt to match matters and procedures is likely to result in repetition of the same point (differently phrased).

- Discuss the assignment with Xzibit's management to determine the purpose, nature and scope of the investigation. In particular, discuss whether any irregularity (theft/fraud) is suspected and, if so, whether evidence gathered will be used:
  - in criminal proceedings;
  - in support of an insurance claim.
- Obtain clarification of terms of reference (TOR) in writing from Xzibit's management.
- The TOR should give the investigating team full access to any aspect of Efex Engineering's operations relevant to their investigation.
- Investigation will involve consideration of:
  - possible understatement of inventory value at 30 June 2006;
  - high material consumption for the quarter ended 30 June 2006.
- Determine the level of experience of staff required for the investigation and the number of staff of each grade.
- The availability of suitable staff may affect the proposed start of the investigation. Alternatively, the timing of other assignments may have to be rescheduled to allow this investigation to be started immediately.
- Xzibit's management will presumably want the investigation completed before the next inventory count (at 30 September 2006) to know if the findings have any implications for the conduct of the count and the determination of year-end inventory.
- The investigation may have been commissioned to give credence to the period-end's accounts. The investigation may therefore be of the nature of a limited audit.

- Produce a budget of expected hours, grades of staff and costs. Agree the anticipated investigative fee with Xzibit's management.
- The depth of the investigation will depend on matters such as:
    - the extent of reliance expected to be placed on the investigation report;
    - whether the report is for Xzibit's internal use only or is it likely to be circulated to bankers and/or shareholders.
- The type of assurance (eg 'negative', reasonable) is likely to have a bearing on:
    - any caveats in the report;
    - the level of risk/potential liability for any errors in conclusions given in the final report;
    - the level of necessary detailed testing required (even if an audit is not requested).
- An engagement letter must be drafted and Xzibit's management must agree to its terms in writing before any investigative work can begin. The letter of engagement should include:
    - details of work to be carried out;
    - likely timescale;
    - basis of determining fee;
    - the reliance that can be placed on the final report and results of the investigation;
    - the extent of responsibilities agreed;
    - any indemnity agreed;
    - the information to be supplied as a basis for the investigation; and
    - any areas specifically excluded.
- Assess the appropriateness of an exclusion clause; for example: 'CONFIDENTIAL – this report has been prepared for the private use of Xzibit only and on condition that it must not be disclosed to any other person without the written consent of the preparing accountant'.

(c) (i) Inventory undervaluation – matters to consider

Physical inventory count
- Inventory will be undervalued at 30 June 2006 if all inventory is not counted. The investigation should consider the adequacy of quarterly physical count procedures. For example, whether or not:
    - all items are marked when counted;
    - management carries out test checks;
    - stocksheets are pre-numbered and prepared in ink;
    - a complete set of stocksheets is available covering all categories of inventory;
    - Efex Engineering's management uses the stocksheets to produce the inventory value.

Tutorial note: *Inventory will not be undervalued if it does not exist (eg because it has been stolen). Theft would be reflected in higher than normal materials consumption (see (d)).*

Cutoff
- Inventory will be undervalued at 30 June 2006 if:
    - any goods set aside for sale in July were excluded from the count;
    - a liability was recognised at 30 June 2006 for goods that were excluded from inventory (eg in transit from the supplier);
    - production did not cease during the physical count and raw materials being transferred between warehouse and production were omitted from inventory.

Scrap materials
- Inventory will be undervalued if any scrap from materials used in production that has a value (eg because it can be recycled) is excluded. Inventory may be undervalued compared with the previous quarter if there is any change in Efex's scrap/wastage policy (eg if previously it was valued in inventory but now it is excluded).
- If production problems increased wastage in the last period this would account for the lower value of inventory and higher materials consumption.

(ii) Tests to quantify the amount of any undervaluation

Tutorial note: *Any tests directed at quantifying an overstatement and/or instead of understatement will not be awarded credit.*

Physical count
- Inspect the warehouse/factory areas to identify high value inventory items and confirm their inclusion on the stocksheets at 30 June 2006 (or otherwise vouch to a delivery note raised after that date).
- Recast all additions and recalculate all extensions on the stocksheets to confirm that there have been no omissions, transposition errors or other computational discrepancies that would account for an undervaluation.

Cutoff
- Ascertain the last delivery notes and despatch notes recorded prior to counting and trace to purchase/sales invoices to confirm that an accurate cutoff has been applied in determining the results for the quarter to 30 June 2006 and the inventory balance at that date.
- Trace any large value purchases in June to the 30 June stocksheets. If not on the stocksheets inquire of management whether they are included in production (or sold). Verify by tracing to production records, goods despatch notes, etc.

Analytical procedures

- Compare large volume/high value items on stocksheets at 31 March with those at 30 June to identify any that might have been omitted (or substantially decreased). Inquire of management if any items so identified have been completely used in production (but not replaced), scrapped or excluded from the count (eg if obsolete). Any inventory excluded should be counted and quantified.
- Compare inventory categories for 30 June against previous quarters. Inventory value at 30 June is 10% less than at 31 March, though revenue is 28% higher. An increase in inventory might have been expected to support increased revenue if there is a general increase in trading activity. (Alternatively, a decrease in inventory may reflect difficulties in obtaining supplies/maintaining inventory levels if demand has increased).

Scrap materials

- Make inquiries of Efex Engineering's warehouse and production officials regarding the company's scrap/wastage policy and any records that are kept.
- Review production records on a month-on-month basis and discuss with the factory manager whether any production problems have increased wastage in the quarter to 30 June 2006.

Pricing test

- Raw materials – select a sample of high value items from the 31 March 2006 inventory valuation and confirm that any unit price reductions as shown by the 30 June 2006 valuation are appropriate (eg vouch lower unit price to recent purchase invoices or write down to net realisable value).
- WIP and finished goods – agree a sample of unit prices to costing records (eg batch costings). Recalculate unit prices on a sample basis and vouch make-up to invoices/payroll records, etc.

(d) (i)   High materials consumption – matters to consider

Tutorial note: Materials consumption has increased from 70% of revenue to 78%. There could be valid business reasons for this (eg there could be an abnormally high level of wastage) or accounting errors that result in overstatement of materials.

Cutoff

- Raw material purchases: Materials consumption will be overstated if goods delivered after the quarter-end have been included (incorrectly) in purchases to 30 June 2006 although excluded (correctly) from the June count.
- Revenue: Materials consumption will be overstated as a percentage of revenue if revenue is understated (eg if goods sold before 30 June 2006 are recorded in the next quarter).

Losses

- Materials consumption will be higher than normal if there is an abnormally high level of raw materials scrapped or wasted during the production process. This could be due to inferior quality raw materials or technical problems with the manufacturing process.
- Materials consumption will also be overstated if raw materials recorded as being used in production are stolen.

Obsolete or redundant inventory

- Materials consumption will appear higher if inventory at 30 June 2006 is lower. For example, if slow-moving, damaged or obsolete inventory identified at the count was excluded or written-down (although included in the previous quarter's inventory valuation).

Individual contracts

- Materials consumption will be higher if the increase in revenue is attributable to a small number of large contracts for which substantial discounts have been negotiated.
- Materials consumption will be higher if the cost of materials on customers' specifications has been underestimated in the determination of selling prices.

Purchasing

- Materials consumed will increase if Efex Engineering has changed to a more expensive supplier in the quarter to 30 June 2006.

(ii)   High materials consumption – tests

Cutoff

- Purchases: Select a sample of invoices included in purchases to 30 June 2006 and match to goods received notes to confirm receipt at 30 June 2006 and hence inclusion in inventory at that date.
- Revenue: Inspect despatch notes raised on or shortly before 30 June 2006 and trace goods sold to invoices raised on or before 30 June 2006.

Scrap

- Inquire of production/factory and warehouse officials the reasons for scrap and wastage and how normal levels are determined.
- Inspect records of materials wastage and confirm the authorisation for scrapping materials and/or reissuing replacement materials to the production process.
- Physically inspect scrap, if any, to confirm that its condition renders it unsuitable for manufacture (and hence confirm its exclusion from inventory at 30 June 2006).
- Review credit notes received after 30 June 2006 to identify materials returned (eg of inferior quality).

Obsolete or redundant inventory
- Inspect the stocksheets at 30 June 2006 for goods identified as obsolete, damaged, etc and compare with the level (and value) of the same items identified at the previous quarter's count.

Individual contracts
- Compare discounts given on new contracts with normal discount levels and confirm the authority of the person approving discounts.
- Calculate actual material cost as a percentage of revenue on individual major contracts and compare with the 70% benchmark.

Tests of controls
- Purchases: Inspect goods received notes to confirm that raw materials are being checked for quality and quantity upon receipt. Inspect invoices recorded to confirm that goods have been received (as evidenced by a goods received note).
    - Review goods returns recorded on pre-numbered goods return notes and confirm matched to subsequent credit notes received.
    - Observe gate controls and other physical security over inventory and review the segregation of duties that seek to prevent or detect theft of inventory.
- Sales: Review goods despatch notes and confirm matching to sales invoices that have been raised promptly and recorded on a timely basis.
- Sales returns: Review credit notes for authorisation and matching to goods returns notes.

3   Ingot & Co

Tutorial note: *Note that as well as the 20 marks for addressing five matters, there are also 'pervasive' issues which can be brought out as overall conclusions on QC policies and procedures at the level of the audit firm. Remember, it is a professional skill to recognise causes and effects or other linkages between the findings.*

(a)   Analytical procedures

Applying analytical procedures at the planning stage, to assist in understanding the business and in identifying areas of potential risk, is an auditing standard and therefore mandatory. Analytical procedures should have been performed (eg comparing the draft accounts to 30 June 2006 with prior year financial statements).

The audit senior may have insufficient knowledge of the waste management service industry to assess potential risks. In particular, Argenta may be exposed to risks resulting in unrecorded liabilities (both actual and contingent) if claims are made against the company in respect of breaches of health and safety legislation or its licence to operate.

The audit has been inadequately planned and audit work has commenced before the audit plan has been reviewed by the AIC. The audit may not be carried out effectively and efficiently.

Tutorial note: *An alternative stance might be that the audit senior did in fact perform the analytical procedures but was careless in completion of the audit planning checklist. This would have quality control implications in that the checklists cannot be relied on by the reviewer.*

(b)   AIC's assignments

The senior has performed work on tangible non-current assets which is a less material (17% of total assets) audit area than trade receivables (58% of total assets) which has been assigned to an audit trainee. Non-current assets also appear to be a lower risk audit area than trade receivables because the carrying amount of non-current assets is comparable with the prior year ($0.6m at both year ends), whereas trade receivables have more than doubled (from $0.9m to $2.1m). This corroborates the implications of (a).

The audit is being inadequately supervised as work has been delegated inappropriately. It appears that Ingot & Co does not have sufficient audit staff with relevant competencies to meet its supervisory needs.

(c)   Direct confirmation

It is usual for direct confirmation of customers' balances to be obtained where trade receivables are material and it is reasonable to expect customers to respond. However, it is already six weeks after the balance sheet date and, although trade receivables are clearly material (58% of total assets), an alternative approach may be more efficient (and cost effective). For example, monitoring of after-date cash will provide evidence about the collectibility of receivables (as well as corroborate their existence).

Tutorial note: *Ingot was only appointed in July and the audit started two weeks ago on 1 August.*

This may be a further consequence of the audit having been inadequately planned.

Alternatively, supervision and monitoring of the audit may be inadequate. For example, if the audit trainee did not understand the alternative approach but mechanically followed circularisation procedures.

(d) **Inventory**

Inventory is relatively immaterial from an auditing perspective, being less than 2.4% of total assets (2005 – 2.1%). Although it therefore seems appropriate that a trainee should be auditing it, the audit approach appears highly inefficient. Such in-depth testing (of controls and details) on an immaterial area provides further evidence that the audit has been inadequately planned.

Again, it may be due to a lack of monitoring of a mechanical approach being adopted by a trainee.

This also demonstrates a lack of knowledge and understanding about Argenta's business – the company has no stock-in-trade, only consumables used in the supply of services.

(e) **Prior period error**

It appears that the subsequent events review was inadequate in that an adjusting event (the out-of-court settlement) was not taken account of. This resulted in material error in the financial statements to 30 June 2005 as the provision for $0.45 million which should have been made represented 12.5% of total assets at that date.

The AIC has not taken any account of the implications of this evidence for the conduct of the audit as the overall audit strategy and audit plan should have been reconsidered. For example:
- the oversight in the subsequent events review may not have been isolated and there could be other errors in opening balances (eg if an impairment was not recognised);
- there may be doubts about the reliability of managements' representations if it confirmed the litigation to be pending and/or asserted that there were no post balance sheet events to be taken account of.

The error has implications for the quality of the prior period's audit that may now require that additional work be carried out on opening balances and comparatives.

As the matter is material it warrants a prior period adjustment (IAS 8 *Accounting Policies, Changes in Accounting Estimates and Errors*). If this is not made Argenta's financial statements for the year ended 30 June 2006 will be materially misstated with respect to the current year and comparatives – because the expense of the out-of-court settlement should be attributed to the prior period and not to the current year's net profit or loss.

The need for additional work may have a consequential effect on the current year's time/fee/staff budgets.

The error should have been brought to the attention of Argenta's management when it was discovered, so that a prior year adjustment could be made. If the AIC did not feel competent to raise the matter with the client he should have discussed it immediately with the audit manager and not merely left it as a file note.

QC policies procedures at audit firm level/Conclusions

That the audit is not being conducted in accordance with ISAs (eg 300 *Planning an Audit of Financial Statements*, 315 *Understanding the Entity and Its Environment and Assessing the Risks of Material Misstatement* and 520 *Analytical Procedures*) means that Ingot's quality control policies and procedures are not established and/or are not being communicated to personnel.

That audit work is being assigned to personnel with insufficient technical training and proficiency indicates weaknesses in procedures for hiring and/or training of personnel.

That there is insufficient direction, supervision and review of work at all levels to provide reasonable assurance that audit work is of an acceptable standard suggests a lack of resources.

Procedures for the acceptance of clients appear to be inadequate as the audit is being conducted so inefficiently (ie audit work is inappropriate and/or not cost-effective). In deciding whether or not to accept the audit of Argenta, Ingot should have considered whether it had the ability to serve the client properly. The partner responsible for accepting the engagement does not appear to have evaluated the firm's (lack of) knowledge of the industry.

The staffing of the audit of Argenta should be reviewed and a more experienced person assigned to its completion and overall review.

4 **Axis & Co**

(a) **Mantis Co**

If a letter of support had **not** been received, then a qualified opinion on the grounds of **disagreement** (about the appropriateness of the going concern presumption) would be required. As the matter is likely to be pervasive an adverse opinion would be appropriate (ISA 570 *Going Concern*).

However, the company has received a letter of support from its parent company to the effect that it will enable Mantis to continue trading. If this evidence (together with other evidence such as management's representations) is considered to be **sufficient** to support the appropriateness of the going concern presumption, a qualified opinion will not be necessary provided that the support is **adequately** disclosed in a note to the financial statements. If the evidence is sufficient, but the disclosure **inadequate**, an 'except for' opinion would be required.

If the letter of support does not provide sufficient evidence (eg if there are doubts about Cube's ability to provide the required finance), the significant uncertainty arising should be disclosed in an emphasis of matter paragraph in the auditor's report. This would not result in a qualified opinion (unless the disclosure relating to it were considered inadequate).

Conclusion

The audit senior's proposal is unsuitable. The auditor's report should be unmodified (assuming that disclosures are adequate).

(b) Lorenze Co

In order to show fair presentation, in all material respects, the financial statements of an entity should contain not only accurate figures, but also sufficient disclosure in relation to those figures in order to allow the user to understand them. As required by IAS 1 *Presentation of Financial Statements*, items should be treated on a consistent basis from year to year. If this is not the case, then any change, together with the financial impact of this change, will need to be disclosed in a note to the financial statements.

Failure to disclose the reasons for change in policy (ie to comply with IFRS 3 *Business Combinations*) and its effects (eg the lack of annual amortisation) means that the financial statements do not comply with IAS 8 *Accounting Policies, Changes in Accounting Estimates and Errors*. A qualified opinion is therefore required on the grounds of disagreement on disclosure (IAS 1 and IAS 8). Assuming the matter to be material (but clearly not pervasive), an 'except for' opinion should be expressed.

The main purpose of an emphasis of matter paragraph is to describe a matter of significant uncertainty which has been taken into account in forming the audit opinion – it does not qualify that opinion. Such a paragraph highlights a note in the financial statements that more extensively discusses the matter. An emphasis of matter paragraph cannot therefore be used to 'make good' a lack of disclosure.

IFRS 3 also requires disclosure of a reconciliation of the carrying amount of goodwill at the beginning and end of the year. This should show no movement for the year ended 30 June 2006.

Conclusion

The audit senior's proposal is unsuitable. Unless all aspects of the change (including reason and effect) are adequately disclosed an 'except for' qualification will be required on the grounds of disagreement.

(c) Abrupt Co

The audit opinion states whether the financial statements:
- are presented fairly, in all material respects (or give a true and fair view) in accordance with the financial reporting framework; and
- comply with statutory requirements (where appropriate).

The directors' report is not a part of financial statements prepared under International Financial Reporting Standards (IFRS). However, auditors have a professional responsibility to read other information in documents containing audited financial statements (eg the directors' report in an annual report) to identify material inconsistencies with the audited financial statements (or material misstatements of fact).

A material inconsistency exists when other information contradicts information contained in the audited financial statements. Clearly, 'major' is inconsistent with 1.6%.

If the inconsistency is resolved (eg because the directors' report is corrected to state '... major part of **other** income...') an unmodified auditor's report will be given.

If the inconsistency is not resolved, the audit opinion on the financial statements cannot be qualified (because the inconsistency is in the directors' report). In this case, an emphasis of matter paragraph may be used to report on this matter that does not affect the financial statements (ISA 700 *The Independent Auditor's Report on a Complete Set of General Purpose Financial Statements*).

Conclusion

An unqualified opinion on the financial statements is appropriate. If, however, the inconsistency is not resolved, it should be reported in a separate emphasis of matter paragraph, after the opinion paragraph.

(d) Jingle Co

The cash transfer is a non-adjusting post balance sheet event. It indicates that Bell was trading after the balance sheet date. However, that does not preclude Bell having commenced trading before the year end.

The finance director's oral representation is wholly insufficient evidence with regard to the existence (or otherwise) of Bell at 30 June 2006. If it existed at the balance sheet date its financial statements should have been consolidated (unless immaterial).

The lack of evidence that might reasonably be expected to be available (eg legal papers, registration payments, etc) suggests a limitation on the scope of the audit. If such evidence has been sought but not obtained then the limitation is imposed by the entity (rather than by circumstances).

Whilst the transaction itself may be immaterial, the information concerning the existence of Bell may be material to users and should therefore be disclosed (as a non-adjusting event). The absence of such disclosure, if the auditor considered necessary, would result in a qualified 'except for', opinion.

Tutorial note: *Any matter that is considered sufficiently material to be worthy of disclosure as a non-adjusting event must result in such a qualified opinion if the disclosure is not made.*

If Bell existed at the balance sheet date and had material assets and liabilities then its non-consolidation would have a pervasive effect. This would warrant an adverse opinion.

Also, the nature of the limitation (being imposed by the entity) could have a pervasive effect if the auditor is suspicious that other audit evidence has been withheld. In this case the auditor should disclaim an opinion.

Conclusion

Additional evidence is required to support an unqualified opinion. If this were not forthcoming a disclaimer may be appropriate.

5   Dedza & Co

(a) Need for ethical guidance

- Accountants (firms and individuals) working in a country that criminalises money laundering are required to comply with anti-money laundering legislation and failure to do so can lead to severe penalties. Guidance is needed because:
    - legal requirements are onerous;
    - money laundering is widely defined; and
    - accountants may otherwise be used, unwittingly, to launder criminal funds.
- Accountants need ethical guidance on matters where there is conflict between legal responsibilities and professional responsibilities. In particular, professional accountants are bound by a duty of confidentiality to their clients. Guidance is needed to explain:
    - how statutory provisions give protection against criminal action for members in respect of their confidentiality requirements;
    - when client confidentiality over-ride provisions are available.
- Further guidance is needed to explain the interaction between accountants responsibilities to report money laundering offences and other reporting responsibilities, for example:
    - reporting to regulators;
    - auditor's reports on financial statements (ISA 700);
    - reports to those charged with governance (ISA 260);
    - reporting misconduct by members of the same body.
- Professional accountants are required to communicate with each other when there is a change in professional appointment (ie 'professional etiquette'). Additional ethical guidance is needed on how to respond to a 'clearance' letter where a report of suspicion has been made (or is being contemplated) in respect of the client in question.

    Tutorial note: *Although the term 'professional clearance' is widely used, remember that there is no 'clearance' that the incumbent accountant can give or withhold.*

- Ethical guidance is needed to make accountants working in countries that do not criminalise money laundering aware of how anti-money laundering legislation may nevertheless affect them. Such accountants may commit an offence if, for example, they conduct limited assignments or have meetings in a country having anti-money laundering legislation (eg UK, Ireland, Singapore, Australia and the United States).

(b) Annual reviews of existing clients

(i)   Tax investigation

- Kora is a relatively new client. Before accepting the assignment(s) Dedza should have carried out customer due diligence (CDD). Dedza should therefore have a sufficient knowledge and understanding of Kora to be aware of any suspicions that the tax authority might have.
- As the investigation has come as a surprise it is possible that, for example:
    - the tax authorities suspicions are unfounded;
    - Dedza has failed to recognise suspicious circumstances.

Tutorial note: *In either case, Dedza should now review relevant procedures.*

- Dedza should review any communication from the predecessor auditor obtained in response to its 'professional inquiry' (for any professional reasons why the appointment should not be accepted).
- A quality control for new audits is that the audit opinion should be subject to a second partner review before it is issued. It should be considered now whether or not such a review took place. If it did, then it should be sufficiently well documented to evidence that the review was thorough and not a mere formality.
- Criminal property includes the proceeds of tax evasion. If Kora is found to be guilty of under-declaring income that is a money laundering offence.
- Dedza's reputational risk will be increased if implicated because it knew (or ought to have known) about Kora's activities. (Dedza may also be liable if found to have been negligent in failing to detect any material misstatement arising in the 31 March 2006 financial statements.)
- Kora's audit working paper files and tax returns should be reviewed for any suspicion of fraud being committed by Kora or error overlooked by Dedza. Tax advisory work should have been undertaken and/or reviewed by a manager/partner not involved in the audit work.

- As tax advisor, Dedza could soon be making disclosures of misstatements to the tax authorities on behalf of Kora. Dedza should encourage Kora to make necessary disclosure voluntarily.
- If Dedza finds reasonable grounds to know or suspect that potential disclosures to the tax authorities relate to criminal conduct, then a suspicious transaction report (STR) should be made to the financial intelligence unit (FIU) also.

Tutorial note: *Though not the main issue credit will be awarded for other ethical issues such as the potential self-interest/ self-review threat arising from the provision of other services.*

(ii) **Advice on payments**
- As compared with (i) there is no obvious tax issue. Xalam is not overstating expenditure for tax purposes.
- Dedza should consider its knowledge of import duties, etc in the destination country before recommending a course of action to Xalam.
- The payments being made for security consultancy services may amount to a bribe. Corruption and bribery (and extortion) are designated categories of money laundering offence under The Forty Recommendations of the Financial Action Task Force on Money Laundering (FATF).

If this is a bribe:
- Xalam clearly benefits from the payments as it receives income from the contract with the major customer. This is criminal property and possession of it is a money laundering offence
- Dedza should consider the seriousness of the disclosure made by the chief executive in the context of domestic law.
- Dedza may be guilty of a money laundering offence if the matter is not reported. If a report to the FIU is considered necessary Dedza should encourage Xalam to make voluntary disclosure. If Xalam does not, Dedza will not be in breach of client confidentiality for reporting knowledge of a suspicious transaction.

Tutorial note: *Making a report takes precedence over client confidentiality.*

(iii) **Financial advisor**
- Customer due diligence (CDD) and record-keeping measures apply to designated non-financial businesses and professions (such as Dedza) who prepare for or carry out certain transactions on behalf of their clients.
- Esau is a 'politically exposed person' ('PEP' ie an individual who is to be entrusted with prominent public functions in a foreign country).
- Dedza's business relationships with Pholey therefore involve reputational risks similar to those with Esau. In addition to performing normal due diligence measures Dedza should:
  - have risk management systems to have determined that Esau is a PEP;
  - obtain senior partner approval for maintaining business relationships with such customers;
  - take reasonable measures to establish the source of wealth and source of funds;
  - conduct enhanced ongoing monitoring of the business relationship.
- Dedza can choose to decline to act for Pholey and/or Esau (if asked).
- If the business relationship is to be continued senior partner approval should be obtained for any transactions carried out on Pholey's behalf in future.

Tutorial note: *The Pholey family is not described as an audit client therefore no familiarity threat arises in relation to an audit (the family may not have any involvement in entities requiring an audit).*

Part 3 Examination – Paper 3.1(INT)
Audit and Assurance Service (International Stream)   December 2006 Answers

1   PAVIA CO

(a) Financial statement risks

Tutorial note: *Note the timeframe. Financial statements for the year to 31 December 2006 are draft. Certain misstatements may therefore exist due to year-end procedures not yet having taken place.*

Revenue

Revenue has increased by 6·4% ($^{(645·4 - 606·5)}/_{606·5}$). Revenue may be overstated through incorrect accounting treatment/cutoff of consignment sales. For example, if consignment sales to dealers before the year end have been included in 2006 revenue but are unsold at the year end.

Tutorial note: *Revenue could be understated if consignment sales to dealers before the year end have been excluded from 2006 revenue but are sold at the year end.*

Other revenue, $17·9 million, has fallen by 59% ($^{(17·9 - 43·7)}/_{43·7}$) and may be understated. For example, because the 2006 financial statements are only draft and year-end procedures may still identify sources of other revenue to be accounted for.

Tutorial note: *An alternative analysis might be to note that other revenue from business activities has fallen to account for only 2·8% of draft revenue (2005 – 7·2%).*

Revenue may be overstated in respect of sales under 0% finance arrangements entered into during the year. Revenue recognised from these vehicle sales should be the discounted amount of the receivable in three years time. The difference, that is finance income, should be recognised as a different source of revenue (if material) over three years.

Other income

Other income has increased by 8·3% ($^{(15·6 - 14·4)}/_{14·4}$) and may be overstated as it includes 'income from the reversal of provision'. A reversal of a provision is not income but a reduction in expense previously recognised. Any reversals should be reflected by a reduction in the line item(s) where the related cost was previously recognised.

Cost of materials/Change in inventories

Cost of materials is the largest expense in the income statement. This cost (as adjusted for change in inventories) is steady at 51% of revenue (2005 – 50%) so if revenue is found to be understated this cost may be understated also (e.g. if year-end inventory is overstated due to insufficient allowance being made for slow-moving/damaged parts).

Tutorial note: *Note that although cost of materials has increased by 16·5%, cost of materials used (i.e. as adjusted for change in inventories) has increased by only 9%. That is, approximately half of the increase is reflected in the replenishment of inventory levels (that fell in the prior period).*

Depreciation/amortisation

Depreciation may be misstated in respect of assets under construction. For example, depreciation will be overstated if it is charged for a period before which the asset was ready for use or if it reclassified to the wrong category of asset with a higher depreciation rate.

Employee benefits expense

Employee benefits expense may be overstated as it has increased by 8·5% ($^{(91·0 - 83·9)}/_{83·9}$) although the average number of employees have fallen (by just 1%). This may be due to changes in year-end provisions (e.g. for holiday pay accruals) that have not yet been taken account of, or the misclassification of other expenses as employee benefits expense.

Other expenses

Other expenses have increased by 15·6% ($^{(116·3 - 100·6)}/_{100·6}$) and may be overstated if, for example:

■ the warranty provision made at 31 December 2006 is overstated;
■ period-end adjustments for pre-paid expenditures have still to be made.

Interest income, net

The net amount has fallen by 41·1% ($^{(12·3 - 20·9)}/_{20·9}$). This compounds the effects of interest income having fallen by a third ($^{(16·8 - 25·1)}/_{25·1}$) and interest expense having increased by 7·1% ($^{(4·5 - 4·2)}/_{4·2}$). Interest income may be understated as cash and cash equivalents have increased by 29·5% ($^{(111·4 - 86·0)}/_{86·0}$). This may be because some interest income accruing during the year to 31 December 2006 has still to be accounted for.

Intangible assets

Intangible assets have increased by 18% ($^{(47\cdot8 - 40\cdot5)}/_{40\cdot5}$). Development costs included in intangible assets will be overstated if:

- any of the IAS 38 *Intangible Assets* recognition criteria cannot be demonstrated in respect of the $12·7 million costs incurred during the year;

- any impairment in the year has not yet been written off in accordance with IAS 36 *Impairment of Assets*.

In particular, $19·0 million ($12·7 million + $6·3 million) development expenditure on the Fox may be impaired as the launch of the new model has been postponed to next year and additional costs may have still to be incurred to correct the problems that arose during trials.

Property plant and equipment

Tangible assets have increased by 21·5% ($^{(124\cdot5 - 102\cdot5)}/_{102\cdot5}$) and will be overstated if, for example:

- revenue expenditure is inappropriately capitalised (e.g. in assets under construction);

- disposals have not yet been accounted for (e.g. on any assets traded-in during the year);

- any depreciation for the year to 31 December 2006 has still to be accounted for (e.g. for the month of December).

Inventories

Inventories may be misstated as a full physical count to ascertain year-end quantities has still to be undertaken. Inventories have increased by 8·6% ($^{(30\cdot3 - 27\cdot9)}/_{27\cdot9}$) and may be overstated if there is insufficient allowance for slow-moving raw materials.

Trade receivables

Trade receivables have increased by 45·3% ($^{(73\cdot1 - 50\cdot3)}/_{50\cdot3}$) and may be overstated if:

- the allowance for non-recoverable debts at the end year has still to be assessed;
- 0% finance sales have been recorded at a gross instead of discounted amount.

Tutorial note: *The discounted amount recorded during the year should then be 'unwound' to amortised cost at the balance sheet date.*

Provisions

Provisions have increased by 31·9% ($^{(160\cdot1 - 121\cdot4)}/_{121\cdot4}$) and will be overstated if items that do not represent liabilities at 31 December 2006 are included. Provision should not be made for future costs of deferred maintenance unless it represents a liability under an onerous contract (e.g. if Pavia took out non-cancellable maintenance contracts on assets that are no longer used).

Similarly, provision cannot be made for a future IT reorganisation as it is highly unlikely to meet the definition of a restructuring (IAS 37 *Provisions, Contingent Liabilities and Contingent Assets*).

Trade payables

Trade payables have increased by only 5·3% ($^{(33\cdot5 - 31\cdot8)}/_{31\cdot8}$) and may be understated (as costs have generally increased by more than this) if year-end accruals have still to be accounted for.

Going concern

There does not appear to be any major threat to going concern, for example, substantial cash balances have increased. However, unpredictable supplies of parts for the assembly of Cipeta models could have consequences for assembly schedules generally and then for delivery of vehicles to dealers and customers, with potential loss of sales.

Profit has fallen substantially, by 25·6% ($^{(61\cdot6 - 82\cdot8)}/_{82\cdot8}$) although revenue increased by 6·4%. There is a risk that overall revenue/income is understated and/or expenses overstated.

(b) Illustration of use of analytical procedures as audit evidence

Tutorial note: *Note that 'as audit evidence' requires consideration of substantive analytical procedures rather that the identification of risks (relevant to part (a)).*

Revenue

Analytical procedures may be used in testing revenue for completeness of recording ('understatement'). The average selling price of a vehicle in 2005 was $68,830 ($526·0 million ÷ 7,642 vehicles). Applying this to the number of vehicles sold in 2006, might be projected to generate $698·8 million ($68,830 × 10,153) revenue from the sale of vehicles. The draft financial statements therefore show a potential shortfall of $110·8 million ($(698·8 − 588·0) million) that is, 15·6%.

This should be investigated and substantiated through more detailed analytical procedures. For example, the number of vehicles sold should be analysed into models and multiplied by the list price of each for a more accurate estimate of potential revenue. The impact of discounts and other incentives (e.g. 0% finance) on the list prices should then be allowed for. If recorded revenue for 2006 (as per draft income statement adjusted for cutoff and consignment inventories) is materially lower than that calculated, detailed substantive procedures may be required in order to show that there is no material error.

'Proof in total'/reasonableness tests

The material correctness, or otherwise, of income statement items (in particular) may be assessed through appropriate 'proof in total' calculations (or 'reasonableness' tests). For example:

- Employee benefits costs: the average number of employees by category (waged/salaried/apprenticed) × the average pay rate for each might prove that in total $91·0 million (as adjusted to actual at 31 December 2006) is not materially misstated. The average number of employees needs to be checked substantively (e.g. recalculated based on the number of employees on each payroll) and the average pay rates (e.g. to rates agreed with employee representatives).

  Tutorial note: An alternative reasonableness might be to take last year's actual adjusted for 2006 numbers of employees grossed-up for any pay increases during the year (pro-rated as necessary).

- Depreciation: the cost (or net book value) of each category of asset × by the relevant straight-line (or reducing balance) depreciation rate. If a 'ballpark' calculation for the year is materially different to the annual charge a more detailed calculation can be made using monthly depreciation calculations. The cost (or net book value) on which depreciation is calculated should be substantively tested, for example by agreeing brought forward balances to prior year working papers and additions to purchase invoices (costings in respect of assets under construction).

  Tutorial note: Alternatively, last year's depreciation charge may be reconciled to this year's by considering depreciation rates applied to brought forward balances with adjustments for additions/disposals.

- Interest income: an average interest rate for the year can be applied to the monthly balance invested (e.g. in deposit accounts) and compared with the amount recognised for the year to 31 December 2006 (as adjusted for any accrued interest per the bank letter for audit purposes). The monthly balances (or averages) on which the calculation is performed should be substantiated to bank deposit statements.

- Interest expense: if the cash balances do not go into overdraft then this may be similar expenses (e.g. prompt payment discounts to customers). If this is to particular dealers then a proof in total might be to apply the discount rate to the amounts invoiced to the dealer during the period.

Immaterial items

For immaterial items analytical procedures alone may provide sufficient audit evidence that amounts in the financial statements are not materially misstated so that detailed substantive procedures are not required. For example, a comparison of administration and distribution, maintenance and insurance costs for 2006 compared with 2005 may be sufficient to show that material error is highly unlikely. If necessary, further reasonableness tests could be performed. For example, considering insurance costs to value of assets insured or maintenance costs to costs of assets maintained.

Ratio analysis

Ratio analysis can provide substantive evidence that income statement and balance sheet items are not materially misstated by considering their inter-relationships. For example:

- Asset turnover: Based on the draft financial statements property, plant and equipment has turned over 5·2 times ($^{\$645·5}/_{124·5}$) compared with 5·9 times in 2005. This again highlights that income may be overstated, or assets overstated (e.g. if depreciation is understated).

- Inventory turnover: Using cost of materials adjusted for changes in inventories this has remained stable at 10·9 times.

  Tutorial note: This is to be expected as in (a) the cost in the income statement has increased by 9% and the value of inventories by 8·5%.

  Inventories represent the smallest asset value on the balance sheet at 31 December 2006 (7·8% of total assets). Therefore substantive procedures may be limited to agreeing physical count of material items (vehicles) and agreeing cutoff.

- Average collection period: This has increased to 41 days ($^{73·1}/_{645·5} \times 365$) from 30 days. Further substantive analysis is required, for example, separating out non-current amounts (for sales on 0% finance terms). Substantive procedures may be limited to confirmation of amounts due from dealers (and/or receipt of after-date cash) and agreeing cutoff of goods on consignment.

- Payment periods: This has remained constant at 37 days (2005 – 38 days). Detailed substantive procedures may be restricted to reconciling only major suppliers' statements and agreeing the cutoff on parts purchased from them.

(c) Principal audit work

   (i) *Development expenditure on the Fox model*

- Agree opening balance, $6·3 million, to prior year working papers.

- Physically inspect assembly plant/factory where the Fox is being developed and any vehicles so far manufactured (e.g. for testing).

■ Substantiate costs incurred during the year, for example:

  – goods (e.g. components) and services (e.g. consultants) to purchase invoices;
  – labour (e.g. design engineers/technicians, mechanics, test drivers) to the payroll analysis;
  – overheads (e.g. depreciation of development buildings and equipment, power, consumables) to management's calculation of overhead absorption and underlying cost accounts.

■ Review of internal trials/test drive results (e.g. in reports to management and video recordings of events).

■ Reperform management's impairment test of development expenditure. In particular recalculate value in use.

  Tutorial note: *It is highly unlikely that a reasonable estimate of fair value less costs to sell could be made for so unique an asset.*

■ Substantiate the key assumptions made by management in calculating value in use. For example:

  – the level of sales expected when the car is launched to advance orders (this may have fallen with the delay in the launch);
  – the discount rate used to Pavia's cost of capital;
  – projected growth in sales to actual sales growth seen last time a new model was launched.

(ii) *Consignment inventory*

■ Agree terms of sale to dealers to confirm the 'principal – agent' relationship between Pavia and dealers.

■ Inspect proforma invoices for vehicles sent on consignment to dealers to confirm number of vehicles with dealers at the year end.

■ Obtain direct confirmation from dealers of vehicles unsold at the year end.

■ Physically inspect vehicles sold on consignment before the year end that are returned unsold by dealers after the year end (if any) for evidence of impairment.

■ Perform cutoff tests on sales to dealers/trade receivables/vehicle inventory.

(iii) *Warranty provision*

■ Agree the principal assumptions in management's estimate of liabilities under warranties to the terms of warranty as set out in contracts for sale of vehicle. For example:

  – the period for which warranties are given;
  – whether for parts replacement only or parts and labour;
  – exclusion clauses, perhaps for vehicles sold into a particular market, or used in a specified industry (e.g. film-making).

■ Agree the reasonableness of management's assumptions in the calculation of the provision. For example, the proportion of vehicles for which claims are made within three months, three to six months, six to nine months, etc.

■ Substantiate the economic reality of the basis of management's calculations. For example:

  – agree the number of vehicles sold each month to a summary sales report;
  – agree the calculation of average cost of a repair under warranty to job records;
  – test costs of repair on a sample basis (e.g. parts replaced to price lists and labour charges to hours worked (per job records) and charge-out rates).

■ Consider the reasonableness of management's estimate by comparing:

  – the actual cost of after-date repairs (say for three months) against the appropriate proportion of the provision made;
  – current year provision per vehicle sold against prior provision per vehicle sold.

■ Assess management's ability to make reliable estimates in this area by comparing last year's provision with the actual repairs under warranty costs incurred during the year in respect of sales made in previous years.

  Tutorial note: *The basis of management's estimate may tend to overstate or understate the provision required and should be revised accordingly.*

■ Agree the extent to which the provision takes account of (has been reduced by) any recourse to suppliers (e.g. in respect of faulty parts). For example:

  – by reviewing terms of purchases from major suppliers;
  – by examining records of replacement parts received free of charge.

2   RBG

(a)   Potential advantages and disadvantages to RBG of outsourcing internal audit services

Advantages

■   Affordability as there should be a cost benefit (budget savings) of replacing fixed cost full-time employees with a variable cost service.

■   Further, if reliance on internal audit by the external auditors is substantially increased, the external audit fee may be reduced.

■   Even if there are some changes in staff within the audit firm providing the internal audit services, there should be greater continuity than currently (as RBG has high employee turnover in this department).

■   A wider range of industry-related expertise might be available to RBG from contracted-in auditors that would be too expensive to maintain internally. This may be particularly beneficial for ad hoc needs such as due diligence reviews for acquisitions or business continuity plans in the event of fire or flood.

■   Experienced internal auditors will be available as and when needed (as typically the audit firm's staff will be experienced) whereas RBG is currently losing its experienced employees to other departments. Outsourcing also offers flexibility to provide more staff at busy times.

■   Outsourcing to an audit firm can provide geographic coverage and more advanced technology.

■   Independent evaluation (e.g. of organisational risk) by the audit firm may provide new ideas for improvements (e.g. enhancing risk management).

■   Better recommendations for improvements as the audit firm can suggest practical, tried and tested solutions and not just theoretical ones.

■   Greater assistance to management in the evaluation of the performance of the external auditors (because the outsourced internal audit firm should be more experienced to make this assessment).

■   Earlier assessment of the impact of changes in financial reporting requirements (because the outsourced internal audit firm should be technically up-to-date).

■   Better utilisation of core competencies, for example, management will have more time to focus on strategic objectives.

■   The audit firm may provide a customer-focussed service that could be lacking in an in-house department.

Disadvantages

■   Over time the audit firm may command a greater premium for internal audit services as RBG becomes dependent on the audit firm's knowledge of the group (i.e. cost savings may be only short term).

■   An out-sourced department may not be as effective as an in-house department if, for example, the audit firm's staff assigned to RBG are changed regularly.

■   The audit firm's staff may not understand RBG's business as well as employed staff if, for example, they work only part-time on the RBG assignment. Employed staff are more likely to have a broader perspective of the group from having worked in other parts of it.

■   The internal audit staff's principle allegiance will be to the audit firm, not RBG. If the services provided by the audit firm are not seen to be an integral part of management, the company may not buy-in to their suggestions.

■   If the audit firm plans to schedule internal audit services to RBG in its 'quiet periods', they may not always be available when needed.

■   RBG will lose a valuable management training ground that provides a source of future managers. The internal audit department's current loss of high performing employees to other departments is a gain to the other departments.

(b)   Principal matters to be included in submission to provide internal audit services

■   Introduction/background – details about York including its organisation (of functions), offices (locations) and number of internal auditors working within each office. The office that would be responsible for managing the contract should be stated.

■   A description of York's services most relevant to RBG's needs (e.g. in the areas of risk management, IT audits, value for money (VFM) and corporate governance).

■   Client-specific issues identified. For example, revenue audits will be required routinely for control purposes and to substantiate the contingent rents due. Other areas of expertise that RBG may be interested in taking advantage of, for example, special projects such as acquisitions and mergers.

■ York's approach to assessing audit needs including the key stages and who will be involved. For example:

    (1) Preliminary – review of business, industry and the entity's operating characteristics

    (2) Planning – including needs analysis and co-ordination with external audit plan

    (3) Post-Audit – assurance that activities were effectively and efficiently executed

    (4) Review – of services provided, reports issued and management's responses.

■ A description of internal audit tools used and methodologies/approach to audit fieldwork including use of embedded audit software and programs developed by York.

■ A description of York's systems-based audit, the IT issues to be addressed and the technological support that can be provided.

■ Any training that will be offered to RBG's managers and staff, for example, in a risk management approach.

■ A description and quantity of resources, in particular the number of full-time staff, to be deployed in providing services to RBG. An outline of RBG's track record in human resource retention and development.

■ Relevant experience – e.g. in internal and external audit in the retail industry. The relative qualifications and skills of each grade of audit staff and the contract manager in particular.

■ Insurance certifications covering, for example, public liability and professional indemnity insurance.

■ Work ethic policies relating to health and safety, equal opportunities' and race relations.

■ How York ensures quality throughout the internal audit process including standards to be followed (e.g. Institute of Internal Auditors' standards).

■ Sample report templates – e.g. for reporting the results of risk analysis, audit plans and quarterly reporting of findings to the Audit and Risk Management Committee.

■ Current clients to whom internal audit services are provided from whom RBG will be able to take up references, by arrangement, if York is short-listed.

■ Any work currently carried out/competed for that could cause a conflict of interest (and the measures to avoid such conflicts).

■ Fees (daily rates) for each grade of staff and travel and other expenses to be reimbursed. An indication of price increases, if any, over the three-year contract period. Invoicing terms (e.g. on presentation of reports) and payment terms (e.g. the end of the month following receipt of the invoice).

■ Performance targets to be met such as deadlines for completing work and submitting and issuing reports.

(c)   **Impact on the audit of the financial statements**

Tutorial note: The answer to this part should reflect that it is not the external auditor who is providing the internal audit services. Thus comments regarding objectivity impairment are not relevant.

■ The appointment will include an evaluation of organisational risk. The results of this will provide Grey with evidence, for example:

    – supporting the appropriateness of the going concern assumption;
    – of indicators of obsolescence of goods or impairment of other assets.

■ As the quality of internal audit services should be higher than previously, providing a stronger control environment, the extent to which Grey may rely on internal audit work could be increased. This would increase the efficiency of the external audit of the financial statements as the need for substantive procedures should be reduced.

■ However, if internal audit services are performed on a part-time basis (e.g. fitting into the provider's less busy months) Grey must evaluate the impact of this on the prevention, detection and control of fraud and error.

■ The internal auditors will provide a body of expertise within RBG with whom Grey can consult on contentious matters.

3   SEYMOUR CO

(a)   Costs of Tournose

(i)   *Matters*

- Development costs at 30 September 2005 have a carrying value of $3 million (i.e. $4 million less 5 years' amortisation at 5% p.a.) that represents 7·4% of total assets at that date (5·6% of total assets at 30 September 2006) and are therefore material.

- Straight line annual amortisation based on 20 year estimate of useful life ($200,000) represents 1·5% of 2006 profit before tax (PBT) and is not material . The patent cost, $11,600 is very immaterial.

- Management must review the useful life of the development costs at 30 September 2006 (IAS 38 *Intangible Assets*).

- The competitor's announcement during the current year (to 30 September 2006) may provide evidence that:

    - the useful life of the development costs is substantially less than the remaining period covered by the patent;

    - there has been a change in the expected pattern of consumption of future economic benefits;

    - development costs are impaired (i.e. recoverable amount is less than carrying value).

Tutorial note: *A 'timeline' is useful to visualise the financial statement impact:*

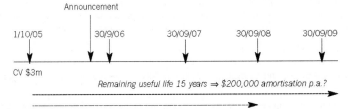

Or just 3 years ⇒ £1 million amortisation p.a?

- A change in the estimated useful life should be accounted for as a change in accounting estimate in accordance with IAS 8 *Accounting Policies, Changes in Accounting Estimates and Errors*. For example, if the development costs have little, if any, useful life after the introduction of the alternative drug ('worst case' scenario), the carrying value ($3 million) should be written off over the current and remaining years, i.e. $1 million p.a. The increase in amortisation/decrease in carrying value ($800,000) is material to PBT (6%) and total assets (1·5%).

- Similarly a change in the expected pattern of consumption of the future economic benefits should be accounted for as a change in accounting estimate (IAS 8). For example, it may be that the useful life is still to 2020 but that the economic benefits may reduce significantly in two years time.

- After adjusting the carrying amount to take account of the change in accounting estimate(s) management should have tested it for impairment and any impairment loss recognised in profit or loss.

(ii)   *Audit evidence*

- $3 million carrying amount of development costs brought forward agreed to prior year working papers and financial statements.

- A copy of the press release announcing the competitor's alternative drug.

- Management's projections of future cashflows from Tournose-related sales as evidence of the useful life of the development costs and pattern of consumption.

- Reperformance of management's impairment test on the development costs: Recalculation of management's calculation of the carrying amount after revising estimates of useful life and/or consumption of benefits compared with management's calculation of value in use.

- Sensitivity analysis on management's key assumptions (e.g. estimates of useful life, discount rate).

- Written management representation on the key assumptions concerning the future that have a significant risk of causing material adjustment to the carrying amount of the development costs. (These assumptions should be disclosed in accordance with IAS 1 *Presentation of Financial Statements*.)

(b) Goodwill

(i) *Matters*

- Cost of goodwill, $1·8 million, represents 3·4% consolidated total assets and is therefore material.

  Tutorial note: *Any assessments of materiality of goodwill against amounts in Aragon's financial statements are meaningless since goodwill only exists in the consolidated financial statements of Seymour.*

- It is correct that the goodwill is not being amortised (IFRS 3 *Business Combinations*). However, it should be tested at least annually for impairment, by management.

- Aragon has incurred losses amounting to $1·1 million since it was acquired (two years ago). The write-off of this amount against goodwill in the consolidated financial statements would be material (being 61% cost of goodwill, 8·3% PBT and 2·1% total assets).

- The cost of the investment ($4·5 million) in Seymour's separate financial statements will also be material and should be tested for impairment.

- The fair value of net assets acquired was only $2·7 million ($4·5 million less $1·8 million). Therefore the fair value less costs to sell of Aragon on other than a going concern basis will be less than the carrying amount of the investment (i.e. the investment is impaired by at least the amount of goodwill recognised on acquisition).

- In assessing recoverable amount, value in use (rather than fair value less costs to sell) is only relevant if the going concern assumption is appropriate for Aragon.

- Supporting Aragon financially may result in Seymour being exposed to actual and/or contingent liabilities that should be provided for/disclosed in Seymour's financial statements in accordance with IAS 37 *Provisions, Contingent Liabilities and Contingent Assets*.

(ii) *Audit evidence*

- Carrying values of cost of investment and goodwill arising on acquisition to prior year audit working papers and financial statements.

- Management's impairment test of Seymour's investment in Aragon and of the goodwill arising on consolidation at 30 September 2006. That is a comparison of the present value of the future cash flows expected to be generated by Aragon (a cash-generating unit) compared with the cost of the investment (in Seymour's separate financial statements).

- Results of any impairment tests on Aragon's assets extracted from Aragon's working paper files.

- Analytical procedures on future cash flows to confirm their reasonableness (e.g. by comparison with cash flows for the last two years).

- Bank report for audit purposes for any guarantees supporting Aragon's loan facilities.

- A copy of Seymour's 'comfort letter' confirming continuing financial support of Aragon for the foreseeable future.

(c) Discontinued operation

(i) *Matters*

- Petcare product revenue represents 12% consolidated revenue and is therefore very material. Consolidated PBT would be 10% higher if the loss on the petcare products was excluded – so also material in relation to Seymour's results.

  Tutorial note: *Consider the 'picture':*

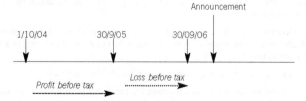

- Although petcare products represent a 'component' of Seymour (as defined by IFRS 5 *Non-Current Assets Held for Sale and Discontinued Operations*), there is no discontinued operation in the current year (to 30 September 2006) because, at the balance sheet date:

  – it had not been disposed of;
  – it did not meet the 'held for sale' classification criteria (e.g. because there was no commitment to a planned sale at the year end).

  Tutorial note: *There is nothing in the question to indicate that management has yet made any plans for a sale.*

- Seymour's management must be persuaded to include the results of this component within continuing operations or the auditor's report should be qualified 'except for' disagreement regarding disclosure.

- The discontinuation of the product line after the balance sheet date provides additional evidence that, as at the balance sheet date, it was of poor quality. Therefore, as at the balance sheet date:

  - an allowance ('provision') may be required for credit notes for returns of products after the year end that were sold before the year end;

  - goods returned to inventory should be written down to net realisable value (may be nil);

  - any plant and equipment used exclusively in the production of the petcare range of products should be tested for impairment;

  - any material contingent liabilities arising from legal claims should be disclosed.

(ii) *Audit evidence*

- A copy of Seymour's announcement (external 'press release' and any internal memorandum).

- Credit notes raised/refunds paid after the year end for faulty products returned.

- Condition of products returned as inspected during physical attendance of inventory count.

- Correspondence from customers claiming reimbursement/compensation for poor quality.

- Direct confirmation from legal adviser (solicitor) regarding any claims for customers including estimates of possible payouts.

4   CLEEVES CO

(a)   Reporting non-compliance

Non-compliance refers to acts of omission or commission by the entity being audited, either intentional or unintentional, that are contrary to the prevailing laws or regulations.

To management

Regarding non-compliance that comes to the auditor's attention the auditor should, as soon as practicable, either:

- communicate with those charged with governance; or
- obtain audit evidence that they are appropriately informed.

However, the auditor need not do so for matters that are clearly inconsequential or trivial and may reach agreement[1] in advance on the nature of such matters to be communicated.

If in the auditor's judgment the non-compliance is believed to be intentional and material, the auditor should communicate the finding without delay.

If the auditor suspects that members of senior management are involved in non-compliance, the auditor should report the matter to the next higher level of authority at the entity, if it exists (e.g. an audit committee or a supervisory board). Where no higher authority exists, or if the auditor believes that the report may not be acted upon or is unsure as to the person to whom to report, the auditor would consider seeking legal advice.

To the users of the auditor's report on the financial statements

If the auditor concludes that the non-compliance has a material effect on the financial statements, and has not been properly reflected in the financial statements, the auditor expresses a qualified (i.e. 'except for disagreement') or an adverse opinion.

If the auditor is precluded by the entity from obtaining sufficient appropriate audit evidence to evaluate whether or not non-compliance that may be material to the financial statements has (or is likely to have) occurred, the auditor should express a qualified opinion or a disclaimer of opinion on the financial statements on the basis of a limitation on the scope of the audit.

Tutorial note: *For example, if management denies the auditor access to information from which he would be able to assess whether or not illegal dumping had taken place (and, if so, the extent of it).*

If the auditor is unable to determine whether non-compliance has occurred because of limitations imposed by circumstances rather than by the entity, the auditor should consider the effect on the auditor's report.

Tutorial note: *For example, if new legal requirements have been announced as effective but the detailed regulations are not yet published.*

To regulatory and enforcement authorities

The auditor's duty of confidentiality ordinarily precludes reporting non-compliance to a third party. However, in certain circumstances, that duty of confidentiality is overridden by statute, law or by courts of law (e.g. in some countries the auditor is required to report non-compliance by financial institutions to the supervisory authorities). The auditor may need to seek legal advice in such circumstances, giving due consideration to the auditor's responsibility to the public interest.

(b) **(i)**   Appropriateness of audit opinion given

Tutorial note: *The answer points suggested by the marking scheme are listed in roughly the order in which they might be extracted from the information presented in the question. The suggested answer groups together some of these points under headings to give the analysis of the situation a possible structure.*

Heading

- The opinion paragraph is not properly headed. It does not state the form of the opinion that has been given nor the grounds for qualification.

- The opinion 'the financial statements do not present fairly' is an 'adverse' opinion.

- That 'provision should be made', but has not, is a matter of disagreement that should be clearly stated as non-compliance with IAS 36. The title of IAS 36 *Impairment of Assets* should be given in full.

- The opinion should be headed 'Disagreement on Accounting Policies – Inappropriate Accounting Method – Adverse Opinion'.

---

[1] ISA 250 does not specify with whom agreement should be reached but presumably with those charged with corporate governance (e.g audit committee or other supervisory board).

Content

■ It is appropriate that the opinion paragraph should refer to the note(s) in the financial statements where the matter giving rise to the modification is more fully explained. However, this is not an excuse for the audit opinion being 'light' on detail. For example, the reason for impairment could be summarised in the auditor's report.

■ The effects have not been quantified, but they *should* be quantifiable. The maximum possible loss would be the carrying amount of the non-current assets identified as impaired.

■ It is not clear why the directors have been 'unable to quantify the amounts'. Since impairments should be quantifiable any 'inability' suggest a limitation in scope of the audit, in which case the opinion should be disclaimed (or 'except for') on grounds of lack of evidence rather than disagreement.

■ The wording is confusing. 'Failure to provide' suggests disagreement. However, there must be sufficient evidence to support any disagreement. Although the directors cannot quantify the amounts it seems the auditors must have been able to (estimate at least) in order to form an opinion that the amounts involved are sufficiently material to warrant a qualification.

■ The first paragraph refers to 'non-current assets'. The second paragraph specifies 'tangible and intangible assets'. There is no explanation why or how both tangible and intangible assets are impaired.

■ The first paragraph refers to 'profit or loss' and the second and third paragraphs to 'loss'. It may be clearer if the first paragraph were to refer to recognition in the income statement.

■ It is not clear why the failure to recognise impairment warrants an adverse opinion rather than 'except for'. The effects of non-compliance with IAS 36 are to overstate the carrying amount(s) of non-current assets (that can be specified) and to understate the loss. The matter does not appear to be pervasive and so an adverse opinion looks unsuitable as the financial statements as a whole are not incomplete or misleading. A loss is already being reported so it is not that a reported profit would be turned into a loss (which is sometimes judged to be 'pervasive').

Prior year

■ As the 2005 auditor's report, as previously issued, included an adverse opinion and the matter that gave rise to the modification:

   – is unresolved; and
   – results in a modification of the 2006 auditor's report,

   the 2006 auditor's report should also be modified regarding the corresponding figures (ISA 710 *Comparatives*).

■ The 2006 auditor's report does not refer to the prior period modification nor highlight that the matter resulting in the current period modification is not new. For example, the report could say 'As previously reported and as more fully explained in notes ....' and state 'increase the loss by $x (2005 – $y)'.

(ii) Implications for audit opinion on consolidated financial statements of Cleeves

■ If the potential adjustments to non-current asset carrying amounts and loss are not material to the consolidated financial statements there will be no implication. However, as Howard is material to Cleeves and the modification appears to be 'so material' (giving rise to adverse opinion) this seems unlikely.

   Tutorial note: *The question clearly states that Howard is material to Cleeves, thus there is no call for speculation on this.*

■ As Howard is wholly-owned the management of Cleeves must be able to request that Howard's financial statements are adjusted to reflect the impairment of the assets. The auditor's report on Cleeves will then be unmodified (assuming that any impairment of the investment in Howard is properly accounted for in the separate financial statements of Cleeves).

■ If the impairment losses are not recognised in Howard's financial statements they can nevertheless be adjusted on consolidation of Cleeves and its subsidiaries (by writing down assets to recoverable amounts). The audit opinion on Cleeves should then be unmodified in this respect.

■ If there is no adjustment of Howard's asset values (either in Howard's financial statements or on consolidation) it is most likely that the audit opinion on Cleeves's consolidated financial statements would be 'except for'. (It should not be adverse as it is doubtful whether even the opinion on Howard's financial statements should be adverse.)

Tutorial note: *There is currently no requirement in ISA 600 to disclose that components have been audited by another auditor unless the principal auditor is permitted to base their opinion solely upon the report of another auditor.*

5   BOLEYN & CO

(a) Professional Accountants

- Professional Accountants are members of an IFAC member body. They may be:
    - in public practice or employed professionals;
    - a sole practitioner, partnership or corporate body.

- Professional Accountants in Public Practice ('practitioners') are:
    - each partner (or person occupying a position similar to that of a partner); and
    - each employee in a practice providing professional services to a client irrespective of their functional classification (e.g. audit, tax or consulting); and
    - professional accountants in a practice having managerial responsibilities.

    This term is also used to refer to a firm of professional accountants in public practice.

- Employed Professional Accountants are professional accountants employed in industry, commerce, the public sector or education.

(b) FAQs

(i) *Information Technology (IT) services*

The greatest threats to independence arise from the provision of any service which involves auditors in:

- auditing their own work;
- the decision-making process;
- undertaking management functions of the client.

IT services potentially pose all these threats:

- self-interest threat – on-going services that provide a large proportion of Boleyn's annual fees will contribute to a threat to objectivity;

- self-review threat – e.g. when IT services provided involve (i) the supervision of the audit client's employees in the performance of their normal duties; or (ii) the origination of electronic data evidencing the occurrence of transactions;

- management threat – e.g. when the IT services involve making judgments and taking decisions that are properly the responsibility of management.

Thus, services that involve the design and implementation of financial IT systems that are used to generate information forming a significant part of a client's accounting system or financial statements is likely to create significant ethical threats.

Possible safeguards include:

- disclosing and discussing fees with the client's audit committees (or others charged with corporate governance);

- the audit client providing a written acknowledgment (e.g. in an engagement letter) of its responsibility for:
    - establishing and monitoring a system of internal controls;
    - the operation of the system (hardware or software); and
    - the data used or generated by the system;

- the designation by the audit client of a competent employee (preferably within senior management) with responsibility to make all management decisions regarding the design and implementation of the hardware or software system;

- evaluation of the adequacy and results of the design and implementation of the system by the audit client;

- suitable allocation of work within the firm (i.e. staff providing the IT services not being involved in the audit engagement and having different reporting lines); and

- review of the audit opinion by an audit partner who is not involved in the audit engagement.

Services in connection with the assessment, design and implementation of internal accounting controls and risk management controls are not considered to create a threat to independence provided that the firm's personnel do not perform management functions.

It would be acceptable to provide IT services to an audit client where the systems are not important to any significant part of the accounting system or the production of financial statements and do not have significant reliance placed on them by the auditors, provided that:

■ a member of the client's management has been designated to receive and take responsibility for the results of the IT work undertaken; and

■ appropriate safeguards are put in place (e.g. using separate partners and staff for each role and review by a partner not involved in the audit engagement).

It would also generally be acceptable to provide and install off-the-shelf accounting packages to an audit client.

(ii) *Corporate hospitality*

A partner in an audit firm is obviously in a position to influence the conduct and outcome of an audit. Therefore a partner being on 'too friendly' terms with an audit client creates a familiarity threat. Other members of the audit team may not exert as much influence on the audit.

A self-interest threat may also be perceived (e.g. if corporate hospitality is provided to keep a prestigious client).

There is no absolute prohibition against corporate hospitality provided:

■ the value attached to such hospitality is 'insignificant'; and
■ the 'frequency, nature and cost' of the hospitality is reasonable.

Thus, flying the directors of an audit client for weekends away could be seen as significant. Similarly, entertaining an audit client on a regular basis could be seen as unacceptable.

Partners and staff of Boleyn will need to be objective in their assessments of the significance or reasonableness of the hospitality offered. (Would 'a reasonable and informed third party' conclude that the hospitality will or is likely to be seen to impair your objectivity?)

If they have any doubts they should discuss the matter in the first instance with the audit engagement partner, who should refer the matter to the ethics partner if in doubt.

(iii) *Cross selling services*

The practice of cross selling is intended to give incentives to members of audit teams to concentrate their efforts on the selling of non-audit services to audit clients.

It is not inappropriate for an audit firm to cross sell or for members of the audit team to recognise on an ongoing basis the need of a client to have non audit services. However it should not be an aim of the audit team member to seek out such opportunities.

Boleyn should have policies and procedures to ensure that, in relation to each audit client:

■ the objectives of the members of the audit team do not include selling of non-audit services to the audit client;

■ the criteria for evaluating the performance of members of the audit team do not include success in selling non-audit services to the audit client;

■ no specific element of remuneration of a member of the audit team and no decision concerning promotion within the audit firm is based on his or her success in selling non-audit services to the audit client; and

■ the ethics partner being available for consultation when needed.

Therefore objectives such as the following are inappropriate:

■ to meet a quota of opportunities;

■ to specifically make time to discuss with clients which non-audit services they should consider;

■ to develop identified selling opportunities.

An audit engagement partner's performance should be judged on the quality and integrity of the audit only. There are no restrictions on normal partnership profit-sharing arrangements.

Review Form & Free Prize Draw – Paper P7 Advanced Audit and Assurance (International stream)
(6/07)

All original review forms from the entire BPP range, completed with genuine comments, will be entered into one of two draws on 31 January 2008 and 31 July 2008. The names on the first four forms picked out on each occasion will be sent a cheque for £50.

Name: _____ Address: _____

_____

_____

How have you used this Kit?
(Tick one box only)

☐ Home study (book only)

☐ On a course: college _____

☐ With 'correspondence' package

☐ Other _____

Why did you decide to purchase this Kit?
(Tick one box only)

☐ Have used the complementary Study text

☐ Have used other BPP products in the past

☐ Recommendation by friend/colleague

☐ Recommendation by a lecturer at college

☐ Saw advertising

☐ Other _____

During the past six months do you recall seeing/receiving any of the following?
(Tick as many boxes as are relevant)

☐ Our advertisement in *Student Accountant*

☐ Our advertisement in *Pass*

☐ Our advertisement in *PQ*

☐ Our brochure with a letter through the post

☐ Our website www.bpp.com

Which (if any) aspects of our advertising do you find useful?
(Tick as many boxes as are relevant)

☐ Prices and publication dates of new editions

☐ Information on product content

☐ Facility to order books off-the-page

☐ None of the above

Which BPP products have you used?

Text	☐	Success CD	☐	Learn Online	☐
Kit	☑	i-Learn	☐	Home Study Package	☐
Passcard	☐	i-Pass	☐	Home Study PLUS	☐

Your ratings, comments and suggestions would be appreciated on the following areas.

	Very useful	Useful	Not useful
Passing ACCA exams	☐	☐	☐
Passing P7	☐	☐	☐
Planning your question practice	☐	☐	☐
Questions	☐	☐	☐
Top Tips etc in answers	☐	☐	☐
Content and structure of answers	☐	☐	☐
'Plan of attack' in mock exams	☐	☐	☐
Mock exam answers			

Overall opinion of this Kit	Excellent ☐	Good ☐	Adequate ☐	Poor ☐

Do you intend to continue using BPP products?   Yes ☐   No ☐

The BPP author of this edition can be e-mailed at: jaitindergill@bpp.com

Please return this form to: Nick Weller, ACCA Publishing Manager, BPP Learning Media, FREEPOST, London, W12 8BR

Review Form & Free Prize Draw (continued)

TELL US WHAT YOU THINK

Please note any further comments and suggestions/errors below.

Free Prize Draw Rules

1   Closing date for 31 January 2008 draw is 31 December 2007. Closing date for 31 July 2008 draw is 30 June 2008.

2   Restricted to entries with UK and Eire addresses only. BPP employees, their families and business associates are excluded.

3   No purchase necessary. Entry forms are available upon request from BPP Learning Media. No more than one entry per title, per person. Draw restricted to persons aged 16 and over.

4   Winners will be notified by post and receive their cheques not later than 6 weeks after the relevant draw date.

5   The decision of the promoter in all matters is final and binding. No correspondence will be entered into.